Stephen Birnbaum Travel Guides

Acapulco
Bahamas, and Turks & Caicos
Barcelona
Bermuda
Boston
Canada
Cancun, Cozumel & Isla Mujeres
Caribbean
Chicago
Disneyland
Eastern Europe
Europe
Europe for Business Travelers
Florence
France
Great Britain
Hawaii
Honolulu
Ireland
Italy
Ixtapa & Zihuatanejo
Las Vegas
London
Los Angeles
Mexico
Miami & Ft. Lauderdale
Montreal & Quebec City
New Orleans
New York
Paris
Portugal
Puerto Vallarta
Rome
San Francisco
South America
Spain
Toronto
United States
USA for Business Travelers
Vancouver
Venice
Walt Disney World
Washington, DC
Western Europe

CONTRIBUTING EDITORS

Marcie Carroll
Rick Carroll
Elizabeth Higgins

SYMBOLS   Gloria McKeown

MAPS   Mark Carlson
          Susan Carlson

A Stephen Birnbaum Travel Guide

Birnbaum's
HONOLULU
1993

Alexandra Mayes Birnbaum
EDITOR

Lois Spritzer
EXECUTIVE EDITOR

Laura L. Brengelman
Managing Editor

Mary Callahan
Jill Kadetsky
Susan McClung
Beth Schlau
Dana Margaret Schwartz
Associate Editors

Gene Gold
Assistant Editor

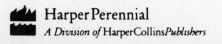

HarperPerennial
A Division of HarperCollins*Publishers*

To Stephen, who merely made all this possible.

FIRST EDITION

ISSN 0749-2561 (Stephen Birnbaum Travel Guides)
ISSN 1060-3875 (Honolulu)
ISBN 0-06-278064-6 (pbk.)

92 93 94 95 96 97 CC/WP 10 9 8 7 6 5 4 3 2 1

Contents

GETTING READY TO GO

All the practical travel data you need to plan your vacation down to the final detail.

When and How to Go

Preparing

On the Road

Sources and Resources

USEFUL WORDS AND PHRASES

THE CITY

A thorough, qualitative guide to Honolulu. Each section offers a comprehensive report on the city's most compelling attractions and amenities, designed to be used on the spot.

DIVERSIONS

A selective guide to more than 15 active and/or cerebral vacation themes, including the best places to pursue them.

For the Experience

For the Body

For the Mind

DIRECTIONS

Five of the most delightful tours through Honolulu.

A Word from the Editor

My husband Steve Birnbaum was a major fan of islands. My travel trail usually led from New York to Los Angeles or San Francisco and on to Hong Kong, or through London, Paris, and Rome, with a fair number of other urban rest stops in between. The constant in my journeying was a surfeit of asphalt and concrete, which I found as relaxing as most people do hammocks and palm trees.

So it took some substantial effort for Steve to get me motivated to meander around any atoll, no matter how attractive. I shared a not uncommon (and admittedly narrow) view that one island was pretty much like any other, and that when you've seen one pristine strand of sand you've pretty much experienced what beaches in general have to offer. That is, until I saw Hawaii.

My Hawaiian port of entry was Honolulu and I won't bore you with a long description of the Hawaiian experiences that left me wide-eyed and a bit slack-jawed, but from the first plumeria lei draped around my neck to my first sight of Pearl Harbor and Diamond Head, I found myself entranced and enchanted by natural wonders and extraordinary vistas that a first-time visitor to Hawaii just doesn't believe possible. My infatuation proved enduring, as my editorship of this volume attests.

Still, all is not swaying palms and shimmering sands even in this idyllic Pacific paradise. As with world news in general, headlines about Hawaii have described some troubles in Eden, and there's no denying that these exist. On the whole, however, Hawaii's — and especially Oahu's — remarkably multi-ethnic and polyglot population has confronted most of the malaise of civilization as intelligently as it is possible to in a world that sometimes seems to defy sense and sanity.

Among these problems are tourists by the jumbo-jetful, and the island's economy, which has come more and more to rely on a sizable, constant influx of tourist currency — in spite of the infusion of Japanese real estate investment. Inevitably, the sheer numbers of these visitors and new landowners have affected island life — and not always for the better. For example, certain segments of Waikiki Beach in midtown Honolulu bear the scars of overzealous development. And street crime is not uncommon. But these are really the only areas that can be cited.

In recent years, the nature of travel to and through the island of Oahu has altered somewhat to reflect changing travel tastes. More and more visitors are leaving their towels on Waikiki Beach to hike into the heart of Koko Crater or take a regal ramble through Iolani Palace. This new guide to Honolulu that you hold in your hand hopes to expand this trend by directing prospective Hawaii visitors to those special corners of the island's capital that are not necessarily part of the most publicized package tours.

Obviously, any guidebook to Honolulu must keep pace with and answer the real needs of today's travelers. That's why we've tried to create a guide that's specifically organized, written, and edited for the more demanding modern traveler, one for whom qualitative information is infinitely more desirable than mere quantities of unappraised data. We think that this book, along with all the other guides in our series, represent a new generation of travel guides — one that is especially responsive to modern needs and interests.

For years, dating back as far as Herr Baedeker, travel guides have tended to be encyclopedic, seemingly much more concerned with demonstrating expertise in geography and history than with a real analysis of the sorts of things that actually concern a typical modern tourist. But today, when it is hardly necessary to tell a traveler where Honolulu is (in many cases, the traveler has been there nearly as often as the guidebook editors), it becomes the responsibility of those editors to provide new perspectives and to suggest new directions in order to make the guide genuinely valuable.

That's exactly what we've tried to do in this series. I think you'll notice a different, more contemporary tone to the text, as well as an organization and focus that are distinctive and more functional. And even a random reading of what follows will demonstrate a substantial departure from the standard guidebook orientation, for we've not only attempted to provide information of a more compelling sort, but we also have tried to present the data in a format that makes it particularly accessible.

Needless to say, it's difficult to decide just what to include in a guidebook of this size — and what to omit. Early on, we realized that giving up the encyclopedic approach precluded our listing every single route and restaurant, a realization that helped define our overall editorial focus. Similarly, when we discussed the possibility of presenting certain information in other than strict geographic order, we found that the new format enabled us to arrange data in a way that we feel best answers the questions travelers typically ask.

Large numbers of specific questions have provided the real editorial skeleton for this book. The volume of mail we regularly receive emphasizes that modern travelers want very precise information, so we've tried to organize our material in the most responsive way possible. Readers who want to know the best restaurants in Honolulu or the best surfing opportunities on the North Shore will have no trouble extracting that data from this guide.

Travel guides are, understandably, reflections of personal taste, and putting one's name on a title page obviously puts one's preferences on the line. But I think I ought to amplify just what "personal" means. Like Steve, I don't believe in the sort of personal guidebook that's a palpable misrepresentation on its face. It is, for example, hardly possible for any single travel writer to visit thousands of restaurants (and nearly as many hotels) in any given year and provide accurate appraisals of each. And even if it were physically possible for one human being to survive such an itinerary, it would of necessity have to be done at a dead sprint, and the perceptions derived therefrom would probably be less valid than those of any other intelligent individual visiting the same establishments. It is, therefore, impossible (especially in a large, annually revised and updated guidebook *series* such as we offer) to have only one person provide all the data on the entire world.

I also happen to think that such individual orientation is of substantially less value to readers. Visiting a single hotel for just one night or eating one hasty meal in a random restaurant hardly equips anyone to provide appraisals that are of more than passing interest. No amount of doggedly alliterative or oppressively onomatopoeic text can camouflage a technique that is essentially specious. We have, therefore, chosen what I like to describe as the "thee and me" approach to restaurant and hotel evaluation and, to a somewhat more limited degree, to the sites and sights we have included in the other sections of our text. What this really reflects is personal sampling tempered by intelligent counsel from informed local sources, and these additional friends-of-the-editors are almost always residents of the city and/or area about which they are consulted.

Despite the presence of several editors, writers, researchers, and local contributors, very precise editing and tailoring keep our text fiercely subjective. So what follows is the gospel according to Birnbaum, and represents as much of our own taste and instincts as we can manage. It is probable, therefore, that if you like your beaches largely unpopulated and your mountainsides mostly uncrowded, prefer small hotels with personality to huge high-rise anonymities, and can't tolerate fresh fish that's been relentlessly overcooked, we're likely to have a long and meaningful relationship. Readers with dissimilar tastes may be less enraptured.

I should also point out something about the person to whom this guidebook is directed. Above all, he or she is a "visitor." This means that such elements as restaurants have been specifically picked to provide the visitor with a representative, enlightening, stimulating, and, above all, pleasant experience. Since so many extraneous considerations can affect the reception and service accorded a regular restaurant patron, our choices can in no way be construed as an exhaustive guide to island dining. We think we've listed all the best places, in various price ranges, but they were chosen with a visitor's enjoyment in mind.

Other evidence of how we've tried to tailor our text to reflect modern travel habits is most apparent in the section we call DIVERSIONS. Where once it was common for travelers to spend an island visit nailed to a single spot, the emphasis today is more likely to be directed toward pursuing some sport or special interest while seeing the surrounding countryside. So we've organized every activity we could reasonably evaluate and arranged the material in a way that is especially accessible to activists of either athletic or cerebral bent. It is no longer necessary, therefore, to wade through a pound or two of superfluous prose just to find the very best surfing spot or the supreme scenic vista within a reasonable distance of your destination.

If there is a single thing that best characterizes the revolution in and evolution of current holiday habits, it is that most travelers now consider travel a right rather than a privilege. No longer is a family trip to the far corners of the world necessarily a once-in-a-lifetime thing; nor is the idea of visiting exotic, faraway places in the least worrisome. Travel today translates as the enthusiastic desire to sample all of the world's opportunities, to find that elusive quality of experience that is not only enriching but comfortable. For that reason, we've tried to make what follows not only helpful and enlightening, but the sort of welcome companion of which every traveler dreams.

Finally, I also should point out that every good travel guide is a living enterprise; that is, no part of this text is carved in stone. In our annual revisions, we refine, expand, and further hone all our material to serve your travel needs better. To this end, no contribution is of greater value to us than your personal reaction to what we have written, as well as information reflecting your own experiences while using the book. We earnestly and enthusiastically solicit your comments about this guide *and* your opinions and perceptions about places you have recently visited. In this way, we will be able to provide the most current information — including the actual experiences of recent travelers — and to make those experiences more readily available to others. Please write to us at 10 E. 53rd St., New York, NY 10022.

We sincerely hope to hear from you.

ALEXANDRA MAYES BIRNBAUM

How to Use This Guide

A great deal of care has gone into the special organization of this guidebook, and we believe it represents a real breakthrough in the presentation of travel material. Our aim is to create a new, more modern generation of travel books, and to make this guide the most useful and practical travel tool available today.

Our text is divided into five basic sections in order to present information in the best way on every possible aspect of a vacation to Honolulu. This organization itself should alert you to the vast and varied opportunities available, as well as indicate all the specific data necessary to plan a successful visit. You won't find much of the conventional "swaying palms and shimmering sands" text here; we've chosen instead to deliver more useful and practical information. Prospective itineraries tend to speak for themselves, and with so many diverse travel opportunities, we feel our main job is to highlight what's where and to provide basic information — how, when, where, how much, and what's best — to assist you in making the most intelligent choices possible.

Here is a brief summary of the five sections of this book, and what you can expect to find in each. We believe that you will find both your travel planning and en route enjoyment enhanced by having this book at your side.

GETTING READY TO GO

This mini-encyclopedia of practical travel facts is a sort of know-it-all companion with all the precise information necessary to create a successful trip to Honolulu. There are entries on more than 25 separate topics, including how to get where you're going, what preparations to make before leaving, what to expect, what your trip is likely to cost, and how to avoid prospective problems. The individual entries are specific, realistic, and, where appropriate, cost-oriented.

We expect you to use this section most in the course of planning your trip, for its ideas and suggestions are intended to simplify this often confusing period. Entries are intentionally concise, in an effort to get to the meat of the matter with the least extraneous prose. These entries are augmented by extensive lists of specific sources from which to obtain even more specialized data, plus some suggestions for obtaining travel information on your own.

USEFUL WORDS AND PHRASES

Though English is spoken throughout the Hawaiian Islands, you often will hear Hawaiian words and phrases used in restaurants, shops, and along the beach — sometimes for emphasis, other times for more accurate description. This section will familiarize you with the Hawaiian alphabet and give you a short course on those words and phrases you are most likely to hear during your stay. By the time you've finished reading it, your vocabulary will include more than just aloha.

THE CITY

The report on Honolulu has been prepared with the aid of researchers, contributors, professional journalists, and experts who live in the city. Although useful at the planning stage, THE CITY is really designed to be taken along and used on the spot. The report offers a short-stay guide, including an essay introducing the city as a contemporary place to visit. *At-a-Glance* material is actually a site-by-site survey of the most important, interesting, and sometimes most eclectic sights to see and things to do. *Sources and Resources* is a concise listing of pertinent tourism information, meant to answer myriad potentially pressing questions as they arise — from simple things such as the address of the local tourist office, how to get around, which sightseeing tours to take, and when special events occur to something more difficult like where to find the best nightspot, which are the shops that have the finest merchandise and/or the most irresistible bargains, and where the best golf, tennis, fishing, and swimming are to be found. *Best in Town* lists our collection of cost-and-quality choices of the best places to eat and sleep on a variety of budgets.

DIVERSIONS

This section is designed to help travelers find the best places in which to engage in a wide range of physical and cerebral activities, without having to wade through endless pages of unrelated text. This very selective guide lists the broadest possible range of activities, including all the best places to pursue them.

We start with a list of special places to stay and eat, move to activities that require some perspiration — sports preferences and other rigorous pursuits — and go on to report on a number of more cerebral and spiritual vacation opportunities. In every case, our suggestion of a particular location — and often our recommendation of a specific resort — is intended to guide you to that special place where the quality of experience is likely to be highest. Whether you opt for golf or tennis, surfing or sport fishing, hula dancing or shopping sprees, each category is the equivalent of a comprehensive checklist of the absolute best in the area.

DIRECTIONS

Here are five walking and driving tours through Honolulu and around the island of Oahu that explore its beaches, its neighborhoods, and its historic districts. The itineraries can be connected for longer sojourns or used individually for short, intensive explorations.

Although each of the book's sections has a distinct format and a special function, they have all been designed to be used together to provide a complete inventory of travel information. To use this book to full advantage, take a few minutes to read the table of contents and random entries in each section to get a firsthand feel for how it all fits together.

Pick and choose needed information. Assume, for example, that your idea of a dream vacation has always been to golf or just bask on a beach in Honolulu, go surfing in the Pacific, feast on mahimahi, and attend an authentic luau — but you never really knew how to organize it or where to go. Turn to DIVERSIONS: *Surf's Up,* for the best places to catch a wave; *Good Golf* for information on the *Turtle Bay* golf course; and *Quintessential Honolulu* for a guide to the best luau. Then choose specific restaurants from the selections offered in "Eating Out" in THE CITY.

In other words, the sections of this book are building blocks designed to help you put together the best possible trip. Use them selectively as a tool, a source of ideas, a reference work for accurate facts, and a guidebook to the best buys, the most exciting sights, the most pleasant accommodations, and the tastiest foods — *the best travel experience* that you can possibly have.

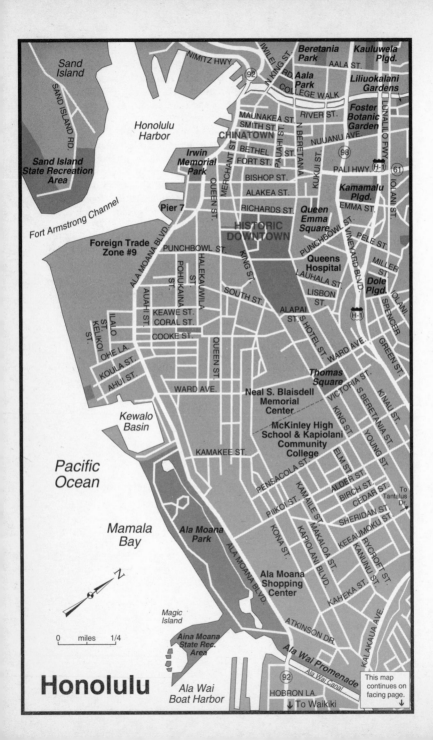

Honolulu

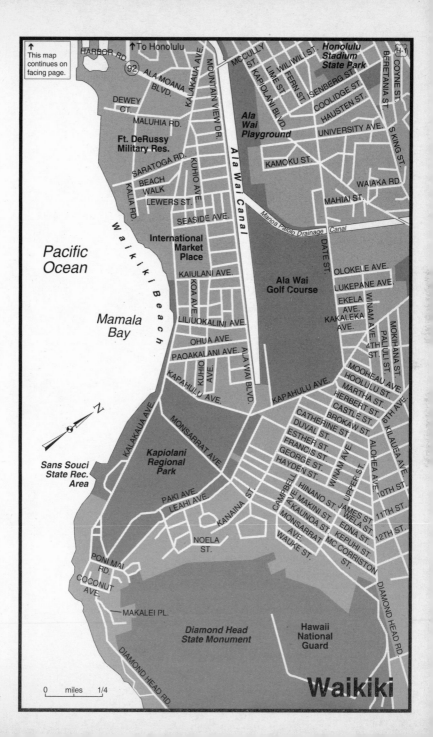

GETTING READY
TO GO

When and How to Go

When to Go

 There isn't really a best time to visit Honolulu, although the two most popular vacation times traditionally are December through February and late May through August. The city enjoys balmy, semitropical weather and only two seasons, with an average temperature in the mid- to upper 80s in summer (May through September) and mid-70s and low 80s, dropping to the low 60s at night, in winter (October through April). Showers can be expected throughout the day in winter, so be prepared with rain gear if you are visiting during that season.

There are good reasons for visiting Honolulu any time of the year. There are no real off-season periods when attractions are closed, so you aren't risking the disappointment of arriving at an attraction and finding the gates locked. However, you can benefit from lower room rates if you visit during the less busy shoulder seasons (March until mid-May and September through November).

■**Note:** When planning the timing of your visit, there is one period during which you must be careful. In the winter, especially during the *Christmas* holidays, hotels are packed and most bargains disappear. This is also the prime meeting and convention season. During this period, make your bookings extra early — preferably 2 to 3 months ahead.

WEATHER: Travelers can get current readings and extended forecasts through *The Weather Channel Connection,* the worldwide weather report center of *The Weather Channel,* a cable TV station. By dialing 900-WEATHER and punching in either the first four letters of the city name or the area code (HONO or 818 for Honolulu) for over 600 cities in the US (including Puerto Rico and the US Virgin Islands), an up-to-date recording will provide such information as current temperature, barometric pressure, relative humidity, and wind speed, as well as a general 2-day forecast. Beach, boating, and highway reports are also provided for some locations. This 24-hour service can be accessed from any touch-tone phone in the US, and costs 95¢ per minute. The charge will show up on your phone bill. For additional information, contact *The Weather Channel Connection,* 2600 Cumberland Pkwy., Atlanta, GA 30339 (phone: 404-434-6800).

CULTURAL EVENTS: As in most Northern Hemisphere cities, autumn signals the beginning of the cultural cycle. The *Honolulu Symphony* and *Chamber Music Hawaii* have seasons September through May, while *Hawaii Opera Theater* offers performances in February and March. For a more Hawaiian feeling, *The Wildest Show in Town* at the *Honolulu Zoo* presents local entertainers in a summer twilight concert series on Wednesdays, while in July the best Hawaiian women artists in music and dance perform at *Na Wahine O Hawaii.* Top island entertainers appear at *Sea Life Park* on Friday nights.

Museums include the *Bishop Museum* with the world's largest collection of

Hawaiiana, the *Mission Houses Museum* demonstrating how the early American settlers in Hawaii lived, and *Queen Emma's Summer Palace* showing how the native royals lived in mid-Victorian times. For other artwork there are the *Honolulu Academy of Arts,* which has an Oriental collection and some American and European works, and the city's newest, *The Contemporary Museum,* devoted to modern art and containing a permanent David Hockney exhibition.

FESTIVALS: A very Hawaiian skill is celebrated in May with the 66th annual *Lei Day Celebration* with competitions, exhibits, and the crowning of a queen. More Hawaiian festivities mark the *King Kamehameha Day* celebration in June, while waterborne events such as an outrigger canoe regatta are part of the *Walter J. MacFarlane Regatta and Surf Race* taking place in July. In August is the Buddhist *Floating Lantern Ceremony* honoring the dead. An *Aloha Week Festival* featuring Hawaiiana pageantry, canoe races, parades and entertainment takes place in September. December sees the *Mission Houses Museum*'s 20th annual *Christmas Fair,* as well as the running of the *Honolulu Marathon.*

Traveling by Plane

 Flying is the quickest, most convenient means of travel between different parts of the country. It *sounds* expensive to travel across the US by air, but when all costs are taken into account for traveling any substantial distance, plane travel usually is less expensive per mile than traveling by car. It also is the most economical way to go in terms of time. Although touring by car, bus, or train certainly is a more scenic way to travel, air travel is far faster and more direct — and the less time spent in transit, the more time spent in Honolulu.

SCHEDULED FLIGHTS: Numerous airlines offer regularly scheduled flights to Honolulu International Airport, which is located 3 miles northwest of the city center and handles international and domestic traffic.

American: 800-433-7300
America West: 800-247-5692
Continental: 800-525-0280
Delta: 800-221-1212
Northwest: 800-225-2525
TWA: 800-221-2000
United: 800-241-6522

Two inter-island carriers link Honolulu with the rest of Hawaii. They are *Aloha Airlines* (phone: 800-367-5250) and *Hawaiian Airlines* (800-367-5320).

Among the international carriers that serve the airport are *Air Canada, Air New Zealand, All Nippon Airways, Canadian International, China Airlines, Garuda Indonesia, Japan Airlines, Korean Airlines, Philippine Airlines, Qantas,* and *Singapore Airlines.*

Tickets – When traveling on regularly scheduled flights, a full-fare ticket provides maximum travel flexibility. There are no advance booking or other ticketing requirements — except seat availability — although cancellation restrictions vary. It pays to check *before* booking your flight. It also is advisable, however, to reserve well in advance during popular vacation periods and around holiday times.

Fares – Full-fare tickets are followed by a wide variety of discount fares, which even experts find hard to keep current. With these fares, the less you pay for your ticket, the more restrictions and qualifications are likely to be attached to the ticket purchase, including the months (and the days of the week) during which you must travel, how far in advance you must purchase your ticket, the minimum and maximum amount of time you may or must remain away, and your willingness to decide and stick with a return date at the time of booking. It is not uncommon for passengers sitting side by side on the same plane to have paid fares varying by hundreds of dollars.

In general, domestic airfares break down to four basic categories — first class, business class, coach (also called economy or tourist class), and excursion or discount fares. In addition, Advance Purchase Excursion (APEX) fares offer savings under certain conditions.

A **first class** ticket admits you to the special section of the aircraft with larger seats, more legroom, better (or more elaborately served) food, free drinks, free headsets for movies and music channels, and above all, personal attention. First class fares cost about twice those of full-fare (often called "regular") economy.

Behind first class often lies **business class**, usually a separate cabin or cabins. While standards of comfort and service are not as high as in first class, they represent a considerable improvement over conditions in the rear of the plane, with roomier seats, more leg and shoulder space between passengers, and fewer seats abreast. Free liquor and headsets, a choice of meal entrées, and a separate counter for speedier check-in are other inducements. Note that airlines often have their own names for their business class service — such as Ambassador Class on *TWA* and Medallion Class on *Delta*.

The terms of the **coach** or **economy** fare may vary slightly from airline to airline, and in fact from time to time airlines may be selling more than one type of economy fare. Coach or economy passengers sit more snugly, as many as 10 in a single row on a wide-body jet, behind the first class and business class sections. Normally, alcoholic drinks are not free, nor are the headsets.

In first, business class, and regular economy, passengers are entitled to reserve seats and are sold tickets on an open reservation system. They may travel on any scheduled flight they wish, buy a one-way or round-trip ticket, and have the ticket remain valid for a year. There are no requirements for a minimum or maximum stay or for advance booking and (often) no cancellation penalties — but beware, the rules regarding cancellation vary from carrier to carrrier. The fare also allows free stopover privileges, although these can be limited in economy.

Excursion and other **discount** fares are the airlines' equivalent of a special sale and usually apply to round-trip bookings only. These fares generally differ according to the season and the number of travel days permitted. They are only a bit less flexible than full-fare economy tickets and are, therefore, often useful for both business and holiday travelers. Most round-trip excursion tickets include strict minimum and maximum stay requirements and can be changed only within the specified time limits. So don't count on extending a ticket beyond the specified time of return or staying less time than required. Different airlines may have different regulations concerning the number of stopovers permitted, and sometimes excursion fares are less expensive during midweek. The availability of these reduced-rate seats is most limited at busy times such as holidays. Discount or excursion fare ticket holders sit with coach passengers and, for all intents and purposes, are indistinguishable from them. They receive all the same basic services, even though they may have paid anywhere between 30% and 55% less for the trip. Obviously, it's wise to make plans early enough to qualify for this less expensive transportation if possible.

These discount or excursion fares may masquerade under a variety of names and invariably have strings attached. A common requirement is that the ticket be purchased a certain number of days — usually between 7 and 21 days — in advance of departure, though it may be booked weeks or months in advance (it has to be "ticketed," or paid for, shortly after booking, however). The return reservation usually has to be made at the time of the original ticketing and often cannot be changed later than a certain number of days (again, usually 7 to 21) before the return flight. If events force a passenger to change the return reservation after the date allowed, the passenger may have to pay the difference between the round-trip excursion rate and the round-trip coach rate, although some carriers permit such scheduling changes for a nominal fee. In addition, some airlines may allow passengers to use their discounted fares by standing by for an empty seat, even if the carrier doesn't otherwise have standby fares. Another common condition is the minimum and maximum stay requirement; for example, 1 to 6 days or 6 to 14 days (but including at least a Saturday night). Last, cancellation penalties of up to 50% of the full price of the ticket have been assessed — if a refund is offered at all — so check the specific penalty in effect when you purchase your discount/excursion ticket.

On some airlines, the ticket bearing the lowest price of all the current discount fares — is the ticket where no change at all in departure and/or return flights is permitted, and where the ticket price is totally nonrefundable. If you do buy such a nonrefundable ticket, you should be aware of a policy followed by some airlines that may make it easier to change your plans if necessary. For a fee — set by each airline and payable at the airport when checking in — you *may* be able to change the time or date of a return flight on a nonrefundable ticket. However, if the nonrefundable ticket price for the replacement flight is higher than that of the original (as often is the case when trading in a midweek for a weekend flight), you also will have to pay the difference. Any such change must be made a certain number of days in advance — in some cases as little as 2 days — of either the original or the replacement flight, whichever is earlier; restrictions are set by the individual carrier. (Travelers holding a nonrefundable or other restricted ticket who must change their plans due to a family emergency should know that some carriers may make special allowances in such situations.)

■**Note:** Due to recent changes in many US airlines' policies, nonrefundable tickets are now available that carry none of the above restrictions. Although passengers still may *not* be able to obtain a refund for the price paid, the time or date of a departing or return flight may be changed at any time (assuming seats are available) for a nominal service charge.

There also is a newer, often less expensive, type of excursion fare, the **APEX**, or **Advanced Purchase Excursion** fare. As with traditional excursion fares, passengers paying an APEX fare sit with and receive the same basic services as any other coach or economy passengers, even though they may have paid 50% less for their seats. In return, they are subject to certain restrictions. In the case of domestic flights, the ticket usually is good for a minimum of 7 days away and a maximum, currently, of 1 to 6 months (depending on the airline and the destination); and as its name implies, it must be "ticketed," or paid for in its entirety a certain period of time before departure — usually 21 days.

The drawback to some APEX fares is that they penalize travelers who change their minds — and travel plans. Usually the return reservation must be made at the time of the original ticketing, and if for some reason you change your schedule, you will have to pay a penalty of $100 or 10% of the ticket value, whichever is greater, as long as you travel within the valid period of your ticket. More flexible APEX fares recently have been introduced, which allow travelers to make changes in the date or time of their flights for a nominal charge (as low as $25).

With either type of APEX fare, if you change your return to a date less than the minimum stay or more than the maximum stay, the difference between the round-trip APEX fare and the full round-trip coach rate will have to be paid. There also is a penalty of anywhere from $50 to $100 or more for canceling or changing a reservation *before* travel begins — check the specific penalty in effect when you purchase your ticket.

In addition, most airlines also offer package deals that may include a car rental, accommodations, and dining and/or sightseeing features along with the basic airfare, and the combined cost of packaged elements usually is considerably less than the cost of the exact same elements when purchased separately.

When you're satisfied that you've found the lowest price for which you can conveniently qualify, make your booking. You may have to call the airline more than once, because different airline reservations clerks have been known to quote different prices, and different fares will be available at different times for the same flight because of a relatively new computerized airline practice called yield management, which adds or subtracts low-fare seats on a given flight depending on how well it is selling.

To protect yourself against fare increases, purchase and pay for your ticket as soon as possible after you've received a confirmed reservation. Airlines generally will honor their tickets, even if the price at the time of your flight is higher than the price you paid. If fares go up between the time you *reserve* a flight and the time you *pay* for it, however, you likely will be out of luck. Finally, with excursion or discount fares, it is important to remember that when a reservations clerk says that you must purchase a ticket by a specific date, this is an absolute deadline. Miss the deadline and the airline usually will automatically cancel your reservation without telling you.

Frequent Flyers – Most of the leading carriers serving Honolulu — including *American, Delta, Northwest,* and *United* — offer a bonus system to frequent travelers. After the first 10,000 miles, for example, a passenger might be eligible for a first class seat for the coach fare; after another 10,000 miles, he or she might receive a discount on his or her next ticket purchase. The value of the bonuses continues to increase as more miles are logged.

Bonus miles also may be earned by patronizing affiliated car rental companies or hotel chains, or by using one of the credit cards that now offers this reward. In deciding whether to accept such a credit card from one of the issuing organizations that tempt you with frequent flyer mileage bonuses on a specific airline, first determine whether the interest rate charged on the unpaid balance is the same as (or less than) possible alternate credit cards, and whether the annual "membership" fee also is equal or lower. If these charges are slightly higher than those of competing cards, weigh the difference against the potential value in airfare savings. Also ask about any bonus miles awarded just for signing up — 1,000 is common, 5,000 generally the maximum.

For the most up-to-date information on frequent flyer bonus options, you may want to send for the monthly *Frequent* newsletter. Issued by Frequent Publications, it provides current information about frequent flyer plans in general, as well as specific data about promotions, awards, and combination deals to help you keep track of the profusion — and confusion — of current and upcoming availabilities. For a year's subscription, send $33 to Frequent Publications, 4715-C Town Center Dr., Colorado Springs, CO 80916 (phone: 800-333-5937).

There also is a monthly magazine called *Frequent Flyer,* but unlike the newsletter mentioned above, its focus is primarily on newsy articles of interest to business travelers and other frequent flyers. Published by Official Airline Guides (PO Box 58543, Boulder, CO 80322-8543; phone: 800-323-3537), *Frequent Flyer* is available for $24 for a 1-year subscription.

Low-Fare Airlines – Increasingly, the stimulus for special fares is the appearance of airlines associated with bargain rates. On these airlines, all seats generally sell for the same price, which tends to be somewhat below the lowest discount fare offered by the larger, more established airlines. It is important to note that tickets offered by these smaller companies frequently are not subject to the same restrictions as some of the discounted fares offered by the more established carriers. They may not require advance purchase or minimum and maximum stays, may involve no cancellation penalties, and may be available one way or round trip. A disadvantage to some low-fare airlines, however, is that when something goes wrong, such as delayed baggage or a flight cancellation due to equipment breakdown, their smaller fleets and fewer flights mean that passengers may have to wait longer for a solution than they would on one of the equipment-rich major carriers.

Taxes and Other Fees – Travelers who have shopped for the best possible flight at the lowest possible price should be warned that a number of extras will be added to that price and collected by the airline or travel agent who issues the ticket. The 10% federal US Transportation Tax applies to travel within the US or US territories. Another fee is charged by some airlines to cover more stringent security procedures, prompted by recent terrorist incidents. Note that these taxes *usually* (but not always) are included in advertised fares and in the prices quoted by airlines reservations clerks.

Reservations – For those who don't have the time or patience to investigate personally all possible air departures and connections for a proposed trip, a travel agent can be of inestimable help. A good agent should have all the information on which flights go where and when, and which categories of tickets are available on each. Most have computerized reservation links with the major carriers, so that a seat can be reserved and confirmed in minutes. An increasing number of agents also possess fare-comparison computer programs, so they often are very reliable sources of detailed competitive price data. (For more information, see *How to Use a Travel Agent,* in this section.)

If making plane reservations through a travel agent, ask the agent to give the airline your home phone number, as well as your daytime business phone number. All too often the agent uses his or her agency's number as the official contact for changes in flight plans. Especially during the winter, weather conditions hundreds or even thousands of miles away can wreak havoc with flight schedules. The airlines are fairly reliable about getting this sort of information to passengers if they can reach them; diligence does little good at 10 PM if the airline has only the agency's or an office number.

Reconfirmation is not generally required on domestic flights. However, it always is wise to call ahead to make sure that the airline did not slip up in entering your original reservation, or in registering any changes you may have made since, and that it has your seat reservation and/or special meal request in the computer.

If you plan not to take a flight on which you hold a confirmed reservation, by all means inform the airline. Because the problem of "no-shows" is a constant expense for airlines, they are allowed to overbook flights, a practice that often contributes to the threat of denied boarding for a certain number of passengers (see "Getting Bumped," below).

Seating – For most types of tickets, airline seats usually are assigned on a first-come, first-served basis at check-in, although some airlines make it possible to reserve a seat at the time of ticket purchase. Always check in early for your flight, even with advance seat assignments. A good rule of thumb for domestic flights is to arrive at the airport *at least* 1 hour before the scheduled departure to give yourself plenty of time in case there are long lines.

Most airlines furnish seating charts, which make choosing a seat much easier, but there are a few basics to consider. You must decide whether you prefer a window, aisle, or middle seat. On those few domestic flights where smoking is permitted (see "Smoking," below), you also should indicate if you prefer the smoking or nonsmoking section.

The amount of legroom provided (as well as chest room, especially when the seat in front of you is in a reclining position) is determined by something called "pitch," a measure of the distance between the back of the seat in front of you and the front of the back of your seat. The amount of pitch is a matter of airline policy, not the type of plane you fly. First class and business class seats have the greatest pitch, a fact that figures prominently in airline advertising. In economy class or coach, the standard pitch ranges from 33 to as little as 31 inches — downright cramped.

The number of seats abreast, another factor determining comfort, depends on a combination of airline policy and airplane dimensions. First class and business class have the fewest seats per row. Economy generally has 9 seats per row on a DC-10 or an L-1011, making either one slightly more comfortable than a 747, on which there normally are 10 seats per row. A 727 has 6 seats per row.

Airline representatives claim that most craft are more stable toward the front and midsections, while the seats farthest from the engines are quietest. Passengers who have long legs and are traveling on a wide-body aircraft might request a seat directly behind a door or emergency exit, since these seats often have greater than average pitch, or a seat in the first row of a given section, which offers extra legroom — although these seats are increasingly being reserved for passengers who are willing (and able) to perform certain tasks in the event of emergency evacuation. It often is impossible, however, to see the movie from seats that are directly behind the plane's exits. Be aware that the first row of the economy section (called a "bulkhead" seat) on a conventional aircraft (not a widebody) does *not* offer extra legroom, since the fixed partition will not permit passengers to slide their feet under it, and that watching a movie from this first-row seat also can be difficult and uncomfortable. These bulkhead seats do, however, provide ample room to use a bassinet or safety seat and often are reserved for families traveling with small children.

A window seat protects you from aisle traffic and clumsy serving carts and also provides a view, while an aisle seat enables you to get up and stretch your legs without disturbing your fellow travelers. Middle seats are the least desirable, and seats in the last row are the worst of all, since they seldom recline fully. If you wish to avoid children on your flight or if you find that you are sitting in an especially noisy section, you usually are free to move to any unoccupied seat — if there is one.

If you are large, you may face the prospect of a long flight with special trepidation. Center seats in the alignments of wide-body 747s, L-1011s, and DC-10s are about 1½ inches wider than those on either side, so larger travelers tend to be more comfortable there.

Despite all these rules of thumb, finding out which specific rows are near emergency exits or at the front of a wide-body cabin can be difficult because seating arrangements on any two same-model planes usually vary from airline to airline. There is, however, a quarterly publication called the *Airline Seating Guide* that publishes seating charts for most major US airlines and many foreign carriers as well. Your travel agent should have a copy, or you can buy the US edition for $39.95 per year. Order from Carlson Publishing Co., Box 888, Los Alamitos, CA 90720 (phone: 800-728-4877 or 310-493-4877).

Simply reserving an airline seat in advance, however, actually may guarantee very little. Most airlines require that passengers arrive at the departure gate at least 45 minutes (sometimes more) ahead of time to hold a seat reservation. It pays to read the fine print on your ticket carefully and follow its requirements.

A far better strategy is to visit an airline ticket office (or one of a select group of travel agents) to secure an actual boarding pass for your specific flight. Once this has been issued, airline computers show you as checked in, and you effectively own the seat you have selected (although some carriers may not honor boarding passes of passengers arriving at the gate less than 10 minutes before departure). This also is good — but not foolproof — insurance against getting bumped from an overbooked flight and is, therefore, an especially valuable tactic at peak travel times.

Smoking – One decision regarding choosing a seat has been taken out of the hands of most domestic travelers who smoke. Effective February 25, 1990, the US government imposed a ban that prohibits smoking on all flights scheduled for 6 hours or less within the US and its territories. The new regulation applies to both domestic and international carriers serving these routes.

Only flights with a *continuous* flying time of over 6 hours between stops in the US or its territories are exempt. Even if the total flying time is longer, smoking is not permitted on segments of domestic flights where the time between US landings is under 6 hours — for instance, flights that include a stopover (even with no change of plane) or connecting flights. To further complicate the situation, several individual carriers ban smoking altogether on certain routes.

On those flights that do permit smoking, the US Department of Transportation has determined that nonsmoking sections must be enlarged to accommodate all passengers who wish to sit in one. The airline does not, however, have to shift seating to accommodate nonsmokers who arrive late for a flight or travelers flying standby. Cigar and pipe smoking are prohibited on all flights, even in the smoking sections.

For a wallet-size guide, which notes in detail the rights of nonsmokers according to these regulations, send a self-addressed, stamped envelope to ASH (Action on Smoking and Health), Airline Card, 2013 H St. NW, Washington, DC 20006 (phone: 202-659-4310).

Meals – If you have specific dietary requirements, be sure to let the airline know well before departure time. The available meals include vegetarian, seafood, kosher, Muslim, Hindu, high-protein, low-calorie, low-cholesterol, low-fat, low-sodium, diabetic, bland, and children's menus (not all of these may be available on every carrier). There is no extra charge for this option. It usually is necessary to request special meals when you make your reservations — check-in time is too late. It's also wise to reconfirm that your request for a special meal has made its way into the airline's computer — the time to do this is 24 hours before departure. (Note that special meals generally are not available on shorter domestic flights, particularly on small local carriers. If this poses a problem, try to eat before you board, or bring a snack with you.)

Baggage – Though airline baggage allowances vary slightly, in general all passengers are allowed to carry on board, without charge, one piece of luggage that will fit easily under a seat of the plane or in an overhead bin, and whose combined dimensions (length, width, and depth) do not exceed 45 inches. A reasonable amount of reading material, camera equipment, and a handbag also are allowed. In addition, all passengers are allowed to check two bags in the cargo hold: one usually not to exceed 62 inches when length, width, and depth are combined, the other not to exceed 55 inches in combined dimensions. Generally no single bag may weigh more than 70 pounds.

Charges for additional, oversize, or overweight bags usually are made at a flat rate; the actual dollar amount varies from carrier to carrier. If you plan to travel with any special equipment or sporting gear, be sure to check with the airline beforehand. Most have specific procedures for handling such baggage, and you may have to pay for transport regardless of how much other baggage you have checked. Golf clubs and skis may be checked through as luggage (most airlines are accustomed to handling them), but tennis rackets should be carried onto the plane. Aqualung tanks, depressurized and appropriately packed with padding, and surfboards (minus the fin and padded) also may go as baggage. Snorkeling gear should be packed in a suitcase, duffel, or tote bag.

To reduce the chances of your luggage going astray, remove all airline tags from previous trips, label each bag inside and out — with your business address, rather than your home address, on the outside, to prevent thieves from knowing whose house might be unguarded. Lock everything and double-check the tag that the airline attaches to make sure that it is correctly coded HNL for Honolulu.

If your bags are not in the baggage claim area after your flight or if they're damaged, report the problem to airline personnel immediately. Keep in mind that policies regarding the specific time limit within which you have to make your claim vary from carrier to carrier. Fill out a report form on your lost or damaged luggage and keep a copy of it and your original baggage claim check. If you must surrender the check to claim a damaged bag, get a receipt for it to prove that you did, indeed, check your baggage on the flight. If luggage is missing, be sure to give the airline your destination and/or the telephone number where you can be reached. Also take the name and number of the person in charge of recovering lost luggage.

Most airlines have emergency funds for passengers stranded away from home without their luggage, but if it turns out that your bags are truly lost and not simply delayed, do not then and there sign any paper indicating you'll accept an offered settlement. Since the airline is responsible for the value of your bags within certain statutory limits ($1,250 per passenger for lost baggage on a US domestic flight) you should take the time to assess the extent of your loss (see *Insurance,* in this section). It's a good idea to keep records indicating the value of the contents of your luggage. A wise alternative is to take a Polaroid picture of the most valuable of your packed items just after putting them in your suitcase.

Considering the increased incidence of damage to baggage, now more than ever it's advisable to keep the sales slips that confirm how much you paid for your bags. These are invaluable in establishing the value of damaged luggage and eliminate any arguments. A better way to protect your precious gear from the luggage-eating conveyers is to try to carry it on board whenever possible.

Getting Bumped – A special air travel problem is the possibility that an airline will accept more reservations (and sell more tickets) than there are seats on a given flight. This is entirely legal and is done to make up for "no-shows," passengers who don't show up for a flight for which they have made reservations and bought tickets. If the airline has oversold the flight and everyone does show up, there simply aren't enough seats. When this happens, the airline is subject to stringent rules designed to protect travelers.

In such cases, the airline first seeks ticket holders willing to give up their seats voluntarily in return for a negotiable sum of money or some other inducement, such as an offer of upgraded seating on the next flight or a voucher for a free trip at some other time. If there are not enough volunteers, the airline may bump passengers against their wishes.

Anyone inconvenienced in this way, however, is entitled to an explanation of the criteria used to determine who does and does not get on the flight, as well as compensation if the resulting delay exceeds certain limits. If the airline can put the bumped passengers on an alternate flight that is *scheduled to arrive* at their original destination within 1 hour of their originally scheduled arrival time, no compensation is owed. If the delay is more than 1 hour but less than 2 hours on a domestic US flight, they must be paid denied-boarding compensation equivalent to the one-way fare to their destination (but not more than $200). If the delay is more than 2 hours after the original arrival time on a domestic flight, the compensation must be doubled (not more than $400). The airline also may offer bumped travelers a voucher for a free flight instead of the denied-boarding compensation. The passenger may be given the choice of either the money or the voucher, the dollar value of which may be no less than the monetary compensation to which the passenger would be entitled. The voucher is not a substitute for the bumped passenger's original ticket; the airline continues to honor that as well. Keep in mind that the above regulations and policies are for US flights only.

To protect yourself as best you can against getting bumped, arrive at the airport early, allowing plenty of time to check in and get to the gate. If the flight is oversold, ask immediately for the written statement explaining the airline's policy on denied-boarding compensation and its boarding priorities. If the airline refuses to give you this information, or if you feel they have not handled the situation properly, file a complaint with both the airline and the appropriate government agency (see "Consumer Protection," below).

Delays and Cancellations – The above compensation rules also do not apply if the flight is canceled or delayed, or if a smaller aircraft is substituted due to mechanical problems. Each airline has its own policy for assisting passengers whose flights are delayed or canceled or who must wait for another flight because their original one was overbooked. Most airline personnel will make new travel arrangements if necessary. If the delay is longer than 4 hours, the airline may pay for a phone call or telegram, a meal, and, in some cases, a hotel room and transportation to it.

■**Caution:** If you are bumped or miss a flight, be sure to ask the airline to notify other airlines on which you have reservations or connecting flights. When your name is taken off the passenger list of your initial flight, the computer usually cancels all of your reservations automatically, unless *you* take steps to preserve them.

CHARTER FLIGHTS: By booking a block of seats on a specially arranged flight, charter tour operators offer travelers air transportation for a substantial reduction over the full coach or economy fare. These operators may offer air-only charters (selling transportation alone) or charter packages (the flight plus a combination of land arrangements such as accommodations, meals, tours, or car rentals). Charters are especially attractive to people living in smaller cities or out-of-the-way places, because they frequently take off from nearby airports, saving travelers the inconvenience and expense of getting to a major gateway.

From the consumer's standpoint, charters differ from scheduled airlines in two main respects: You generally need to book and pay in advance, and you can't change the itinerary or the departure and return dates once you've booked the flight. In practice, however, these restrictions don't always apply. Today, although most domestic charter flights still require advance reservations, some permit last-minute bookings (when there are unsold seats available), and some even offer seats on a standby basis. Though charters almost always are round trip, and it is unlikely that you would be sold a one-way seat on a round-trip flight, on rare occasions one-way tickets on charters are offered.

Things to keep in mind about the charter game:

1. It cannot be repeated often enough that if you are forced to cancel your trip, you can lose much (and possibly all) of your money unless you have cancellation insurance, which is a *must* (see *Insurance,* in this section). Frequently, if the cancellation occurs far enough in advance (often 6 weeks or more), you may forfeit only a $25 or $50 penalty. If you cancel only 2 or 3 weeks before the flight, there may be no refund at all unless you or the operator can provide a substitute passenger.
2. Charter flights may be canceled by the operator up to 10 days before departure for any reason, usually underbooking. Your money is returned in this event, but there may be too little time for you to make new arrangements.
3. Most charters have little of the flexibility of regularly scheduled flights regarding refunds and the changing of flight dates; if you book a return flight, you must be on it or lose your money.
4. Charter operators are permitted to assess a surcharge, if fuel or other costs warrant it, of up to 10% of the airfare up to 10 days before departure.
5. Because of the economics of charter flights, your plane almost always will be full, so you will be crowded, though not necessarily uncomfortable. (There is, however, a new movement among charter airlines to provide flight accommodations that are more comfort-oriented, so this situation may change in the near future.)

To avoid problems, *always* choose charter flights with care. When you consider a charter, ask your travel agent who runs it and carefully check the company. The Better Business Bureau in the company's home city can report on how many complaints, if any, have been lodged against it in the past. Protect yourself with trip cancellation and interruption insurance, which can help safeguard your investment if you, or a traveling companion, are unable to make the trip and must cancel too late to receive a full refund from the company providing your travel services. (This is advisable whether you're buying a charter flight alone or a tour package for which the airfare is provided by charter or scheduled flight.)

Bookings – If you do fly on a charter, read the contract's fine print carefully and pay particular attention to the following:

Instructions concerning the payment of the deposit and its balance and to whom the check is to be made payable. Ordinarily, checks are made out to an escrow account, which means the charter company can't spend your money until your flight has safely returned. This provides some protection for you. To ensure the safe handling of your money, make out your check to the escrow account, the number of which must appear by law on the brochure, though all too often it is on the back in fine print. Write the details of the charter, including the destination and dates, on the face of the check; on the back, print "For Deposit Only." Your travel agent may prefer that you make out your check to the agency, saying that it will then pay the tour operator the fee minus commission. It is perfectly legal to write the check as we suggest, however, and if your agent objects too vociferously (he or she should trust the tour operator to send the proper commission), consider taking your business elsewhere. If you don't make your check out to the escrow account, you lose the protection of that escrow should the trip be canceled. Furthermore, recent bankruptcies in the travel industry have served to point out that even the protection of escrow may not be enough to safeguard a traveler's investment. More and more, insurance is becoming a necessity. The charter company should be bonded (usually by an insurance company), and if you want to file a claim against it, the claim should be sent to the bonding agent. The contract will set a time limit within which a claim must be filed.

Specific stipulations and penalties for cancellations. Most charters allow you to cancel up to 45 days in advance without major penalty, but some cancellation dates are 50 to 60 days before departure.

Stipulations regarding cancellation and major changes made by the charterer. US rules say that charter flights may not be canceled within 10 days of departure except when circumstances — such as natural disasters or political upheavals — make it physically impossible to fly. Charterers may make "major changes," however, such as in the date or place of departure or return, but you are entitled to cancel and receive a full refund if you don't wish to accept these changes. A price increase of more than 10% at any time up to 10 days before departure is considered a major change; no price increase at all is allowed during the last 10 days immediately before departure.

At the time of this writing, the following companies regularly offered charter flights within the US:

> *Amber Tours* (7337 W. Washington St., Indianapolis, IN 46251; phone: 800-225-9920). Goes to Honolulu. Retails to the general public.
>
> *Apple Vacations East* (7 Campus Blvd., Newtown Sq., PA 19073; phone: 800-727-3400). This agency is a wholesaler, so use a travel agent.
>
> *Funway Holidays* (PO Box 1460, Milwaukee, WI 53201-1460; phone: 800-558-3050). This agency is a wholesaler, so use a travel agent.
>
> *MLT Vacations* (5130 Hwy. 101, Minnetonka, MN 55345; phone: 800-328-0025). Goes to Honolulu. This agency is a wholesaler, so use a travel agent.
>
> *Morris Air Service* (260 E. Morris Ave., Salt Lake City, UT 84115-3200; phone: 800-444-5660). Retails to the general public.
>
> *MTI Vacations* (1220 Kensington Ct., Oak Brook, IL 60521; phone: 800-323-7285 or 708-990-8028). This agency is a wholesaler, so use a travel agent.

Suntrips (2350 Paragon Dr., San Jose, CA 95131; phone: 800-SUNTRIP in California; 408-432-0700 elsewhere in the US). Goes to Honolulu. Retails to the general public.

You also may want to subscribe to the travel newsletter *Jax Fax,* which regularly features a list of charter companies and packagers offering seats on US charter flights. For a year's subscription, send a check or money order for $12 to *Jax Fax,* 397 Post Rd., Darien, CT 06820 (phone: 203-655-8746).

DISCOUNTS ON SCHEDULED FLIGHTS: Promotional fares often are called discount fares because they cost less than what used to be the standard airline fare — full-fare economy. Nevertheless, they cost the traveler the same whether they are bought through a travel agent or directly from the airline. Tickets that cost less if bought from some outlet other than the airline do exist, however. While it is likely that the vast majority of travelers flying within the US in the near future will be doing so on a promotional fare or charter rather than on a "discount" air ticket of this sort, it still is a good idea for cost-conscious consumers to be aware of the latest developments in the budget airfare scene. Note that the following discussion makes clear-cut distinctions among the types of discounts available based on how they reach the consumer; in actual practice, the distinctions are not nearly so precise.

Net Fare Sources – The newest notion for reducing the costs of travel services comes from travel agents who offer individual travelers "net" fares. Defined simply, a net fare is the bare minimum amount at which an airline or tour operator will carry a prospective traveler. It doesn't include the amount that normally would be paid to the travel agent as a commission. Traditionally, such commissions amount to about 10% on domestic fares — not counting significant additions to these commission levels that are paid retroactively when agents sell more than a specific volume of tickets or trips for a single supplier. At press time, at least one travel agency in the US was offering travelers the opportunity to purchase tickets and/or tours for a net price. Instead of earning its income from individual commissions, this agency assesses a fixed fee that may or may not provide a bargain for travelers; it requires a little arithmetic to determine whether to use the services of a net travel agent or those of one who accepts conventional commissions. One of the potential drawbacks of buying from agencies selling travel services at net fares is that some airlines refuse to do business with them, thus possibly limiting your flight options.

Travel Avenue is a fee-based agency that rebates its ordinary agency commission to the customer. They will find the lowest retail fare, then rebate 7% to 10% (depending on the airline) of that price, minus a ticket-writing charge of $10 for domestic flights. The ticket-writing charge is imposed per ticket; if the ticket includes more than eight separate flights, an additional $10 fee is charged. Customers using free flight coupons pay the ticket-writing charge, plus an additional $5 coupon-processing fee.

Travel Avenue will rebate its commissions on all tickets, including heavily discounted fares and senior citizen passes. Available 7 days a week, reservations should be made far enough in advance to allow the tickets to be sent by first class mail, since extra charges accrue for special handling. It's possible to economize further by making your own airline reservation, then asking *Travel Avenue* only to write/issue your ticket. For travelers outside the Chicago area, business may be transacted by phone and purchases charged to a credit card. For information, contact *Travel Avenue* at 641 W. Lake, Suite 201, Chicago, IL 60606-1012 (phone: 312-876-1116 in Illinois; 800-333-3335 elsewhere in the US).

Consolidators and Bucket Shops – Other vendors of travel services can afford to sell tickets to their customers at an even greater discount because the airline has sold the tickets to them at a substantial discount (usually accomplished by sharply increasing commissions to that vendor). Many airlines indulge in this practice, albeit discreetly, preferring that the general public not know they are undercutting their own "list" prices. Airlines anticipating a slow period on a particular route sometimes sell off a certain portion of their capacity at a very great discount to a wholesaler, or consolidator. The wholesaler sometimes is a charter operator who resells the seats to the public as though they were charter seats, which is why prospective travelers perusing the brochures of charter operators with large programs frequently see a number of flights designated as "scheduled service." As often as not, however, the consolidator, in turn, sells the seats to a travel agency specializing in discounting. Airlines also can sell seats directly to such an agency, which thus acts as its own consolidator. The airline offers the seats either at a net wholesale price, but without the volume-purchase requirement that would be difficult for a modest retail travel agency to fulfill, or at the standard price, but with a commission override large enough (as high as 50%) to allow both a profit and a price reduction to the public.

Travel agencies specializing in discounting sometimes are called "bucket shops," a term fraught with connotations of unreliability in this country. But in today's highly competitive travel marketplace, more and more conventional travel agencies are selling consolidator-supplied tickets, and the old bucket shops' image is becoming respectable. Agencies that specialize in discounted tickets exist in most large cities, and usually can be found by studying the smaller ads in the travel sections of local Sunday newspapers.

Before buying a discounted ticket, whether from a bucket shop or a conventional, full-service travel agency, keep the following considerations in mind: To be in a position to judge how much you'll be saving, first find out the "list" prices of tickets to your destination. Then do some comparison shopping among agencies. Also bear in mind that a ticket that may not differ much in price from one available directly from the airline may, however, allow the circumvention of such things as the advance-purchase requirement. If your plans are less than final, be sure to find out about any other restrictions, such as penalties for canceling a flight or changing a reservation. Most discount tickets are non-endorsable, meaning that they can be used only on the airline that issued them, and they usually are marked "nonrefundable" to prevent their being cashed in for a list-price refund.

A great many bucket shops are small businesses operating on a thin margin, so it's a good idea to check the local Better Business Bureau for any complaints registered against the one with which you're dealing — before parting with any money. If you still do not feel reassured, consider buying discounted tickets only through a conventional travel agency, which can be expected to have found its own reliable source of consolidator tickets — some of the largest consolidators, in fact, sell only to travel agencies.

A few bucket shops require payment in cash or by certified check or money order, but if credit cards are accepted, use that option. Note, however, if buying from a charter operator selling both scheduled and charter flights, that the scheduled seats are not protected by the regulations — including the use of escrow accounts — governing the charter seats. Well-established charter operators, nevertheless, may extend the same protections to their scheduled flights, and when this is the case, consumers should be sure that the payment option selected directs their money into the escrow account.

Listed below are some of the consolidators frequently offering discounted domestic fares:

> *Bargain Air* (655 Deep Valley Dr., Suite 355, Rolling Hills, CA 90274; phone: 800-347-2345 or 213-377-2919).
>
> *Maharaja/Consumer Wholesale Travel* (34 W. 33rd St., Suite 1014, New York, NY 10001; phone: 212-213-2020 in New York State; 800-223-6862 elsewhere in the US).
>
> *TFI Tours International* (34 W. 32nd St., 12th Floor, New York, NY 10001; phone: 212-736-1140 in New York State; 800-825-3834 elsewhere in the US).

25 West Tours (2490 Coral Way, Miami, FL 33145; phone: 305-856-0810 in Florida; 800-252-5052 elsewhere in the US).

Unitravel (1177 N. Warson Rd., St. Louis, MO 63132; phone: 314-569-0900 in Missouri; 800-325-2222 elsewhere in the US).

Check with your travel agent for other sources of consolidator-supplied tickets.

■**Note:** Although rebating and discounting are becoming increasingly common, there is some legal ambiguity concerning them. Strictly speaking, it is legal to discount domestic tickets but not international tickets. On the other hand, the law that prohibits discounting, the Federal Aviation Act of 1958, is consistently ignored these days, in part because consumers benefit from the practice and in part because many illegal arrangements are indistinguishable from legal ones. Since the line separating the two is so fine that even the authorities can't always tell the difference, it is unlikely that most consumers would be able to do so, and in fact it is not illegal to *buy* a discounted ticket. If the issue of legality bothers you, ask the agency whether any ticket you're about to buy would be permissible under the above-mentioned act.

Last-Minute Travel Clubs – Still another way to take advantage of bargain airfares is open to those who have a flexible schedule. A number of organizations, usually set up as last-minute travel clubs and functioning on a membership basis, routinely keep in touch with travel suppliers to help them dispose of unsold inventory at discounts of between 15% and 60%. A great deal of the inventory consists of complete package tours and cruises, but some clubs offer air-only charter seats and, occasionally, seats on scheduled flights.

Members generally pay an annual fee and receive a toll-free hotline telephone number to call for information on imminent trips. In some cases, they also receive periodic mailings with information on bargain travel opportunities for which there is more advance notice. Despite the suggestive names of the clubs providing these services, last-minute travel does not necessarily mean that you cannot make plans until literally the last minute. Trips can be announced as little as a few days or as much as 2 months before departure, but the average is from 1 to 4 weeks' notice.

Among the organizations regularly offering such discounted travel opportunities in the US are the following:

Discount Travel International (Ives Building, 114 Forrest Ave., Suite 205, Narberth, PA 19072; phone: 800-334-9294 or 215-668-7184). Annual fee: $45 per household.

Encore/Short Notice (4501 Forbes Blvd., Lanham, MD 20706 (phone: 301-459-8020; 800-638-0930 for customer service). Annual fee: $48 per family for Encore (main discount travel program), $36 per family for Short Notice program.

Last Minute Travel (1249 Boylston St., Boston MA 02215; phone: 800-LAST-MIN or 617-267-9800). No fee.

Moment's Notice (425 Madison Ave., New York, NY 10017; phone: 212-486-0503). Annual fee: $45 per family.

Traveler's Advantage (3033 S. Parker Rd., Suite 1000, Aurora, CO 80014; phone: 800-548-1116). Annual fee: $49 per family.

Vacations to Go (2411 Fountain View, Suite 201, Houston, TX 77057; phone: 800-338-4962). Annual fee: $19.95 per family.

Worldwide Discount Travel Club (1674 Meridian Ave., Miami Beach, FL 33139; phone: 305-534-2082). Annual fee: $40 per person; $50 per family.

Generic Air Travel – Organizations that apply the same flexible-schedule idea to air travel only and arrange for flights at literally the last minute also exist. Their service sometimes is known as "generic" air travel, and it operates somewhat like an ordinary airline standby service except that the organizations running it do not guarantee flights to a specific destination, but only to a general region, and offer seats on not one but several scheduled and charter airlines.

One pioneer of generic flights is *Airhitch* (2790 Broadway, Suite 100, New York, NY 10025; phone: 212-864-2000), which offers flights to Hawaii from the West Coast through its Hawaiihitch program. Prospective travelers stipulate a range of at least 5 consecutive departure dates and their desired destination, along with alternate choices, and pay the fare in advance. They are then sent a voucher good for travel *on a space-available basis* on flights to Hawaii during this time period. The week before this range of departure dates begins, travelers must contact *Airhitch* for specific information about flights on which seats may be available and instructions on how to proceed for check-in. (Return fights are arranged in the same manner as the outbound flights — a specified period of travel is decided upon, and a few days before this date range begins, prospective passengers contact *Airhitch* for details bout flights that may be available.) If the client does not accept any of the suggested flights or cancels his or her travel plans after selecting a flight, the amount paid may be applied toward a future fare or the flight arrangements can be transferred to another individual (although, in both cases, an additional fee may be charged). No refunds are offered unless the prospective passenger does not ultimately get on any flight in the specified date range; in such a case, the full fare is refunded. (Note that *Airhitch*'s slightly more expensive Target program, which provides confirmed reservations on specific dates to specific destinations, offers passengers greater — but not guaranteed — certainty regarding destinations and other flight arrangements.)

Bartered Travel Sources – Suppose a hotel buys advertising space in a newspaper. As payment, the hotel gives the publishing company the use of a number of hotel rooms in lieu of cash. This is barter, a common means of exchange among hotels, airlines, car rental companies, cruise lines, tour operators, restaurants, and other travel service companies. When a bartering company finds itself with empty airline seats (or excess hotel rooms, or cruise ship cabin space, and so on) and offers them to the public, considerable savings can be enjoyed.

Bartered travel clubs often can give discounts of up to 50% to members, who pay an annual fee (approximately $50 at press time) which entitles them to select from the flights, cruises, hotel rooms, or other travel services that the club obtained by barter. Members usually present a voucher, club credit card, or scrip (a dollar-denomination voucher negotiable only for the bartered product) to the hotel, which in turn subtracts the dollar amount from the bartering company's account.

Selling bartered travel is a perfectly legitimate means of retailing. One advantage to club members is that they don't have to wait until the last minute to obtain flight or room reservations.

Among the companies specializing in bartered travel, several that frequently offer members travel services throughout the US include the following:

> *Travel Guild* (18210 Redmond Way, Redmond, WA 98052; phone: 206-861-1900). Annual fee: $48 per family.
>
> *Travel World Leisure Club* (225 W. 34th St., Suite 2203, New York, NY 10122; phone: 800-444-TWLC or 212-239-4855). Annual fee: $50 per person; $20 for each additional member of a family.

OTHER DISCOUNT TRAVEL SOURCES: An excellent source of information on economical travel opportunities is the *Consumer Reports Travel Letter,* published monthly by Consumers Union. It keeps abreast of the scene on a wide variety of fronts, including package tours, rental cars, insurance, and more, but it is especially helpful for its comprehensive coverage of airfares, offering guidance on all the options, from scheduled flights on major or low-fare airlines to charters and discount sources. For a year's subscription, send $37 ($57 for 2 years) to *Consumer Reports Travel Letter* (PO Box 53629, Boulder, CO 80322-3629; phone: 800-999-7959). For information on other travel newsletters, see *For More Information,* in this section.

CONSUMER PROTECTION: Consumers who feel that they have not been dealt with fairly by an airline should make their complaints known. Begin with the customer service representative at the airport where the problem occurred. If your complaint cannot be resolved there to your satisfaction, write to the airline's consumer office. In a businesslike, typed letter, explain what reservations you held, what happened, the names of the employees involved, and what you expect the airline to do to remedy the situation. Send copies (never the originals) of the tickets, receipts, and other documents that back your claims. Ideally, all correspondence should be sent via certified mail, return receipt requested. This provides proof that your complaint was received.

Passengers with consumer complaints — lost baggage, compensation for getting bumped, violation of smoking and nonsmoking rules, deceptive practices by an airline — who are not satisfied with the airline's response should contact the Department of Transportation (DOT), Consumer Affairs Division (400 7th St. SW, Room 10405, Washington, DC 20590; phone: 202-366-2220). DOT personnel stress, however, that consumers initially should direct their complaints to the airline that provoked them.

Remember, too, that the federal Fair Credit Billing Act permits purchasers to refuse to pay for credit card charges for services which have not been delivered, so the onus of dealing with the receiver for a bankrupt airline, for example, falls on the credit card company. Do not rely on another airline to honor any ticket you're holding from a failed airline, since the days when virtually all major carriers subscribed to a default protection program that bound them to do so are long gone. Some airlines may voluntarily step forward to accommodate the stranded passengers of a fellow carrier, but this is now an entirely altruistic act.

The deregulation of US airlines has meant that travelers must find out for themselves what they are entitled to receive. The Department of Transportation's informative consumer booklet, *Fly Rights,* is a good place to start. To receive a copy, send $1 to the Superintendent of Documents (US Government Printing Office, Washington, DC 20402-9325; phone: 202-783-3238). Specify its stock number, 050-000-00513-5, and allow 3 to 4 weeks for delivery.

On Arrival

FROM THE AIRPORT TO THE CITY: Honolulu International Airport is located 6 miles northwest of Honolulu's city center. The ride from the airport to downtown usually takes about 20 to 25 minutes. (In the following listings, the area code is 808 unless otherwise indicated.)

Bus Service – Two companies transfer passengers between the airport and Waikiki hotels. Each one charges $6 for the trip. *Airport Motorcoach* (phone: 926-4747) picks up passengers at the *Aloha* and *Hawaiian* airlines terminals and at the median strip in front of the International Arrivals building. *Airport Bus* (phone: 942-2177) also picks up at the inter-island terminals and at Baggage Claim Area H of International Arrivals.

At 60¢ a ride, *TheBus,* Oahu's public transit system, is the cheapest way to get into the city — but only if you're carrying a minimal amount of luggage, such as a bag that fits on your lap.

CAR RENTAL: Most travelers who want to drive while on vacation can rent a car through a travel agent or national rental firm before leaving home, or from a local company once they arrive in Honolulu. Another possibility, also arranged before departure, is to rent the car as part of a larger travel package.

It's tempting to wait until arrival to scout out the lowest-priced rental from the company located the farthest from the airport high-rent district and offering no pick-up services. But if your arrival coincides with a holiday or a peak travel period, you may be disappointed to find that even the most expensive car in the city was reserved months ago. Whenever possible, it is best to reserve in advance, anywhere from a few days in slack periods to a month or more during the busier seasons.

Often, the easiest place to rent (or at least pick up) the car is at the airport on arrival. The majority of the national car rental companies have locations at Honolulu International Airport, where shuttle buses from each company pick up clients from the terminals and take them to the car rental locations. Travel agents can arrange rentals for clients, but it is just as easy to call and rent a car yourself. Listed below are the nationwide, toll-free telephone numbers of the major national rental companies that have locations in Honolulu:

Alamo: 800-327-9633
American International Rent-A-Car: 800-527-0202
Avis: 800-831-8000
Budget Rent-A-Car: 800-527-0700
Dollar Rent-A-Car: 800-367-7006
Hertz: 800-654-3131
National Car Rental: 800-CAR-RENT
Sears Rent-A-Car: 800-527-0770
Thrifty Rent-A-Car: 800-367-2277

If you decide to wait until after you arrive, you'll often find a surprising number of small companies listed in the local yellow pages. (All of the following are in the 808 area code.) One such company is *Aloha Funway Rentals* with a variety of locations, including one near the airport at 3165 N. Nimitz Hwy. (phone: 834-1016), and in Waikiki at 1778 Ala Moana Blvd. (phone: 942-9696). Two other companies are *Tropical Rent A Car* (phone: 800-678-6000) with a location at the airport and in Waikiki at 205 Lewers St., and *Island Rent A Car* (839-2222) at 530 Paiea St. near the airport.

To economize on a car rental, also consider one of the firms that rents 3- to 5-year-old cars that are well worn but (presumably) mechanically sound; one such company is *Waikiki Rent-a-Car* at 1958 Kalakaua Ave. (phone: 946-2181). While the company cannot make airport pick-ups, it might well be worth the taxi ride, especially since it is in such a convenient location in the city for tourists.

At the other extreme, for those who feel like splurging, *Ferrari Rentals* (1958 Kalakaua Ave.; phone: 942-8725) offers Porsches, Jaguars, Corvettes, and, of course, Ferraris. And for a little bit of nostalgia, *Classic Car Rentals* at the same address (phone: 951-8331) will fit you out in a Model A roadster or an *American Graffiti*-style "street rod."

Requirements – Whether you decide to rent a car in advance from a large national rental company or wait to rent from a local company, you should know that renting a car is rarely as simple as signing on the dotted line and roaring off into the night. If you are renting for personal use, you must have a valid driver's license and will have to convince the renting agency that (1) you are personally creditworthy, and (2) you will bring the car back at the stated time. This will be easy if you have a major credit card; most rental companies accept credit cards in lieu of a cash deposit, as well as for payment of your final bill. If you prefer to pay in cash, leave your credit card imprint as a "deposit," then pay your bill in cash when you return the car.

Note that *Avis, Budget, Hertz,* and other national companies usually *will* rent to travelers paying in cash and leaving either a credit card imprint or a substantial amount of cash as a deposit. This is not necessarily standard policy, however, as other national chains and a number of local companies will *not* rent to an individual who doesn't have a valid credit card. In this case, you will have to call around to find a company that accepts cash.

Also keep in mind that although the minimum age to drive in most states is 16, the minimum age to rent a car is set by the rental company. (Restrictions vary from company to company, as well as at different locations.) Many firms have a minimum age requirement of 21 years, some raise that to 23 or 25 years, and for some models of cars it rises to 30 years. The upper age limit at many companies is between 69 and 75; others have no upper limit or may make drivers above a certain age subject to special conditions.

Costs – Finding the most economical car rental will require some telephone shopping on your part. As a *general* rule, expect to hear lower prices quoted by the smaller, strictly local companies than by the well-known international names.

Comparison shopping always is advisable, however. Even the international giants offer discount plans whose conditions are easy for most travelers to fulfill. For instance, *Budget* and *National* sometimes offer discounts of anywhere from 10% to 30% off their usual rates (according to the size of the car and the duration of the rental), provided that the car is reserved a certain number of days before departure (usually 7 to 14 days, but it can be less), is rented for a minimum period (5 days or, more often, a week), is paid for at the time of booking, and, in most cases, is returned to the same location that supplied it or to another in the same area. Similar discount plans include *Hertz*'s Leisure Rates and *Avis*'s Supervalue Rates.

If driving short distances for only a day or two, the best deal may be a per-day, per-mile rate: You pay a flat fee for each day you keep the car, plus a per-mile charge. An increasingly common alternative is to be granted a certain number of free miles each day and then be charged on a per-mile basis over that number.

Most companies also offer a flat per-day rate with unlimited free mileage; this certainly is the most economical rate if you plan to drive over 100 miles. Make sure that the low, flat daily rate that catches your eye, however, is indeed a per-day rate: Often the lowest price advertised by a company turns out to be available only with a minimum 3-day rental — fine if you want the car that long, but not the bargain it appears if you really intend to use it no more than 24 hours. Flat weekly rates also are available, as are some flat monthly rates that represent a further saving over the daily rate.

Another factor influencing the cost is the type of car you rent. Rentals are based on a tiered price system, with different sizes of cars — variations of budget, economy, regular, and luxury — often listed as A (the smallest and least expensive) through F, G, or H, and sometimes even higher. Charges may increase by only a few dollars a day through several categories of subcompact and compact cars — where most of the competition is — then increase by great leaps through the remaining classes of full-size and luxury cars and passenger vans. The larger the car, the more it costs to rent and the more gas it consumes, but for some people the greater comfort and extra luggage space of a larger car (in which bags and sporting gear can be safely locked out of sight) may make it worth the additional expense. Also more expensive are sleek sports cars, but again, for some people the thrill of driving such a car — for a week or a day — may be worth it.

Electing to pay for collision damage waiver (CDW) protection will add considerably to the cost of renting a car. Some companies, such as *Hertz* and *Avis,* call the option a loss damage waiver (LDW). You may be responsible for the *full value* of the vehicle being rented if it is damaged or stolen, but you can dispense with all of the possible liability by buying the offered waiver at a cost of around $5 to $13 a day. Before making any decisions about optional collision damage waivers, however, check with your own insurance agent and determine whether your personal automobile insurance policy covers rented vehicles; if it does, you probably won't need to pay for the waiver. Be aware, too, that increasing numbers of credit cards automatically provide CDW coverage if the car rental is charged to the appropriate credit card. However, the specific terms of such credit card coverage differ sharply among individual card companies, so check with the credit card company for information on the nature and amount of coverage provided. Business travelers also should be aware that, at the time of this writing, *American Express* had withdrawn its automatic CDW coverage from some corporate *Green* card accounts and limited the length of coverage — watch for similar cutbacks by other credit card companies.

When inquiring about CDW or LDW coverage and costs, be aware that a number of car rental companies now are automatically including the cost of this waiver in their quoted prices. This does not mean that they are absorbing this cost and you are receiving free coverage — in many cases total rental prices have increased to include the former CDW charge. The disadvantage of this inclusion is that you probably will not have the option to refuse this coverage, and will end up paying the added charge — even if you already are adequately covered by your own insurance policy or through a credit card company.

Another cost to be added to the price tag is drop-off charges or one-way service fees. The lowest price quoted by any given company may apply only to a car that is returned to the same location from which it was rented. A slightly higher rate may be charged if the car is to be returned to a different location (even within the same city).

Package Tours

 If the mere thought of buying a package for your visit to Honolulu conjures up visions of a trip spent marching in lockstep through the city's attractions with a horde of frazzled fellow travelers, remember that packages have come a long way. For one thing, not all packages necessarily are escorted tours, and the one you buy does not have to include any organized touring at all — nor will it necessarily include traveling companions. If it does, however, you'll find that people of all sorts — many just like yourself — are taking advantage of packages today because they are economical and convenient and save an immense amount of planning time. Given the high cost of travel these days, packages have emerged as a particularly wise buy.

In essence, a package is just an amalgam of travel services that can be purchased in a single transaction. A package (tour or otherwise) may include any or all of the following: round-trip transportation, local transportation (and/or car rentals), accommodations, some or all meals, sightseeing, entertainment, transfers to and from the hotel, taxes, tips, escort service, and a variety of incidental features that might be offered as options at additional cost. In other words, a package can be any combination of travel elements, from a fully escorted tour offered at an all-inclusive price to a simple fly/drive booking that allows you to move about totally on your own. Its principal advantage is that it saves money: The cost of the combined arrangements invariably is well below the price of all of the same elements if bought separately, and, particularly if transportation is provided by discount flight, the whole package could cost less than just a round-trip economy airline ticket on a regularly scheduled flight. A package provides more than economy and convenience: It releases the traveler from having to make individual arrangements for each separate element of a trip.

Tour programs generally can be divided into two categories — "escorted" (or locally hosted) and "independent." An escorted tour means that a guide will accompany the group from the beginning of the tour through to the return flight; a locally hosted tour means that the group will be met upon arrival at each location by a different local host.

On independent tours, there generally is a choice of hotels, meal plans, and sightseeing trips, as well as a variety of special excursions. The independent plan is for travelers who do not want a totally set itinerary, but who do prefer confirmed hotel reservations. Whether choosing an escorted or an independent tour, always bring along complete contact information for your tour operator in case a problem arises, although tour operators often have local affiliates who can give additional assistance or make other arrangements on the spot.

To determine whether a package — or more specifically, *which* package — fits your travel plans, start by evaluating your interests and needs, deciding how much and what you want to spend, see, and do. Gather brochures on Honolulu tours. Be sure that you take the time to read each brochure *carefully* to determine precisely what is included. Keep in mind that they are written to entice you into signing up for a package tour. Often the language is deceptive and devious. For example, a brochure may quote the lowest prices for a package tour based on facilities that are unavailable during the off-season, undesirable at any season, or just plain nonexistent. Information such as "breakfast included" or "plus tax" (which can add up) should be taken into account. Note, too, that the prices quoted in brochures almost always are based on double occupancy: The rate listed is for each of two people sharing a double room, and if you travel alone, the supplement for single accommodations can raise the price considerably (see *Hints for Single Travelers,* in this section).

In this age of erratic airfares, the brochure most often will *not* include the price of an airline ticket in the price of the package, though sample fares from various gateway cities usually will be listed separately, as extras to be added to the price of the ground arrangements. Before figuring your actual costs, check the latest fares with the airlines, because the samples invariably are out of date by the time you read them. If the brochure gives more than one category of sample fares per gateway city — such as an individual tour-basing fare, a group fare, an excursion, APEX, or other discount ticket — your travel agent or airline tour desk will be able to tell you which one applies to the package you choose, depending on when you travel, how far in advance you book, and other factors. (An individual tour-basing fare is computed as part of a package that includes land arrangements, thereby entitling a carrier to reduce the air portion almost to the absolute minimum. Though it always represents a saving over full-fare coach or economy, lately the individual tour-basing fare has not been as inexpensive as the excursion and other discount fares that also are available to individuals. The group fare usually is the least expensive, and it is the tour operator who makes up the group.) When the brochure does include round-trip transportation in the package price, don't forget to add the cost of round-trip transportation from your home to the departure city to come up with the total cost of the package.

Finally, read the general information regarding terms and conditions and the responsibility clause (usually in fine print at the end of the descriptive literature) to determine the precise elements for which the tour operator is — and is not — liable. Here the tour operator frequently expresses the right to change services or schedules as long as equivalent arrangements are offered. This clause also absolves the operator of responsibility for circumstances beyond human control, such as avalanches, earthquakes, or floods, or injury to you or your property. While reading, ask the following questions:

1. Does the tour include airfare or other transportation, sightseeing, meals, transfers, taxes, baggage handling, tips, or any other services? Do you want all these services?
2. If the brochure indicates that "some meals" are included, does this mean a welcoming and farewell dinner, two breakfasts, or every evening meal?
3. What classes of hotels are offered? If you will be traveling alone, what is the single supplement?
4. Does the tour itinerary or price vary according to the season?

5. Are the prices guaranteed; that is, if costs increase between the time you book and the time you depart, can surcharges unilaterally be added?
6. Do you get a full refund if you cancel? If not, be sure to obtain cancellation insurance.
7. Can the operator cancel if too few people join? At what point?

One of the consumer's biggest problems is finding enough information to judge the reliability of a tour packager, since individual travelers seldom have direct contact with the firm putting the package together. Usually, a retail travel agent is interposed between customer and tour operator, and much depends on his or her candor and cooperation. So ask a number of questions about the tour you are considering. For example:

- Has the travel agent ever used a package provided by this tour operator?
- How long has the tour operator been in business? Check the Better Business Bureau in the area where the tour operator is based to see if any complaints have been filed against it.
- Is the tour operator a member of the *United States Tour Operators Association* (*USTOA;* 211 E. 51st St., Suite 12B, New York, NY 10022; phone: 212-944-5727)? *USTOA* will provide a list of its members on request; it also offers a useful brochure called *How to Select a Package Tour.*
- How many and which companies are involved in the package?

■ **A word of advice:** Purchasers of vacation packages who feel they're not getting their money's worth are more likely to get a refund if they complain in writing to the operator — and bail out of the whole package immediately. Alert the tour operator to the fact that you are dissatisfied, that you will be leaving for home as soon as transportation can be arranged, and that you expect a refund. They may have forms to fill out detailing your complaint; otherwise, state your case in a letter. Even if difficulty in arranging immediate transportation home detains you, your dated, written complaint should help in procuring a refund from the operator.

SAMPLE PACKAGES FOR HONOLULU: Following is a list of some of the major tour operators that offer Honolulu packages. Most companies offer several departure dates, depending on the length of the tour and intinerary.

American Express Travel Related Services (offices throughout the US; phone: 800-241-1700 for information and local branch offices). Offers flexible city stays in Honolulu as well as independent and escorted tours throughout the US. The tour operator is a wholesaler, so use a travel agent.

Cartan Tours (2809 Butterfield Rd., Oak Brook, IL 60521; phone: 800-422-7826). Operates a variety of escorted and independent programs.

Empire Tours (562 Mission St., Suite 500, San Francisco, CA 94105; phone: 800-833-3333 or 415-543-8111). Operates all-inclusive air/land and land-only programs lasting from 3 days to 2 weeks. The company is a wholesaler, so use a travel agent.

Globus-Gateway (*Group Voyagers, Inc.,* 95-25 Queens Blvd., Rego Park, NY 11374; phone: 800-221-0090 or 718-268-7000). Their new 10-day tour of Hawaii's national parks includes 3 days in Honolulu.

GoGo Tours (69 Spring St., Ramsey, NJ 07446-0507; phone: 800-229-4999). Features 2- to 7-night air-inclusive programs with car options.

MTI Vacations, Inc. (1220 Kensington Ct., Oak Brook, IL 60521; phone: 800-323-7285 or 708-990-8028). This charter operator also offers city packages that include air transportation and use of a car for a minimum of 2 nights. It is a wholesaler, so consult a travel agent.

Sheraton Travel Service (PO Box 8559, Honolulu, HI 96830; phone: 800-634-4747 or 808-924-5180). Hotel chain offers a variety of packages featuring its numerous properties.

SuperCities (Radisson Reservations Center, 11340 Blondo St., Omaha, NE 68164; phone: 800-333-1234). Offers highly flexible mix-and-match city packages. This tour operator is a wholesaler, so use a travel agent.

The following operators offer flexible city stays that start with 1 or 2 hotel nights, with a choice of locations and prices available, to which may be added more nights and a wide variety of options, such as sightseeing, transfers, car rental, and, in some cases, dine-around plans. Most companies offer air-inclusive and land-only programs. These operators mostly are wholesalers and will deal only with a travel agent unless otherwise noted.

Classic Hawaii (1 N. First St., 3rd Floor, San Jose, CA 95113; phone: 800-221-3949 or 408-287-9101).

Creative Leisure International (951 Transport Way, Petaluma, CA 94954; phone: 800-426-6367 or 707-778-1800).

Haddon Holidays (1120 Executive Plaza, Suite 375, Mt. Laurel, NJ 08054; phone: 800-257-7488 or 609-273-8666).

Jetour Hawaii/Jet Hawaii (92255 Kuhio Ave., Suite 700, Honolulu, HI 96815; phone: 800-367-2380 or 808-926-1551).

Pleasant Hawaiian Holidays (2404 Townsgate Rd., Westlake Village, CA 91361; phone: 800-2-HAWAII, 800-FOR-POSH, or 818-991-3390). Will accept direct bookings.

Runaway Tours (120 Montgomery St., Suite 800, San Francisco, CA 94104; phone: 800-622-0723 or 415-956-3750).

For runners, *Marathon Tours* (108 Main St., Charlestown, MA 02129; phone: 800-783-0024 or 617-242-7845) will make the arrangements to run in marathons throughout the country, including the one in Honolulu every December. The company is the official travel agency for the Chicago and Boston races.

Many of the major air carriers maintain their own tour departments or subsidiaries to stimulate vacation travel to the cities they serve. In all cases, the arrangements may be booked through a travel agent or directly with the airline. Air/hotel Honolulu packages are offered by the following tour operations of airlines serving the city:

American Airlines FlyAAway Vacations (Southern Reservation Center, Mail Drop 1000, Box 619619, Dallas/Ft. Worth Airport, TX 75261-9619; phone: 800-321-2121).

America West Vacations (1150 E. University, Suite 201, Tempe, AZ 85281; phone: 800-356-6611).

Continental's Grand Destinations (PO Box 1460, Milwaukee, WI 53201-1460; phone: 800-634-5555).

Delta's Dream Vacations (PO Box 1525, Ft. Lauderdale, FL 33302; phone: 800-872-7786).

Northwest Vacations Center (5101 Northwest Dr., St. Paul, MN 55111-3034; phone: 800-692-8687).

TWA Getaway (10 E. Stow Rd., Marlton, NJ 08053; phone: 800-GETAWAY).

United Vacations/Pacific (P.O. Box 24580, Milwaukee, WI 53224; phone: 800-328-6877).

Whether visiting Honolulu independently or on one of the above packages, if you would like to include some organized touring, *E Noa Tours* (1110 University Ave., Room 306, Honolulu, HI 96826; 808-599-2561) operates the open-air *Old Town Honolulu Trolley* between Waikiki and shops and attractions in the city where, for $15, visitors can get on and off as they please all day. The company also offers half- and full-day sightseeing programs, as does *Akamai Tours* (2270 Kalakaua Ave., Suite 1708, Honolulu, HI 96815; phone: 800-922-6485 or 808-971-4545). Another good locally owned sightseeing operator is *Polynesian Adventure Tours* (1049 Kikowaena Place, Honolulu, HI 96819; 800-622-3011 or 808-922-0888).

■ **Note:** Frequently, the best city packages are offered by the hotels, which are trying to attract guests during the weekends, when business travel drops, and during other off periods. These packages are sometimes advertised in local newspapers and in the Sunday travel sections of major metropolitan papers, such as *The New York Times,* which has a national edition available in most parts of the US. The two local dailies, the morning *Honolulu Advertiser* and the afternoon *Honolulu Star-Bulletin,* run hotel and other package ads that are aimed at the locals but can be a good buy for visitors; it's worth looking at them. It's also worthwhile asking about packages, especially family and special-occasion offerings, when you call to make a hotel reservation. Calling several hotels can garner you a variety of options from which to choose.

Preparing

Calculating Costs

DETERMINING A BUDGET: A realistic appraisal of travel expenses is the most crucial bit of planning before any trip. It also is, unfortunately, one for which it is most difficult to give precise practical advice.

Estimating travel expenses for Honolulu depends on the mode of transportation you choose and how long you will stay, as well as the kind of trip you are planning.

When calculating costs, start with the basics, the major expenses being transportation, accommodations, and food. For Honolulu that will mean $160 or more a night for a double at an expensive hotel, $70 to $150 for a moderate property, and somewhat under $70 for an inexpensive one. Dinner for two runs to over $60 at an expensive restaurant, $25 to $55 at a moderate one, and under $25 at an inexpensive one. Then there are breakfast and lunch to consider.

Don't forget such extras as local transportation, shopping, and such miscellaneous items as laundry and tips. The reasonable cost of these items often is a positive surprise to your budget. And ask about discount passes on local transportation. For example, if you want to do some sightseeing on another Hawaiian island, *Hawaiian Airlines* (phone: 800-367-5320) offers a Hawaiian AirPass good for unlimited travel over a fixed period. The pass costs $129 for 5 days, $199 for 10 days, and $239 for 14 days. Seniors 60 and over and children under 12 pay $20 less. Rival *Aloha Airlines* (phone: 800-367-5250) also offers a 5-day pass, the Island Hopper, for $129 ($20 less for seniors and children).

Other expenses, such as the cost of local sightseeing tours and other excursions, should be included. Tourist information offices and most of the better hotels will have someone at the front desk to provide a rundown on the cost of local tours and full-day excursions in and out of Honolulu. Travel agents also can provide this information.

In planning any travel budget, it also is wise to allow a realistic amount for both entertainment and recreation. Are you planning to spend time sightseeing and visiting local tourist attractions? Is tennis or golf a part of your plan? Are you traveling with children who want to visit every site? Finally, allow for the extra cost of nightlife, if such is your pleasure. This one item alone can add a great deal to your daily expenditures.

If at any point in the planning process it appears impossible to estimate expenses, consider this suggestion: The easiest way to put a ceiling on the price of all these elements is to buy a package tour with transportation, rooms, meals, sightseeing, local travel, tips, and a dinner show or two included and prepaid. This provides a pretty exact total of what the trip will cost beforehand, and the only surprise will be the one you spring on yourself by succumbing to some irresistible souvenir.

Planning a Trip

123 Travelers fall into two categories: those who make lists and those who do not. Some people prefer to plot the course of their trip to the finest detail, with contingency plans and alternatives at the ready. For others, the joy of a voyage is its spontaneity; exhaustive planning only lessens the thrill of anticipation and the sense of freedom.

For most travelers, however, a week-plus trip can be too expensive for an "I'll take my chances" attitude. At least some planning is crucial. This is not to suggest that you work out your itinerary in minute detail before you go, but it's still wise to decide certain basics at the very start: where to go, what to do, and how much to spend. These decisions require a certain amount of consideration. So before rigorously planning specific details, you might want to establish your general travel objectives:

1. How much time will you have for the entire trip, and how much of it are you willing to spend getting where you're going?
2. What interests and/or activities do you want to pursue while on vacation?
3. At what time of year do you want to go?
4. Do you want peace and privacy or lots of activity and company?
5. How much money can you afford to spend for the entire vacation?

You now can make almost all of your own travel arrangements if you have time to follow through with hotels, airlines, tour operators, and so on. But you'll probably save considerable time and energy if you have a travel agent make arrangements for you. The agent also should be able to advise you of alternative arrangements of which you may not be aware. Only rarely will a travel agent's services cost a traveler any money, and they may even save you some (see *How to Use a Travel Agent,* below).

Make plans early. For December through February and from late May through August, make hotel reservations at least a month in advance. If you are flying at these times and want to benefit from savings offered through discount fares, purchase tickets as far ahead as possible. Many hotels require deposits before they will guarantee reservations, and this most often is the case during peak travel periods. (Be sure to get a receipt for any deposit or, better yet, charge the deposit to a credit card.)

When packing, make a list of any valuable items you are carrying with you, including credit card numbers and the serial numbers of your traveler's checks. Put copies in your purse or pocket, and leave other copies at home. Put a label with your name and home address on the inside of your luggage for identification in case of loss. Put your name and business address — *never your home address* — on a label on the outside of your luggage. (Those who run businesses from home should use the office address of a friend or relative.)

Review your travel documents. If you are traveling by air, check that your ticket has been filled in correctly. The left side of the ticket should have a list of each stop you will make (even if you are stopping only to change planes), beginning with your departure point. Be sure that the list is correct, and count the number of copies to see that you have one for each plane you will take. If you have confirmed reservations, be sure that the column marked "status" says "OK" beside each flight. Have in hand vouchers or proof of payment for any reservation for which you've paid in advance; this includes hotels, transfers to and from the airport, sightseeing tours, car rentals, and tickets to special events.

Although policies vary from carrier to carrier, it's still smart to reconfirm your flight 48 to 72 hours before departure, both going and returning. If you are traveling by car, bring your driver's license, car registration, and proof of insurance, as well as gasoline credit cards and auto service card (if you have them).

Finally, you always should bear in mind that despite the most careful plans, things do not always occur on schedule. If you maintain a flexible attitude and try to accept minor disruptions as less than cataclysmic, you will enjoy yourself a lot more.

How to Use a Travel Agent

 A reliable travel agent remains the best source of service and information for planning a trip, whether you have a specific itinerary and require an agent only to make reservations or you need extensive help in sorting through the maze of airfares, tour offerings, hotel packages, and the scores of other arrangements that may be involved in your trip.

Know what you want from a travel agent so that you can evaluate what you are getting. It is perfectly reasonable to expect your travel agent to be a thoroughly knowledgeable travel specialist, with information about your destination and, even more crucial, a command of current airfares, ground arrangements, and other wrinkles in the travel scene.

Most travel agents work through computer reservations systems (CRS). These are used to assess the availability and cost of flights, hotels, and car rentals, and through them they can book reservations. Despite reports of "computer bias," in which a computer may favor one airline over another, the CRS should provide agents with the entire spectrum of flights available to a given destination and the complete range of fares, in considerably less time than it takes to telephone the airlines individually — and at no extra cost to the client.

Make the most intelligent use of a travel agent's time and expertise; understand the economics of the industry. As a client, traditionally you pay nothing for the agent's services; with few exceptions it's all free, from hotel bookings to advice on package tours. Any money the travel agent makes on the time spent arranging your itinerary — booking hotels, resorts, or flights, or suggesting activities — comes from commissions paid by the suppliers of these services — the airlines, hotels, and so on. These commissions generally run from 10% to 15% of the total cost of the service, although suppliers often reward agencies that sell their services in volume with an increased commission called an override.

A travel agent sometimes may charge a fee for special services. These chargeable items may include long-distance telephone costs incurred in making a booking, for reserving a room in a place that does not pay a commission (such as a small, out-of-the way hotel), or for a special attention such as planning a highly personalized itinerary. A fee also may be assessed in instances of deeply discounted airfares.

Choose a travel agent with the same care with which you would choose a doctor or lawyer. You will be spending a good deal of money on the basis of the agent's judgment, so you have a right to expect that judgment to be mature, informed, and interested. At the moment, unfortunately, there aren't many standards within the travel agent industry to help you gauge competence, and the quality of individual agents varies enormously.

At present, only nine states have registration, licensing, or other forms of travel agent–related legislation on their books. Rhode Island licenses travel agents; Florida, Hawaii, Iowa, and Ohio register them; and California, Illinois, Oregon, and Washington have laws governing the sale of transportation or related services. While state licensing of agents cannot absolutely guarantee competence, it can at least ensure that an agent has met some minimum requirements.

Perhaps the best-prepared agents are those who have completed the CTC Travel Management program offered by the *Institute of Certified Travel Agents (ICTA)* and carry the initials CTC (Certified Travel Counselor) after their names. This indicates a relatively high level of expertise. For a free listing of CTCs in your area, send a self-addressed, stamped, #10 envelope to *ICTA,* 148 Linden St., Box 56, Wellesley, MA 02181 (phone: 617-237-0280 in Massachusetts; 800-542-4282 elsewhere in the US).

An agent's membership in the *American Society of Travel Agents (ASTA)* can be a useful guideline in making a selection. But keep in mind that *ASTA* is an industry organization, requiring only that its members be licensed in those states where required; be accredited to represent the suppliers whose products they sell, including airline and cruise tickets; and adhere to its Principles of Professional Conduct and Ethics code. *ASTA* does not guarantee the competence, ethics, or financial soundness of its members, but it does offer some recourse if you feel you have been dealt with unfairly. Complaints may be registered with *ASTA* (Consumer Affairs Dept., 1101 King St., Alexandria, VA 22314; phone: 703-739-2782). First try to resolve the complaint directly with the supplier. For a list of *ASTA* members in your area, send a self-addressed, stamped, #10 envelope to *ASTA,* Public Relations Dept., at the address above.

There also is the *Association of Retail Travel Agents (ARTA),* a smaller but highly respected trade organization similar to *ASTA.* Its member agencies and agents similarly agree to abide by a code of ethics, and complaints about a member can be made to *ARTA*'s Grievance Committee, 1745 Jefferson Davis Hwy., Suite 300, Arlington, VA 22202-3402 (phone: 800-969-6069 or 703-553-7777).

Perhaps the best way to find a travel agent is by word of mouth. If the agent (or agency) has done a good job for your friends over a period of time, it probably indicates a certain level of commitment and competence. Always ask for the name of the company *and* for the name of the specific agent with whom your friends dealt, for it is that individual who will serve you, and quality can vary widely within a single agency.

Insurance

It is unfortunate that most decisions to buy travel insurance are impulsive and usually are made without any real consideration of the traveler's existing policies. Therefore, the first person with whom you should discuss travel insurance is your own insurance broker, not a travel agent or the clerk behind the airport insurance counter. You may discover that the insurance you already carry — homeowner's policies and/or accident, health, and life insurance — protects you adequately while you travel and that your real needs are in the more mundane areas of excess value insurance for baggage or trip cancellation insurance.

TYPES OF INSURANCE: To make insurance decisions intelligently, however, you first should understand the basic categories of travel insurance and what they cover. Then you can decide what you should have in the broader context of your personal insurance needs, and you can choose the most economical way of getting the desired protection: through riders on existing policies; with onetime, short-term policies; through a special program put together for the frequent traveler; through coverage that's part of a travel club's benefits; or with a combination policy sold by insurance companies through brokers, automobile clubs, tour operators, and travel agents.

There are seven basic categories of travel insurance:

1. Baggage and personal effects insurance
2. Personal accident and sickness insurance
3. Trip cancellation and interruption insurance

4. Default and/or bankruptcy insurance
5. Flight insurance (to cover injury or death)
6. Automobile insurance (for driving your own or a rented car)
7. Combination policies

Baggage and Personal Effects Insurance – Ask your insurance agent if baggage and personal effects are included in your current homeowner's policy, or if you will need a special floater to cover you for the duration of a trip. The object is to protect your bags and their contents in case of damage or theft anytime during your travels, not just while you're in flight, where only limited protection is provided by the airline. Baggage liability varies from carrier to carrier, but generally speaking, on domestic flights, luggage usually is insured to $1,250 — that's per passenger, not per bag. This limit should be specified on your airline ticket, but to be awarded any amount, you'll have to provide an itemized list of lost property, and if you're including new and/or expensive items, be prepared for a request that you back up your claim with sales receipts or other proof of purchase.

If you are carrying goods worth more than the maximum protection offered by the airlines, consider excess value insurance. Additional coverage is available from airlines at an average, currently, of $1 to $2 per $100 worth of coverage, up to a maximum of $5,000. This insurance can be purchased at the airline counter when you check in, though you should arrive early to fill out the necessary forms and to avoid holding up other passengers.

Major credit card companies provide coverage for lost or delayed baggage — and this coverage often also is over and above what the airline will pay. The basic coverage usually is automatic for all cardholders who use the credit card to purchase tickets, but to qualify for additional coverage, cardholders generally must enroll.

American Express: Provides $500 coverage for checked baggage; $1,250 for carry-on baggage; and $250 for valuables, such as cameras and jewelry.

Carte Blanche and Diners Club: Provide $1,250 free insurance for checked or carry-on baggage that's lost or damaged.

Discover Card: Offers $500 insurance for checked baggage and $1,250 for carry-on baggage — but to qualify for this coverage cardholders first must purchase additional flight insurance (see "Flight Insurance," below).

MasterCard and Visa: Baggage insurance coverage set by the issuing institution.

Additional baggage and personal effects insurance also is included in certain of the combination travel insurance policies discussed below.

■ **A note of warning:** Be sure to read the fine print of any excess value insurance policy; there often are specific exclusions, such as cash, tickets, furs, gold and silver objects, art, and antiques. Insurance companies ordinarily will pay only the depreciated value of the goods rather than their replacement value. The best way to protect your property is to take photos of your valuables, and keep a record of the serial numbers of such items as cameras, typewriters, laptop computers, radios, and so on. If an airline loses your luggage, you will be asked to fill out a Property Irregularity Report before you leave the airport. Also report the loss to the police (since the insurance company will check with the police when processing the claim).

Personal Accident and Sickness Insurance – This covers you in case of illness during your trip or death in an accident. Most policies insure you for hospital and doctors' expenses, lost income, and so on. In most cases, it is a standard part of existing health insurance policies (especially where domestic travel is concerned), though you should check with your insurance broker to be sure of the conditions for which your policy will pay. If your coverage is insufficient, take out a separate vacation accident policy or an entire vacation insurance policy that includes health and life coverage.

Trip Cancellation and Interruption Insurance – Most package tour passengers pay for their travel well before departure. The disappointment of having to miss a vacation because of illness or any other reason pales before the awful prospect that not all (and sometimes none) of the money paid in advance might be returned. So cancellation insurance for any package tour is a must.

Although cancellation penalties vary (they are listed in the fine print of every tour brochure, and before you purchase a package tour you should know exactly what they are), rarely will a passenger get more than 50% of this money back if forced to cancel within a few weeks of scheduled departure. Therefore, if you book a package tour, you should have trip cancellation insurance to guarantee full reimbursement or refund should you, a traveling companion, or a member of your immediate family get sick, forcing you to cancel your trip or *return home early*.

The key here is *not* to buy just enough insurance to guarantee full reimbursement for the cost of the package in case of cancellation. The proper amount of coverage should include reimbursement for the cost of having to catch up with a tour after its departure or having to travel home at the full economy airfare if you have to forgo the return flight tied to the package. There usually is quite a discrepancy between an excursion or other special airfare and the amount charged to travel the same distance on a regularly scheduled flight at full economy fare.

Trip cancellation insurance is available from travel agents and tour operators in two forms: as part of a short-term, all-purpose travel insurance package (sold by the travel agent); or as specific cancellation insurance designed by the operator for a specific tour. Generally, tour operators' policies are less expensive, but also less inclusive. Cancellation insurance also is available directly from insurance companies or their agents as part of a short-term, all-inclusive travel insurance policy.

Before you decide on a policy, read each one carefully. (Either type can be purchased from a travel agent when you book the package tour.) Be sure to check the fine print for stipulations concerning "family members" and "pre-existing medical conditions," as well as allowances for living expenses if you must delay your return due to injury or illness.

Default and/or Bankruptcy Insurance – Although trip cancellation insurance usually protects you if *you* are unable to complete — or begin — your trip, a fairly recent innovation is coverage in the event of default and/or bankruptcy on the part of the tour operator, airline, or other travel supplier. In some travel insurance packages, this contingency is included in the trip cancellation portion of the coverage; in others, it is a separate feature. Either way, it is becoming increasingly important. Whereas sophisticated travelers have long known to beware of the possibility of default or bankruptcy when buying a tour package, in recent years more than a few respected airlines have unexpectedly revealed their shaky financial condition, sometimes leaving hordes of stranded ticket holders in their wake. While default/bankruptcy insurance will not ordinarily result in reimbursement in time to pay for new arrangements, it can ensure that you will get your money back, and even independent travelers buying no more than an airplane ticket may want to consider it.

Flight Insurance – US airlines' liability for injury or death to passengers on domestic flights currently is determined on a case-by-case basis in court — this means potentially unlimited liability. But remember, this liability is not the same thing as an insurance policy; every penny that an airline eventually pays in the case of death or injury likely will be subject to a legal battle.

But before you buy last-minute flight insurance from an airport vending machine, consider the purchase in light of your total existing insurance coverage. A careful review of your current policies may reveal that you already are amply covered for accidental death. Be aware that airport insurance, the kind typically bought at a counter or from a vending machine, is among the most expensive forms of life insurance coverage, and that even within a single airport, rates for approximately the same coverage vary widely.

If you buy your plane ticket with a major credit card, you generally receive automatic insurance coverage at no extra cost. Additional coverage usually can be obtained at extremely reasonable prices, but a cardholder must sign up for it in advance.

Automobile Insurance – If you have an accident in a state that has "no fault" insurance, each party's insurance company pays his or her expenses up to certain specified limits. When you rent a car, the rental company is required to provide you with collision protection.

In your car rental contract, you'll see that for about $5 to $13 a day, you may buy optional collision damage waiver (CDW) protection. Some companies, such as *Hertz* and *Avis,* now call the option a loss damage waiver (LDW). (If partial coverage with a deductible is included in the rental contract, the CDW will cover the deductible in the event of an accident, and can cost as much as $25 per day.) If you do not accept the CDW coverage, you may be liable for as much as the full retail value of the rental car if it is damaged or stolen; by paying for the CDW, you are relieved of all responsibility for any damage to the car. Before agreeing to this coverage, however, check with your own broker about your own existing personal automobile insurance policy. It very well may cover your entire liability exposure without any additional cost, or you automatically may be covered by the credit card company to which you are charging the cost of your rental. To find out the amount of rental car insurance provided by major credit cards, contact the issuing institutions.

Combination Policies – Short-term insurance policies, which may include a combination or all of the types of insurance discussed above, are available through retail insurance agencies, automobile clubs, and many travel agents. These combination policies are designed to cover you for the duration of a single trip.

The following companies provide such coverage for the insurance needs discussed above:

Access America International: A subsidiary of the Blue Cross/Blue Shield plans of New York and Washington, DC, now available nationwide. Contact *Access America,* P.O. Box 90310, Richmond, VA 23230 (phone: 800-284-8300 or 804-285-3300).

Carefree: Underwritten by The Hartford. Contact *Carefree Travel Insurance,* Arm Coverage, PO Box 310, Mineola, NY 11501 (phone: 800-645-2424 or 516-294-0220).

NEAR Services: In addition to a full range of travel services, this organization offers a comprehensive travel insurance package. An added feature is coverage for lost or stolen airline tickets. Contact *NEAR Services,* 450 Prairie Ave., Suite 101, Calumet City, IL 60409 (phone: 708-868-6700 in the Chicago area; 800-654-6700 elsewhere in the US and Canada).

Tele-Trip: Underwritten by the Mutual of Omaha Companies. Contact *Tele-Trip Co.,* PO Box 31685, 3201 Farnam St., Omaha, NE 68131 (phone: 402-345-2400 in Nebraska; 800-228-9792 elsewhere in the US).

Travel Assistance International: Provided by Europ Assistance Worldwide Services, and underwritten by Transamerica Occidental Life Insurance Company. Contact *Travel Assistance International,* 1133 15th St. NW, Suite 400, Washington, DC 20005 (phone: 202-331-1609 in Washington, DC; 800-821-2828 elsewhere in the US).

Travel Guard International: Underwritten by the Insurance Company of North America, it is available through authorized travel agents; or contact *Travel*

Guard International, 1145 Clark St., Stevens Point, WI 54481 (phone: 715-345-0505 in Wisconsin; 800-826-1300 elsewhere in the US).

Travel Insurance PAK: Underwritten by The Travelers. Contact *The Travelers Companies,* Ticket and Travel Plans, One Tower Sq., Hartford, CT 06183-5040 (phone: 203-277-2319 in Connecticut; 800-243-3174 elsewhere in the US).

Wallach & Co.: This organization offers two health insurance plans as well as other coverage. Contact *Wallach & Co.,* 243 Church St. NW, Suite 100-D, Vienna, VA 22180 (phone: 703-281-9500 in Virginia; 800-237-6615 elsewhere in the US).

Hints for Handicapped Travelers

From 40 to 50 million people in the US alone have some sort of disability, and over half this number are physically handicapped. Like everyone else today, they — and the uncounted disabled millions around the world — are on the move. More than ever before, they are demanding facilities they can use comfortably, and they are being heard. With the 1990 passage of the Americans with Disabilities Act, the physically handicapped increasingly will be finding better access to places and services throughout the US. The provisions of the act relating to public accommodations and transportation, which took effect in January 1992, mandate that means of access be provided except where the cost would be prohibitive, and creative alternatives are being encouraged. As the impact of the law spreads across the country, previous barriers to travel in the US should be somewhat ameliorated.

PLANNING A TRIP: Collect as much information as you can about your specific disability and facilities for the disabled in Honolulu. Make your travel arrangements well in advance and specify to services involved the exact nature of your condition or restricted mobility, as your trip will be much more comfortable if you know that there are accommodations and facilities to suit your needs.

One of the best sources of information on facilities for the disabled in Hawaii, including Honolulu, is the 2-part brochure, *Aloha Guide to Accessibility in the State of Hawaii.* Part I covers airports, transportation and parking, and medical and support services; Part II deals with hotels, theaters, shopping centers, and government buildings. The publication is available from the Communications Department, Hawaii Visitors Bureau (2770 Kalakaua Plaza, Honolulu, HI 96815; phone: 808-923-1811).

It is also advisable to call the hotel you are considering and ask specific questions. If you require a corridor of a certain width to maneuver a wheelchair or if you need handles on the bathroom walls for support, ask the manager (many large hotels have rooms specially designed for the handicapped). A travel agent or the local chapter or national office of the organization that deals with your particular disability — for example, the *American Foundation for the Blind* or the *American Heart Association* — will supply the most up-to-date information on the subject.

The following organizations also offer general information on access:

ACCENT on Living (PO Box 700, Bloomington, IL 61702; phone: 309-378-2961). This information service for persons with disabilities provides a free list of travel agencies specializing in arranging trips for the disabled; for a copy send a self-addressed, stamped envelope. It also offers a wide range of publications, including a quarterly magazine ($10 per year; $17.50 for 2 years) for persons with disabilities.

Direct Link (PO Box 1036, Solvang, CA 93463; phone: 805-688-1603). This company provides an on-line computer service and links the disabled and their families with a wide range of information, including accessibility, attendant care, transportation, and travel necessities.

Disabled Individuals Assistance Line (DIAL; 100 W. Randolph St., Suite 8-100, Chicago, IL 60601; 800-233-DIAL; both voice and TDD — telecommunications device for the deaf). This toll-free hotline provides information about public and private resources available to people with disabilities.

Information Center for Individuals with Disabilities (Ft. Point Pl., 1st Floor, 27-43 Wormwood St., Boston, MA 02210; phone: 800-462-5015 in Massachusetts; 617-727-5540/1 elsewhere in the US; both numbers provide voice and TDD). The center offers information and referral services on accessibility of the transportation system, cultural sites, and other attractions. Also provides a referral service on disability-related issues, publishes fact sheets on travel agents, tour operators, and other travel resources, and can help you research your trip.

Mobility International USA (MIUSA; PO Box 3551, Eugene, OR 97403; phone: 503-343-1284; both voice and TDD). This US branch of *Mobility International* (the main office is at 228 Borough High St., London SE1 1JX, England; phone: 011-44-71-403-5688), a nonprofit British organization with affiliates worldwide, offers members advice and assistance — including information on accommodations and other travel services, and publications applicable to the traveler's disability. *Mobility International* also offers a quarterly newsletter and a comprehensive sourcebook, *A World of Options for the 90s: A Guide to International Education Exchange, Community Service and Travel for Persons with Disabilities* ($14 for members; $16 for non-members). Membership includes the newsletter and is $20 a year; subscription to the newsletter alone is $10 annually.

National Rehabilitation Information Center (8455 Colesville Rd., Suite 935, Silver Spring, MD 20910; phone: 301-588-9284). A general information, resource, research, and referral service.

Paralyzed Veterans of America (PVA; PVA/ATTS Program, 801 18th St. NW, Washington, DC 20006; phone: 202-416-7708 in Washington, DC; 800-424-8200 elsewhere in the US). The members of this national service organization all are veterans who have suffered spinal cord injuries, but it offers advocacy services and information to all persons with a disability. *PVA* also sponsors *Access to the Skies (ATTS),* a program that coordinates the efforts of the national and international air travel industry in providing airport and airplane access for the disabled. Members receive several helpful publications, as well as regular notification of conferences on subjects of interest to the disabled traveler.

Society for the Advancement of Travel for the Handicapped (SATH; 347 Fifth Ave., Suite 610, New York, NY 10016; phone 212-447-7284). To keep abreast of developments in travel for the handicapped as they occur, you may want to join *SATH,* a nonprofit organization whose members include consumers, as well as travel service professionals who have experience (or an interest) in travel for the handicapped. For an annual fee of $45 ($25 for students and travelers who are 65 and older), members receive a quarterly newsletter and have access to extensive information and referral services. *SATH* also offers two useful publications: *Travel Tips for the Handicapped* (a series of informative fact sheets) and *The United States Welcomes Handicapped Visitors* (a 48-page guide covering domestic transportation and accommodations, as well as useful hints for travelers with disabilities); to order, send a self-addressed, #10 envelope and $1 per title for postage to the address above.

Travel Information Service (Moss Rehabilitation Hospital, 1200 W. Tabor Rd., Philadelphia, PA 19141-3099; phone: 215-456-9600 for voice; 215-456-9602 for TDD). This service assists physically handicapped people in planning trips and supplies detailed information on accessibility, for a nominal fee.

Blind travelers should contact the *American Foundation for the Blind* (15 W. 16th St., New York, NY 10011; phone: 800-829-0500 or 212-620-2147) and *The Seeing Eye* (Box 375, Morristown, NJ 07963-0375; phone: 201-539-4425); both provide useful information on resources for the visually impaired.

In addition, there are a number of publications — from travel guides to magazines — of interest to handicapped travelers. Among these are the following:

Access to the World, by Louise Weiss, offers sound tips for the disabled traveler. Published by Facts on File (460 Park Ave. S., New York, NY 10016; phone: 212-683-2244 in New York State; 800-322-8755 elsewhere in the US; 800-443-8323 in Canada), it costs $16.95 and is available only in paperback. Check with your local bookstore; it also can be ordered by phone with a credit card.

The Diabetic Traveler (PO Box 8223 RW, Stamford, CT 06905; phone: 203-327-5832) is a useful quarterly newsletter for travelers with diabetes. Each issue highlights a single destination or type of travel and includes information on general resources and hints for diabetics. A 1-year subscription costs $18.95. When subscribing, ask for the free fact sheet including an index of special articles; back issues are available for $4 each.

Guide to Traveling with Arthritis, a free brochure available by writing to the Upjohn Company (PO Box 307-B, Coventry, CT 06238), provides lots of good, commonsense tips on planning your trip and how to be as comfortable as possible when traveling by car, bus, train, cruise ship, or plane.

Handicapped Travel Newsletter is regarded as one of the best sources of information for the disabled traveler. It is edited by wheelchair-bound Vietnam veteran Michael Quigley, who has traveled to 93 countries around the world. Issued every 2 months (plus special issues), a subscription is $10 per year. Write to *Handicapped Travel Newsletter,* PO Box 269, Athens, TX 75751 (phone: 903-677-1260).

Handi-Travel: A Resource Book for Disabled and Elderly Travellers, by Cinnie Noble, is a comprehensive travel guide full of practical tips for those with disabilities affecting mobility, hearing, or sight. To order this book, send $12.95, plus shipping and handling, to the *Canadian Rehabilitation Council for the Disabled,* 45 Sheppard Ave. E., Suite 801, Toronto, Ontario M2N 5W9, Canada (phone: 416-250-7490; both voice and TDD).

The Itinerary (PO Box 2012, Bayonne, NJ 07002-2012; phone: 201-858-3400). This bimonthly travel newsletter for people with disabilities includes information on accessibility, listings of tours, news of adaptive devices, travel aids, and special services, as well as numerous general travel hints. A subscription costs $10 a year.

The Physically Disabled Traveler's Guide, by Rod W. Durgin and Norene Lindsay, rates accessibility of a number of travel services and includes a list of organizations specializing in travel for the disabled. It is available for $9.95, plus shipping and handling, from Resource Directories, 3361 Executive Pkwy., Suite 302, Toledo, OH 43606 (phone: 419-536-5353 in the Toledo area; 800-274-8515 elsewhere in the US).

Ticket to Safe Travel offers useful information for travelers with diabetes. A reprint of this article is available free from local chapters of the *American Diabetes Association.* For the nearest branch, contact the central office at 505 Eighth Ave., 21st Floor, New York, NY 10018 (phone: 212-947-9707 in New York State; 800-232-3472 elsewhere in the US).

Travel for the Patient with Chronic Obstructive Pulmonary Disease, a publication of the George Washington University Medical Center, provides some sound practical suggestions for those with emphysema, chronic bronchitis, asthma, or other lung ailments. To order, send $2 to Dr. Harold Silver, 1601 18th St. NW, Washington, DC 20009 (phone: 202-667-0134).

Traveling Like Everybody Else: A Practical Guide for Disabled Travelers, by Jacqueline Freedman and Susan Gersten, offers the disabled tips on traveling by car, cruise ship, and plane, as well as lists of accessible accommodations, tour operators specializing in tours for disabled travelers, and other resources. It is available for $11.95, plus postage and handling, from Modan Publishing, PO Box 1202, Bellmore, NY 11710 (phone: 516-679-1380).

Travel Tips for Hearing-Impaired People, a free pamphlet for deaf and hearing-impaired travelers, is available from the *American Academy of Otolaryngology* (One Prince St., Alexandria, VA 22314; phone: 703-836-4444). For a copy, send a self-addressed, stamped, business-size envelope to the academy.

Travel Tips for People with Arthritis, a free 31-page booklet published by the *Arthritis Foundation,* provides helpful information regarding travel by car, bus, train, cruise ship, or plane, planning your trip, medical considerations, and ways to conserve your energy while traveling. It also includes listings of helpful resources, such as associations and travel agencies that operate tours for disabled travelers. For a copy, contact your local *Arthritis Foundation* chapter, or send $1 to the national office, PO Box 19000, Atlanta, GA 30326 (phone: 404-872-7100).

The Wheelchair Traveler, by Douglass R. Annand, lists accessible hotels, motels, restaurants, and other sites by state throughout the US. This valuable resource is available directly from the author. For the price of the most recent edition, contact Douglass R. Annand, 123 Ball Hill Rd., Milford, NH 03055 (phone: 603-673-4539).

A few more basic resources to look for are *Travel for the Disabled,* by Helen Hecker ($19.95), and by the same author, *Directory of Travel Agencies for the Disabled* ($19.95). *Wheelchair Vagabond,* by John G. Nelson, is another useful guide for travelers confined to a wheelchair (hardcover, $14.95; paperback, $9.95). All three titles are published by Twin Peaks Press, PO Box 129, Vancouver, WA 98666 (phone: 800-637-CALM or 206-694-2462). The publisher also offers a catalogue of 26 other books on travel for the disabled for $2.

PLANE: The US Department of Transportation (DOT) has ruled that US airlines must accept all passengers with disabilities. As a matter of course, US airlines were pretty good about accommodating handicapped passengers even before the ruling, although each airline has somewhat different procedures. Ask for specifics when you book your flight.

Disabled passengers always should make reservations well in advance and should provide the airline with all relevant details of their conditions. These details include information on mobility and equipment that you will need the airline to supply — such as a wheelchair for boarding or portable oxygen for in-flight use. Be sure that the person to whom you speak fully understands the degree of your disability — the more details provided, the more effective help the airline can give you.

On the day before the flight, call back to make sure that all arrangements have been prepared, and arrive early on the day of the flight so that you can board before the rest of the passengers. It's a good idea to bring a medical certificate with you, stating your specific disability or the need to carry particular medicine.

Because most airports have jetways (corridors connecting the terminal with the door of the plane), a disabled passenger usually can be taken as far as the plane, and sometimes right onto it, in a wheelchair. If not, a narrow boarding chair may be used to take you to your seat. Your own wheelchair, which will be folded and put in the baggage compartment, should be tagged as escort luggage to assure that it's available at planeside upon landing rather than in the baggage claim area. Travel is not quite as simple if your wheelchair is battery-operated: Unless it has non-spillable batteries, it might not be accepted on board, and you will have to check with the airline ahead of time to find out how the batteries and the chair should be packaged for the flight. Usually people in wheelchairs are asked to wait until other passengers have disembarked. If you are making a tight connection, be sure to tell the attendant.

Passengers who use oxygen may not use their personal supply in the cabin, though it may be carried on the plane as cargo (the tank must be emptied) when properly packed and labeled. If you will need oxygen during the flight, the airline will supply it to you (there is a charge) provided you have given advance notice — 24 hours to a few days, depending on the carrier.

The free booklet, *Air Transportation of Handicapped Persons,* explains the general guidelines that govern air carrier policies. For a copy, write to the US Department of Transportation (Distribution Unit, Publications Section, M-443-2, Washington, DC 20590) and ask for "Free Advisory Circular #AC-120-32." *Access Travel: A Guide to the Accessibility of Airport Terminals,* a free publication of the *Airport Operators Council International,* provides information on more than 500 airports worldwide and offers ratings of 70 features, such as accessibility to bathrooms, corridor width, and parking spaces. For a copy, contact the Consumer Information Center (Dept. 563W, Pueblo, CO 81009; phone: 719-948-3334).

The following airlines have TDD toll-free lines in the US for the hearing-impaired:

American: 800-582-1573 in Ohio; 800-543-1586 elsewhere in the US
America West: 800-526-8077
Continental: 800-343-9195
Delta: 800-831-4488
Northwest: 800-328-2298
TWA: 800-252-0622 in California; 800-421-8480 elsewhere in the US
United: 800-942-8819 in Illinois: 800-323-0170 elsewhere in the US
US Air: 800-242-1713 in Pennsylvania; 800-245-2966 elsewhere in the US

GROUND TRANSPORTATION: Perhaps the simplest solution to getting around is to travel with an able-bodied companion who can drive. If you are accustomed to driving your own hand-controlled car and want to rent one, you are in luck. Some rental companies will fit cars with hand controls. *Avis* (phone: 800-331-1212) can convert a car to hand controls with as little as 24 hours' notice, though it's a good idea to arrange for one more than a day in advance. *Hertz* (phone: 800-654-3131) requires 2 days to install the controls. Neither company charges extra for hand controls, but *Avis* will fit them only on a full-size car, and both request that you bring your handicapped driver's permit with you. Other car rental companies provide hand-control cars at some locations; however, as there usually are only a limited number available, call well in advance.

A relatively new company, *Wheelchair Getaways,* rents vans accommodating one or two wheelchairs and up to five passengers. Each vehicle has 4-point straps to secure wheelchairs, air conditioning, and stereo. The renter provides the driver. The Pennsylvania-based company (PO Box 819, Newtown, PA 18940; phone: 800-642-2042 or 215-579-9120) has franchises in a number of US cities, although at press time, nothing in the Honolulu area. It would be worthwhile, however, to call the headquarters when making travel plans to find out if the company has extended service to Hawaii.

The *American Automobile Association (AAA)* publishes a useful booklet, *The Handicapped Driver's Mobility Guide.* Contact the central office of your local *AAA* club for availability and pricing, which may vary at different branch offices.

TOURS: Programs designed for the physically impaired are run by specialists who have researched hotels, restaurants, and sites to be sure they present no insurmountable obstacles. The following travel agencies and tour operators specialize in making group and individual arrangements for travelers to Honolulu with physical or other disabilities:

Access: The Foundation for Accessibility by the Disabled (PO Box 356, Malverne, NY 11565; phone: 516-887-5798). A travelers' referral service that acts as an intermediary with tour operators and agents worldwide, and provides information on accessibility at various locations.

Accessible Journeys (412 S. 45th St., Philadelphia, PA 19104; phone: 215-747-0171). Arranges for traveling companions who are medical professionals — registered or licensed practical nurses, therapists, or doctors (all are experienced travelers). Several prospective companions' profiles and photos are sent to the client for perusal, and if one is acceptable, the "match" is made. The client usually pays all travel expenses for the companion, plus a certain amount in "earnings" to replace wages the companion would be making at his or her usual job.

Accessible Tours/Directions Unlimited (720 N. Bedford Rd., Bedford Hills, NY 10507; phone: 914-241-1700 in New York State; 800-533-5343 elsewhere in the continental US). Arranges group or individual tours for disabled persons traveling in the company of able-bodied friends or family members. Accepts the unaccompanied traveler if completely self-sufficient.

Beehive Business and Leisure Travel (1130 W. Center St., N. Salt Lake, UT 84054; phone: 800-777-5727 or 801-292-4445). John Warner runs Dialysis in Wonderland, a guided tour program for dialysis patients, which includes arrangements for treatment en route. Among destinations offered last year was Hawaii.

Dahl Good Neighbor Travel Service (124 S. Main St., Viroqua, WI 54665: phone: 608-637-2128; and 535 N. St. Mary's Rd., Libertyville, IL 60048; phone: 708-362-0129). This agency can arrange a full range of services and provide necessities to travelers with any special needs, mental or physical.

Evergreen Travel Service (4114 198th St. SW, Suite 13, Lynnwood, WA 98036-6742; phone: 800-435-2288 or 206-776-1184 throughout the continental US and Canada). Offers worldwide tours and cruises for the disabled (Wings on Wheels Tours), sight-impaired/blind (White Cane Tours), hearing-impaired/deaf (Flying Fingers Tours), and mentally retarded (Happiness Tours). Most programs are first class or deluxe, and include a trained escort.

First National Travel Ltd. (Thornhill Sq., 300 John St., Suite 405, Thornhill, Ontario L3T 5W4, Canada; phone: 416-731-4714). Handles tours and individual arrangements.

Flying Wheels Travel (143 W. Bridge St., Box 382, Owatonna, MN 55060; phone: 800-535-6790 or 507-451-5005). Handles both tours and individual arrangements.

Guided Tour (613 W. Cheltenham Ave., Suite 200, Melrose Park, PA 19126-2414; phone: 215-782-1370). Arranges tours for people with developmental and learning disabilities and sponsors separate tours for members of the same population who also are physically disabled or who simply need a slower pace.

Hinsdale Travel (201 S. Ogden Ave., Hinsdale, IL 60521; phone: 708-325-1335 or 708-469-7349). Janice Perkins, the tour leader, has been in a wheelchair for years and leads an active life. She takes groups of handicapped travelers on the road, making arrangements to meet their special needs.

USTS Travel Horizons (11 E. 44th St., New York, NY 10017; phone: 800-487-8787 or 212-687-5121). Travel agent and registered nurse Mary Ann Hamm designs trips for individual travelers requiring all types of kidney dialysis and handles arrangements for the dialysis.

Weston Travel Agency (134 N. Cass Ave., PO Box 1050, Westmont, IL 60559; phone: 708-968-2513 in Illinois; 800-633-3725 elsewhere in the US; fax: 708-968-2539). This agency specializes in travel services for people with cerebral palsy and those who are wheelchair-bound.

Whole Person Tours (PO Box 1084, Bayonne, NJ 07002-1084; phone: 201-858-3400). Handicapped owner Bob Zywicki travels the world with his wheelchair and offers a lineup of escorted tours (many conducted by him) for the disabled. *Whole Person Tours* also publishes *The Itinerary,* a bimonthly newsletter for disabled travelers (see the publication source list above).

Travelers who would benefit from being accompanied by a nurse or physical therapist also can hire a companion through *Traveling Nurses' Network,* a service provided by Twin Peaks Press (PO Box 129, Vancouver, WA 98666; phone: 800-637-CALM or 206-694-2462). For a $10 fee, clients receive the names of three nurses, whom they can then contact directly; for a $125 fee, the agency will make all the hiring arrangements for the client. Travel arrangements also may be made in some cases — the fee for this further service is determined on an individual basis.

A similar service is offered by *MedEscort International* (ABE International Airport, PO Box 8766, Allentown, PA 18105; phone: 800-255-7182 in the continental US; elsewhere, call 215-791-3111). Clients can arrange to be accompanied by a nurse, paramedic, respiratory therapist, or physician through *MedEscort.* The fees are based on the disabled traveler's needs. This service also can assist in making travel arrangements.

Hints for Single Travelers

 Just about the last trip in human history on which the participants were neatly paired was the voyage of Noah's Ark. Ever since, passenger lists and tour groups have reflected the same kind of asymmetry that occurs in real life, as countless individuals set forth to see the world unaccompanied (or unencumbered, depending on your outlook) by spouse, lover, friend, companion, or relative.

The truth is that the travel industry is not very fair to people who vacation by themselves. People traveling alone almost invariably end up paying more than individuals traveling in pairs. Most travel bargains, including package tours, accommodations, resort packages, and cruises, are based on *double occupancy* rates. This means that the per-person price is offered on the basis of two people traveling together and sharing a double room (which means they each will spend a good deal more on meals and extras). The single traveler will have to pay a surcharge, called a single supplement, for exactly the same package. In extreme cases, this can add as much as 35% to the basic per-person rate.

Don't despair, however. Throughout the US, there are scores of smaller hotels and other hostelries where, in addition to a cozier atmosphere, prices still are quite reasonable for the single traveler.

The obvious, most effective alternative is to find a traveling companion. Even special "singles' tours" that promise no supplements usually are based on people sharing double rooms. Perhaps the most recent innovation along these lines is the creation of organizations that "introduce" the single traveler to other single travelers. Some charge fees, while others are free, but the basic service offered is the same: to match an unattached person with a compatible travel mate. Among such organizations are the following:

Jane's International (2603 Bath Ave., Brooklyn, NY 11214; phone: 718-266-2045). This service puts potential traveling companions in touch with one another. It has started a new organization, *Sophisticated Women Travelers,* to create groups for single women to travel together. No age limit, no fee for either.

Partners-in-Travel (PO Box 491145, Los Angeles, CA 90049; phone: 213-476-4869). Members receive a list of singles seeking traveling companions; prospective companions make contact through the agency. The membership fee is $40 per year and includes a chatty newsletter (6 issues per year).

Travel Companion Exchange (PO Box 833, Amityville, NY 11701; phone: 516-454-0880). This group publishes a newsletter for singles and a directory of individuals looking for travel companions. On joining, members fill out a lengthy questionnaire and write a small listing (much like an ad in a personal column). Based on these listings, members can request copies of profiles and contact prospective traveling companions. It is wise to join well in advance of your planned vacation so that there's enough time to determine compatibility and plan a joint trip. Membership fees, including the newsletter, are $30 for 6 months or $60 a year for a single-sex listing; $66 and $120, respectively, for a complete listing. Subscription to the newsletter alone costs $24 for 6 months or $36 per year.

In addition, a number of tour packagers cater to single travelers. These companies offer packages designed for individuals interested in vacationing with a group of single travelers or in being matched with a traveling companion. Among the better established of these agencies are the following:

Gallivanting (515 E. 79 St., Suite 20F, New York, NY 10021; phone: 800-933-9699 or 212-988-0617). Offers matching service for singles ages 25 through 55 willing to share accommodations in order to avoid paying single supplement charges, with the agency guaranteeing this arrangement if bookings are paid for at least 75 days in advance.

Marion Smith Singles (611 Prescott Pl., N. Woodmere, NY 11581; phone: 516-791-4852, 516-791-4865, or 212-944-2112). Specializes in tours for singles ages 20 to 50, who can choose to share accommodations to avoid paying single supplement charges.

Odyssey Network (118 Cedar St., Wellesley, MA 02181; phone: 800-487-6059 or 617-237-2400). Originally founded to match single female travelers, this company now includes men in its enrollment. *Odyssey* offers a quarterly newsletter for members who are seeking a travel companion and makes independent arrangements for them. A $50 membership fee includes the newsletter.

Saga International Holidays (120 Boylston St., Boston MA 02116; phone: 800-343-0273 or 617-451-6808). A subsidiary of a British company specializing in older travelers, many of them single, *Saga* offers a broad selection of packages for people age 60 and over or those 50 to 59 traveling with someone 60 or older. Although anyone can book a *Saga* trip, a $15 club membership includes a subscription to their newsletter, as well as other publications and travel services — such as a matching service for single travelers.

Singles in Motion (545 W. 236th St., Suite 1D, Riverdale, NY 10463; phone: 718-884-4464). Has a scheduled program.

Travel in Two's (239 N. Broadway, Suite 3, N. Tarrytown, NY 10591; phone: 914-631-8409). For city programs, this company matches up solo travelers and then customizes programs for them. The firm also puts out a quarterly *Singles Vacation Newsletter,* which costs $7.50 per issue or $20 per year.

A good book for single travelers is *Traveling On Your Own,* by Eleanor Berman, which offers tips on traveling solo and includes information on trips for singles. Available in bookstores, it also can be ordered by sending $12.95, plus postage and handling, to Random House, Order Dept., 400 Hahn Rd., Westminster, MD 21157 (phone: 800-733-3000).

Single travelers also may want to subscribe to *Going Solo,* a newsletter that offers helpful information on going on your own. Issued eight times a year, a subscription costs $36. Contact Doerfer Communications, PO Box 1035, Cambridge, MA 02238 (phone: 617-876-2764).

Those interested in a particularly cozy type of accommodation should consider going the bed and breakfast route. Though a single person will likely pay more than half of the rate quoted for a couple even at a bed and breakfast establishment, the prices still are quite reasonable, and the homey atmosphere will make you feel less conspicuously alone.

Another possibility is the *United States Servas Committee* (11 John St., Room 407, New York, NY 10038; phone: 212-267-0252), which maintains a list of hosts around the world, including Honolulu, who are willing to take visitors into their homes as guests. *Servas* will send an application form and a list of interviewers at the nearest locations for you to contact. After the interview, if you are accepted as a *Servas* traveler, you'll receive a membership certificate. The membership fee is $45 per year for an individual, with a $15 deposit to receive the host list, refunded upon its return.

Hints for Older Travelers

Special discounts and more free time are just two factors that have given Americans over age 65 a chance to see the world at affordable prices. Senior citizens make up an ever-growing segment of the travel population, and the trend among them is to travel more frequently and for longer periods of time.

PLANNING: When planning a vacation, prepare your itinerary with one eye on your own physical condition and the other on your interests. One important factor to keep in mind is not to overdo anything and to be aware of the effects that the weather may have on your capabilities.

Older travelers may find the following publications of interest:

Discount Guide for Travelers Over 55, by Caroline and Walter Weintz, is an excellent book for budget-conscious older travelers. Published by Penguin USA, it is currently out of print; check your local library.

International Health Guide for Senior Citizen Travelers, by Dr. W. Robert Lange, covers such topics as trip preparations, food and water precautions, adjusting to weather and climate conditions, finding a doctor, motion sickness, jet lag, and so on. Also includes a list of resource organizations that provide medical assistance for travelers. It is available for $4.95 postpaid from Pilot Books, 103 Cooper St., Babylon, NY 11702 (phone: 516-422-2225).

Mature Traveler is a monthly newsletter that provides information on travel discounts, places of interest, useful tips, and other topics of interest for travelers 49 and up. To subscribe, send $24.50 to GEM Publishing Group, PO Box 50820, Reno, NV 89513 (phone: 702-786-7419).

Senior Citizen's Guide to Budget Travel in the US and Canada, by Paige Palmer, provides specific information on economical travel options for senior citizens. To order, send $4.95, plus $1 for postage and handling, to Pilot Books (address above).

Take a Camel to Lunch and Other Adventures for Mature Travelers, by Nancy O'Connell, offers offbeat and unusual adventures for travelers over 50. Available for $8.95 at bookstores or directly from Bristol Publishing Enterprises (include $2.75 for shipping and handling), PO Box 1737, San Leandro, CA 94577 (phone: 800-346-4889 or 510-895-4461).

Travel Easy: The Practical Guide for People Over 50, by Rosalind Massow, discusses a wide range of subjects — from trip planning, transportation options, and preparing for departure to avoiding and handling medical problems en route. The book is out of print, so check your local library.

Unbelievably Good Deals & Great Adventures That You Absolutely Can't Get Unless You're Over 50, by Joan Rattner Heilman, offers travel tips for older travelers, including discounts on accommodations and transportation, as well as a list of organizations for seniors. It is available for $7.95, plus shipping and handling, from Contemporary Books, 180 N. Michigan Ave., Chicago, IL 60601 (phone: 312-782-9181).

HEALTH: Pre-trip medical and dental checkups are strongly recommended. In addition, be sure to take along any prescription medication you need, enough to last *without a new prescription* for the duration of your trip; pack all medications with a note from your doctor for the benefit of airport authorities. If you have specific medical problems, bring prescriptions and a "medical file" composed of the following:

1. A summary of your medical history and current diagnosis.
2. A list of drugs to which you are allergic.
3. Your most recent electrocardiogram, if you have heart problems.
4. Your doctor's name, address, and telephone number.

DISCOUNTS AND PACKAGES: Since guidelines change from place to place, it is a good idea to inquire in advance about discounts on transportation, hotels, concerts, movies, museums, and other activities. For instance, the National Park Service has a Golden Age Passport, which entitles people over 62 (and those in the car with them) to free entrance to all national parks and monuments (available by showing a Medicare card or driver's license as proof of age at any national park).

Many hotel chains, airlines, cruise lines, bus companies, car rental companies, and other travel suppliers offer discounts to older travelers. For instance, *United Airlines* offers senior citizen coupon books — with either four or eight coupons each — that can be exchanged for tickets on domestic flights of up to 2,000 miles. These coupons are good 7 days a week for travel in all 50 states, although some peak travel periods are omitted. Other airlines also offer discounts for passengers age 60 (or 62) and over, which may be applicable to one traveling companion per senior. Among the airlines that often offer such discounted airfares are *America West, Continental,* and *TWA.* Given the continuing changes in the airline industry, however, these discounted fares may not be available when you purchase your tickets. For information on current prices and applicable restrictions, contact the individual carriers.

In order to take advantage of these discounts, you should carry proof of your age (or eligibility). A driver's license, membership card in a recognized senior citizens organization, or a Medicare card should be adequate. Among the organizations dedicated to helping older travelers see the world are the following:

American Association of Retired Persons (AARP; 601 E St. NW, Washington, DC 20049; phone: 202-434-2277). The largest and best known of these organizations. Membership is open to anyone 50 or over, whether retired or not; dues are $8 a year, $20 for 3 years, or $45 for 10 years, and include spouse. The *AARP* Travel Experience Worldwide program, available through *American Express Travel Related Services,* offers members tours and other travel programs designed exclusively for older travelers. For example, it offers an independent Honolulu city program. Members can book these services by calling *American Express* at 800-927-0111 for land and air travel.

Mature Outlook (Customer Service Center, 6001 N. Clark St., Chicago, IL 60660; phone: 800-336-6330). Through its *TravelAlert,* tours, cruises, and other vacation packages are available to members at special savings. Hotel and car rental discounts and travel accident insurance also are available. Membership is open to anyone 50 years of age or older, costs $9.95 a year, and includes a bimonthly newsletter and magazine, as well as information on package tours.

National Council of Senior Citizens (1331 F St., Washington, DC 20005; phone: 202-347-8800). Here, too, the emphasis is on keeping costs low. This nonprofit organization offers members a different roster of package tours each year, as well as individual arrangements through its affiliated travel agency *(Vantage Travel Service)*. Although most members are over 50, membership is open to anyone (regardless of age) for an annual fee of $12 per person or couple. Lifetime membership costs $150.

Certain travel agencies and tour operators offer special trips geared to older travelers. Among them are the following:

Evergreen Travel Service (4114 198th St. SW, Suite 13, Lynnwood, WA 98036-6742; phone: 800-435-2288 or 206-776-1184 throughout the continental US and Canada). This specialist in trips for persons with disabilities recently introduced Lazybones Tours, a program offering leisurely tours for older travelers. Most programs are first class or deluxe, and include an escort.

Gadabout Tours (700 E. Tahquitz Canyon Way, Palm Springs, CA 92262; phone: 619-325-5556 or 800-521-7309 in California; 800-952-5068 elsewhere in the US). Offers escorted tours and cruises to a number of destinations, including Honolulu.

Saga International Holidays (120 Boylston St., Boston, MA 02116; phone: 800-343-0273 or 617-451-6808). A subsidiary of a British company catering to older travelers, *Saga* offers a broad selection of packages for people age 60 and over or those 50 to 59 traveling with someone 60 or older. Although anyone can book a *Saga* trip, a $15 club membership includes a subscription to their newsletter, as well as other publications and travel services.

Many travel agencies, particularly the larger ones, are delighted to make presentations to help a group of senior citizens select destinations. A local chamber of commerce should be able to provide the names of such agencies. Once a time and place are determined, an organization member or travel agent can obtain group quotations for transportation, accommodations, meal plans, and sightseeing. Larger groups usually get the best breaks.

Another choice open to older travelers is a trip that includes an educational element. *Elderhostel,* a nonprofit organization, offers programs at educational institutions in the US, including Honolulu, and worldwide. The domestic programs generally last 1 week, and include double occupancy accommodations in hotels or student residence halls and all meals. Travel to the programs usually is by designated scheduled flights, and participants can arrange to extend their stay at the end of the program. Elderhostelers must be at least 60 years old (younger if a spouse or companion qualifies), in good health, and not in need of special diets. For a free catalogue describing the program and current offerings, write to *Elderhostel* (75 Federal St., Boston, MA 02110; phone: 617-426-7788). Those interested in the program also can borrow slides at no charge or purchase an informational videotape for $5.

Hints for Traveling with Children

What better way to encounter Honolulu's historic past and exciting present than in the company of the young, wide-eyed members of your family? Their presence does not have to be a burden or an excessive expense. The current generation of discounts for children and family package deals can make a trip together quite reasonable.

A family trip to Honolulu will be an investment in your children's future, making the geography and history of our country's expansionist years come alive to them, leaving a memory that will be among the fondest you will share with them someday. Their insights will be refreshing to you; their impulses may take you to unexpected places with unexpected dividends. The experience will be invaluable to them at any age.

PLANNING: Here are several hints for making a trip with children easy and fun:

1. Children, like everyone else, will derive more pleasure from a trip if they know something about their destination before they arrive. Begin their education about a month before you leave. Using maps, travel magazines, and books, give children a clear idea of where you are going and how far away it is.
2. Children should help to plan the itinerary, and where you go and what you do should reflect some of their ideas. If they already know something about the city and the sites they will visit, they will have the excitement of recognition when they arrive.
3. Give children specific responsibilities: The job of carrying their own flight bags and looking after their personal things, along with some other light chores, will give them a stake in the journey.
4. Give each child a travel diary or scrapbook to take along.

Children's books about Honolulu and its place in the history of our country provide an excellent introduction and can be found at children's bookstores (see *Books and Bookstores*), many general bookstores, and in libraries.

And for parents, *Travel With Your Children* (*TWYCH;* 80 Eighth Ave., New York, NY 10011; phone: 212-206-0688) publishes a newsletter, *Family Travel Times,* that focuses on families with young travelers and offers helpful hints. An annual subscription (10 issues) is $35 and includes a copy of the "Airline Guide" issue (updated every other year), which focuses on the subject of flying with children. This special issue is available separately for $10.

Another newsletter devoted to family travel is *Getaways.* This quarterly publication provides reviews of family-oriented literature, activities, and useful travel tips. To subscribe, send $25 to *Getaways,* Att. Ms. Brooke Kane, PO Box 8282, McLean, VA 22107 (phone: 703-534-8747).

Also of interest to parents traveling with their children is *How to Take Great Trips with Your Kids,* by psychologist Sanford Portnoy and his wife, Joan Flynn Portnoy. The book includes helpful tips from fellow family travelers, tips on economical accommodations and touring by car, as well as over 50 games to play with your children en route. It is available for $8.95, plus shipping and handling, from Harvard Common Press, 535 Albany St., Boston, MA 02118 (phone: 617-423-5803). Another title worth looking for is *Great Vacations with Your Kids,* by Dorothy Jordan (Dutton; $12.95).

Another book on family travel, *Travel with Children* by Maureen Wheeler, offers a wide range of practical tips on traveling with children. It is available for $10.95, plus shipping and handling, from Lonely Planet Publications, Embarcadero West, 112 Linden St., Oakland, CA 94607 (phone: 510-893-8555).

Also look for the Hawaiian Islands volume of the "Kidding Around" series on US cities, published by John Muir Publications. It starts with an overview of the city, along with some interesting background information, and then it is divided into areas, with descriptions of the various attractions in the general order in which you might encounter them. The book can be ordered for $9.95, plus shipping, from John Muir Publications, PO Box 613, Santa Fe, NM 87504, or by calling 800-888-7504 or 505-982-4078.

Finally, parents arranging a trip with their children may want to deal with an agency specializing in family travel such as *Let's Take the Kids* (1268 Devon Ave., Los Angeles, CA 90024; phone: 800-726-4349 or 213-274-7088). In addition to arranging and booking trips for individual families, this group occasionally organizes trips for single-parent families traveling together. They also offer a parent travel network, whereby parents who have been to a particular destination can evaluate it for others.

PLANE: Begin early to investigate all available family discount flights, as well as any package deals and special rates offered by the major airlines. When you make your reservations, tell the airline that you are traveling with a child. Children ages 2 through 11 generally travel at about a 20% to 30% discount off regular full-fare adult ticket prices on domestic flights. This children's fare, however, usually is much higher than the excursion fare, which may be used by any traveler, regardless of age. An infant under 2 years of age usually can travel free if it sits on an adult's lap. A second infant without a second adult would pay the fare applicable to children ages 2 through 11.

Although some airlines will, on request, supply bassinets for infants, most carriers encourage parents to bring their own safety seat on board, which then is strapped into the airline seat with a regular seat belt. This is much safer — and certainly more comfortable — than holding the child in your lap. If you do not purchase a seat for your baby, you have the option of bringing the infant restraint along on the off-chance that there might be an empty seat next to yours — in which case some airlines will let you use that seat at no charge for your baby and infant seat. However, if there is no empty seat available, the infant seat no doubt will have to be checked as baggage (and you may have to pay an additional charge), since it generally does not fit under the airplane seats or in the overhead racks. The safest bet is to pay for a seat.

Be forewarned: Some safety seats designed primarily for use in cars do not fit into plane seats properly. Although nearly all seats manufactured since 1985 carry labels indicating whether they meet federal standards for use aboard planes, actual seat sizes may vary from carrier to carrier. At the time of this writing, the FAA was in the process of reviewing and revising the federal regulations regarding infant travel and safety devices — it was still to be determined if children should be *required* to sit in safety seats and whether the airlines will have to provide them.

If using one of these infant restraints, you should try to get bulkhead seats, which will provide extra room to care for your child during the flight. You also should request a bulkhead seat when using a bassinet — again, this is not as safe as strapping the child in. On some planes the bassinet hooks into a bulkhead wall; on others it is placed on the floor in front of you. (Note that bulkhead seats often are reserved for families traveling with small children.) As a general rule, babies should be held during takeoff and landing.

Request seats on the aisle if you have a toddler or if you think you will need to use the bathroom frequently. Carry onto the plane all you will need to care for and occupy your children during the flight — formula, diapers, a sweater, books, favorite stuffed animals, and so on. Dress your baby simply, with a minimum of buttons and snaps, because the only place you may have to change a diaper is at your seat or in a small lavatory.

You also can ask for a hot dog or hamburger instead of the airline's regular dinner if you give at least 24 hours' notice. Some, but not all, airlines have baby food aboard, and the flight attendant can warm a bottle for you. While you should bring along toys from home, also ask about children's diversions. Some carriers have terrific free packages of games, coloring books, and puzzles.

When the plane takes off and lands, make sure your baby is nursing or has a bottle, pacifier, or thumb in its mouth. This sucking will make the child swallow and help to clear stopped ears. A piece of hard candy will do the same for an older child.

Parents traveling by plane with toddlers, children, or teenagers may want to consult *When Kids Fly,* a free booklet published by Massport (Public Affairs Department, 10 Park Plaza, Boston, MA 02116-3971; phone: 617-973-5600), which includes helpful information on airfares for children, infant seats, what to do in the event of overbooked or canceled flights, and so on.

■**Note:** Newborn babies, whose lungs may not be able to adjust to the altitude, should not be taken aboard an airplane. And some airlines may refuse to allow a pregnant woman in her 8th or 9th month to fly. Check with the airline ahead of time, and carry a letter from your doctor stating that you are fit to travel — and indicating the estimated date of birth.

Things to Remember

1. If you are visiting many sites, pace the days with children in mind. Break the trip into half-day segments, with running around or "doing" time built in.
2. Don't forget that a child's attention span is far shorter than an adult's. Children don't have to see every sight or all of any sight to learn something from their trip; watching, playing with, and talking to other children can be equally enlightening.
3. Let your children lead the way sometimes; their perspective is different from yours, and they may lead you to things you would never have noticed on your own.
4. Remember the places that children love to visit: aquariums, zoos, amusement parks, beaches, nature trails, and so on. Among the activities that may pique their interest are bicycling, horseback riding, boat trips, visiting planetariums and children's museums, and viewing natural habitat exhibits. The perennial Honolulu attractions for children are the *Bishop Museum,* the *Polynesian Cultural Center,* *Sea Life Park,* and the *Honolulu Zoo.*

On the Road

Credit Cards and Traveler's Checks

It may seem hard to believe, but one of the greatest (and least understood) costs of travel is money itself. Your one single objective in relation to the care and retention of your travel funds is to make them stretch as far as possible. When you do spend money, it should be on things that expand and enhance your travel experience, with no buying power lost due to carelessness or lack of knowledge. This requires more than merely ferreting out the best airfare or the most charming budget hotel. It means being canny about the management of money itself. Herewith, a primer on making money go as far as possible while traveling.

TRAVELER'S CHECKS: It's wise to carry traveler's checks while on the road instead of (or in addition to) cash, since it's possible to replace them if they are stolen or lost; in the US, you usually can receive partial or full replacement funds the same day if you have your purchase receipt and proper identification. Issued in various denominations, with adequate proof of identification (credit cards, driver's license, passport), traveler's checks are as good as cash in most hotels, restaurants, stores, and banks. Don't assume, however, that restaurants, small shops, and other establishments are going to be able to change checks of large denominations. More and more establishments are beginning to restrict the face amount of traveler's checks they will accept or cash, so it is wise to purchase at least some of your checks in small denominations — say, $10 and $20.

Every type of traveler's check is legal tender in banks around the world, and each company guarantees full replacement if checks are lost or stolen. After that the similarity ends. Some charge a fee for purchase, while others are free; you can buy traveler's checks at almost any bank, and some are available by mail. Most important, each traveler's check issuer differs slightly in its refund policy — the amount refunded immediately, the accessibility of refund locations, the availability of a 24-hour refund service, and the time it will take you to receive replacement checks. For instance, *American Express* offers a 3-hour replacement of lost or stolen traveler's checks at any *American Express* office — other companies may not be as prompt. (Note that *American Express*'s 3-hour policy is based on the traveler's being able to provide the serial numbers of the lost checks. Without these numbers, refunds can take much longer.) *American Express*'s offices in Honolulu are located at 1778 Ala Moana Blvd. in the *Discovery Bay Shopping Center* (phone: 946-7741), at 2301 Kalakaua Ave. in the *Royal Hawaiian Center* (phone: 924-6555), and in the following hotels: the *Hawaiian Regent* (phone: 924-6555), *Hilton Hawaiian Village* (phone: 947-2607, *Hyatt Regency Waikiki* (phone: 925-5441), *Ilikai* (phone: 945-2679), *Pacific Beach Hotel* (phone: 922-2363), and the *Waikiki Beachcomber* (phone: 924-9202).

We cannot overemphasize the importance of knowing how to replace lost or stolen checks. All of the traveler's check companies have agents throughout the US, both in their own name and at associated agencies (usually, but not necessarily, banks), where refunds can be obtained during business hours. Most of them also have 24-hour toll-free telephone lines, and some even will provide emergency funds to tide you over on a Sunday.

Be sure to make a photocopy of the refund instructions that will be given to you by the issuing institution at the time of purchase. To avoid complications should you need to redeem lost checks (and to speed up the replacement process), keep the purchase receipt and an accurate list, by serial number, of the checks that have been spent or cashed. You may want to incorporate this information in an "emergency packet," also including the numbers of the credit cards you are carrying, and any other bits of information you shouldn't be without. Always keep these records separate from the checks and the original records themselves (you may want to give them to a traveling companion to hold).

Several of the major traveler's check companies charge 1% for the acquisition of their checks; others don't. To receive fee-free traveler's checks you may have to meet certain qualifications — for instance, *Thomas Cook*'s checks issued in US currency are free if you make your travel arrangements through its travel agency. *American Express* traveler's checks are available without charge to members of the *American Automobile Association (AAA).* Holders of some credit cards (such as the *American Express Platinum* card) also may be entitled to free traveler's checks. The issuing institution (e.g., the particular bank at which you purchase them) may itself charge a fee. If you purchase traveler's checks at a bank in which you or your company maintains significant accounts (especially commercial accounts of some size), the bank may absorb the 1% fee as a courtesy.

American Express, Bank of America, Citicorp, MasterCard, Thomas Cook, and *Visa* all offer traveler's checks. Here are the numbers to call for more information on purchasing traveler's checks or to report lost or stolen checks throughout the US:

American Express: 800-221-7282
Bank of America: 800-227-3460
Citicorp: 800-645-6556
MasterCard: Note that *Thomas Cook Mastercard* (below) is now handling all *MasterCard* traveler's check inquiries and refunds (see below).
Thomas Cook MasterCard: 800-223-7373
Visa: 800-227-6811

CREDIT CARDS: Some establishments you may encounter during the course of your travels may not honor any credit cards and some may not honor all cards, so there is a practical reason to carry more than one. The following is a list of credit cards that enjoy wide domestic and international acceptance:

American Express: Cardholders can cash personal checks for traveler's checks and cash at *American Express* or its representatives' offices in the US up to the following limits (within any single 21-day period): $1,000 for *Green* and *Optima* cardholders; $5,000 for *Gold* cardholders; and $10,000 for *Platinum* cardholders. Check cashing also is available to cardholders who are guests at participating hotels (up to $250), and for holders of airline tickets at participating airlines (up to $50). Free travel accident, baggage, and car rental insurance is provided if the ticket or rental is charged to the card; additional insurance also is available for additional cost. For further information or to report a lost or stolen *American Express* card, call 800-528-4800 throughout the US.
Carte Blanche: Free travel accident, baggage, and car rental insurance if ticket or rental is charged to card; additional insurance also is available at additional cost. For medical, legal, and travel assistance, call 800-356-3448 throughout the US. For further information or to report a lost or stolen *Carte Blanche* card, call 800-525-9135 throughout the US.
Diners Club: Emergency personal check cashing for cardholders staying at participating hotels and motels (up to $250 per stay). Free travel accident, baggage,

and car rental insurance if ticket or rental is charged to card; additional insurance also is available for an additional fee. For medical, legal, and travel assistance worldwide, call 800-356-3448 throughout the US. For further information or to report a lost or stolen *Diners Club* card, call 800-525-9135 throughout the US.

Discover Card: Offered by a subsidiary of Sears, Roebuck & Co., it provides cardholders with cash advances at numerous automatic teller machines and *Sears* stores throughout the US. For further information or to report a lost or stolen *Discover* card, call 800-DISCOVER throughout the US.

MasterCard: Cash advances are available at participating banks worldwide. Check with your issuing bank for information. *MasterCard* also offers a 24-hour emergency lost card service; call 800-826-2181 throughout the US.

Visa: Cash advances are available at participating banks worldwide. Check with your issuing bank for information. *Visa* also offers a 24-hour emergency lost card service; call 800-336-8472 throughout the US.

SENDING MONEY: If you have used up your traveler's checks, cashed as many emergency personal checks as your credit card allows, drawn on your cash advance line to the fullest extent, and still need money, have it sent to you via one of the following services:

American Express (phone: 800-543-4080). Offers a service called "Moneygram," completing money transfers in as little as 15 minutes. The sender can go to any *American Express* office in the US and transfer money by presenting cash, a personal check, money order, or credit card — *Discover, Mastercard, Visa,* or *American Express Optima* (no other *American Express* or other credit cards are accepted). *American Express Optima* cardholders also can arrange for this transfer over the phone. The minimum transfer charge is $12, which rises with the amount of the transaction; the sender can forward funds of up to $10,000 per transaction (credit card users are limited to the amount of their pre-established credit line). To collect at the other end, the receiver must show identification (driver's license or other picture ID) at an *American Express* branch office. The company's offices in Honolulu are listed above in the *Traveler's Checks* section.

Western Union Telegraph Company (phone: 800-325-4176 throughout the US). A friend or relative can go, cash in hand, to any *Western Union* office in the US, where, for a *minimum* charge of $11 (it rises with the amount of the transaction), the funds will be transferred to a centralized *Western Union* account. When the transaction is fully processed — generally within 30 minutes — you can go to any *Western Union* branch office to pick up the transferred funds; for an additional fee of $2.95 you will be notified by phone when the money is available. For a higher fee, the sender may call *Western Union* with a *MasterCard* or *Visa* number to send up to $2,000, although larger transfers will be sent to a predesignated location. Two convenient Honolulu locations to receive money are at the *Star Markets* at 2470 S. King St. (phone: 973-1666) and the *Kahala Shopping Center* (phone: 733-1366).

CASH MACHINES: Automatic teller machines (ATMs) are now common throughout the US. If your bank participates in one of the international ATM networks (most do), the bank will issue you a "cash card" along with a personal identification code or number (also called a PIC or PIN). You can use this card at any ATM in the same electronic network to check your account balances, transfer monies between checking and savings accounts, and — most important for a traveler — withdraw cash instantly. Network ATMs generally are located in banks, commercial and transportation centers, and near major tourist attractions.

Some financial institutions offer exclusive automatic teller machines for their own customers only at bank branches. At the time of this writing, ATMs that *are* connected generally belong to one of the following two international networks:

Cirrus: Has over 70,000 ATMs in more than 45 countries, including over 65,000 locations in the US — about 125 in Honolulu. *MasterCard* holders also may use their cards to draw cash against their credit lines. For further information on the *Cirrus* network, call 800-4-CIRRUS.

Plus System: Has over 70,000 automatic teller machines worldwide, including over 50,000 locations in the US — over 170 of them in Honolulu. *MasterCard* and *Visa* cardholders also may use their cards to draw cash against their credit lines. For further information on the *Plus System* network, call 800-THE-PLUS.

Information about the *Cirrus* and *Plus* systems also is available at member bank branches, where you can obtain free booklets listing the locations worldwide. Note that a recent change in banking regulations permits financial institutions to subscribe to *both* the *Cirrus* and *Plus* systems, allowing users of either network to witraw funds from ATMs at participating banks.

Time Zone and Business Hours

TIME ZONE: Honolulu is in the Hawaiian time zone, which means that it is 2 hours behind Pacific standard time and 5 hours behind eastern standard time. Since the state does not observe daylight saving time, the difference is increased by an hour during that period, from the first Sunday in April until the last Sunday in October.

BUSINESS HOURS: Honolulu maintains business hours that are fairly standard throughout the country: 9 AM to 5 PM, Mondays through Fridays. When there is any variation, the tendency is for the business to open and close earlier.

Banks generally are open weekdays from 9 AM to 3 PM, and 24-hour ATMs are common (for information on national networks, see *Credit Cards and Traveler's Checks,* in this section).

Retail stores usually are open from 9:30 or 10 AM to 5:30 or 6 PM, Mondays through Saturdays. The stores at some of the larger malls are open until 9 PM, until 10 PM on holidays. Many retail establishments also remain open on Sundays until 5 PM or so.

Mail, Telephone, and Electricity

MAIL: The main Honolulu post office is located at 3600 Aolele (phone: 423-3930); counter hours are 8 AM to 7:30 PM weekdays and until 2:30 PM on Saturdays. A self-service section with stamp machines and a scale for weighing packages is open 24 hours a day. Other locations are downtown (335 Merchant St. at Richards St.; phone: 541-1962), open 8 AM to 4:30 PM, and in Waikiki (330 Saratoga Rd.; phone: 941-1062). A substation in the *Royal Hawaiian Shopping Center* (phone: 926-3710) is open 9 AM to 4:30 PM.

Stamps also are available at most hotel desks. There are vending machines for stamps in drugstores, transportation terminals, and other public places. Stamps cost more from these machines than they do at the post office.

For rapid, overnight delivery to other cities, *Federal Express* can be useful. The phone number to call for pick-up in Honolulu is 395-3339, while convenient drop-off addresses include downtown (at 841 Bishop St.) and in Waikiki (at 2255 Kuhio Ave. and 2255 Kalakaua Ave. in the *Sheraton Waikiki,* 2nd Floor). The pick-up number for another convenient express service, *DHL Worldwide Courier Express,* is 836-0441.

TELEPHONE: Public telephones are available just about everywhere — including transportation terminals, hotel lobbies, restaurants, drugstores, libraries, post offices, and other municipal buildings, as well as major tourist centers.

The Hawaii area code, including Honolulu, is 808.

Although you can use a telephone company credit card number on any phone, pay phones that take major credit cards (*American Express, MasterCard, Visa,* and so on) are increasingly common, particularly in transportation and tourism centers. Also now available is the "affinity card," a combined telephone calling card/bank credit card that can be used for domestic and international calls. Cards of this type include the following:

> *AT&T/Universal* (phone: 800-662-7759)
> *Executive Telecard International* (phone: 800-950-3800)

Similarly, *MCI VisaPhone* (phone: 800-866-0099) can add phone card privileges to the services available through your existing *Visa* card. This service allows you to use your *Visa* account number, plus an additional code, to charge calls on any touch-tone phone.

You must first dial 1 to indicate that you are making a long-distance call. The nationwide number for information is 555-1212. If you need a number in another area code, dial 1 + the area code + 555-1212. (If you don't know the area code, simply dial 0 for an operator who will tell you.)

Long-distance rates are charged according to when the call is placed: weekday daytime; weekday evenings; and nights, weekends, and holidays. Least expensive are the calls you dial yourself from a private phone at night and on weekends and major holidays. It generally is more expensive to call from a pay phone than it is to call from a private phone, and you must pay for a minimum 3-minute call. If the operator assists you, calls are more expensive. This includes credit card, bill-to-a-third-number, collect, and time-and-charge calls, as well as person-to-person calls, which are the most expensive. Rates are fully explained in the front of the white pages of every telephone directory.

Hotel Surcharges – Before calling from any hotel room, inquire about any surcharges the hotel may impose. These can be excessive, but are avoidable by calling collect, using a telephone credit card (see above), or calling from a public pay phone. (Note that when calling from your hotel room, even if the call is made collect or charged to a credit card number, some establishments still may add on a nominal line usage charge — so ask before you call.)

Emergency Number – As in most cities, 911 is the number to dial in the event of an emergency in Honolulu. Operators at this number will get you the help you need from the police, fire department, or ambulance service. It is, however, a number that should be used for real emergencies only.

■**Note:** An excellent resource for planning your trip is *AT&T's Toll-Free 800 Directory,* which lists thousands of companies with 800 numbers, both alphabetically (white pages) and by category (yellow pages), including a wide range of travel services — from travel agents to transportation and accommodations. Issued in a consumer edition for $9.95 and a business edition for $14.95, both are available from *AT&T Phone Centers* or by calling 800-426-8686. Other useful directories for use before you leave and on the road include the *Toll-Free Travel & Vacation Information Directory* ($4.95 postpaid from Pilot Books, 103 Cooper St., Babylon, NY 11702; phone: 516-422-2225) and *The Phone Booklet,* which lists the nationwide, toll-free (800) numbers of travel information sources and suppliers — such as major airlines, hotel and motel chains, car rental companies, and tourist information offices (send $2 to Scott American Corporation, Box 88, West Redding, CT 06896).

ELECTRICITY: All 50 US states have the same electrical current system: 110 volts, 60 cycles, alternating current (AC). Appliances running on standard current can be used throughout the US without adapters or converters.

Staying Healthy

The surest way to return home in good health is to be prepared for medical problems that might occur en route. Below, we've outlined everything about which you need to think before you go.

BEFORE YOU GO: Older travelers or anyone suffering from a chronic medical condition, such as diabetes, high blood pressure, cardiopulmonary disease, asthma, or ear, eye, or sinus trouble, should consult a physician before leaving home. Those with conditions requiring special consideration when traveling should consider seeing, in addition to their regular physician, a specialist in travel medicine. For a referral in a particular community, contact the nearest medical school or ask a local doctor to recommend such a specialist. Dr. Leonard Marcus, a member of the *American Committee on Clinical Tropical Medicine and Travelers' Health,* provides a directory of more than 100 travel doctors across the country. For a copy, send a 9x12-inch addressed, stamped envelope, to Dr. Marcus at 148 Highland Ave., Newton, MA 02165 (phone: 617-527-4003).

Also be sure to check with your insurance company ahead of time about the applicability of your hospitalization and major medical policies while you're away. If your medical policy does not protect you while you're traveling, there are comprehensive combination policies specifically designed to fill the gap. (For a discussion of medical insurance and a list of inclusive combination policies, see *Insurance,* in this section.)

FIRST AID: Put together a compact, personal medical kit including Band-Aids, first-aid cream, antiseptic, nose drops, insect repellent, aspirin or non-aspirin pain reliever, an extra pair of prescription glasses or contact lenses (and a copy of your prescription for glasses or contact lenses), sunglasses, over-the-counter remedies for diarrhea, indigestion, and motion sickness, a thermometer, and a supply of those prescription medicines you take regularly.

In a corner of your kit, keep a list of all the drugs you have brought and their purpose, as well as duplicate copies of your doctor's prescriptions (or a note from your doctor). As brand names may vary in different parts of the US, it's a good idea to ask your doctor for the generic name of any drugs you use so that you can ask for their equivalent should you need a refill.

It also is a good idea to ask your doctor to prepare a medical identification card that includes such information as your blood type, your social security number, any allergies or chronic health problems you have, and your medical insurance information. Considering the essential contents of your medical kit, keep it with you, rather than in your checked luggage.

MEDICAL ASSISTANCE: If a bona fide emergency occurs, dial 911, the emergency number, and immediately state the nature of your problem and your location. If you are able to, another alternative is to go directly to the emergency room of the nearest hospital.

In Honolulu, a major medical institution with top emergency facilities is the *Kuakini Health System* (347 N. Kuakini; phone: 547-9540 for emergencies, 536-2236 for other business). Another medical institution is the *Queen's Medical Center* (1301 Punchbowl; phone: 538-9011). The *Straub Clinic & Hospital* has an affiliated service, *Doctors on Call,* which operates offices in four Honolulu hotels and provides house calls. The office at the *Hyatt Regency Waikiki* (2424 Kalakaua Ave., Diamondhead Tower, 4th Floor; phone: 926-4777) is open 24 hours. The other offices are at the *Hawaiian Regent Hotel* (2552 Kalakaua Ave., Kuhio Tower, 2nd Floor; phone: 923-3666; open 8 AM TO 4:40 PM weekdays), the *Hilton Hawaiian Village* (2005 Kalia Rd., Rainbow Bazaar, upper level; phone: 973-5252; open 8 AM TO 5PM daily), and the *Reef Tower Hotel* (227 Lewers St., Suite 242; phone: 926-0664; open 8 AM to 4:30 PM weekdays).

For other medical emergencies, in Waikiki, the *Kuhio Pharmacy* at the *Outrigger West Hotel* (2330 Kuhio Ave.; phone: 923-4466) is open from 8:30 AM to 10:45 PM 7 days a week, although the pharmacist leaves at 5 PM. In the rest of the city, *Long's Drug Stores* has several locations, one in the *Ala Moana Center* (1450 Ala Moana; phone 941-4433) that is open from 9 AM until 9 PM on weekdays, until 5:30 PM on Saturdays, and until 5 PM on Sundays; the one downtown (1088 Bishop St.; phone 536-4551) is open from 6:30 AM to 6 PM weekdays, 7 AM to 5 PM on Saturdays, and 8:30 AM to 5 PM on Sundays. The pharmacy that stays open the latest is the *Pillbox* (1133 11th Ave.; phone: 737-1777), which is open from 7 AM until 11 PM every day except Sunday, when it shortens its hours to 7 PM until 11 PM.

If a doctor is needed for something less than an emergency, there are several ways to find one. If you are staying in a hotel, ask for help in reaching a doctor or other emergency services, or for the house physician, who may visit you in your room or ask you to visit an office. When you check in at a hotel, it's not a bad idea to include your home address and telephone number; this will facilitate the process of notifying friends, relatives, or your own doctor in case of an emergency.

If you need to refill a prescription from your own doctor, you should be aware that in some states pharmacists will fill only prescriptions made out by a doctor licensed to practice in that state, so you may have to have a local doctor rewrite a prescription. In Hawaii, a pharmacist can fill an original out-of-state prescription but not a refill; thus, if you run out of your medication, your physician could send you the prescription by Express Mail or *Federal Express* at less expense than going to a local doctor. In an emergency — such as a diabetic needing insulin — a traveler more than likely will be given only enough of a drug to last until a local prescription can be obtained. Generally a hospital emergency room or walk-in clinic can provide a refill from its pharmaceutical department or a prescription that can be filled at a nearby pharmacy.

Medical assistance also is available for travelers who have chronic ailments or whose illness requires them to return home. If you have a health condition that may not be readily perceptible to the casual observer — one that might result in a tragic error in an emergency situation — *Medic Alert Foundation* (2323 N. Colorado, Turlock, CA 95380; phone: 800-ID-ALERT or 209-668-3333) offers identification emblems specifying such conditions. The foundation also maintains a computerized central file from which your complete medical history is available 24 hours a day by phone (the telephone number is clearly inscribed on the emblem). The onetime membership fee (between $25 and $45) is based on the type of metal from which the emblem is made — the choices range from stainless steel to 10K gold-filled.

■ **Note:** Those who are unable to take a reserved flight due to personal illness or who must fly home unexpectedly due to a family emergency should be aware that airlines may offer a discounted airfare (or arrange a partial refund) if the traveler can demonstrate that his or her situation is indeed a legitimate emergency. Your inability to fly or the illness or death of an immediate family member usually must be substantiated by a doctor's note or the name, relationship, and funeral home where the deceased will be buried. In such cases, airlines often will waive certain advance purchase restrictions or you may receive a refund check or voucher for future travel at a later date. Be aware, however, that this bereavement fare may not necessarily be the least expensive fare available and, if possible, it is best to have a travel agent check all possible flights through a computer reservations system (CRS).

HELPFUL PUBLICATIONS: Practically every phase of health care — before, during, and after a trip — is covered in *The New Traveler's Health Guide* by Drs. Patrick J. Doyle and James E. Banta. It is available for $4.95, plus postage and handling, from Acropolis Books Ltd., 13950 Park Center Rd., Herndon, VA 22071 (phone: 800-451-7771 or 703-709-0006).

The *Traveling Healthy Newsletter,* which is published six times a year, also is brimming with healthful travel tips. For an annual subscription, which costs $24, contact Dr. Karl Neumann (108-48 70th Rd., Forest Hills, NY 11375; phone: 718-268-7290). Dr. Neumann also is the editor of the useful free booklet, *Traveling Healthy,* which is available by writing to the *Travel Healthy Program* (PO Box 10208, New Brunswick, NJ 08906-9910; phone: 908-732-4100).

Legal Aid

LEGAL AID: The best way to begin looking for legal aid in an unfamiliar area is to call your own lawyer. If you don't have, or cannot reach, your own attorney, most cities offer legal referral services (sometimes called attorney referral services) maintained by county bar associations. Such referral services see that anyone in need of legal representation gets it. (Attorneys also are listed in the yellow pages.) The referral service is almost always free. In Honolulu, call the *Hawaii State Bar Association*'s referral service (1136 Union Mall, Penthouse 1; phone: 537-9140) or the *Legal Aid Society of Hawaii* (1108 Nuuanu Ave.; phone: 536-4302). If your case goes to court, you are entitled to court-appointed representation if you can't get a lawyer or can't afford one.

In the case of minor traffic accidents (such as fender benders), it is often most expedient to settle the matter before the police get involved. If you get a traffic or parking ticket, pay it. For most violations, you will receive a citation at most, and be required to appear in court on a specified date.

Drinking and Drugs

DRINKING: As in all 50 states, the legal drinking age in Hawaii is 21. Liquor may be served every day of the week in hotels from 6 AM until 4 AM, while restaurants, bars, and lounges may start at the same time but must close at 2 AM. Cabarets may not open until 10 AM but may do business until 4 AM. For retail purchases, liquor, wine, and beer are sold at package stores, supermarkets, and convenience stores from 6 AM until midnight.

DRUGS: Despite the US government's intensified and concerted effort to stamp out drugs, illegal narcotics still are prevalent in the US, as elsewhere. Enforcement of drug laws is becoming increasingly strict throughout the nation, however, and local narcotics officers are renowned for their absence of understanding and lack of a sense of humor.

Possession of small amounts of marijuana is a misdemeanor in Hawaii, while being caught with crack, cocaine, or heroin brings exposure to a felony charge, with conviction leading to sentences of 20 years to life in prison. It is important to bear in mind that the quantity of drugs involved is of minor importance. The best advice we can offer is this: Don't carry, use, buy, or sell illegal drugs.

To avoid difficulties during spot luggage inspections at the airport, if you carry medicines that contain such controlled drugs as codeine or codeine derivatives, be sure to bring along a current doctor's prescription.

Tipping

 While tipping is at the discretion of the person receiving the service, 50¢ is the rock-bottom tip for anything, and $1 is the current customary minimum for small services. In restaurants, tip between 10% and 20% of the bill. For average service in an average restaurant, a 15% tip to the waiter is reasonable, although one should never hesitate to penalize poor service or reward excellent and efficient attention by leaving less or more.

Although it's not necessary to tip the maître d' of most restaurants — unless he has been especially helpful in arranging a special party or providing a table (slipping him something *may*, however, get you seated sooner or procure a preferred table) — when tipping is desirable or appropriate, the least amount should be $5. In the finest restaurants, where a multiplicity of servers are present, plan to tip 5% to the captain in addition to the gratuity left for the waiter. The sommelier (wine waiter) is tipped approximately 10% of the price of the bottle of wine.

In allocating gratuities at a restaurant, pay particular attention to what has become the standard credit card charge form, which now includes separate places for gratuities for waiters and/or captains. If these separate boxes are not on the charge slip, simply ask the waiter or captain how these separate tips should be indicated. In some establishments, tips indicated on credit card receipts may not be given to the help, so you may want to leave tips in cash.

In a large hotel, where it is difficult to determine just who out of a horde of attendants actually performed particular services, it is perfectly proper for guests to ask to have an extra 10% to 15% added to their bill. For those who prefer to distribute tips themselves, a chambermaid generally is tipped at the rate of around $1 a day. Tip the concierge or hall porter for specific services only, with the amount of such gratuities dependent on the level of service provided. For any special service you receive in a hotel, a tip is expected — $1 being the minimum for a small service.

Bellhops, doormen, and porters at hotels and transportation centers generally are tipped at the rate of $1 per piece of luggage, along with a small additional amount if a doorman helps with a cab or car. Taxi drivers should get about 15% of the total fare.

Miscellaneous tips: Sightseeing tour guides should be tipped. If you are traveling in a group, decide together what you want to give the guide and present it from the group at the end of the tour ($1 per person is a reasonable tip). If you have been individually escorted, the amount paid should depend on the degree of your satisfaction, but it should not be less than 10% of the tour price. Museum and monument guides also are usually tipped a few dollars. Coat checks are worth about 50¢ to $1 a coat, and washroom attendants are tipped — there usually is a little plate with a coin already in it suggesting the expected amount. In barbershops and beauty parlors, tips also are expected, but the percentages vary according to the type of establishment — 10% in the most expensive salons; 15% to 20% in less expensive establishments. (As a general rule, the person who washes your hair should get a small additional tip.)

Tipping always is a matter of personal preference. In the situations covered above, as well as in any others that arise where you feel a tip is expected or due, feel free to express your pleasure or displeasure. Again, never hesitate to reward excellent and efficient attention or to penalize poor service. Give an extra gratuity and a word of thanks when someone has gone out of his or her way for you. Either way, the more personal the act of tipping, the more appropriate it seems. And if you didn't like the service — or the attitude — don't tip.

Religion on the Road

 The surest source of information on religious services in an unfamiliar community is the desk clerk of the hotel or resort in which you are staying; the local tourist information office or a church of another religious affiliation also may be able to provide this information. For a full range of options, joint religious councils often provide circulars with the addresses and times of services of other houses of worship in the area. These often are printed as part of general tourist guides provided by the local tourist and convention center, or as part of a "what's going on" guide to the city. Many newspapers also offer a listing of religious services in their area in weekend editions.

You may want to use your vacation to broaden your religious experience by joining an unfamiliar faith in its service. This can be a moving experience, especially if the service is held in a church, synagogue, or temple that is historically significant or architecturally notable. You almost always will find yourself made welcome and comfortable.

Sources and Resources

Tourist Information

For information, maps, and brochures on Hawaii, contact the Hawaii Visitors Bureau (2270 Kalakaua Ave., Suite 1108, Honolulu, HI 96815; phone: 808-923-1811). For local tourist information, see *Local Sources and Resources* in THE CITY.

For More Information

BOOKS AND BOOKSTORES: The variety and scope of books and other travel information in and on the United States today is astounding. Every city and region are represented, so before you leave on your journey you can prepare by perusing books relevant to your special travel interests. These can usually be found in bookshops devoted to travel, among them the following:

Book Passage (51 Tamal Vista Blvd., Corte Madera, CA 94925; phone: 415-927-0960 in California; 800-321-9785 elsewhere in the US). Travel guides and maps to all areas of the world. A free catalogue is available.

The Complete Traveller (199 Madison Ave., New York, NY 10016; phone: 212-685-9007). Travel guides and maps. A catalogue is available for $2.

Forsyth Travel Library (PO Box 2975, Shawnee Mission, KS 66201-1375; phone: 800-367-7984 or 913-384-3440). Travel guides and maps, old and new, to all parts of the world. Ask for the "Worldwide Travel Books and Maps" catalogue.

Gourmet Guides (2801 Leavenworth Ave., San Francisco, CA 94133; phone: 415-771-9948). Travel guides and maps, along with cookbooks. Mail-order lists available on request.

Phileas Fogg's Books and Maps (87 *Stanford Shopping Center*, Palo Alto, CA 94304; phone: 800-533-FOGG or 415-327-1754). Travel guides, maps, and language aids.

Powell's Travel Store (Pioneer Courthouse Sq., 701 SW 6th Ave., Portland, OR 97204; phone: 503-228-1108). A wealth of travel-related books (over 15,000 titles) and reference materials (globes, an extensive selection of maps, language aids, for example), as well as luggage and travel accessories (travel irons, electrical converters, and the like). There is even a travel agency on the premises.

Tattered Cover (2955 E. First Ave., Denver, CO 80206; phone: 800-833-9327 or 303-322-7727). The travel department alone of this enormous bookstore carries over 7,000 books, as well as maps and atlases. No catalogue is offered (the list is too extensive), but a newsletter, issued three times a year, is available on request.

Thomas Brothers Maps & Travel Books (603 W. Seventh St., Los Angeles, CA 90017; phone: 213-627-4018). Maps (including road atlases, street guides, and wall maps), guidebooks, and travel accessories.

Traveller's Bookstore (22 W. 52nd St., New York, NY 10019; phone: 212-664-0995). Travel guides, maps, literature, and accessories. A catalogue is available for $2.

MAGAZINES: As sampling the regional fare is likely to be one of the highlights of any visit, you will find reading about local edibles worthwhile before you go or after you return. *Gourmet,* a magazine specializing in food, frequently features mouth-watering articles on food and restaurants in the US, although its scope is much broader than domestic fare alone. It is available at newsstands nationwide for $2.50 an issue or for $18 a year from *Gourmet,* PO Box 53780, Boulder, CO 80322 (phone: 800-365-2454).

There are numerous additional magazines for every special interest available; check at your library information desk for a directory of such publications, or look over the selection offered at a well-stocked newsstand.

NEWSLETTERS: One of the very best sources of detailed travel information is *Consumer Reports Travel Letter.* Published monthly by Consumers Union (PO Box 53629, Boulder, CO 80322-3629; phone: 800-999-7959), it offers comprehensive coverage of the travel scene on a wide variety of fronts. A year's subscription costs $37; 2 years, $57.

In addition, the following travel newsletters provide useful up-to-date information on travel services and bargains:

Entree (PO Box 5148, Santa Barbara, CA 93150; phone: 805-969-5848). Monthly; a year's subscription costs $59. Subscribers also have access to a 24-hour hotline providing information on restaurants and accommodations around the world. This newsletter caters to a sophisticated, discriminating traveler with the means to explore the places mentioned.

The Hideaway Report (Harper Associates, Subscription Office: PO Box 300, Whitefish, MO 59937; phone: 406-862-3480; Editorial Office: PO Box 50, Sun Valley, ID 83353; phone: 208-622-3193). This monthly source highlights retreats — including domestic idylls — for sophisticated travelers. A year's subscription costs $90.

Romantic Hideaways (217 E. 86th St., Suite 258, New York, NY 10028; phone: 212-969-8682). This newsletter leans toward those special places made for those traveling in twos. A year's subscription to this monthly publication costs $65.

Travel Smart (Communications House, 40 Beechdale Rd., Dobbs Ferry, NY 10522; phone: 914-693-8300 in New York; 800-327-3633 elsewhere in the US). This monthly newsletter covers a wide variety of trips and travel discounts. A year's subscription costs $44.

COMPUTER SERVICES: Anyone who owns a personal computer and a modem can subscribe to a database service providing everything from airline schedules and fares to restaurant listings. Two such services to try:

CompuServe (5000 Arlington Center Blvd., Columbus, OH 43220; phone: 800-848-8199 or 614-457-8600). It costs $39.95 to join, plus hourly usage fees of $6 to $12.50.

Prodigy Services (445 Hamilton Ave., White Plains, NY 10601; phone: 800-822-6922 or 914-993-8000). A month's subscription costs $12.95, plus variable phone charges.

■**Note:** Before using any computer bulletin-board services, be sure to take precautions to prevent downloading of a computer "virus." First install one of the programs designed to screen out such nuisances.

Cameras and Equipment

Vacations (and even some business trips) are everybody's favorite time for taking pictures and home movies. After all, most of us want to remember the places we visit — and to show them off to others. Here are a few suggestions to help you get the best results from your travel photography or videography.

BEFORE THE TRIP

If you're taking your camera or camcorder out after a long period in mothballs, or have just bought a new one, check it thoroughly before you leave to prevent unexpected breakdowns or disappointing pictures.

1. Still cameras should be cleaned carefully and thoroughly, inside and out. If using a camcorder, run a head cleaner through it. You also may want to have your camcorder professionally serviced (opening the casing yourself will violate the manufacturer's warranty). Always use filters to protect your lens while traveling.
2. Check the batteries for your camera's light meter and flash, and take along extras just in case yours wear out during the trip. For camcorders, bring along extra Nickel-Cadmium (Ni-Cad) batteries; if you use rechargeable batteries, a recharger will cut down on the extras.
3. Using all the settings and features, shoot at least one test roll of film or one videocassette, using the type you plan to take along with you.

EQUIPMENT TO TAKE ALONG

Keep your gear light and compact. Items that are too heavy or bulky to be carried comfortably on a full-day excursion will likely remain in your hotel room.

1. Invest in a broad camera or camcorder strap if you now have a thin one. It will make carrying the camera much more comfortable.
2. A sturdy canvas, vinyl, or leather camera or camcorder bag, preferably with padded pockets (not an airline bag), will keep your equipment organized and easy to find. If you will be doing much shooting around the water, a waterproof case is best.
3. For cleaning, bring along a camel's hair brush that retracts into a rubber squeeze bulb. Also take plenty of lens tissue, soft cloths, and plastic bags to protect equipment from dust and moisture.

FILM AND TAPES: If you are concerned about airport security X-rays damaging rolls of undeveloped still film (X-rays do not affect processed film) or tapes, store them in one of the lead-lined bags sold in camera shops. This possibility is not as much of a threat as it used to be, however. In the US, incidents of X-ray damage to unprocessed film (exposed or unexposed) are few because low-dosage X-ray equipment is used virtually everywhere. If you're traveling without a protective bag, you may want to ask to have your photo equipment inspected by hand. One type of film that should never be subjected to X-rays is the very high speed ASA 1000 film; there are lead-lined bags made especially for it — and, in the event that you are refused a hand inspection, this is the only way to save your film. The walk-through metal detector devices at airports do not affect film, though the film cartridges may set them off.

You should have no problem finding film or tapes in Honolulu. When buying film, tapes, or photo accessories the best rule of thumb is to stick to name brands with which you are familiar. The availability of film processing labs and equipment repair shops will vary.

For tips on some of Honolulu's most photogenic spots, see *A Shutterbug's View* in DIVERSIONS.

USEFUL WORDS
AND PHRASES

Useful Words and Phrases

 A visitor to the Hawaiian Islands may hear as many as nine languages — Chinese, English, Filipino, Hawaiian, Japanese, Korean, Portuguese, Samoan, and a smattering of Spanish — spoken during even a brief stay. This diversity simply adds to the romance of the visit and does not cause problems, because English has been the spoken language of Hawaii since the 1850s and is the language taught in all island schools, even though certain conversations liberally laced with "pidgin" may belie this fact at times.

Unfortunately, a fluent speaker of Hawaiian is a rare bird, and usually an elderly one. Hawaiian is a language that is gradually disappearing, scarcely spoken at home, taught in only a few schools and at the University of Hawaii, and transmitted to the new generation as a mother tongue only on the tiny, isolated, private island of Niihau (whose population is less than 250).

Visitors will, however, hear many Hawaiian words and phrases animating ordinary English sentences. In addition, because of the present cultural renaissance, many songs are sung in the Hawaiian language only, most major choirs sing in Hawaiian, and several churches, particularly Kawaiahao Church in Honolulu, present sermons in Hawaiian. All but a few street names and the names of most public buildings are in Hawaiian. Therefore, a traveler with some small knowledge of what Hawaiian is all about and able to pronounce the names of new native friends will be more comfortable in this paradise of the Pacific and, homeward bound, will have something to show off.

The Hawaiian language, as written today, has the shortest alphabet in the world, with only twelve letters. Five of them are vowels — *a, e, i, o,* and *u* — and seven are consonants — *h, k, l, m, n, p,* and *w*. All vowels are pronounced, there is a vowel at the end of each syllable, and a vowel always appears between consonants. Some words contain a glottal stop (") rather than a written consonant. The glottal stop, which could be considered the eighth consonant, is pronounced the way the breathy pause in "oh-oh" is pronounced.

Most words are stressed on the next to last syllable and some words have an even stress. Consonants are pronounced as in English except for *w*. When it is the first letter of a word, as in Waikiki, it is pronounced like a *w;* when it follows the vowels *e* or *i,* it is pronounced like a *v,* as in Ewa or Iwalani.

Anyone familiar with Spanish will have no trouble with Hawaiian vowels in general (and beginners shouldn't worry about exceptions). They are pronounced as follows:

a like *a* in far
e like *e* in bed
i like *ee* in see
o like *o* in sole
u like *oo* in moon

Spoken, Hawaiian is melodious and dramatic, with a lilting, romantic sound. Its vocabulary, as passed down through the written language, has only about 20,000 words, and considering how recently it became a written language — the early-19th-century missionary era — it has generated an overwhelming number of books, manuscripts, and other writings. The language is ingenious and sophisticated, often figurative in meaning, and tales and poems are filled with symbolism and plays on words. Given this complexity, it is sometimes difficult to read correctly unless glottal stops are stressed or accented vowels are marked in the text as they would be heard in speech; words otherwise pronounced the same way can have several different meanings: *ka'u* is mine, *"kau* is yours; *pua'a* is pig or pork and *pu"a'a* is confused or frightened. (These refinements in transcription do not appear in this guidebook because the only Hawaiian words included are those few, easily recognized words in almost universal use in Hawaii, or the names of people or places. Glottal stops are not used on Hawaiian street signs, incidentally.)

Hawaiian differs from the Polynesian languages of other Pacific islands principally in the use of *k* for *t*, *l* for *r*, *n* for *nd* or *ng*, and *h* for *f* or *s*, and in its ambivalence about *w* for *v* (that is, using the written *w* and pronouncing it both ways).

Most Pacific sociologists and phylogenists believe that the languages of the Pacific islands derive from the root languages of Indonesia and Malaya. There are many similar words of everyday use and meaning. Coconut in Indonesian is *niur;* in Hawaiian, Samoan, and Tongan it is *niu.* Fire in Indonesian is *api,* in Hawaiian it is *ahi,* and in Samoan and Tongan it is *afi.* Sky in Indonesian is *langit,* in Samoan and Tongan it is *langi,* and in Hawaiian it is *lani.* If the missionaries who created the Hawaiian alphabet had not been so arbitrary in their choice of letters to represent the sounds they heard, these root words might be even closer in spelling and pronunciation.

The early Hawaiians carved their messages to posterity in the smooth lava rocks of their islands. Excellent petroglyph examples are on the Big Island of Hawaii at Puuloa near Kalapana Beach, at Kaupulehu near Kona Village, and at Puako near Kawaihae, South Kohala. Though each island has areas of petroglyphs, Hawaii seems to have more of them, probably because it is so much bigger.

Petroglyphs were once highly rated by romantic scholars and were considered transported derivatives of Egyptian hieroglyphics. In recent years they have been accepted for what they appear to be — stick pictures of people, animals, fish, canoes, battles, maps — depictions of a variety of aspects of ancient Hawaiian life. Some students say the pictures' deep and real meanings still have not been established, but most historians feel they are no more than what they seem, that they record a king's death, a good fish catch, the arrival of a great canoe from Tahiti, a family tree, or a war party.

This does not negate their importance as primitive art nor diminish the interest of the stories they tell. But it is obvious they are neither remnants of a forgotten written language nor the beginnings of one.

The Hawaiians did not have a written language until missionaries to the Sandwich Islands produced one so that the "pagans" could be taught to read the Bible. In January 1822, every *alii* (noble) in Honolulu was invited to watch the first book printed in Hawaiian, a little four-page primer, come off the small mission press. A number of the stalwart chiefs even gave printer Elisha Loomis a hand in turning the level of the old Ramage.

A full year and 9 months' work had gone into the little book, all of it spent in creating an alphabet for the Hawaiian language. Each minister, doctor, carpenter, and missionary wife had given the project every available moment. Before a sentence could be written, speech variations had to be tabulated; before speech variations could be tabulated, sounds had to be distinguished. A spelling system had to be conceived, and before any of the problems could be solved, an alphabet had to be devised.

In the beginning, this diligent company identified 90 different sounds and for a few brief weeks was tempted to create an alphabet to match. But they thought it was hardly likely that the illiterate Hawaiians would be able to master an alphabet if they themselves couldn't, so they cut it as much as possible and wound up with just twelve letters, with "nine biblical consonants reserved for biblical names and Sunday school books."

Beginning with Captain James Cook, who was the first person known to have transliterated the Hawaiian spoken word, explorers and traders had given the language a confusing variety of spellings. But the phonetic decisions made by the missionaries were final. Hanarooru, Whyteetee, Owahoo, and Owhyhee became Honolulu, Waikiki, Oahu, and Hawaii forever, and *pule* (prayer) and *palapala* (writing) became the basis of the new kingdom.

Kaahumanu, a widow of Kamehameha I and the regent for the absent Liholiho (King Kamehameha II), quickly issued a decree that everyone in the kingdom was obliged to learn reading and writing. She herself ably demonstrated that the Hawaiians had the intellect to do so.

During this period only adults went to school. There wasn't room for the youngsters, whose turn, most Hawaiians felt, would come later. Besides, the alphabet was so simple that even the dullest citizen could master it. As fast as the students graduated, they were sent to organize other schools. Some classes were held under banyan trees, some under palm frond lean-tos, and some simply on the open plains, where students held their slates as often above their heads to ward off rain and sun as on their laps.

Twenty thousand copies of the Old Testament came off the presses in Honolulu and Lahaina in 1831 and 50,000 copies of the New Testament in 1832. By 1844, more than half of the adult Hawaiian population had been taught to read.

In their extreme simplification of the alphabet, the missionaries created difficulties for Hawaiians of the 20th century, for a major part of their cultural renaissance is the attempt to reclaim the rich linguistic expressiveness of their ancestors. The Hawaiian language was one of great descriptive beauty, with many nuances, but during these early "learning" years, much was lost, dual meanings were abandoned, and some words were irreparably forgotten. Today's Hawaiian scholars are making every effort to record the speech of their *kupunas* (elders) before these last few contacts with the past are gone. This undertaking is described by Mary Kawena Pukui and Samuel H. Elbert in the introduction to the second edition of their definitive *Hawaiian Dictionary,* which begins with the saying *He loa ka"imina o ke ala o Hawai"i "imi loa* ("Long is the search for the way of Hawaii's thinkers").

There's a tenth language spoken to a degree by everyone in Hawaii — pidgin. Pidgin is the catalyst of many Hawaiian conversations, and although it is now basically a language of fun and the peer language in all island schools, it also crops up in many a business dialogue, where it is the common medium of exchange. Hawaiian pidgin developed as a mixture of English and the various immigrant patois, to which schoolchildren have added the refinements of their own colloquial dialect. It varies not only from one island to another but from one school to another.

The ubiquitous pidgin expression is *da kine,* which can be used anywhere to describe anything. More expressive than whatchamacallit, *da kine* can cover weather, cars, lost articles, gadgets, and so on, and it can also be a flattering or a derogatory description depending upon the tone of voice. It is used when other people know what you mean and when you can't remember the name of something. Other expressions used in everyday conversations include:

> *an' den:* and then what? so what else? I'm bored!
>
> *brah:* friend, buddy, as in "Howzit, brah?"
>
> *cockaroach:* steal or sneak away with
>
> *geev um:* go for it, beat them, give it all you've got; similar to "go for broke," which is about the same exhortation
>
> *li' dat:* like that, and so; used to explain something one doesn't want to bother explaining
>
> *mo' bettah:* better, best, a good idea

shaka: very good, right on, this is really OK; combined with a hand signal, with the thumb and little finger extended, is a "Howzit?" greeting

s'koshi: a small thing or person, just a little bit

talk story: gossip, shooting the breeze, bull session

The current dictionary of pidgin in Hawaii is *Pidgin to da Max,* by Peppo, found in most Hawaiian bookstores. It is lovingly done, interesting, amusing, and informative.

Pidgin is a very personal thing with the people of Hawaii, who use it every day. It's not an affectation and doesn't mix well with mainland English. Visitors can avoid embarrassing themselves and the Hawaiians by saving pidgin practice for friends and the tour escort and not including it in conversations with strangers. Using it does not make one an instant *kamaaina,* anyway. Mo' bettah to listen for it, sit back and enjoy it, but not try to get involved.

USEFUL, COMMON HAWAIIAN EXPRESSIONS

aikane (eye-*kah*-nay): friend

akamai (ah-kah-my): smart, clever

ala (ah-lah): road or pathway

alii (ah-*lee*-ee): chief, nobility

aloha (ah-*loh*-hah): welcome, love, greetings, sympathy, farewell

auwe (ow-way): too bad, oh damn

ewa (*eh*-vah): toward Ewa or westerly direction

haole (*how*-lee): Caucasian, foreigner

hapa (hah-pah): half

hapa haole (hah-pah *hah*-oh-lay): half- or part-Caucasian

holoku (*ho*-loh-koo): long fitted dress with a train

hoolaulea (ho-oh-lah-oo-lay-ah): celebration

hoomalimali (ho-oh-mah-lee-mah-lee): flattery, blarney

huhu (hoo-*hoo*): miffed, angry

kai (kah-ee): sea

kamaaina (kah-mah-*aye*-nah): native, local resident

kane (*kah*-ney): man, sign on men's room

keiki (kay-*ee*-kee): child

kokua (koh-*koo*-ah): help, assistance, aid

lanai (lah-*nye*): balcony or patio

lei (lay): necklace or garland of flowers

lua (loo-ah): bathroom, not to be confused with luau

luau (loo-*ow*): party, feast, cooked taro leaves

mahalo (mah-*hah*-low): thank you

makai (mah-*kah*-ee): direction toward the sea

malihini (mah-lih-*hee*-nee): newcomer, visitor

mauka (*mau*-kah): direction toward the mountains

mele (*meh*-lay): chant, song

muumuu (moo-oo-moo-oo): very loose, long dress for all occasions

ohana (oh-*hah*-nah): family, extended family

okole (oh-koh-leh): butt, rear, bottom

okolemaluna (oh-koh-leh-mah-*loo*-nah): as in a toast "bottoms up"; literally "bottom to the moon" (luna)

ono (*oh*-noh): tastes good
opu (oh-*poo*): stomach
pahu (pah-hoo): drum
pali (*pah*-lee): cliff, escarpment
paniolo (pah-nee-*oh*-loh): cowboy
pau (pow): the end, finished
pehea oe (peh-hay-ah *oh-ee*): how are you?
pilikia (pee-lee-*key*-ah): trouble
poi (poy-ee): cooked taro corm pounded into paste
puka (*poo*-kah): doorway, entrance, hole, parking space
pupule (poo-*poo*-ley): crazy, pixilated
wahine (wah-*hee*-ney): girl, woman, sign on ladies' room
wai (wah-ee): water
wikiwiki (*wee*-kee-*wee*-kee): be quick, hurry, quickly

Hauoli la hanau (hah-oo-*oh*-lee lah hah-*nah*-oo): Happy Birthday
Mele Kalikimaka (meh-lay kah-lee-*kee*-mah-kah): Merry Christmas
Hauoli makahiki hou (hah-oo-*oh*-lee mah-kah-*hee*-kee ho-oo): Happy
  New Year

THE CITY

HONOLULU

Honolulu stretches along a 25-mile strip of land between the Pacific Ocean and Oahu's 3,000-foot Koolau Mountains, on the major island of the state of Hawaii. In the past 30 years the city has outgrown this narrow strip and risen up the mountains along ridges and deeply cleft valleys; it reaches into the sea with a multitude of docks and marinas that run, off and on, from Pearl Harbor to the first grand sweep of magnificent Waikiki Beach — and magnificent it is, even poised against a backdrop of high-rise hotels several blocks deep. At night the homes up in the heights glitter above the city, and beyond them — 15 minutes from downtown — are the tropical mountain rain forests, as prolific and luxuriant as ever.

Private sailors and yachtsmen know Honolulu as one of America's trimmest, cleanest port cities. To land-bound Americans it is something more — the country's most foreign metropolis, an American city that stubbornly refuses to feel quite like America. Small wonder, when you consider that less than 100 years ago — until 1893, to be exact — it was the capital of a foreign country, a monarchy ruled by a queen: a Pacific Ocean island nation with its own distinct culture, arts, and world view rooted in the South Seas. In 1893, reigning Queen Liliuokalani was overthrown by Americans living in the islands, and 5 years later the islands were annexed as a US territory. They became American, but they were — are — still the islands, and that ain't canned pineapple. About 2,500 miles southwest of Los Angeles, Honolulu is about a third of the way between the continental US and Tokyo, a relationship that more than once has given rise to awe and some misgivings, particularly since investment has made the Japanese the major force in the islands' economy.

The sense of disorientation is not all one-sided. The "mainland" is what residents call the rest of the United States (and if you want to keep their respect you never will refer to it as "stateside" since Hawaii, too, is a state, and proud of it), and to many residents the other 49 states represent the strange and sometimes rather frightening culture of the *haoles.* Pronounced *how*-lees, this old Hawaiian word for outsiders has, in the 20th century, come to mean Caucasians — a segment of the population well outnumbered by Asians and Polynesians in Hawaii. To native Hawaiians, *haoles* in the past have represented Yankees who don't understand pidgin and who seem eager to bully their way into business and social success. The fact that they no longer automatically succeed in these objectives represents a change not uniformly felt, and sometimes overlooked, in the islands today.

Islanders in general, and Honolulu residents in particular, are unabashedly fond of dubbing their island home "paradise." But it is sometimes an uneasy Eden, with a history that has often been violent and tragic. Early-19th-century American missionaries experienced severe hardships here; but in the pitched battles between missionaries, western shippers, and merchants for the hearts and minds of the native population, it was the Hawaiians who lost almost everything. They were converted to Christianity and lost almost all of their ancient culture; they were taught to read, write, and count, and were decimated by foreign diseases to which they had no immunity. Only today is the long-dormant pride of traditional heritage emerging among descendants of the original Polynesian Hawaiians.

Other groups came to live in the islands, too, gradually making Honolulu a cosmopolitan city. When the economy required hard labor for the sugar plantations in the late 19th century, unskilled workers were recruited from all over, especially from Japan, China, and the Portuguese islands of Madeira and the Azores. When their contracts expired, many stayed on, marrying and contributing genes to the lovely racial mix that characterizes contemporary Honolulu society. At the turn of the century, large numbers of Filipino and Korean immigrants were added to the melting pot. In recent years, transplanted mainlanders and South Pacific islanders have arrived in large numbers. More than half the marriages in Hawaii today are interracial.

With the attack on Pearl Harbor — December 7, 1941 — Honolulu entered the consciousness of most mainland Americans. Martial law was declared throughout the islands, and for millions of American servicemen Hawaii became the jumping-off point for the Pacific theater. They called Oahu "the Rock," and they hated it.

They don't hate it anymore. Nearly 7 million visitors a year pour into the Honolulu airport and drop almost $11 billion into the Hawaiian coffers. Honolulu's green outback may be carpeted with sugar and pineapple plantations, but plantations no longer support the economy. Tourism is the vital juice of Hawaii, and much of it gets squeezed out in Honolulu. (And among the visitors are a good number of former GIs who once upon a time hated the Rock. The most popular attraction is the beautiful memorial that floats over the sunken USS *Arizona*. More than a million people a year visit it.)

Honolulu — the 25th-largest city in the country — is a modern metropolis struggling with modern problems. A few decades ago Waikiki was a sparsely settled peninsula along a swamp, 4 miles southeast of town. There was an unobstructed view of Diamond Head, and the tallest structure in town was the 10-story Aloha Tower, from which ship traffic in the harbor was controlled. No more, no more. Forests of high-rises now dwarf the Tower, which is slated to become the heart of a harbor revitalization plan, and Waikiki has its share of dope dealers, pickpockets, and prostitutes. But Chinatown, while slowly being gentrified, is still in the center of the city, with its noodle factories and small restaurants so reminiscent of a port town 100 years ago. And within Honolulu is a taste of everything Hawaiian and a flavor of seas far beyond.

HONOLULU AT-A-GLANCE

 SEEING THE CITY: For an eye-popping view of the shoreline, take the outdoor glass elevator to the top of the *Ilikai* hotel (1777 Ala Moana Blvd.; phone: 949-3811). There are equally spectacular views from the *Hanohano Room* atop the *Sheraton Waikiki* (2255 Kalakaua Ave.; phone: 922-4422)

and from *Nicholas Nickolas,* atop the *Ala Moana* hotel (410 Atkinson Dr.; phone: 955-4811). For another good perspective, visit the 10th-floor observatory in the Aloha Tower, with a panorama that stretches from the airport to Diamond Head (at the bottom of *Fort Street Mall;* phone: 537-9260). The popular Tantalus Lookout provides a sweeping perspective that takes in much of Honolulu, Waikiki, Diamond Head, and Manoa Valley, wherein lies the campus of the University of Hawaii. The lookout from Punchbowl Crater offers another panoramic perspective of the city, all the way from downtown Honolulu to Waikiki.

SPECIAL PLACES: Although it is now considerably overbuilt, Waikiki is nonetheless an interesting place to wander. We suggest getting to know your neighborhood first with a 3-mile walking tour.

Diamond Head – Guarding the southeasternmost boundary of Waikiki, this 760-foot volcanic crater is a world-famous landmark. You can climb around the slopes of Diamond Head along the tricky trail that begins at a gate off Makalei Place. It is also possible to drive into the crater through a tunnel to a state park inside, where there is a half-hour hike to the summit, which passes by World War II bunkers. Open 6 AM to 6 PM. For park information, call the State Parks Department at 548-7455.

Kapiolani Park – This 170-acre park, named for the wife of Kalakaua, the last King of Hawaii, has enough to keep you busy for more than a few hours. Just off Monsarrat Avenue, the *Kodak Hula Show* (phone: 833-1661) is performed at 10 AM Tuesdays through Thursdays. Get there early if you want a good seat. Drift along toward the scent of the Kapiolani Rose Garden on the corner of Paki and Monsarrat. Other attractions in the park include the *Waikiki Aquarium, Honolulu Zoo,* tennis courts, beaches, jogging trails, and the *Shell,* featuring entertainment under the stars. Kalakaua Avenue, named after the good king, begins here. Pronounced Ka-la-*cow*-wah, it is the principal thoroughfare of Waikiki.

Waikiki Beach – Just outside the park, alongside Kalakaua Avenue, begins the famous, 2½-mile-long curve of Waikiki Beach, one of the most famous beaches and surfing spots in the world. The 2- to 5-foot waves that are standard along the shoreline for much of the year are perfect for novices and amateurs. (On the few days in the summer when they reach 10 feet, Waikiki's waves should be avoided by all but experts.) Several hotels along Waikiki — for example, the *Outrigger* (2335 Kalakaua Ave.; phone: 923-0711; ask for Beach Services) — provide instruction and surfboards.

International Market Place – A great place to poke around outdoor stalls underneath a giant banyan tree festooned with lanterns. (A souk, Hawaiian-style is what we call it.) You can pick up all kinds of exotic junk and treasures you can't live without. At press time, plans to construct a major convention center at the site were still under consideration. 2330 Kalakaua Ave. (phone: 923-9871).

Royal Hawaiian Shopping Center – Right in the middle of Waikiki on the ocean side of Kalakaua Avenue, this 3-block-long mall is a conglomeration of glitz and geegaws, appealing primarily to tourists and definitely worth exploring. Here, European and American boutiques, including *Cartier, Van Cleef & Arpels, Hermès, Chanel,* and *Coach,* stand side by side with shops selling Chinese art imports, beach and sportswear, jewelry kiosks, candy and cookie counters, restaurants, and the ubiquitous souvenir shops. 2201 Kalakaua Ave. (phone: 922-0588).

Ft. DeRussy Army Museum – Weapons used by ancient Hawaiians, weapons captured from the Japanese, and weapons used by US soldiers in campaigns from the Spanish-American to the Korean War are on display here. In addition, there are uniforms worn at various times by US forces as well as those of the enemy. The most fascinating items are the Hawaiian weapons made long ago from shark's teeth and the newspaper accounts of the US involvement in World War II following the invasion of Pearl Harbor. Closed Mondays. No admission charge. Kalia Rd. (phone: 955-9552).

Tantalus Drive – The country road that winds its way up Mount Tantalus provides some of the most beautiful urban scenery found anywhere. The panoramas from lookouts en route through lush rain forest include Waikiki, Diamond Head, downtown Honolulu, and the distant Waianae Mountains. A state park provides one of several places to relax, picnic, or hike.

DOWNTOWN HONOLULU

Mission Houses Museum – This museum complex contains the earliest American buildings in Hawaii. The frame houses, shipped around Cape Horn in pieces and then reassembled in 1821 by the first missionaries, used to be a school and a minister's home, as well as a mission. They contain furniture and artifacts more reminiscent of New England than Hawaii, as well as a rare archive of the islands' history. In the Printing House, constructed from coral, is a replica of the original printing press used to produce religious tracts and primers for schoolchildren, mostly in Hawaiian. On Saturdays, the Living History program populates the mission grounds with volunteers dressed in 19th-century garb. Open Tuesdays through Saturdays from 9 AM to 4 PM; tours offered from 9:30 AM to 3 PM. Open Sundays from noon to 4 PM. Closed Mondays. Admission charge. 553 S. King St. (phone: 531-0481).

Kawaiahao Church – Across from the *Mission Houses,* Kawaiahao Church also is known as the Westminster Abbey of Hawaii, and indeed, those remnants of the old Hawaiian royal and princely families who have retained their Congregational faith occasionally do use the church for baptisms, marriages, and funerals. It's the oldest church in Honolulu, built in 1842 on the site of Hawaii's first mission, which was a thatch-roofed hut standing close to an ancient and sacred *hao* (spring). Tall *kahilis* (feather-decorated staffs symbolic of royalty) placed on either side of the altar testify to its distinguished past. It was here that King Kamehameha III used the expression *Ua mau ke ea o ka aina i ka pono* ("The life of the land is perpetuated in righteousness"), which now is the state motto. Services are conducted in English and Hawaiian at 8 and 10:30 AM on Sundays. Open daily. King and Punchbowl Sts. (phone: 522-1333).

Chinatown – Chinatown is on the westernmost fringe of downtown and spills across the Nuuanu Stream into Aala Triangle Park. There are open-air meat, fish, and vegetable markets; herb shops selling age-old medications; and elderly people who still dress in traditional costume. This also is the "sin" quarter of Honolulu, where sleazy sex shows compete for customers with family-style chop suey houses. Recent gentrification is under way, however, bringing new shops and galleries into renovated turn-of-the-century buildings. A walking tour of Chinatown with an optional lunch (a real bargain) takes place on Tuesdays at 9:30 AM, starting from the Chinese Chamber of Commerce, 42 N. King St. (phone: 533-3181). If you prefer to go at your own pace, seee *Walk 2: Chinatown* in DIRECTIONS.

Maunakea Marketplace – At the core of the neighborhood, the marketplace serves as a commercial centerpiece for Chinatown's on-going renewal. The use of Chinese architectural detail is particularly beautiful. The central courtyard is filled with vendors, shops, restaurants, and food stalls which offer a variety of Asian tastes. Maunakea and Pauahi Sts.

Hawaii Maritime Museum – Pier 7 is the home of the four-masted *Falls of Clyde* and the outrigger voyaging canoe *Hokulea,* returned from its three transpacific voyages along Polynesian migration routes. There also are displays related to Hawaii's maritime history, plus a library and photo archive. Open daily. Admission charge. Pier 7, near Aloha Tower (phone: 536-6373).

Iolani Palace – With elaborate surroundings, Iolani Palace sits in state, receiving tribute from admirers. Highly revered by historians and sentimentalists alike, the palace was the royal residence of monarch and songwriter Queen Liliuokalani. In fact, she was imprisoned here following the 1893 revolution and wrote some of her famous songs, including "Aloha Oe," while in detention. Iolani was built by her brother, King David Kalakaua, between 1878 and 1882. In 1883, he placed a crown on his own head in what is now *Coronation Bandstand,* where, every Friday at noon, the *Royal Hawaiian Band* gives free, informal concerts. Palace tours are given Wednesdays through Saturdays. Admission charge. King and Richards Sts. (phone: 522-0832).

State Capitol – Built in 1969, the capitol takes its inspiration from the natural history of the islands. All of its features — columns, reflecting pools, courtyard — reflect aspects of Hawaii's environment. Outside the capitol stands a beautiful bronze statue of Queen Liliuokalani and the controversial modern statue of Father Damien, the hero of the leprosy settlement at Kalaupapa on the island of Molokai. Open daily. Admission charge. 415 S. Beretania St. (phone: 548-2211).

OTHER SPECIAL PLACES

Ala Moana Center – Among the largest shopping centers in the world, it was built in 1959 and has undergone several renovations and many expansions. (The latest addition is a 3-story wing that added 40 shops to the 200-store roster, including the first *Neiman Marcus* west of Los Angeles.) The Pacific's major retail center, it is said to attract 56 million customers a year. The open-air mall often features performances of island music and dance on its outdoor stage, and includes several large department stores — *Liberty House, Shirokiya,* and *Sears* — as well as a many European designer boutiques, mainland specialty stores and such local favorites as the *Coral Grotto* and *Honolulu Book Shop.* Don't miss the *Makai Market Food Court,* 20 stalls dispensing Chinese, Japanese, Korean, Italian, Mexican, Hawaiian, and American fare. Open daily. Ala Moana Blvd. opposite Ala Moana Park (phone: 946-2811).

Arizona **Memorial** – More than a million people a year come to honor the American sailors who perished on the USS *Arizona,* sunk when the Japanese bombed Pearl Harbor on December 7, 1941. Something of a surprise is the number of Japanese among the visitors. The only boat tour of the memorial departs from the visitors' center daily. The National Park Service operates a large museum, with exhibitions and films. *Paradise Cruises* (phone: 536-3641) departs from Kewalo Basin (hotel transfers are included) for the half-day tour that passes the memorial but does not allow for a visit. *Pearl Harbor Day* is commemorated every December 7, with a service at the memorial. The USS *Bowfin Pacific Submarine Museum* (11 Arizona Memorial Place; phone: 423-1341) is adjacent to the visitors' center. Open daily. Admission charge.

Bishop Museum – Near the beginning of Likelike (pronounced *Leekay-leekay*) Highway, in the working class neighborhood called Kalihi, this prestigious museum houses the greatest collection of Hawaiiana in the world. Founded in 1899, it is the center for most of the anthropological research done throughout Polynesia and the Pacific. In addition to excellent displays, the museum features daily performances of Hawaiian music and dance. Shows are also featured at the adjacent planetarium. Open daily. Admission charge. 1525 Bernice St. (phone: 847-3511, or 848-4129 for recorded information).

Foster Botanical Garden – Often overlooked by tourists, this cool, tranquil retreat in the middle of the city is a living museum of growing things. The No. 4 bus from Waikiki will bring you close to the garden at Nuuanu and Vineyard. Open daily. Admission charge. 50 N. Vineyard Blvd. (phone: 522-7065).

Honolulu Academy of Arts – Across Thomas Square from *Blaisdell Center,* the *Academy of Arts* has Oriental art and some European and American works. Interesting items include a Japanese ink and color handscroll dating to 1250, John Singleton Copley's *Portrait of Nathaniel Allen,* and Segna di Bonaventura's *Madonna and Child.* Lunch is served in the museum garden café Tuesdays through Saturdays from 11:30 AM to 1 PM. Thursday evenings dinner is served at 6 PM. Reservations necessary. Closed Mondays. No admission charge. 900 S. Beretania St. (phone: 538-3693).

Pacific Aerospace Museum – Recently opened in the terminal of the Honolulu International Airport, this $1.75-million, high-tech museum — dedicated to aviation and aerospace achievement in the Pacific — traces the history of Pacific exploration: from the celestial navigation of the ancient Polynesians to the scientific study of space, now under way at nine international observatories atop 14,000-foot Mauna Kea on the Big Island of Hawaii. There are flight simulators, a NASA space shuttle flight deck, actual recorded voices of famous aviators, and a mission control exhibit that re-creates space launches. At the *Great Skyquest Theater,* a 3-room, 3-dimensional multimedia production, original artifacts, models, art, and music are used to re-create the glory days of such aviators as Amelia Earhart, Charles Kingford-Smith, and US Navy Commander John Rodgers. Open 8 AM to 5 PM daily. Admission charge. Central Waiting Lobby, Honolulu International Airport (phone: 839-0777).

Queen Emma's Summer Palace – This royal retreat in the cool highlands of Nuuanu Valley was the summer home of Kamehameha IV and Queen Emma, presented to them as a gift by the queen's aunt and uncle. Built sometime between 1847 and 1850, it is a simple building with Doric columns and a roof that overhangs a broad lanai (verandah). The building, which was abandoned when Queen Emma died in 1885, was rescued from wreckers by the Daughters of Hawaii, a civic group that has operated it as a museum since 1915. Both furnishings and artifacts are on display, including a Gothic-design cabinet, a gift of Queen Victoria's consort, Prince Albert; a stereopticon presented to Queen Emma by Napoleon III; and the christening robe made for the royal couple's only child, Prince Albert, the last child born to a ruling Hawaiian monarch, who died tragically at the age of 4. Open daily. Admission charge. 2913 Pali Hwy. (phone: 595-3167).

National Memorial Cemetery of the Pacific – Also known as Punchbowl Crater, this cemetery is the Arlington of the Pacific. In prehistoric times it was the site of human sacrifices. Now, more than 26,000 servicemen lie buried among its 112 peaceful acres overlooking downtown Honolulu. Commercial bus and van tours visit Punchbowl, but if you're on your own, you'll need a car or taxi. A lookout from the crater's rim offers panoramic city views. Take Puowaina Drive to its end.

Polynesian Cultural Center – The closest thing Hawaii has to *Disneyland,* this 42-acre "living" theme park, run by the Hawaii branch of Brigham Young University, features replicas of villages and displays from the cultures of old Hawaii, the Marquesas, Samoa, Tonga, Fiji, Tahiti, and New Zealand. It's not the same as visiting all those places, but for most people, already at the end of their geographic leash on Oahu, this South Pacific sampler suffices. Although it is 45 miles west of Waikiki, the park attracts more than 800,000 people each year who pay as much as $75 to walk, ride on trams, or float on canoes on artificial streams through historic villages, have dinner and watch a show in which natives (actually Brigham Young students from various Pacific islands) appear in traditional costume to sing and dance. A shuttle bus rounds up parkgoers outside Waikiki hotels each morning and whisks them over to Laie, on the north side of Oahu, and back (phone: 293-3333).

Contemporary Museum – Situated on the Tantalus hillside, with a beautiful view of the city, it features contemporary sculpture, paintings, graphics, and more, most of it in well-displayed, changing exhibitions. There's a major permanent display of the works of David Hockney. In addition, a satellite gallery is in the news building of the Honolulu Newspaper Agency on Kapiolani Boulevard. Open Tuesdays through Saturdays from 10 AM to 4 PM; Sundays from noon to 4 PM; closed Mondays. Donations requested. 2411 Makiki Heights Dr. (phone: 526-0232).

Dole Cannery Square – A 60-year-old, still-operational pineapple cannery, with adjacent areas transformed into a visitors' center complete with shops and a hands-on children's museum. The best part of a visit is the escorted tour of the cannery itself, where the sweet smell of the spiky fruit hangs heavy in the air. Shuttle service links the cannery to Waikiki. Open daily. Admission charge. 650 Iwilei Rd. (just west of downtown Honolulu, off Nimitz Hwy.; phone: 531-8855).

■**EXTRA SPECIAL:** Honolulu is the great jumping-off point for island-hopping expeditions. *Hawaiian Air* (phone: 537-5100) flies to the islands of Kauai, Maui, Hawaii, Molokai, and Lanai daily; *Aloha Airlines* (phone: 836-1111) serves all but Lanai; *Aloha Island Air* (phone: 833-3219) is the largest of several commuter airlines that fly among the islands. Both *Hawaiian Air* and *Aloha Airlines* offer unlimited inter-island passes (for more information, see *Traveling by Plane* in GETTING READY TO GO). Commuter flights link both major airports as well as more isolated communities like Hana, Maui, or Waimea on the Big Island. On runs to Molokai, commuter fares are lower than those charged for the jet service of the majors. Kauai, the oldest of the islands, is known for golf at the *Princeville* and *Kauai Lagoons* resort courses, sunny Poipu Beach, and the spectacular beauty of Waimea Canyon and the Na Pali Coast. Maui offers valleys, waterfalls, beaches, and the crater of the dormant Haleakala Volcano. The small Kapalua/West Maui Airport serves direct flights to Lahaina, Kaanapali, Kahana, Napili, and Kapalua resorts. The island of Hawaii, also called the Big Island, is the home of Mauna Loa and Kilauea, two of the most active volcanoes in the world, as well as Hawaii's premier archaeological sites including Puuhonua O'Honaunau and Paukuhoa *heiau.* On Lanai, only 17 miles long, the main draws are plenty of pineapples, two new resort hotels, the *Lodge at Koele* and *Manele Bay,* and a sense of away-from-it-all isolation. Molokai, 37 miles long, a relatively untouched ranchers' island, offers tourists the opportunity to see a rural side of Hawaii, or visit the isolated leper's settlement at Kalaupapa, now administered as a National Historic Park. There also is a resort at Kaluakoi and several small condos and hotels along the east coast for those who wish to stay awhile.

SOURCES AND RESOURCES

TOURIST INFORMATION: The Hawaii Visitors Bureau (2270 Kalakaua Ave., Room 801, Honolulu, HI 96815; phone: 923-1811) has a large number of illustrated guides, brochures, maps, and leaflets for all the islands, including materials distributed by hotels and tour guide operators.

Visitor publications such as *Oahu Destinations, Here in Hawaii, Guide to Oahu, This Week, Spotlight Hawaii, Island News,* and the *Waikiki Beach Press* are available in hotel lobbies and at sidewalk stands. At car rental counters you can pick up the *Oahu Drive Guide,* designed for the motorist but with useful information for the tourist on foot as well. All the above are free and can point you in the direction of the more obvious tourist attractions and places to eat. In addition, they sometimes contain discount coupons. Also see our own *Birnbaum's Hawaii 1993* (edited by Alexandra Mayes Birnbaum; HarperCollins, $17).

Local Coverage – The *Honolulu Advertiser,* a morning daily, and the *Honolulu Star-Bulletin,* an afternoon paper, are major newspapers that cover world, national, and local events. They combine to produce a Sunday newspaper, which has a week-long review of events and a dining section containing restaurants, including some lesser-known "ethnic" places, and entertainment (editorial coverage is largely influenced by advertisers). Check the *Advertiser*'s Honolulu Calendar or the *Star-Bulletin*'s Pulse of Paradise for listings of the city's often overlooked selection of movies, concerts, and shows. (Top name performers frequently include a Honolulu stopover on Asia or Australia tours.) The *Los Angeles Times* and *USA Today* are usually available in Honolulu by 9 AM on the day of publication; *The New York Times* generally arrives a day after publication. They are sold in the sundries stores of most large hotels. *Honolulu,* a monthly magazine, covers island topics, people, and places, and also features a useful calendar of events. *Aloha* (bimonthly) also publishes a calendar of statewide events; *Aloha* features a restaurant directory and listing of gallery exhibits.

Television Stations – KHON Channel 2–NBC; KITV Channel 4–ABC; KGMB Channel 9–CBS; KHET Channel 11–PBS.

Radio Stations – AM: KSSK 590 (oldies and contemporary); KHVH 990 (news). FM: KHPR 88.1 (classical); KUMU 94.7 (easy listening); KQMQ 96.3 (soft rock); KPOI 98 (rock); KHHH 98.5 (jazz and popular music).

TELEPHONE: The area code for Honolulu and all of Hawaii is 808.

SALES TAX: There is a 4% sales tax and a 5% hotel tax in Honolulu.

GETTING AROUND: Bus – *TheBus:* TheMarvell! A proofreader's and typographer's nightmare, *TheBus* is a dream come true for everyone else. It not only circulates through all the suburban veins of Honolulu but runs along most of the coastline and through central Oahu, too. Whether you go one stop or 80 miles around the island, it costs the same, 60¢ (at press time), which you must pay with exact change. *TheBus* is painted in shades of yellow, black, and gray. The main terminus on Oahu is at the *Ala Moana Shopping Center* on the Kona Street side of the ground-floor parking lot. The No. 8 bus is a shuttle between Kapiolani Park, near Diamond Head, and the *Ala Moana Center,* and passes through the main Waikiki hotel district en route. If you are coming from Waikiki, it will drop you on the *makai* (ocean) side of the shopping center. To reach the terminus, walk through the parking lot. Passengers proceeding by another bus can ask for a transfer upon boarding the first bus; this can be used only for a continuing journey in the same direction. If you are making several stops along a particular route, ask for a transfer each time you pay a fare.

A favorite trip on *TheBus* is the journey around the island: For 60¢ it's an extraordinary way to see a great deal of Oahu, besides being one of the best ways to meet local people. If you stay on the bus, the trip takes 4 hours. There are two ways to go: north across central Oahu, eastward along the North Shore, and south down the Windward Coast on bus No. 52, marked Wahiawa/Kaneohe or Wahiawa/Circle Island; or north along the Windward Coast, west along the North Shore, and south through central Oahu on bus No. 52, marked Kaneohe/Wahiawa or Kaneohe/Circle Island. Either way, the ride is splendid. Waimea Falls and the Polynesian Cultural Center are served by these routes; take the former for the falls and the latter for the center. To get to Pearl Harbor direct from Waikiki, take bus No. 20, marked Airport. You can also ride the No. 8 bus to Ala Moana and change to bus No. 50, 51, or 52, marked Wahiawa/Kaneohe or Wahiawa/Circle Island. Some buses that pass through Waikiki but do not require a trip to *Ala Moana* are the No. 58 Hawaii Kai bus, which can be boarded on Kuhio Avenue and makes stops at the entrance to Diamond Head Crater and *Sea Life Park,* and the No. 2 School Street bus, which passes the *Bishop Museum. TheBus* No. 19 Airport runs between Waikiki and Honolulu International Airport; however, there is no room for luggage on board, and what cannot be carried on your lap cannot be brought on. Telephone information lines provide route information at *Ala Moana Center*. Two publications that can be purchased for a couple of dollars are *TheBus Guide*, with details on 71 destinations and a great deal of other useful information, and *Honolulu and Oahu by TheBus*, which contains maps of Oahu, Greater Honolulu, and Waikiki showing every bus route as well as 35 small maps indicating the bus stops at some of the most frequently visited points of interest. For further information, contact the Honolulu Department of Transport, Mass Transit Lines (MTL), 811 Middle St., Honolulu, HI 96819 (phone: 848-4444).

A private enterprise, *Airport Motorcoach* (phone: 926-4747), provides hotel/airport transfers for $5 (it's possible to reserve seats in advance) and makes runs to the Arizona Memorial for $4 per person, round-trip.

Car Rental – For information on renting a car, see "On Arrival" in GETTING READY TO GO.

Ferry – A new passenger ferry connecting downtown Honolulu and west Oahu during rush hours — and offering service between Oahu, Maui, and Kauai at other times — began operating at press time. The Barbers Point–downtown Honolulu run will take 27 minutes, the trips between Oahu and Maui about 1½ hours, and those between Oahu and Kauai will take 2 hours. *San Diego Shipbuilding and Repair* (phone: 619-691-1091).

Helicopter Tours – *Papillon Hawaii Pacific* (phone: 836-1566) offers a series of aerial tours. *Cherry Helicopter* (phone: 833-4339) departs from the *Turtle Bay* resort on the North Shore.

Moped and Motorcycle – They're a breezy way to see the island or just to cruise around Waikiki and the southeast. Be careful: Pickup truck drivers on the Waianae Coast tend to look askance at riders of these motorized "toys," and driving them on newly wet surfaces can be tricky if you're not completely accustomed to them. *Aloha Funway Rentals* (1778 Ala Moana Blvd.; phone: 942-9696) is the best-known motorcycle/moped rental outfit in Honolulu. In Haleiwa, you can rent from *Fantasy Cycles* (66-134 Kam Hwy.; phone: 637-3221).

Taxi – Technically, taxis are not allowed to cruise or pick up passengers on the street. However, most cabs will stop if they are not on radio call, and if the cabs are not creating a nuisance, the police usually turn a blind eye. Generally, to be sure of finding a cab, it is wise to call one yourself or through a hotel bell captain. *SIDA (State Independent Drivers Association)* taxis are owner-driven and have a good reputation for reliability (phone: 836-0011). Other major companies are *Aloha State Taxi* (phone: 847-3566), which serves the whole island and is especially popular with military personnel; and *Charley's* (phone: 955-2211 or 531-1333), which will take you to any point on the island from the airport or drive you around the island in a Cadillac Fleetwood for about $55 an hour, with a 2-hour minimum. If you want to show up at your hotel in a Rolls-Royce, call *Cloud Nine* (phone: 524-7999). *Handicabs* (phone: 524-3866) specializes in transport for handicapped people and operates vehicles that will accommodate passengers in their wheelchairs. Best to call a day in advance.

Trolley – *Waikiki Trolley* (phone: 599-2561) has launched a fleet of motorized, open-air reproductions of the horse-drawn trolleys that operated at the turn of the century. Today, they provide tour and point-to-point service between Waikiki and such shopping and cultural attractions as Kewalo Basin, *Ala Moana Center*, Chinatown, and the Aloha Tower. The trolleys run from 8:30 AM to 4 PM, and tours run between 9 AM and 4 PM; all-day passes cost $10.

 LOCAL SERVICES: Baby-sitting – *Aloha Baby-sitting* (phone: 732-2029) or check with the hotel concierge or activity desk.

Business Services – *Una May Young*, Suite 3206, Manor Wing, *Sheraton Waikiki Hotel*, 2255 Kalakaua Ave. (phone: 922-4422).

Dry Cleaner/Tailor – *Al Phillips the Cleaner,* 2310 Kuhio Ave. (phone: 923-1971).

Limousine – *Executive Limousine* (phone: 941-1999); *Silver Cloud Limousine* (phone: 524-7999).

Mechanic – *Toguchi Chevron Service Station,* 825 N. Vineyard Blvd. (phone: 845-6422).

Medical Emergency – *Queen's Hospital* open to 10 PM, at Discovery Bay (phone: 943-1111).

Messenger Services – *Courier Express* (phone: 955-0079); *ADDS Messenger Service* (phone: 946-1565 or 947-4228).

National/International Courier – *Federal Express* (phone: 359-3339); *DHL Worldwide Courier Express* (phone: 836-0441).

Pharmacy – *Pillbox,* open until 11 PM (1133 11th Ave.; phone: 737-1777); *Outrigger Pharmacy* (2335 Kalakaua Ave.; phone: 923-2529); any *Long's* drugstore (phone: 941-4433).

Photocopies – *Island Instant Printers* (2270 Kalakaua Ave.; phone: 922-1225); *Second Image* (2600 S. King St.; phone: 955-7498); *Ditto's,* open 24 hours (833 Kapiolani Blvd.; phone: 531-0544).

Post Office – Several locations downtown (at 335 Merchant St. at Richards St.; phone: 541-1962); in Waikiki (330 Saratoga Rd.; phone: 941-1062); and at substations in the *Royal Hawaiian Shopping Center* (phone: 926-3710), the *Hilton Hawaiian Village* (phone: 949-4321), and at the airport (phone: 423-3930).

Professional Photographer – *David Cornwell* (phone: 949-7000); *Creative Focus* (phone: 942-0202).

Secretary/Stenographer – *Kelly Services* (phone: 536-9343).

Teleconference Facilities – *Kahala Hilton* (phone: 734-2211).

Translator – *Academia Language School* (phone: 946-5599); *A-1 Kanner Language Systems* (phone: 415-365-3046).

Western Union/Telex – Many offices located around the city (phone: 942-2274).

Word Processing/Typewriter Rental – *Pacific Business Machines,* 1- and 2-week minimums, depending on equipment (phone: 946-5059); *Alexander Brothers,* hourly in-office use or 2-week minimum rentals (phone: 837-7828); *Computer House,* rentals and repairs (phone: 472-7253).

Other – *Lyn's Video Rental* (phone: 941-1253); *Ditto's,* fax services (phone: 531-0544).

 SPECIAL EVENTS: Special events are held year-round. Here are a few highlights:

January – The annual *Hula Bowl College All-Star Football Classic* is played in *Aloha Stadium,* and the *Chinese New Year* is celebrated in Chinatown (sometimes in February).

February – Early in the month, the nationally televised 4-day *Hawaiian Open International Golf Tournament* is played at the *Waialae Country Club* in the Kahala District (sometimes late in January).

March – The Irish and the would-be Irish celebrate with a lot of green and the traditional (and not so traditional) varieties of good cheer along Waikiki's Kalakaua Avenue on *St. Patrick's Day* (March 17). *Prince Kuhio Day* (March 26) acknowledges the birthday of the Kauai-born prince who was Hawaii's first delegate to the US Congress.

May – On *Lei Day* (May 1), a queen is crowned at the *Waikiki Band Shell* in Kapiolani Park, where there is also a lei making contest and at sunset, a hula show.

June – The week-long *Festival of the Pacific,* highlighting the songs, dances, arts and crafts, and competitive sports of more than 40 Pacific Rim nations, is held in early June.

The most spectacular annual parade in the islands is held on *King Kamehameha Day* (June ll), when the king's statue (opposite the Judiciary Building in downtown Honolulu) is draped with 40-foot leis.

July – In even-numbered years, the *Trans-Pacific Yacht Race* finishes off Diamond Head. *The Prince Lot Hula Festival* is held in a lovely outdoor setting at Moanalua Gardens.

September – The *Waikiki Rough Water Swim* is held over a 2-mile course, ending at Duke Kahanamoku Beach in front of the *Hilton Hawaiian Village* hotel. *Aloha Week* is Honolulu's biggest celebration. It features canoe races, luaus, balls, athletic events, parades and more. September also marks the beginning of symphony season.

October – The *Honolulu Orchid Society Show* is held at the *Neal S. Blaisdell Center,* with lei making and flower arranging demonstrations as well as floral displays.

December – December 7 is *Pearl Harbor Day,* commemorated by a service at the USS *Arizona* Memorial. Contestants in the *Honolulu Marathon* run from the Aloha Tower to the bandshell in Kapiolani Park. The *Triple Crown* of surfing competitions is held along Oahu's North Shore. Late in November or early December, the *Pacific International Film Festival* presents a week of free movies. Streets are ablaze with *Christmas* lights between mid-December and *New Year's Eve* in the heart of downtown Honolulu.

 MUSEUMS: The *Bishop Museum, Contemporary Museum, Ft. DeRussy Army Museum, Hawaii Maritime Museum, Honolulu Academy of Arts, Mission Houses Museum, Pacific Aerospace Museum, Polynesian Cultural Center,* and *Queen Emma's Summer Palace* are described in *Special Places.*

Damien Museum and Archives – This museum is dedicated to Father Damien Joseph de Veuster, the Belgian priest who worked with the lepers at Kalaupapa on Molokai for 16 years, contracting leprosy himself before he died. On display are his mementos and personal papers. Open weekdays 9 AM to 3 PM, Saturdays until noon. No admission charge. 130 Ohua Ave. (phone: 923-2690).

Hawaii Children's Museum – First of its kind in Hawaii, this $1.5-million "hands-on, minds-on" exploratorium is geared to children between the ages of 3 and 13, but appeals to their parents as well. See what insects look like magnified on the optech bioscanner, send a fax to grandma, build a dome out of bubbles, meet Einstein the dog inside a giant toy box, or make a video visit to a faraway city. Open daily except Mondays. Admission charge. 650 Iwilei Rd. (phone: 522-0040).

Hawaii Plantation Village – Located in central Oahu in the former sugar plantation town of Waipahu, this unusual cultural museum provides a look back at plantation life on the island. Primarily an architectural park, it features 28 houses of various styles imported to Hawaii during sugar's heyday, (the years between 1897 and 1910); the houses are replicas of those occupied by immigrant laborers who came from Japan, China, the Philippines, and Portugal to harvest sugarcane. 94-695 Waipahu St., Waipahu (phone: 676-6727).

 MAJOR COLLEGES AND UNIVERSITIES: Honolulu is the center of higher learning in Hawaii and the Pacific. The island boasts five colleges and universities, including the University of Hawaii, with a total enrollment of about 43,000 students. The university (in Manoa Valley; phone: 956-8855) offers degrees in more than 80 disciplines, including astronomy, oceanography, travel industry management, tropical agriculture, and Asian studies. Other private universities and colleges include Brigham Young University (at Laie; phone: 293-3211); Chaminade University of Honolulu (phone: 735-4711); Hawaii Pacific College (downtown; phone: 544-0239); and Hawaii Loa College (phone: 235-3647).

SHOPPING: If you can drag yourself away from the beach long enough, you'll discover that Honolulu is a tropical shopping heaven — not so much for bargains, although there are some, but for the incredible diversity of wares that stream into this Pacific capital from Asia, Europe, and the US mainland, as well as from the other South Pacific and Hawaiian islands. With some exceptions, the Honolulu shopping scene is centered around its malls; many have an architectural or commercial theme, usually Oriental or Hawaiian, and are occasionally outdoors. The emphasis is on high-priced, designer goods; aloha-and other resortwear; vacation sundries such as lotions, beach towels, and mats; Polynesian handicrafts; and other gift items. Mixed in are some boutiques that carry such famous international names as Chanel and Gucci, and high-fashion sportswear. Most shopping malls are open daily from 10 AM to 9 PM; Sundays until 5 PM. Waikiki shopping malls have longer hours, 9 AM to 11 PM daily. The following is a selection of shops and shopping areas.

SHOPPING CENTERS

Ala Moana Shopping Center – Among the largest shopping centers in the world, this 3-story mall has more than 200 stores, plus a food court with over 20 fast-food specialty restaurants. The center is also the main *TheBus* terminus on Oahu. The No. 8 bus leaves for and comes from Waikiki every 10 minutes, and the No. 20 bus stops here on the Airport-Waikiki run. (For more information, see *Special Places.*) Ala Moana Blvd. opposite Ala Moana Park (phone: 946-2811).

Aloha Flea Market – This market sets up in the parking lot at *Aloha Stadium* in Aiea every Wednesday, Saturday, and Sunday, and on many holidays. Sundays are the busiest days, with about 1,000 vendors. Go early in the day; it's cooler and easier to park. Look for fresh fruits and vegetables, including exotic produce unknown to most mainlanders, as well as seashells, baskets, flowers, and plants. Shoppers also find T-shirts, eel-skin and leather goods, souvenirs, and Asian imports — some of the same things that are sold in Waikiki, but offered here at substantially lower prices. Don't be afraid to bargain. Trucks dispense *manapua* (a local version of *char siu bow,* a steamed Chinese bun with barbecued pork inside) and cool drinks. Open 6 AM to 3 PM. *Aloha Stadium* (phone: 486-1529).

Hyatt Regency Center – The first 3 floors of the *Hyatt* complex are dominated by more than 70 shops that surround a 3-tier waterfall and pool. A fashion show is held each Wednesday at 4 PM outside *Harry's Bar* beside the pool. 2424 Kalakaua Ave. (phone: 923-1234).

International Market Place – Famous for its huge banyan tree, it's a bustling, noisy bazaar of shops and booths, including South Seas and Hawaiian products, such as bamboo and rattanwork, baskets woven of *lau hala* or pandanus leaves, and tikis, platters, and bowls carved from monkeypod and other woods. Almost every store has its racks of alohawear and shelves of straw hats, and you'll find that quality, styles, and prices vary little from place to place. Numerous kiosks are draped with earrings, necklaces, and bracelets made of shell and semi-precious stones, including amethyst, coral, jade, opal, puka, and so on. You can bargain with these dealers, and very often a feigned disinterest can drop the asking price by half. At press time, plans to construct a major convention center at the site were still under consideration. 2330 Kalakaua Ave. (phone: 923-9871).

Kahala Mall – This 86-shop mall, a smaller upscale alternative to *Ala Moana,* is located in an exclusive neighborhood east of downtown Honolulu. A popular cinema eight-plex here will keep movie fans happy (phone: 735-9744). 4211 Waialae Ave. (phone: 732-7736).

Kilohana Square – Located on Waikiki's eastern border, this small complex is in the 1000-block of Kapahulu Street and includes Western and Asian antiques shops, art galleries, and specialty stores. 2863 Kihei Pl.

King's Village – This pastel complex of quaint townhouse-style buildings and cobblestone walkways at the back of the *Hyatt Regency* hotel is designed to resemble urban Honolulu in the days of the 19th-century monarchs. The result is slightly reminiscent of *Disneyland,* although the *Rose and Crown Pub* (phone: 923-5833), with its horse brasses, etched-glass mirrors, and timber beams, manages to be a fair replica of an English country pub. The *Changing of the Guard* occurs nightly at 6:15 PM. 131 Kaiulani Ave.

Rainbow Bazaar – A collection of 30 or so boutiques selling ethnic handicrafts and antiques from Polynesia and Asia. *Hilton Hawaiian Village* (phone: 949-4321).

Royal Hawaiian Shopping Center – An ultramodern, 4-story arcade of boutiques and restaurants that covers 6½ acres. The shopping center runs along the south side of Kalakaua Avenue east from Lewers Street in front of the *Sheraton* and *Royal Hawaiian* hotels. This is where some of Waikiki's best shops have moved, which lends a Rodeo Drive elegance to the area. The center also has numerous restaurants and fast-food kiosks, and sponsors a wide range of free musical and cultural presentations throughout the year. 2201 Kalakaua Ave. (phone: 922-0588).

Waikiki Shopping Center – The merchandise in this complex has to compete with a 5-story water display that is part fountain and part Plexiglas sculpture. There are a few shops of interest as well as some fine restaurants on the upper floors. 2270 Kalakaua Ave. (phone: 923-1191).

Waikiki Trade Center – An architecturally distinctive office building, it has several stories of shops and restaurants. 2255 Kuhio Ave., at the juncture of Kuhio and Royal Hawaiian (phone: 922-7444).

Ward Center – On Ala Moana Boulevard, across the street from *Ward Warehouse* and from Ala Moana Beach Park, this low-key mall has a selection of upscale shops and art galleries as well as many popular eateries, including *Sushi Masa* (phone: 536-1007); *Il Fresco,* with fine Italian specialties (phone: 523-5191); *Compadres,* a spacious, plant-filled place serving Mexican fare (phone: 523-1307); and *Mary Catherine's,* which serves delicious coffee (531-3525).

Ward Warehouse – Also on Ala Moana Boulevard opposite the Kewalo Boat Basin, this 2-story complex of 70 boutiques and restaurants is constructed from stout timbers painted brown. A lot of people come here just to sip fine coffee at *The Coffee Works* and to munch on candy from *Fudge Works.*

SPECIALTY AND DISCOUNT SHOPS

WAIKIKI

ABC Discount – As the name suggests, this 35-store chain carries vacation essentials: straw beach mats (less expensive here than most places), cold drinks and chilled half-papayas for the thirsty beach crowd, snacks, sundries, film and souvenirs (phone: 538-6743).

Alfred Dunhill – Located in the elegantly restored Moana wing of the *Moana Surfrider* hotel, its cherrywood fixtures, plush velvet, and who-can-afford-it prices are as awesome as the jewelry, leather goods, and accessories that carry the Dunhill imprint (phone: 921-2020).

Betty's Imports – Real bargains on all kinds of jewelry and imported bric-a-brac, often at prices 30% to 50% lower than other shops. Fifth floor of the *Waikiki Shopping Center* (phone: 922-3010).

Center Art Gallery – Although the store has signed prints by Chagall, Dalí, and some other prolific printmakers, its specialty is canvases by celebrities such as Elke Sommer and Red Skelton. If you would like an original painting of Woody Woodpecker — commanding an outrigger canoe — by his creator, Walter Lantz, hurry on over. *Royal Hawaiian Shopping Center* (phone: 926-2727).

Chanel – Every Chanel item ever imagined and then some at prices that maybe you hadn't. Accessories, perfumes, jewelry, and more. *Ala Moana Shopping Center* (phone: 942-5555); *Royal Hawaiian Shopping Center* (phone: 923-0255).

Chapman's – This once traditional men's clothing chain has added a line of contemporary, high-fashion designs. *Hyatt Regency Center* (phone: 923-7010); *King's Village* (phone: 923-5920).

Chaumet – More than 200 years after the first shop opened in Paris, a branch of this fine jewelry store now can be found in Waikiki. The collection includes one-of-a-kind watches, accessories, and objets d'art. *Royal Hawaiian Shopping Center* (phone: 923-8055).

Circle Gallery – For a comprehensive selection of serigraphs, lithographs, and other graphics by Erté and other, lesser-known artists. *Hyatt Regency Center* (phone: 923-6040).

Cotton Cargo – This shop offers a refreshing change from alohawear, featuring 100% cotton fashion for women. The clothes have style; most are imported from India, Bali, Turkey, Greece, and Central America. *Hyatt Regency Center* (phone: 923-5811).

Down Under Honolulu – One of the best sources for men's swimwear in Hawaii, with designer labels as well as merchandise designed in-house. Everything from nearly revealing to very revealing, plus a fine selection of generic shorts and T-shirts. 2139 Kuhio Ave. (phone: 922-9229).

The Fossil Shop – Unique fossilized and crystallized items made from minerals and shells can be found here. *King's Village* (phone: 924-9314).

Gucci – This exclusive emporium has two branches in Honolulu; each one carries the usual elegant shoes, leather goods, and fashionable clothing. *Ala Moana Center* (phone: 942-1148); *Hyatt Regency Center* (phone: 923-2968).

Hermès of Paris – An elegant shop, featuring the finest silk scarves, leatherware, fragrances, bath accessories, jewelry, watches, and riding gear from the famous French maker. *Royal Hawaiian Shopping Center* (phone: 922-5780).

Kitamura's – An exquisite collection of antique Japanese dolls. Call in advance for an appointment. *King's Village* (phone: 293-1725).

Little Hawaiian Craft Shop – One of Hawaii's best collections of carved wood objects and museum-quality reproductions of Hawaiian sculpture. It's also known for handicrafts made from such materials as nuts, gourds, bones, fossil ivory, and seaweed, and for jewelry, ornaments, and "conversation pieces" made from cowrie shells. *Royal Hawaiian Shopping Center* (phone: 926-2662).

Loewe – This Spanish leather goods shop focuses on high quality, high fashion, and high prices. Worth a browse, if not a buy. *Royal Hawaiian Shopping Center* (phone: 922-1950).

Louis Vuitton – This is the Waikiki flagship for luggage and other leather goods and accessories imprinted with the famous intertwining initials. *Royal Hawaiian Shopping Center* (phone: 926-0621).

Lowe's Rare Coins – If you're numismatically inclined, this an interesting place to browse. *Waikiki Shopping Center* (phone: 923-3372).

McInerny Galleria – A small department store that's one of the best places in town for designer clothing for men, women, and children. Some of the labels sold in the store include Giorgio Armani and Ferragamo. *Royal Hawaiian Shopping Center* (phone: 971-4200).

Real Estate Showcase – The place to get an idea of what it costs to buy a piece of paradise. Displays that highlight condominium options on all islands make for interesting browsing and comparing. The Japanese are the big buyers here. *Royal Hawaiian Shopping Center* (phone: 926-5677).

Sawada Golf – Fill all your tee-time essentials at this large duffer's depot. *Waikiki Shopping Center* (phone: 923-0144).

Tiffany & Co. – The Waikiki branch of this world-renowned jeweler offers unique pieces as well as simpler items, all examples of Tiffany quality and style. In the *Sheraton Moana Surfrider* (phone: 922-2722).

Van Brugge House – Designer labels from the land down under — Australia, that is — as well as a cache of that country's pink, champagne, and cognac-colored diamonds. *Royal Hawaiian Shopping Center* (phone: 971-6678).

Villa Roma – It has a nice selection of contemporary women's fashions. *Waikiki Shopping Center* (phone: 923-4447).

Waldenbooks – Most of the sundries stores have pulp romances and spy novels, but if it's the new Paul Theroux or Tom Clancy (or *Birnbaum* guide) you're after, head here. The shop receives shipments barely days after mainland stores, and if you're staying a month or so, the staff will order anything not in stock. *Waikiki Shopping Center* (phone: 922-4154); *Ward Warehouse* (phone: 533-2711).

Yokohama-Okadaya – The chief reason for stopping in this international gift shop is its fine collection of designer leather goods. *Royal Hawaiian Shopping Center* (phone: 922-5731); *Waikiki Shopping Center* (phone: 922-5731).

DIAMOND HEAD

As Time Goes By – Antique jewelry, paintings, and silver are showcased at this antiques shop. *Kilohana Square,* 1016 Kapahulu Ave. (phone: 732-1174).

Apropos – Women's clothing with a European flair. *Kahala Mall* (phone: 735-1611).

Bailey's Antique & Thrift Shop – Prime vintage aloha shirts now fetch a cool grand here, although not all the goods are that pricey. 758 Kapahulu Ave. (phone: 734-7628).

Bebe Sport – Trendy men's and women's fashions are for sale at this shop. *Kahala Mall* (phone: 734-6444).

Carriage House – The mix at this store is European, Oriental, and American antiques. *Kilohana Square* (phone: 737-2622).

Corner Loft – An alluring selection of antiques, silver, and jewelry. *Kahala Mall* (phone: 732-4149).

Hawaii Quilts – Collectible Hawaiian quilts, as well as more contemporary designs. 2338 S. King St. (phone: 942-3195).

Juma – Colorful clothing for men and women, highlighted by the eye-popping designs of Jams, Baik Baik, and other style-conscious lines. *Kahala Mall* (phone: 739-5303).

Max Davis – High-quality Oriental antiques are the thing here. *Kilohana Square* (phone: 735-2341).

Needlepoint, Etc. – This shop sells kits and patterns with tropical flowers and other Hawaii motifs. *Kilohana Square* (phone: 737-3944).

Riches – A costume-jewelry kiosk with an impressive collection of earrings. *Kahala Mall* (phone: 737-3303).

Vue Hawaii – Locally created artworks, gifts, clothing, and koa wood items. *Kilohana Square* (phone: 735-8774).

MIDTOWN

Artlines – All sorts of artistic to mystic collectibles from all over the globe. Plenty to browse through and maybe even be unable to resist buying. *Ala Moana Shopping Center* (phone: 941-1445).

Banana Republic – The Hawaii branch of this outfitter of the urban adventurer is a good place for well-made, sanely priced, all-cotton clothing, as well as a location to find the unusual — especially if it's travel-related. *Ala Moana Shopping Center* (phone: 955-2602).

Bruno Magli – A beautiful selection of Italian-style shoes and accessories for men and women. *Ala Moana Shopping Center* (phone: 955-1448).

Cartier – Its first boutique located in Hawaii stocks a full range of the famous jewelers' gems and leather goods. The store is a replica of the original *Cartier's* in Paris. *Ala Moana Shopping Center* (phone: 955-5533).

Celine – A full range of French women's and men's ready-to-wear and accessories, with the eponymous logo as the lure. *Ala Moana Shopping Center* (phone: 973-3366).

Chocolates for Breakfast – The women's clothing sold here is often elegant, sometimes daring, and occasionally counter-chic, but always sophisticated. For the pure of heart there are muslins that *look* innocent enough. *Ala Moana Shopping Center* (phone: 947-3434).

Coral Grotto – If it's coral jewelry you're after, this shop (part of a chain) is known for its good-quality merchandise. The rings are particularly lovely — in pink, black, and gold coral; prices start at about $80. *Hyatt Regency Center* (phone: 923-3454); *Ala Moana Shopping Center* (phone: 955-6760).

Crack Seed Center – Preserved seeds and fruits, including dried cherries, plums, ginger, and lemon peel, are featured. *Ala Moana Shopping Center* (phone: 949-7200).

Emporio Armani – Italian men's and women's fashions in all their stylish glory. *Ala Moana Shopping Center* (phone: 523-5020).

Extra Dimension – Beautiful silk flowers and floral arrangements are made in this shop with the same traditional techniques used in Japan. *Ward Warehouse* (phone: 521-5512).

Foot Locker – It bills itself as "America's Most Complete Athletic Store," and it might be right. *Ala Moana Shopping Center* (phone: 944-8390).

Hale Kukui – Candles from all over the world, including scented, dripless, and/or smokeless varieties. Charming candle-powered windmills and unusual Hawaiian *Christmas* decorations, too. *Ala Moana Shopping Center* (phone: 949-6500).

Honolulu Book Shop – One of the largest and most comprehensive of its kind in Hawaii. *Ala Moana Shopping Center* (phone: 941-2274).

Iida's – Specializing in things Japanese, from bronze statues to porcelains to back massage rollers. It's fun to explore just to see what's being offered; good gift ideas, too. *Ala Moana Shopping Center* (phone: 973-0320).

Images International/Otsuka Gallerie – The photographs of Japan's Hisashi Otsuka are worth seeing, even if the price tags are high. *Ala Moana Shopping Center* (phone: 947-8844).

Imago – High-fashion women's clothing from American designers. *Ward Center* (phone: 521-1112).

Laise Adzer – A distinctive mix of ethnic fabrics and haute couture for women is offered at the Hawaiian branch of this high-fashion designer. The prices are high, but the clothes are simply beautiful. *Ala Moana Shopping Center* (phone: 944-1564).

Liberty House – Hawaii's leading department store, of which you will find a token version in hotels on all the major islands. The emphasis is on middle-of-the-road men's, women's, and children's fashions — not quite designer creations, but not simply aloha-wear, either. The *Ala Moana* store also has housewares, toys, books, and so on. Visits to more than a dozen *Liberty House* stores indicate that the staff is, on the whole, more than usually helpful. *Ala Moana Shopping Center* (phone: 941-2345).

MCM – Offering the finest in German leather goods, this shop takes its initials from designer Michael Cromer of Munich. *Ala Moana Shopping Center* (phone: 955-8700).

Neon Leon – What started as a neon lighting specialty shop has become a place to find inexpensive, offbeat, humorous gifts, plus one of Hawaii's best selections of humorous greeting cards. *Ward Warehouse* (phone: 545-7666).

Nohea Gallery – Superior Hawaiian arts and crafts are on display and for sale. Among these items are prints, drawings, woven goods, chimes, ceramics, pottery, and scrimshaw with nautical etchings. *Ward Warehouse* (phone: 599-7927).

North Beach Leather – From coats to dresses, pants to accessories, everything you might want to wear made of leather — with high-fashion design and price tags to match. *Ala Moana Shopping Center* (phone: 949-6719).

Pocketbook Man – Perhaps Hawaii's most complete selection of luggage and handbags, with some very elegant choices, is here. *Ala Moana Shopping Center* (phone: 949-3535).

Polo Ralph Lauren – This shop carries a full collection of the luxurious Polo designs. *Ala Moana Shopping Center* (phone: 947-7656).

Pomegranates in the Sun – The name's a bit far-fetched, but the selection of hand-painted and ethnic clothing for men and women is intriguing. *Ward Warehouse* (phone: 531-1108).

Prides of New Zealand – Everything in sheepskin, from stadium rugs to car seat covers, toys to golf club warmers. Golf club warmers? In Hawaii? Anyway, you'll find it all here. *Ala Moana Shopping Center* (phone: 944-5590).

Products of Hawaii – Hawaiian perfume, Hawaiian tiki carvings, Hawaiian *lau hala* mats, Hawaiian-designed greeting cards are sold here — as advertised. It's a good spot to do all your souvenir shopping at one time. *Ala Moana Shopping Center* (phone: 949-6866).

Royal Hawaiian Heritage – The place to visit if you've become enamored of the black and gold Hawaiian-style jewelry that graces many local women. Across from the *Ala Moana Center* at 1430 Kona St. (phone: 973-4343).

Sharper Image – This adult "toy" store is bound to have something to please, be it products of high-tech electronics or space-age imagination. The prices are neither low nor ridiculous. *Ala Moana Shopping Center* (phone: 949-4100).

Tahiti Imports – Polynesian fashions for women, a lot of them quite classy in their brief way, are sold here. The *pareu,* in simple and elegant designs, can be turned into intriguing cover-ups and skirts. *Ala Moana Shopping Center* (phone: 941-4539).

Waterford/Wedgwood – Here is a complete selection of England's finest porcelain and crystal. *Ala Moana Shopping Center* (phone: 943-9630).

Willowdale Gallery – Items featured are of the antique sort, most hailing from Europe. *Ward Center* (phone: 536-2080).

DOWNTOWN

Aala Lei Shop – An excellent selection of leis and flower arrangements can be found here at good prices. 1104 Maunakea St. (phone: 521-5766).

Bo Wah Trading Co. Liberty House – The offerings run from practical to kitschy at this shop. 1149 Maunakea St. (phone: 537-2017).

Honolulu Chocolate Company – Chocoholics beware, your taste buds will confirm the initial impulse to surrender to temptation. The prices are steep, but worth it. Restaurant Row (phone: 531-2997) and Manoa Valley (phone: 988-4999).

Jenny's Lei Shop – One of a number of shops downtown that specialize in the traditional Hawaiian art of lei making, with a larger and better-priced selection than that found in Waikiki. 1151 Maunakea St. (phone: 521-1595).

Lai Fong – This long-established store features Oriental antiques and bric-a-brac. 1118 Nuuanu Ave. (phone: 537-3497).

Liberty House – A branch of this Hawaiian store that carries clothing for men, women, and children. 1032 Fort St. (phone: 945-5151).

Mellow's – Fans of antique jewelry will want to visit this store. 841 Bishop St. (phone: 533-6313).

Pauahi Nuuanu Gallery – The emphasis is on Hawaiian arts ranging from wood-carving to feathered leis to Niihau shell jewelry. 1 N. Pauahi St. (phone: 531-6088).

Pegge Hopper Gallery – Pricey outputs of this artist's palette are featured. 1164 Nuuanu Ave. (phone: 524-1160).

Penthouse – A reduced-price merchandise outlet, where some real bargains can be found. 1 N. King St. (phone: 945-5151).

Ramsey Galleries – Changing exhibits of high-quality watercolors, pen-and-ink drawings, ceramicware, and other art forms are shown here. 1128 Smith St. (phone: 537-ARTS).

William Waterfall Gallery – Art photography, graphics, jewelry, and collector's quality ceramics are featured here, along with a fine selection of Balinese, Burmese, and Thai objets d'art. 1160A Nuuanu Ave. (phone: 521-6863).

ELSEWHERE

Barnfield's Raging Isle Sports – This is the place to witness a slice-of-the-surf-scene life. Adjacent to the *North Shore Center,* it's where some of the best custom surfboards in Hawaii are made. 66-250 Kamehameha Hwy., Hailewa (phone: 637-7707).

Charlie's Country Store – Apart from the distressingly familiar souvenirs, this place also sells excellent books on the flora and fauna of the islands. In Waimea Falls Park, 59-864 Kamehameha Hwy., Haleiwa (phone: 638-8525).

Deeni's Boutique – Good for beach towels, bikinis, and muumuus, especially when there's an "odd lot" table. 66-079 Kamehameha Hwy., Haleiwa (phone: 637-9871).

Elizabeth's Fancy – Handmade Hawaiian quilts, wall hangings, and pillows as well as custom design kits and patterns. 767 Kailua Rd., Kailua (phone: 262-7513).

Fettig Art Gallery – Large and colorful paintings of Hawaiian rural and maritime scenes. 66-030 Kamehameha Hwy., Haleiwa (phone: 637-4933).

Kukui Nuts of Hawaii – This is the place where kukui nuts are transformed into shiny black and brown leis. Also available: an array of products, from lotions to shampoos, created from healthful kukui oil. 66-935 Kaukonahua Rd., between Haleiwa and Waialua (phone: 637-9889).

Mahalo Mona – Owned by *Kahala Creations* owner Mona Link, this shop has stylish and unusual imported tropical-weight women's clothes and accessories. 767 Kailua Rd., Kailua (phone: 262-6366).

Outrigger Trading Co. – Inside *Jameson's by the Sea* restaurant, this small shop specializes in hand-crafted Hawaiian-made pottery, glass, wood, and so on. 62-540 Kamehameha Hwy., Haleiwa (phone: 637-4737).

Pacific Island Arts – Located in the *North Shore Center,* this gallery fills its 5,000 square feet with the works of some of Hawaii's finest artists. Particularly noteworthy are Dan Van Zyle (serigraphs), Norman Nagai (watercolors), Laka Morton (Hawaiian portraiture), and mother/daughter Mary Koski and Cathy Long (painting, pen and ink drawings, etchings). 66-250 Kamehameha Hwy. Hailewa (phone: 637-7880).

Platinor – Oriental art and antiques, many from owner Engelbert "Angelo" Klockner's collection. In the lobby of the *Turtle Bay Hilton* (phone: 293-8777).

Tusitala Bookshop – A secondhand bookstore with a great collection of Hawaiiana books and the artful old-fashioned Hawaiian song sheets and menu covers suitable for framing. 116 Hekili St., Kailua (phone: 262-6343).

Windward Antiques – Browse here for home furnishings, primitives, and jewelry. 760 Kailua Rd., Kailua (phone: 262-5526).

Wyland Gallery – Whaling Wall artist Wyland has opened a gallery featuring his primarily nautical paintings, as well as the work of other Hawaiian artists. 66-150 Kamehameha Hwy., Haleiwa (phone: 637-7498).

 SPORTS AND FITNESS: Hawaii is one of the world's great centers for water sports. Surfing and swimming contests are held often. *Aloha Stadium* is the site of the *Hula Bowl* college football game each January; football and baseball games at other times take place in Halawa Heights (phone: 486-

9300). Basketball and boxing events are held at the *Neal S. Blaisdell Center* (777 Ward Ave.; phone: 521-2911).

Bicycling – *Island Triathlon & Bike* (569 Kapahulu Ave., near Waikiki; phone: 732-7227) and *Island Bike and Surf Rentals* (2084 Kalakaua Ave.; phone: 949-2453) are two choices for good-quality rentals.

Fishing – Fishing enthusiasts from all over the world flock to Hawaiian waters. Fishing boats can be chartered from *Coreene C's I Sport Fishing Charters* (phone: 536-7472), *Golden Eagle Marine Charter Services* (phone: 531-4966), or *Island Charters* (phone: 536-1555). Most boats leave from Kewalo Basin, at the end of Ward Avenue, on Ala Moana Boulevard.

Fitness Centers – The *YMCA* has a pool, racquetball court, sauna, exercise machines, and weights (401 Atkinson Dr., across from *Ala Moana Center;* phone: 941-3344).

Football – Enthusiasts of the sport can participate in the NFL *Pro Bowl Dream Week,* where amateurs are coached by and play with such gridiron legends as Gale Sayers, Willie Lanier, Mel Blount, and Don Maynard. Everyone competes at the end of the week in a big pre–*Pro Bowl* football game at *Aloha Stadium* — and survivors get to attend the *Pro Bowl* game itself the next day. For information, contact *Dream Week, Inc.,* 2337 Philmont Ave., Huntingdon Valley, PA 19006 (phone: 215-938-1200 or 800-888-4376).

Gliding – *Hawaii Glider Rides* has 3-seat sailplanes departing about every 20 minutes daily from 10:30 AM to 5 PM at the North Shore's Dillingham Airfield (phone: 677-3404).

Golf – There are numerous public golf courses on Oahu, with more in the planning stage. Resorts courses include *Ko Olina* (phone: 676-5300), near the Ewa district, west of Honolulu; *Sheraton Makaha* (phone: 695-9544); *Hawaii Prince Country Club* (phone: 956-1111); and the *Turtle Bay Hilton* (phone: 293-8811), near Kahuku on the North Shore. Among the public courses are *Ala Wai,* the closest course to Waikiki (phone: 296-4653); *Pali,* in Kaneohe (phone: 261-9784); and *Makaha Valley Country Club* (phone: 695-7111). Military personnel, active or retired, can tee up on the island's first-rate military courses, most of which have reasonable greens fees. Among the best are *Hickam Mamala Bay* (phone: 449-6490), a championship course with a view of the silvery-blue waters of Mamala Bay, and near Schofield Barracks, *Kalakaua* (phone: 655-9833) and *Leilehua* (phone: 655-4653). For additional information, see *Great Golf* in DIVERSIONS.

Jogging – Run along Kalakaua Avenue to Kapiolani Park, where a group meets at the bandstand at 7:30 AM every Sunday from March through December for a short lecture and a run. The distance around the park is 1.8 miles; to tack on more mileage, continue along Kalakaua to Diamond Head Road and circle the base of Diamond Head. The road turns into Monsarrat Avenue, which leads back to Kalakaua (4½ miles altogether). Or take Diamond Head Road as far as Kahala Avenue, one of the island's most beautiful runs. Also popular: the 2-mile perimeter of Ala Moana Beach Park.

Kayaking – *Adventure Kayaking International* conducts a series of kayak tours, including 2-hour sunset and full-moon excursions, along the Diamond Head–Waikiki coast. They also offer day trips for beginners, starting at $45 a day, and 1- to 5-day overnight kayaking excursions to the Big Island and Molokai plus Tahiti and Fiji. Prices for overnight trips start at $150 a day and include kayaks, guides, gear, and food (but not airfare to or from the final destination). Excursions arranged for groups of 4 to 12 (children welcome, too). 53-352 Kam Hwy., in Ponaluu (phone: 924-8898 or 800 52-KAYAK).

Skin Diving – *Dan's Dive Shop* (660 Ala Moana Blvd.; phone: 536-6181) rents diving gear, offers instructions for beginners, and has brush-up courses for those with some experience. Other Honolulu-based dive shops include *Waikiki Diving Center* (1734 Kalakaua Ave.; phone: 955-5151); *Aloha Dive Shop* (Koko Marina, Hawaii Kai; phone:

395-5922); *South Seas Aquatics* (870 Kapahulu Ave.; phone: 735-0437); and *Steve's Diving Adventures* (1860 Ala Moana Blvd.; phone: 947-8900). Out near Makaha, call *Leeward Dive Center* (phone: 696-3414). On the North Shore, call *Underwater Hawaii* (at the *Turtle Bay Hilton,* 57091 Kam Hwy., Kahuku, HI 96731; phone: 293-8811) for lessons, or *Surf and Sea* in Haleiwa (phone: 637-9887) for rentals. Snorkelers can take an inexpensive day trip to Hanauma Bay with *Hanauma Bay Snorkeling Tours* (phone: 944-8828). *Barefoot Charters* (phone: 522-1533) departs Kewalo Basin for half-day sails that include snorkeling in the marine preserve off Diamond Head.

Surfing – The quest for the perfect wave attracts surfers from all over the world. Most hotels along Waikiki Beach have surfing instructors and concessions that rent surfboards, canoes, and catamarans. The most famous surfing beaches are Sunset, Ehukai, and Waimea, on the north side of the island. Major international competitions are held here in late November through early January. In Honolulu, learn to surf with *Waikiki Beach Services* (phone: 924-4940 or 924-4941) or the *Sheraton Waikiki* (phone: 922-4422). The *Haleiwa Surf Center* (phone: 637-5051) on the North Shore has free surfing classes on weekends.

Swimming – With Waikiki Beach generally very crowded, an alternative is to head to nearby Ala Moana or Diamond Head beach parks, or to beaches on the other side of the island. Equally spectacular settings include Sandy Beach and Makapuu, where just about everyone body-surfs; Waimanalo and Kailua, where swimming and wind-surfing are popular; and on up the coast to Kahana and the legendary surfing beaches of the North Shore. Many beaches are dangerous for swimming; stick to those with lifeguards.

Tennis – There are public courts at 40 places around Oahu. Try Ala Moana Park (phone: 522-7031), *Diamond Head Tennis Center* (phone: 971-7150), or *Kapiolani Tennis Courts* (no phone), or *Honolulu Tennis Club* (phone: 944-9696). The *Ilikai* hotel has 6 courts (1 lighted for night play), the *Hawaiian Regent* has 1 court, while the *Kahala Hilton* offers 6 courts (all night-lighted) at the *Maunalua Bay Club.*

Windsurfing – *Kailua Beach School* (phone: 261-3539) and *Naish Hawaii* (phone: 261-6067) feature rentals and lessons in Waikiki or windward Oahu.

THEATER: You can get tickets at the door for most plays and musicals in Honolulu. The main theaters are the *Blaisdell Center Concert Hall* (Ward and King Sts.; phone: 537-6191); *Diamond Head Theater* (Makapuu and Aloha Aves.; phone: 734-0274); and *Hawaii Performing Arts Company's Manoa Theatre* (2833 E. Manoa Rd.; phone: 988-6131). Also check for under-the-stars performances at the *Waikiki Shell* (phone: 521-2911).

MUSIC: The *Honolulu Symphony* plays at the *Blaisdell Center Concert Hall* (phone: 537-6191). Rock musicians appear at the *Blaisdell Center Arena* (phone: 521-2911) or sometimes at *Aloha Stadium* (phone: 486-9300) or the *Waikiki Shell* (phone: 521-2911). If the *Brothers Cazimero* are performing at the *Royal Hawaiian,* it's worth a visit.

NIGHTCLUBS AND NIGHTLIFE: When the sun goes down, Honolulu after dark is traditional, often corny, but always fun, and nearly nonstop. One of the world's great playgrounds, something is always going on here.

Polynesian spectaculars (dinner, luau, or cocktail options) that provide Hollywood-cum-Broadway versions of Pacific island music and dance are of most interest to first-time visitors to Honolulu. The best location is the beachside luau and revue at the *Outrigger* hotel (2335 Kalakaua Ave.; phone: 923-0711) on Tuesdays, Fridays, and Sundays. At the *Sheraton Princess Kaiulani* (2342 Kalakaua Ave.; phone: 922-5811) there is a nightly show, and the *Royal Hawaiian* (2259 Kalakaua Ave.;

phone: 923-7311) is the site for a luau and revue on Mondays. *Voyage* is the latest variation on the theme. The *Aloha Showroom* (on the fourth floor of the *Royal Hawaiian Shopping Center*) features Waikiki's largest and most extravagant showroom. The setting is a Hollywood vision of Hawaii, complete with waterfalls, streams, a rain forest, and "erupting volcanoes," with performers telling the story of a missionary's arrival in 19th-century Hawaii in music and dance. Tickets to the show can be purchased independently ($25) or in conjunction with many dinner packages in restaurants in the *Royal Hawaiian* complex.

Dinner cruises have been part of the Honolulu scene for years. *Royal Hawaiian Cruises* (phone: 848-6360) departs Kewalo Basin on the *Navatek,* a jet-propelled catamaran, on sunset and moonlight cruises. Although the cost, which includes an elegant steak and lobster dinner along with first class entertainment, is high ($130), it is a fine choice for a very romantic evening. *Paradise Cruises* (phone: 536-3641) leaves from Kewalo Basin (hotel pickups are provided), and offers drinks and food during the sail back along Waikiki Beach to Diamond Head. *Aikane Catamarans* (phone: 522-1533; 800-522-1538) and *Windjammer Cruises* (phone: 521-0036) also offer popular sunset sails, with drinks, dinner, and all-too-often noisy entertainment. Cruises include transfers between Kewalo Basin and Waikiki.

Another Honolulu tradition is the luau, an ancient Hawaiian ceremony of cooking a pig in an *imu,* an earthen pit lined with lava rock and heated by burning kiawe wood. The pig is stuffed with red-hot rocks, wrapped in wet ti and banana leaves, and covered with earth. Other ingredients such as yams, taro, fish, breadfruit, and whatever else is available are placed in the *imu* beside the pig. Hours later, the pig is removed, at which time it is referred to as kalua pork. Removing the pig from the *imu* is a ceremony in itself, often accompanied by songs. There are a number of commercial luaus that include the removal ceremony and a torchlighting ritual, a heavy meal of pork and accompanying traditional foodstuffs, "all you can drink," and Polynesian entertainment. In Waikiki there's a Monday luau at the *Royal Hawaiian* hotel (2259 Kalakaua Ave.; phone: 923-7311). Other luaus take place on beaches out of town but with pick-up buses serving most hotels. At the *Paradise Cove Luau* there is an *imu* ceremony, torchlighting ritual, beachfront *hukilau* (communal net fishing), Hawaiian arts and crafts displays, and a Polynesian revue (phone: 973-5828). *Paradise Cove* and *Germaine's Luau* both take place on beaches near Ewa, about 40 minutes from Waikiki (transportation provided). *Germaine's* features a net-throwing demonstration during which, for a brief moment, there's the splendid sight of a fishing net extended in silhouette against the late evening sky. Before the removal of the pig, there is also a procession, with young people modeling costumes worn by ancient Hawaiian royalty. In the Polynesian extravaganza that follows ($40), the audience is invited to participate in various dances and songs in an exhibition that may turn even strong stomachs after a generous number of free mai tais and blue Hawaiis (phone: 949-6626).

Sea Life Park (phone: 923-1531) has exhibits and shows from 7 to 10 PM on Thursday, Friday, and Sunday evenings. At the *Bishop Museum* (phone: 848-4129 or 847-8200), a state-of-the-art planetarium show is presented at 7 PM Fridays and Saturdays; admission $2.50. Pack a picnic and seat yourself on the lawn for one of the symphonic, jazz, or Hawaiian shows often presented at the *Waikiki Shell* (box office phone: 521-2911), with Diamond Head as a backdrop. Gates open at 5:30 PM; showtime is usually 7:30 PM. When the moon is full, consider the free escorted walks at Waimea Falls Park (phone: 638-8511).

Headliners in Honolulu usually mean entertainers who have made their name in the islands. The most famous is Don Ho, the smooth-crooning, still-island-boyish man who turned "Tiny Bubbles" into gold. Ho's performances, at Waikiki's *Hula Hut* (286 Beach Walk; phone: 923-8411), can be erratic; they are best on Fridays and Saturdays, when he attracts a good number of *kamaainas* who will request songs that the stranger does not know. Also, Charo stars in a good, Vegas-style revue at the *Hilton Hawaiian*

Village's *Tropic Room,* evenings except Sundays. Dinner and cocktail seatings available. Another favorite is the *Society of Seven,* a group performing a mix of contemporary music and comedy at the *Outrigger Waikiki* showroom (2335 Kalakaua Ave.; phone: 923-0711). Check the entertainment guides for details. The *Brothers Cazimero,* Roland and Robert, are also very popular. They have a great respect for the music of the islands, and their show in the *Royal Hawaiian's Monarch Room* (phone: 923-7311) is one of Hawaii's best. Again, check newspapers and guides to find out where they are appearing. Illusionist and magician John Hirokawa stars in Magic of Polynesia, a spectacular David Copperfield–style show that mixes magic, illusions, and Hawaiian music and song. Nightly in the *Hilton Dome,* at 5 PM for the dinner show ($44.50), and at 6 PM for the cocktail show ($25). Fans of stand-up comedy can head to the *Honolulu Comedy Club* Tuesdays through Sundays at the *Ilikai* hotel. Reservations advised; $10 cover (177 Ala Moana Blvd.; phone: 922-5998). Check Oahu newspapers to find out where a favorite local funny man, Frank Delima, is appearing. His Imelda Marcos impression is priceless.

Other Honolulu hot spots, from rock 'n' roll joints to steamy discos and mellow piano bars, include the following:

Anna Bannanas – A funky college hangout, with a second-story dance hall, which is home to the *Pagan Babies,* Hawaii's world-touring *World Beat* band. 2440 S. Beretania St. (phone: 946-5190).

Annabelle's – Located atop the *Ilikai* hotel, this disco features contemporary music and panoramic views. *Ilikai Hotel,* 1777 Ala Moana Blvd. (phone: 949-3811).

Andrew's – Hawaiian vocalist Mahi Beamer sings at the piano every weekend in the lounge of this Italian restaurant. *Ward Center,* 1200 Ala Moana Blvd. (phone: 523-8677).

Banyan Verandah – Authentic live Hawaiian entertainment daily on a Victorian verandah by the sea. *Sheraton Moana Surfrider,* 2353 Kalakaua Ave. (phone: 922-3111).

Black Orchid – There's entertainment nightly in this chic lounge; the music is Top 40 and you can dance on the mini-floor in the bar. Restaurant Row, 500 Ala Moana Blvd. (phone: 521-3111).

Bobby McGee's – Located just below Diamond Head on the edge of Waikiki, this is a popular disco with a young crowd and lively atmosphere. 2885 Kalakaua Ave. (phone: 922-1282).

Café Sistina – Amid murals and frescoes, this hip Italian bistro features live local jazz and blues on weekends. 1314 S. King St. (phone: 526-0071).

Flashback – The reason Elvis-sightings keep happening in Waikiki is because Jonathon Von Brana, "the king of the King's impressionists" appears here nightly with other faux celebs such as *The Andrew Sisters,* George Michael, and Madonna. *Waikiki Terrace Hotel,* 2045 Kalakaua Ave. (phone: 955-8444).

Gussie L'Amours – A rock 'n' roll boogie joint in a warehouse district that keeps the good times rolling with live, Top 40 entertainment and occasional appearances by big-name stars of the 1960s and 1970s. 3251 N. Nimitz Hwy. (phone: 836-9180).

Hala Terrace – Home of Hawaiian singer Danny Kaleikini, whose Hawaiian-Polynesian variety show packs them in nightly. *Kahala Hilton,* 5000 Kahala Ave. (phone: 734-2211).

Hard Rock Café – An "in" spot for the young crowd (twenties and thirties); there's lots of mingling and noise at the bar. 1837 Kapiolani Blvd. (phone: 955-7383).

House Without a Key – The *Halekulani's* open-air restaurant and bar has mellow Hawaiian music and hula to complement Waikiki's spectacular sunsets. *Halekulani Hotel,* 2199 Kalia Rd. (phone: 923-2311).

Horatio – This second-story restaurant lounge, overlooking Kewalo Basin, features live classic rock music Wednesdays through Saturdays. *Ward Warehouse,* 1050 Ala Moana Blvd. (phone: 521-5002).

Hula's – Drinks and dancing are the draw at this open-air tropical-style bar, which draws a primarily gay crowd. 2103 Kuhio Ave. (phone: 923-0669).

Jazz Cellar – The name's a misnomer; there's no jazz here — just live bands playing hard-core rock 'n' roll. 205 Lewers St., Waikiki (phone: 923-9952).

Jolly Roger East – Right in the heart of Waikiki, this fun, local-crowd establishment has dancing to live music, pop, and light rock. 150 Kaiulani Ave. (phone: 923-2172).

Jolly Roger Waikiki Crow's Nest – Known for their mai tais, this spot features comedy shows, and live folk and bluegrass music 7 nights a week. 2244 Kalakaua Ave. (phone: 923-2422).

Jubilee – The last stand of authentic Hawaiian music, stop here to hear slack key (guitar playing with loosened strings), steel guitar, falsetto singers, and Honolulu's most popular Hawaiian artists. 1007 Dillingham Blvd. (phone: 845-1568).

Langing – Primarily a *pau hana* (after-work) watering hole, this downtown Honolulu establishment features live blues and jazz on Friday evenings. 700 Bishop St. (phone: 528-4335).

Lewers Lounge – This clubby 1950s-style room draws the after-dinner set for cognac and the sound of Loretta Able's jazzy tunes. *Halekulani Hotel,* 2199 Kalia Rd. (phone: 923-2311).

Maharaja – A flashy disco with a large dance floor, the DJs here spin mainly Top 40 hits on the best sound system in town. *Waikiki Trade Center,* Kuhio and Seaside (phone: 922-3030).

Mahina Lounge – A very mellow piano bar with music nightly. Don't miss the cool sound of jazz singer Andrea Young on Thursdays, Fridays, and Saturdays. *Ala Moana Hotel,* 410 Atkinson Dr. (phone: 955-4811).

Maila's Cantina – A slice of Mexico in Waikiki, this hot tamale restaurant turns into a lively tequila bar after 9 PM with live contemporary Hawaiian music. 311 Lewers St. (phone: 922-7808).

Maile Lounge – Kit Samson's *Sound Advice* plays ballroom jazz here Tuesdays through Saturdays. Dancing is popular at this dress-up spot. *Kahala Hilton Hotel,* 5000 Kahala Ave. (phone: 734-2211).

Monterey Bay Canners – Popular with a local crowd, this well-known restaurant lounge features "Jawaiian" (local reggae) and other local music. *Ward Warehouse,* 1200 Ala Moana Blvd. (phone: 536-6197).

Moose McGillycuddy – Expect dancing and live bands nightly at this Waikiki hot spot, which attracts a young singles crowd. At the other branch of the *Moose,* near the University of Hawaii, there's contemporary Hawaiian music Friday and Saturday nights, dancing Thursdays and Sundays. 310 Lewers St., Waikiki (phone: 923-0751); 1035 University Ave. (phone: 944-5525).

New Orleans Bistro – One of the few dedicated jazz spots in Honolulu, this open-air sidewalk café has jazz nightly and features Betty Loo Taylor on weekends. 2139 Kuhio Ave., Waikiki (phone: 926-4444).

Nicholas Nickolas – This popular nightspot features spectacular views of the Waikiki lights from its top-floor perch. Dancing and live music, Top 40 to salsa, every night. *Ala Moana Hotel,* 410 Atkinson Dr. (phone: 955-4466).

Nick's Fishmarket – With its great dance floor and live bands, this is a popular spot to see and be seen. *Waikiki Gateway Hotel,* 2070 Kalakaua Ave. (phone: 955-6333).

Oasis – A mainly local crowd gathers here for live contemporary Hawaiian music Wednesdays through Saturdays, karaoke Sundays through Tuesdays. 2888 Waialae Ave. (phone: 734-3772).

Paradise Lounge – Effervescent Jimmy Borges presents jazz stylings of George Gershwin, Cole Porter, and Jerome Kern. *Hilton Hawaiian Village,* 2005 Kalia Rd. (phone: 949-4321).

Pecos River Café – Expect dancing aplenty at this hopping country/western bar, featuring live entertainment by *Good Ole Byes* and *Warren Johnson's Gator Creek Band.* 99-016 Kamehameha Hwy., Aiea (phone: 487-7980).

Pink's Garage – A young crowd comes here for the big-name bands, punk and progressive, that play in this warehouse setting. 955 Waimanu St. (phone: 537-1555).

Ramsay Galleries and Café – A piano player tickles the ivories in the loft of this Chinatown bistro. 1128 Smith St. (phone: 537-ARTS).

Reni's – Founded by "Magnum P.I." co-star Roger Mosley, this Pearl City hangout in a light industrial district features rock, jazz, and soul music. 98-713 Kuahao Pl., Pearl City (phone: 487-3625).

Row Bar – Where Honolulu meets after work, this is an open-air oasis with a noisy crowd and live music weekends and most nights. Restaurant Row, 500 Ala Moana Blvd. (phone: 528-2345).

Rumors – Popular flashy disco dance club. *Ala Moana Hotel,* 410 Atkinson Dr. (phone: 955-4811).

Scruples – The late-night crowd ends up here; this hot nightclub plays Top 40 songs for a dance crowd. 310 Kuhio Ave., Waikiki (phone: 923-9530).

Shell Bar – At this beautiful indoor/outdoor tropical lounge, two pianists play dueling back-to-back white baby grand pianos. *Hilton Hawaiian Village,* 2005 Kalia Rd. (phone: 949-4321).

Shore Bird – Home of the world's longest-running bikini contest, this beachfront bar features Hawaiian music every evening until 8; after that, it's karaoke time. 2169 Kalia Rd. (phone: 922-6906).

Silver Fox Lounge – A street-corner bar in Chinatown, this place has lots of local color, a pool table and *Mojo Hand,* a house band with a hot harmonica man. 49 N. Hotel St. (phone: 536-9215).

Spats – This steamy disco has a large dance floor and a late-night pasta bar for those who dance up an appetite. *Hyatt Regency Waikiki,* 2424 Kalakaua Ave. (phone: 923-1234).

Studebaker's – A rock 'n' roll disco where the music jumps the decades, and every now and again the staff takes to the tabletops to dance. 500 Ala Moana Blvd. (phone: 526-9888).

Trapper's – An Art Deco discotheque, where the sound ranges from Top 40 tunes to the best of the 1950s and 1960s. *Hyatt Regency Waikiki,* 2424 Kalakaua Ave. (phone: 923-1234).

Tropics Surf Bar Showroom – Five nights a week, this cabaret vibrates to the never-ending, Vegas-style energy of Charo. Closed Sundays and Mondays. *Hilton Hawaiian Village,* 2005 Kalia Rd. (phone: 949-4321).

Waikiki Broiler – Expect live contemporary Hawaiian music in this mainly dinner atmosphere. 200 Lewers St., Waikiki (phone: 923-8836).

Wave Waikiki – Dance to the max at this rock 'n' and roll club, whose live bands cater to a young crowd. 1877 Kalakaua Ave. (phone: 941-0424).

BEST IN TOWN

CHECKING IN: Honolulu hotels vary in personality, so do a bit of careful checking before picking one. Remember, it's not just a place to sleep; it also will serve as your tropical headquarters during your visit. Expect to pay $250 or more for a double at those places we've listed as very expensive; around $160 and up at hotels classed as expensive; between $70 and $150 at those designated moderate; under $70 at hotels listed as inexpensive. For a "superior double" room in a condominium, expect to pay around $150 and up; for a standard condominium, the charge is $80 to $145 a night. Unless otherwise stated, the same rate applies for one to four people, though there often is a nominal (under $10) charge for each person after the first two. For bed and breakfast accommodations, contact *Bed & Breakfast Hawaii* (Box 449, Kapaa, HI 96746; phone: 822-7771), *Pacific Hawaii Bed & Breakfast* (970 N. Kalaheo Ave.; Suite A218, Kailua, HI 96734; phone: 254-5030), or *Bed and Breakfast Honolulu Statewide* (3242 Kaohinani Dr., Honolulu, HI 96817; phone: 595-7533). All telephone numbers are in the 808 area code unless otherwise indicated.

WAIKIKI

Aston Waikiki Beachside – Small and sumptuous, this luxurious establishment is perfect for those who appreciate lovely surroundings. Inside, European and Oriental period pieces add to the elegant ambience, while the service is undeniably impeccable. A minor drawback for those who crave lots of space are the guestrooms, some of which are fairly small, albeit appealingly appointed. In-room VCRs are just one of the extras, as are French toiletries. Although there are no restaurants on the premises, it's merely a 5-minute walk to the *Hyatt Regency* or other resort complexes in the area. Conveniently located just across Kalakaua from the beach. Amenities include a concierge desk, photocopiers, and CNN. 2452 Kalakaua Ave. (phone: 931-2100; 800-922-7866; fax: 931-2129; telex: 634479). Very expensive to expensive.

Halekulani – This contemporary, recently refurbished mid-rise incorporates the old Lewers home, which served as the original hotel. Among its features are 456 rooms, a fitness room, and an open-air, oceanfront lounge — *House Without a Key* — featuring Hawaiian music and fine views of Diamond Head and sunsets. Its restaurants, *Orchids* and *La Mer* (see *Eating Out*), are among Honolulu's best. The hotel, designed to reestablish Waikiki as a destination for the carriage trade, is the essence of contemporary elegance. This is a place for which the adjective "luxury" is no exaggeration. Among the business conveniences are 6 meeting rooms, a concierge, secretarial services, A/V equipment, photocopiers, and computers. CNN and express checkout are also pluses. 2199 Kalia Rd. (phone: 923-2311; 800-367-2343; fax: 926-8004; telex: 8382). Very expensive to expensive.

Hawaii Prince – Waikiki's newest luxury hotel is the second Hawaii property for Japan's Prince Hotel chain (the other is on Maui). Attention to detail, carefully prepared cuisine at the hotel's five restaurants, including the *Prince Court* (see *Eating Out*), and panoramic views of the neighboring Ala Wai Yacht Tower are the main justifications for top-of-the-scale rates. Guests are also offered complimentary shuttle service to golf courses, a nearby health spa, downtown, and Waikiki. Located on the western edge of Waikiki, it is a short walk from either Ala Moana Beach or Waikiki Beach. Twenty-four–hour room service is available, as are 6 meeting rooms. A concierge and secretarial services are on call. Other pluses are A/V equipment, photocopiers, CNN, and express checkout. 100 Holomoana St. (phone: 956-1111; 800-321-6284; fax: 946-0811; telex: 628-48648). Very expensive.

Hilton Hawaiian Village – With close to 2,600 rooms and 22 acres (plans to build a new high-rise tower were recently announced), it is Hawaii's largest hotel, and the western terminus of Waikiki Beach. Standing between the Duke Kahanamoku Lagoon and the beach, it boasts a colorful shopping center, its own post office, and a catamaran that offers both day and night cruises. The Rainbow Tower, famed for its 30-story rainbow mosaic, and the Tapa Tower, with 250 corner suites, have the best views. The Alii Tower is the hotel's most elegant segment, and features its own pool and full concierge services. The village has lots that visitors want from a Hawaiian vacation — pools, beaches, fine dining, luaus, and Polynesian extravaganzas featuring Don Ho — but lacks much peace and serenity. The hotel did a $100-million renovation in 1988 that brought all the parts of the village together around a pool area that also highlights the beach, rather than obscuring it. "Aloha Friday," a weekly celebration dedicated to King David Kalakaua, features crafts displays, hula dancing, and a luau-style dinner from 5 to 9:30 PM at the *Rainbow Lanai.* The evening is capped off by fireworks starting at 7:30 PM, or after dark, whichever is later. There are 32 meeting rooms, plus secretarial services, A/V equipment, photocopiers, and computers. A concierge desk, CNN, and express checkout are other pluses. 2005 Kalia Rd. (phone: 949-4321; 800-445-8667; fax: 947-7914). Very expensive to expensive.

Hawaiian Regent – Just across the road from the beach, the two tall towers possess little architectural distinction. The interiors, however, are a bit more appealing, with inner courtyards paved in tile and marble, and an outdoor-café atmosphere in the main lobby. The Ocean Terrace pool area is also inviting, and the rooms are large and comfortable. There are several first class restaurants in the hotel, including the prestigious *The Secret,* which boasts a 6,000-bottle wine room (see *Eating Out*). *The Library,* where there's not a book in sight, has some unusually good soft music starting at 8:30 PM. Business services include 12 meeting rooms, a concierge, secretarial services, A/V equipment, photocopiers, computers, CNN, and express checkout. 2552 Kalakaua Ave. (phone: 922-6611; 800-367-5370). Expensive.

Sheraton Moana Surfrider – This beautifully restored Victorian hostelry has been standing at the edge of the Waikiki surf since 1901. The Japanese firm that owns it (Sheraton manages it) finished a $50-million renovation in 1989 that brought back the glow of its early days. Until its exotic neighbor, the *Royal Hawaiian,* was opened in 1927, the *Moana* was the only hotel in the area. Brass headboards, white wicker chairs, antique lamps, and Victorian armoires adorn many of the rooms. These touches, and in many cases a ceiling fan, help to obscure the more modern iconography of Waikiki outside. When making reservations, it is wise to specify a room in the old building, if that is what you want, as the Surfrider wing is more contemporary in style and decor. Be sure to book a meal at *W.C. Peacock* (see *Eating Out*). Among the amenities here are 24-hour room service, 7 meeting rooms, a concierge, secretarial services, A/V equipment, photocopiers, computers, CNN, and express checkout. 2365 Kalakaua Ave. (phone: 922-3111; 800-325-3535; fax: 737-2478; telex: 397148). Expensive.

Hawaiian Waikiki Beach – Although the rooms at the recently renamed *Holiday Inn Waikiki Beach* provide the chain's standard level of style and comfort, this hotel boasts magnificent views of the ocean and Diamond Head. It also has a terrific site: just outside the hustle-bustle of the strip, next door to Kapiolani Park and the Honolulu Zoo, and across the street from the loveliest stretch of Waikiki Beach. Its *Captain's Table,* an easygoing eatery that looks out at the sea, is a good place to sample your first mahimahi. Two meeting rooms are available for business needs, as well as A/V equipment, photocopiers, and CNN. 2570 Kalakaua Ave. (phone: 922-2511; 800-877-7666; fax: 923-3656; telex: 634226). Expensive to moderate.

Hyatt Regency – The hotel's two octagonal towers are a visual landmark among the concrete blocks along Kalakaua Avenue. The Great Hall, with its outdoor tropical garden, 3-story waterfall, and massive hanging sculpture, is a sightseeing spot in its own right. Each of its 1,230 rooms is handsomely furnished, and the art on the walls is invariably worth looking at. The suites feature some exceptional Japanese and European antiques. Guests in the Regency Club, as the 39th- and 40th-floor accommodations are known, have their own private, complimentary bar and a concierge. The pool deck is one of the most attractive in Honolulu, and the bars, cafés, and restaurants in the complex — they include *Ciao Mein, Spats* (see *Eating Out* for both), *Trapper's,* and *Harry's* — are among the very best in Waikiki. The service here is exemplary. Amenities include 24-hour room service, 8 meeting rooms, A/V equipment, photocopiers, CNN, and express checkout. 2424 Kalakaua Ave. (phone: 923-1234; 800-233-1234; fax: 923-7839; telex: 723-8278). Expensive to moderate.

Ilikai – Located at the western edge of Waikiki, this 800-room property recently underwent a multimillion-dollar face-lift, sprucing up its spacious guestrooms (some with kitchenettes; many have panoramic views) and public areas. The hotel has Waikiki's best tennis facilities, with 6 courts and pros available to provide instruction. The open area at the lobby level has pools, terraces, and fountains. The beach, Duke Kahanamoku Lagoon, and the yacht marina are just a stone's throw away. Atop the hotel sits *Annabelle's,* a disco reached via a spectacular ride in an exterior elevator that opens up vast panoramas of the Pacific as you ascend. Among the business conveniences are 12 meeting rooms, a concierge desk, secretarial services, A/V equipment, photocopiers, CNN, and express checkout. 1777 Ala Moana Blvd. (phone: 949-3811; 800-367-8434; fax: 947-4523; telex: 634555). Expensive to moderate.

Outrigger Reef – With 885 rooms, this is the largest moderately priced beachfront hotel in Waikiki. All rooms and public areas have been nicely upgraded, resulting in somewhat higher rates. Popular with young couples and singles traveling in pairs, it's right on the beach, with most of the rooms facing either toward Diamond Head or across Ft. DeRussy Beach Park to the ocean. Guests here seem to use their lanais more than those at any other hotel in the neighborhood; it's a friendly sight. Four meeting rooms, secretarial services, A/V equipment, photocopiers, computers, CNN, and express checkout are among the business amenities. 2169 Kalia Rd. (phone: 923-3111; 800-367-5170; fax: 924-4957). Expensive to moderate.

Outrigger Waikiki – Recently fully renovated and refurbished, this beachfront property features extras like a beachside health club with an exercise room and lockers for beachgoers' convenience. Four restaurants are on the property, including *Monterey Bay Canners* (see *Eating Out*). This is one of the better-priced Waikiki beachfront hotels. One meeting room is available for business needs, as well as secretarial services, A/V equipment, photocopiers, computers, and express checkout. 2335 Kalakaua Ave. (phone: 923-0711; 800-733-7777; fax: 921-9749). Expensive to moderate.

Pacific Beach – Standing on the site of the summer home of Queen Liliuokalani, this property is famous for its 280,000-gallon indoor oceanarium, which can be viewed from the hotel's bars and restaurants. Along with the swimming pool, there are tennis courts and a Jacuzzi. Recently renovated, this place is a good buy. Other pluses are 7 meeting rooms, a concierge, secretarial services, A/V equipment, photocopiers, computers, CNN, and express checkout. 2490 Kalakaua Ave. (phone: 922-1233; 800-367-6060; fax: 922-0129; telex: 633101). Expensive to moderate.

Royal Hawaiian – "The Pink Lady," as this flamingo-colored, 6-story landmark of Spanish-Moorish design is best known, is flanked by two other Sheraton properties that seem to stand in an adversary, rather than a neighborly, stance. And indeed, rumor has it along the beach that there are entrepreneurs who would not object to seeing the Lady deposed in favor of something more modern (and anonymous). Never mind. While it lasts — and one hopes it will last a long time — this is one of the two grand old hotels in Waikiki (the *Moana* is the other). The pink color scheme runs, perhaps a smidgin too obviously, throughout the hotel. Most of the rooms have either a pink sofa, quilt, or drapes. Usually it works, sometimes it doesn't. In any case, once away from the bustle of the lobby, which attracts ten times more spectators than guests, this remains the most charming hotel in Waikiki. There are 5 meeting rooms, secretarial services, A/V equipment, photocopiers, CNN, and express checkout. Reservations through the *Sheraton Waikiki,* 2259 Kalakaua Ave. (phone: 923-7311; 800-325-3535; fax: 924-7098; telex: 743-1240). Expensive to moderate.

Sheraton Waikiki – With 1,852 rooms, this establishment, the second-largest in Waikiki (surpassed only by the *Hilton Hawaiian Village*), still has the greatest number of units in one building of any hotel on the beach. Lanais on the Pacific side loom over the ocean as precipitously as a cliff. It's a splendid sensation if you don't suffer from vertigo, and the sunsets can be memorable. Happily, subtle tans and casually tropical styling have replaced the garish greens and floral designs that made the rooms and lobby rather hard on the eyes. This place has all that's expected from a big hotel: There is never a dearth of taxis, it's a pick-up point for every major tour operator, *TheBus* stops nearby, and there is just about every kind of restaurant you could crave, except a truly first class one. Ten meeting rooms, secretarial services, A/V equipment, photocopiers, computers, CNN, and AP wire service round out the business amenities. There's also a concierge desk and express checkout. 2255 Kalakaua Ave. (phone: 922-4422; 800-325-3535; fax: 923-8785; telex: 743-0115). Expensive to moderate.

Waikiki Joy – Upscale and contemporary, this hostelry has a pleasant marble entry and lounge. Steer clear of the studios on the lower-level floors, as they can be a bit noisy. The suites on the upper floors boast wonderful views of Waikiki. Fine continental fare is served at *Cappucino's* restaurant. A complimentary continental breakfast is served in the lobby each morning. There's a concierge desk, and room service is available during meal times. Secretarial services, A/V equipment, photocopiers, CNN, and express checkout are pluses. 320 Lewers St. (phone: 923-2300; 800-733-5569; fax: 955-1313). Expensive to moderate.

Ilima – Near the Ala Wai Canal, about 3 blocks from the *Royal Hawaiian Beach,* it offers the additional convenience of full kitchens in all rooms, as well as a restaurant, cocktail lounge, sauna, and pool. Business pluses include 1 meeting room, A/V equipment and photocopiers, and CNN. 2500 Kuhio Ave. (phone: 922-0811; 800-733-7777; fax: 923-0330). Moderate.

Outrigger Prince Kuhio – Quietly set on Kuhio Avenue, just 1 block from the beach, it manages to feel like a small hotel despite its 620 rooms on 37 floors. There are a maximum of 18 rooms to a floor, and each room is individually decorated and furnished, with its own wet bar and marble bathroom. The lobby is a graceful and airy place where complimentary coffee is poured from a silver samovar every morning. Rooms high on the Diamond Head side have stunning views of the crater. The top 3 floors are part of the exclusive Kuhio Club (where guests can take advantage of a concierge and other special services). There's a concierge desk, as well as 7 meeting rooms, secretarial services, A/V equipment, photocopiers, computers, CNN, and express checkout. 2500 Kuhio Ave. (phone: 922-0811; 800-733-7777; fax: 923-0330). Moderate.

Outrigger Reef Lanais – A small gem, with 54 rooms (some with kitchenettes) that look out over the expanse of Ft. DeRussy and the beach. Recent renovations have transformed this place into a stylish, well-priced alternative to the big hotels that predominate in Waikiki. One block from the beach and convenient to shops and restaurants. 225 Saratoga Ave. (phone: 923-3881; 800-737-7777). Moderate.

Outrigger Reef Towers – Although it is hard to believe that a street of concrete blocks can have character, the section of Lewers Street between Kalia Road and Kalakaua Avenue does — it's narrow and shaded by very tall, spindly coconut palms. One of the concrete blocks is this hotel. Though gorgeous vistas are not a selling point here, some people find it an excellent buy. Rooms with kitchenettes are available. Photocopiers, A/V equipment, CNN, and express checkout are all available. 227 Lewers St. (phone: 923-3111; 800-733-7777; fax: 924-6042). Moderate.

Waikiki Beachcomber – Whether you look toward the ocean, Diamond Head, or downtown, the lanais here are a pleasant spot for breakfast or cocktails. For the price, its rooms are surprisingly large, with separate dressing areas and capacious closets, and their layout and color scheme give them a feeling of coolness and comfort. The lobby has facilities for booking tours, and the hotel is a short walk from the beach. Room service is available until 9 PM, and there is a concierge, A/V equipment, photocopiers, and express checkout. 2300 Kalakaua Ave. (phone: 922-4646; 800-622-4646; fax: 923-4889). Moderate.

Waikiki Parc – Opened by the same Japanese company that owns the neighboring *Halekulani,* this hotel focuses its attention on service and high-tech features like computer-coded room locks on its 298 rooms. It's an easy walk to Waikiki Beach, a fact that isn't immediately obvious from its towering proximity to the *Halekulani* and the *Sheraton Waikiki.* The hotel's *Parc Café* serves fine fare (see *Eating Out*). There is a concierge desk, secretarial services, photocopiers, express checkout, and CNN, too. 2233 Helumoa Rd. (phone: 921-7272; 800-422-0450; fax: 923-1336). Moderate.

Waikiki Shores – By a stroke of luck, this apartment hotel stands next to the *Ft. DeRussy Army Museum* and has an unobstructed view across the museum grounds. From each wide lanai there is a panorama of both ocean and mountains. Under Aston management, some apartments have been refurbished; others are a little worse for wear. Linen, cooking utensils, and dishes are provided. There are fully equipped kitchens and weekly maid service. Cost and location combine to make this one of the best buys on the beach, especially for families. 2161 Kalia Rd. (phone: 926-4733; 800-922-7866; fax: 922-2902). Moderate.

Waikiki Terrace – Reopened in 1990 after a major overhaul, its decor has made use of grays, greens, and mauves in appealing and innovative ways. Surrounded by Fort DeRussy, most of the 255 rooms have gorgeous views from their lanais. Downstairs, the *Mezzanine* restaurant serves tasty fare (see *Eating Out*). 2045 Kalakaua Ave. (phone: 955-6000; 800-445-8811; fax: 943-8555). Moderate.

Waikikian – For many returning visitors, the torches that blaze outside each night signal that they are once more entering the fabled resort area. More torches line the narrow path that passes between the Polynesian cabañas that are the hotel's salient feature. These are decorated in Hawaiian motifs, with ceiling fans, exposed timber ceilings, and wooden lanais, all contributing to the South Seas atmosphere. Some units also have kitchenettes. An adjacent 6-story contemporary building offers more conventional accommodations. The beach, a romantic lagoon, and a particularly attractive palm-fringed poolside area with a popular outdoor café called the *Tahitian Lanai* (see *Eating Out*) complete the amenities. Room service is available until 10 PM, and there's a concierge desk, photocopiers, and CNN. 1811 Ala Moana Blvd. (phone: 949-5331; 800-922-7866; fax: 946-2843). Moderate.

Ocean Resort Hotel Waikiki – Just 1 block from 220-acre Kapiolani Park at the foot of Diamond Head, the formerly named *Quality Inn Waikiki* has always enjoyed a good reputation for service and comfort. Some rooms in the older Diamond Head Tower and all the rooms in the newer Pali Tower have kitchenettes, although the newer accommodations tend to be larger and more subdued in decor. There are 2 swimming pools for people who find the 3-minute stroll to the beach too strenuous. 175 Paoakalani Ave. (phone: 922-3861; 800-228-5151; fax: 924-1982). Moderate to inexpensive.

Outrigger Edgewater – This small hostelry manages to look more like a seaside apartment house than a hotel and exudes an air of calm and quiet. For those who find the hurly-burly of large establishments either intimidating or just plain exhausting, this is the ideal spot at an ideal price. An added attraction is the *Trattoria,* a well-regarded Italian restaurant. A concierge, CNN, and express checkout are pluses. 2168 Kalia Rd. (phone: 922-6424; 800-733-7777; fax: 922-6424; telex: 634178). Moderate to inexpensive.

Outrigger Waikiki Village – Brightly decorated with an emphasis on greens and blues, this member of the Outrigger chain is popular with young couples making a first visit to Hawaii. The poolside area is, if anything, busier than many others in the district, considering that the ocean is just 2 blocks away. Perhaps what attracts so many is its underwater viewing area. Some rooms have kitchenettes; all have CNN. Photocopiers are available for guests' use. 240 Lewers St. (phone: 923-3881; 800-733-7777; fax: 922-2330). Moderate to inexpensive.

Pleasant Holiday Isle – Right in the heart of Waikiki and just a block from the beach, this is a compact hotel, though it's beginning to look a bit faded. The rates are reasonable, which more than compensates for the fact that from most of the lanais, the view is less than indelible, and the street noise is occasionally audible. There's 1 meeting room, photocopiers, and CNN. 270 Lewers St. (phone: 923-0777). Moderate to inexpensive.

Royal Islander – Another stopping place where smallness is an advantage. The front-desk personnel usually manage to remember guests' names. Recently renovated rooms are on the small side, though not oppressively so, and each has a lanai, refrigerator, and coffee makers on request. Street noise may prove bothersome. The property is now managed by the Outrigger chain and is opposite the *Reef* hotel, behind which is the beach. 2164 Kalia Rd. (phone: 922-1961; 800-733-7777; fax: 456-4329). Moderate to inexpensive.

Waikiki Parkside – Overlooking Fort DeRussy and Ala Moana Boulevard, it offers CNN, indoor parking ($4), with shopping, restaurants, and the beach minutes away. One meeting room is available for business needs. 1850 Ala Moana Blvd. (phone: 955-1567; 800-237-9666; fax: 955-6010). Moderate to inexpensive.

Royal Grove – A small apartment hotel with personality. Like the *Royal Hawaiian,* it is painted pink. There are very comfortable, cheerful studios as well as 1-bedroom units. Although the ocean, a block and a half away, is visible from some of the lanais, many people prefer to look out on the pool and tropical gardens. Most rooms have air conditioning and kitchenettes. There is maid service but no room service. 151 Uluniu Ave. (phone: 923-7691). Inexpensive.

Waikiki Surf – One of the "finds" of Honolulu. In a semi-residential part of Waikiki, it's friendly, clean, decorated in blue and green, quiet, and delightfully inexpensive. Some rooms have kitchenettes. Perhaps best of all, the 288-room hotel has two companions — the 102-room *Waikiki Surf East* (422 Royal Hawaiian Ave.) and the 110-room *Waikiki Surf West* (412 Lewers St.) — owned and run by the same very friendly people. The original *Waikiki Surf* is at 2200 Kuhio Ave. (switchboard for all three properties: 923-7671; 800-733-7777; fax: 921-4804). Inexpensive.

CONDOMINIUMS

Aston Waikiki Beach Tower – With only four 2-bedroom apartments to a floor, this is Waikiki's most exclusive rentable condominium. The views, particularly on floors 25 to 40, are magnificent, with large lanais offering front-row seats as the sun slides into the Pacific. Another prime asset is privacy — the perfect antidote to the street energy of Waikiki. Full concierge service, with the beach just across the street. 2470 Kalakaua Ave. (phone: 926-6400; 800-922-3368; fax: 926-7380). Very expensive to expensive.

Aston's Waikiki Sunset – Recent renovations and refurbishing have added to the appeal of this high-rise property, which is convenient to Waikiki Beach and Kapiolani Park. Besides swimming in the large pool, guests can play tennis or shuffleboard. Daily maid service. 229 Paoakalani Ave. (phone: 922-0511; 800-922-7866; fax: 923-8580). Expensive to moderate.

Coconut Plaza Waikiki – This 84-studio unit condominium faces a small landscaped garden and the Ala Wai Canal. The ambience is relaxed, with complimentary continental breakfast served alfresco. Some units have kitchenettes; the complex also has a restaurant and a pool. A good buy. 450 Lewers St. (phone: 923-8828; 800-882-9696). Expensive to moderate.

Foster Tower – For location alone — right across Kalakaua Avenue from the beach — this is one of Waikiki's better buys. All rooms have color television sets, and on the property are a pool and shops. No maid service. 2500 Kalakaua Ave. (phone: 523-7785; 800-367-7040; fax: 537-3701). Moderate.

Island Colony – Another luxury high-rise looking out on the Koolau Mountains and the canal, it is decorated with bleached-wood furniture, light brown walls and textiles, and beige carpets, giving it a pleasantly restful appearance. It also has a restaurant, pool, sauna, and hydromassage facilities, as well as a Jacuzzi. Daily maid service. 445 Seaside Ave. (phone: 923-2345; 800-92-ASTON; fax: 922-0991). Moderate.

Pacific Monarch – Close to the *Kings Alley* shopping bazaar and a few minutes from the beach, the property offers spectacular views from its upper-floor 1-bedroom and studio units and the rooftop pool area. Laundry facilities and daily maid service. 142 Uluniu Ave. (phone: 923-9805; 800-367-6046 or 800-777-1700; fax: 924-3220). Moderate.

Royal Kuhio – Two blocks away from the beach and the *International Market Place,* it has upper-floor units that offer some of the best views of Diamond Head in Waikiki. On the 7th-floor deck, there is a pool and shuffleboard. Maid service. 2240 Kuhio Ave. (phone: 923-0555; 800-367-8047). Moderate.

Waikiki Banyan – One of the largest condos in Waikiki, it's a short walk from the beach, zoo, and the *Ala Wai* golf course. The living rooms are handsomely decorated and have attractive breakfast counters that separate them from the kitchen. The building contains a sauna, a large recreation area with tennis courts and a swimming pool, laundry facilities on each floor, and daily maid service. From the top floor on the Diamond Head side you see beyond the crater to Maunalua Bay. 201 Ohua Ave. (phone: 922-0555; 800-366-7765; fax: 922-0906). Moderate.

Waikiki Lanais – With its attractively furnished 1- and 2-bedroom apartments on one of Waikiki's quieter streets, this well-maintained condominium features a mix of vacation rentals and full-time residences that adds to its appeal, as does its location near the beach and the commercial heart of Waikiki. 2452 Tusitala St. (phone: 923-0994; 800-367-7042; or call *Condo Rentals of Waikiki;* phone: 923-0555; fax: 544-1868). Moderate.

DIAMOND HEAD

Colony Surf – A true Hollywood-style condominium right on the beach, it is one of the most delightful places to stay in Honolulu. Apartments are decorated in the plush, off-white tones that many people associate with seaside living. There are no lanais, but large windows with glorious views. Kitchens are modern and fully equipped, and there is daily maid service and adequate laundry facilities. The small, elegant lobby leads to *Michel's* restaurant (see *Eating Out*). Studios with lanais and kitchenettes are available in the adjacent *Colony East* hotel, which is owned and operated by the same company at the same address, but lacks the flair and views of the main building. 2895 Kalakaua Ave. (phone: 923-5751; 800-252-7873; fax: 922-8433). Expensive to moderate.

Diamond Head Beach – This 14-story structure on the beach was completely refurbished in 1986 to make it one of the more attractive places in terms of price and location in Honolulu. Units range from hotel rooms to 1-bedroom apartments. Rooms are smallish but comfortable, with good-size lanais. Although there is little in the way of a lobby and no shops, pool, or tour desks, these are available close by, in the *New Otani*. Services include a concierge desk and photocopiers. CNN is available. 2947 Kalakaua Ave. (phone: 922-1928; 800-367-6046; fax: 924-8980). Expensive to moderate.

New Otani Kaimana Beach – The location is the thing here: on the Diamond Head side of Kapiolani Park, just a few minutes away from Waikiki by foot or bus. The beach is right outside, and beautiful reefs are within easy snorkeling distance. The *Hau Tree Lanai* terrace restaurant overlooks the beach and is edged by (and named for) large hau trees, and *Miyako* serves *shabu shabu*–style cooking (see *Eating Out* for both). Oceanside rooms have stunning views. Families seem to like this hotel, and women traveling alone have found it a friendly, hospitable, and safe haven. There's a concierge desk, as well as secretarial services, 2 meeting rooms, A/V equipment, photocopiers, CNN, and express checkout. 2863 Kalakaua Ave. (phone: 923-1555; 800-657-7949; fax: 922-9404; telex: 743-0470). Expensive to moderate.

MIDTOWN

Ala Moana – Bright, sunny rooms in lively tropical colors and just about every kind of hotel service imaginable are two of the things that help this 36-story property compensate for not being close enough to the Waikiki beaches to be in the swing. The hotel's size can sometimes be a disadvantage; although the room staff and managers seem very helpful, a somewhat impersonal feeling pervades. A concierge, CNN, and express checkout all are available, as are 7 meeting rooms, secretarial services, A/V equipment, photocopiers, and computers. 410 Atkinson Dr. (phone: 955-4811; 800-367-6025; fax: 944-2974; telex: 947-4705). Expensive to moderate.

Manoa Valley Inn – This may be Honolulu's most complete bed and breakfast facility, with 8 bedrooms in a beautifully restored turn-of-the-century Manoa Valley home or a separate cottage, and it is highly recommended. Rates include an ample continental breakfast, afternoon pupus, and sunset cocktails. Bus connections to *Ala Moana Center,* and from there to all other parts of Oahu, are available. About 2 miles from Waikiki, at 2001 Vancouver Dr. (phone: 947-6019; 800-634-5115; fax: 946-6168). Expensive to moderate.

GREATER HONOLULU

Kahala Hilton – Operated by Hilton International (which is now run by Britain's Ladbrooke group), this is one of the chain's prime showpieces. Queen Elizabeth II spent a couple of nights here, and King Juan Carlos of Spain came for part of his honeymoon with Queen Sophia. The main structure of this lavish hostelry is 12 stories high and overlooks a glorious 800-foot stretch of beach that loses nothing by being manmade. Additional beachside bungalows and a 2-story wing watch over a large lagoon in which dolphins, turtles, and penguins cavort. Rooms in the main building have charming semicircular lanais decorated with bougainvillea. Relatively recent renovation and refurbishing have put them at least on a par with those in the finest hotels. The lobby is an absolute masterpiece — with handsome chandeliers and a stunning circular carpet — that manages to look plush and airy at the same time. Guests are greeted with chilled whole pineapple, and an orchid is laid on each pillow when beds are turned down in the evening. Besides ocean and pool swimming, the hotel provides kayaks and snorkeling equipment and can arrange deep-sea fishing and scuba diving; and there are several fine restaurants (see *Eating Out*). "Kamp Kahala" keeps children ages 6 to 12 happily occupied with a series of activities designed to entertain energetic youngsters. European efficiency at the executive level and island good humor at the service level are the keynotes here. They work together like a charm. Business amenities include 3 meeting rooms, secretarial services, A/V equipment, photocopiers, and computers. CNN, 24-hour room service, a concierge, and express checkout are also available. 5000 Kahala Ave., Kahala (phone: 734-2211; 800-367-2525; fax: 947-7914). Very expensive to expensive.

ELSEWHERE

Ke Iki Hale – Set on an acre and a half of palm-fringed beachfront in Haleiwa, about an hour's drive from Honolulu, these charming cottages contain 1 or 2 bedrooms, full kitchens; and large picture windows afford fine views. Recreational facilities include a volleyball court, barbecues, and picnic tables overlooking the water. Maid service is not available. 59-579 Ke Iki Rd., Haleiwa (phone: 638-8229). Expensive.

Plantation Spa – This 7-acre holistic retreat on the Windward Coast, owned and run by Dave and Bodil Anderson, provides a place for 18 guests to enjoy week-long programs that include kayaking, hiking, snorkeling, yoga, aquacize aerobics, massage, and evening speakers who discourse on things healthful and Hawaiian. There's no regimented schedule to follow, just a wide range of daily activities designed to get you out there and generate some nature-induced high energy. Accommodations are in the main house or in cozy nearby cottages, and all meals are prepared for strict vegetarians. Two-night programs start at $357, with the full 6-night program priced at $995 (includes two massages and an herbal wrap). 51-550 Kamehameha Hwy., Kaaawa (phone: 237-8685; 800-422-0307). Expensive.

Sheraton Makaha – The cottages at this resort in central Oahu are among the most attractive accommodations on the island, handsomely furnished in bold tropical motifs set off by cut flowers and plants and surrounded by well-tended lawns and groves of blossoming trees. The beautiful golf course has a resident pro to help those whose game is not quite up to championship standards. There are also tennis courts, riding stables, a croquet lawn, a large swimming pool, and a beautifully restored *heiau* (ancient Hawaiian temple). From its elegant patio you can see the ocean a mile down the valley. Perhaps the only drawback is its distance from the ocean, although to compensate, the resort offers a complete beach program of scuba, snorkeling, swimming, even canoeing in an outrigger, all supervised by experts who know the caprices of the waters around here. 84-626 Makaha Valley Rd., Makaha (phone: 695-9511; 800-325-3535). Expensive.

Turtle Bay Hilton – This North Shore resort has just about everything that you could possibly want on a vacation. There are miles of beautiful beach, including tiny, idyllic Kuilima Cove, one of the few places on this side of the island where you can swim year-round. In addition, the hotel offers the new Arnold Palmer–designed course (a second Palmer course, available for play at the end of next year, will replace the original George Fazio course), tennis, scuba diving, snorkeling, and horseback riding. Tennis programs and tennis camp are offered by the *Nick Bollettieri Tennis Academy* (phone: 800-USA-NICK). The guestrooms are large and on the whole quite elegant, particularly since a property-wide renovation was completed in 1990. Winter, when it is damp and cloudy, may not be the best time to visit if you are looking for a placid ocean and a deep tan, but once you have been lulled to sleep by the pounding surf along the Kuilima beaches, any other sleeping aid will seem ineffectual. The range of accommodations here is wide, from bay-view rooms to ocean-view rooms to separate cottages, cabañas, and executive suites. 57-091 Kamehameha Hwy., Kahuku (phone: 293-8811; 800-445-8667; fax: 293-9147). Expensive.

EATING OUT: Once a culinary wasteland that thrived on Spam and two scoops of rice with macaroni salad, Honolulu now sits close to the apex of an emerging regional cuisine that blends the best foods and spices of Asia and the Pacific with European styles and sauces. Don't expect Paris on the Pacific, but today, many Honolulu restaurants delight visitors with dishes that utilize local Hawaiian fish and tropical fruits and vegetables in imaginative ways (although finding authentic Hawaiian fare in Honolulu takes some doing). With Hawaii's proximity to Asia, places serving authentic Pacific Rim specialties abound, as do traditional continental restaurants. These are old favorites and new, to be enjoyed by anyone looking for a delightful meal in pleasant surroundings. Expect to pay $100 or more for two people at those places we've described as very expensive; between $60 and $95 at those places listed as expensive; between $25 and $55 for moderate; and under $25, inexpensive. Prices don't include drinks, wine, or tips. All telephone numbers are in the 808 area code unless otherwise indicated.

WAIKIKI

La Mer – The distinctive menu suits one of Hawaii's most refined restaurants. Start with an appetizer of grilled filet with steamed asparagus and orange sauce, then move on to roast duck with cherries marmalade and port wine sauce. The service is excellent and the decor an appealing blend of Oriental styles. Open daily from 6 to 10 PM. Reservations necessary. Major credit cards accepted. *Halekulani,* 2199 Kalia Rd. (phone: 923-2311). Very expensive to expensive.

The Secret – One of the top dining rooms in Honolulu, it has consistently won prizes for its cooking. Guests dine in a setting of high-backed rattan chairs with red velvet cushions, strolling musicians, a carp pool, and a fountain. Among the house specialties are medallions of veal *forêt noire* and rack of spring lamb. For dessert there are Polynesian fruits with kirsch, followed by well-made Irish coffee. Oenophiles can select a rare vintage or two from the vast 6,000-bottle wine room. Open daily for dinner. Reservations advised. Major credit cards accepted; there is a $15 minimum charge. In the *Hawaiian Regent Hotel,* 2552 Kalakaua Ave. (phone: 922-6611). Very expensive to expensive.

Bali by the Sea – Contemporary elegance, enhanced by a mix of cool whites and Mediterranean pastels, sets the scene for seaside dining. The food is excellent, with appetizers like *coquille* of shrimp and scallops with ginger sauce, enticing entrées such as Kaiwi Channel opakapaka with fresh basil, and a concluding irresistible dessert tray. Open daily for dinner. Reservations advised. Major credit cards accepted. Valet parking is available. *Hilton Hawaiian Village Rainbow Tower,* 2005 Kalia Rd. (phone: 949-4321). Expensive.

Chez Michel – The same Michel who lent his name to the *Colony Surf* hotel also created this place. He's retired, but the restaurant remains popular. Just outside the *Hilton Hawaiian Village* end of Waikiki in Eaton Square, it is lush with plants and boasts a rich French decor. The menu is varied, well prepared, and nicely presented. Open daily. Reservations advised. Major credit cards accepted. 444 Hobron La. (phone: 955-7866). Expensive.

Hy's Steak House – Entering this place is like walking into a magnificent Victorian private library, full of velvet chairs and etched glass. But the gleaming brass broiler inside a glassed-in gazebo, where steaks and chops are prepared with loving care, demonstrates that it is something more. Although the menu indicates that chicken and seafood are available, the main attraction is steaks, which are merely superb. Open daily for dinner. Reservations advised. Major credit cards accepted. 2440 Kuhio Ave. (phone: 922-5555). Expensive.

Musashi – This very elegant Japanese restaurant in the *Hyatt Regency Waikiki* features three styles of at-the-table preparation as well as a wide-ranging menu of Japanese specialties. Tabletop *teppanyaki* grill; cooked-in broth *shabu shabu* dishes; and cooked-in-sauce sukiyaki dishes are all prepared at the table. There's also an excellent sushi bar. Appealing multilevel decor includes small rock gardens and pools. Open daily for dinner. Reservations advised. Major credit cards accepted. 2424 Kalakana Ave. (phone: 923-1234). Expensive.

Nick's Fishmarket – One of the best fish places in Honolulu. Don't let the earthy name confuse you; this is a plush establishment with individually controlled lighting systems for those customers seated at banquettes and rather too many staffers per customer — the attention can occasionally be stifling. Live Maine lobsters are available at substantial cost, but this is also the ideal place to sample fresh island fish, such as opakapaka, mahimahi, and ulua. The combination seafood Louis salad is enormous and beautifully prepared. Open daily for dinner. Reservations advised. Major credit cards accepted. In the *Waikiki Gateway Hotel,* 2070 Kalakaua Ave. (phone: 955-6333). Expensive.

Prince Court – Chef Gary Strehl is the secret behind the success of this elegant spot featuring imaginative Hawaii regional cookery and specializing in local fish. Highlights of the menu include blackened blue ahi and kiawe grilled capon. Everything is artistically arranged, and the service is impeccable. Open daily for breakfast, lunch and dinner, as well as Sunday brunch. Reservations advised. Major credit cards accepted. *Hawaii Prince Hotel,* 100 Holomoana St. (phone: 956-1111). Expensive.

Ship's Tavern – This elegant place is decorated in an appealing mix of gray, white, and celadon green, complementing its natural backdrop of Diamond Head and the Pacific. The menu is nothing short of superb, with selections ranging from familiar standbys (such as New England clam chowder) to more unusual offerings (like sautéed filet of veal in morel sauce). Dinner nightly from 5 to 10 PM. Reservations advised. Major credit cards accepted. In the *Sheraton Moana Surfrider Hotel* (phone: 922-3111). Expensive.

Bon Appetit – Perhaps Honolulu's best French dining place, it has the look of an elegant bistro in the French provinces with its cane-back chairs and light pink linen. The menu is imaginative and includes an unusual scallop mousse, bouillabaisse, and snails in puff pastry. Closed Sundays. Reservations advised. Major credit cards accepted. In the Discovery Bay complex at 1778 Ala Moana Blvd. (phone: 942-3837). Expensive to moderate.

Ciao Mein – The *Hyatt Regency*'s original signature restaurant, *Bagwell's,* has been replaced by this gem. An eclectic menu of Italian and Chinese dishes includes delicate fried spring rolls, inspired fettuccine Alfredo, and tender pieces of lobster wrapped in noodles. Without a doubt, this is some of the finest fare in Hawaii. It offers indoor and alfresco seating nightly from 6 to 10 PM. Reservations advised. Major credit cards accepted. In the *Hyatt Regency Hotel,* 2424 Kalakaua Ave. (phone: 923-1234). Expensive to moderate.

Furusato – There are two branches of this Japanese restaurant in Waikiki. Each has its own menu and ambience; both are comfortable if not elegant. The kitchens generally offer a range of steaks, seafood, and sushi. Open daily for lunch and dinner. Reservations advised. Major credit cards accepted. *Hyatt Regency* (phone: 922-4991) and *Foster Tower* condominium (phone: 922-5502). Expensive to moderate.

Golden Dragon – Perhaps Hawaii's most elegant Chinese dining room, the food happily lives up to the surroundings. One specialty, Imperial Beggar's chicken, is wrapped in lotus leaves with spices, then cooked for 6 hours inside a sealed clay pot to retain natural juices and flavor. Another specialty is the Peking roast duck, and be sure to leave room for the celestial desserts. Thanks to the exquisite decorative flourishes, dining indoors is as appealing as alfresco. Open daily for dinner. Reservations advised. Major credit cards accepted. Valet parking available. *Hilton Hawaiian Village Rainbow Tower,* 2005 Kalia Rd. (phone: 949-4321). Expensive to moderate.

Matteo's – Low lighting, pleasant decor, and high-backed banquettes all conspire to make this a place for quiet dining. The service is good, as is the food which includes such highly recommended dishes as calamari, chicken, and veal. Open daily for dinner, from 6 PM to midnight; the bar is open until 2 AM. Reservations advised. Major credit cards accepted. In the *Marine Surf Hotel,* 364 Seaside Ave. (phone: 922-5551). Expensive to moderate.

Orchids – Sliding French doors that open onto a green lawn and expansive views of Diamond Head and the sea are a perfect backdrop for crisp white linen and tables elegantly set with silver, crystal, and fresh flowers. Breakfast is a highlight, as is the Sunday brunch, though lunch and dinner also are first-rate. Open daily. Reservations necessary. Major credit cards accepted. *Halekulani Hotel,* 2199 Kalia Rd. (phone: 923-2311). Expensive to moderate.

Roy's Park Bistro – Master chef Roy Yamaguchi, whose first restaurant put Hawaii Kai on the map with an exceptional Eurasian menu, goes Mediterranean in Waikiki, with amazing results. This is food to savor, accompanied by a wine list that is also worthy of praise. Open for breakfast, lunch, and dinner. Reservations advised. Major credit cards accepted. In the *Park Plaza Waikiki Hotel,* 1956 Ala Moana Blvd. (phone: 944-4624). Expensive to moderate.

Zuke Bistro – This classy remake of a once-humble spot now offers a setting compatible with the high quality of the fish, meat, and poultry dishes cooked by the owner-chef. Be prepared for a bit of a wait at the table — each order is prepared from scratch, which takes time. Open daily for dinner, except Sundays. Reservations advised. Major credit cards accepted. 2171 Ala Wai Blvd. (phone: 922-0102). Expensive to moderate.

Baci – Located in the *Waikiki Trade Center,* this modern eatery is a popular spot for business lunches and makes a convenient stop for shopping breaks. Sample the northern Italian pasta specialties — they're the best in the islands. Open for lunch weekdays, dinner daily, 5:30 to 11 PM. Reservations advised. Major credit cards accepted. Ground level, *Waikiki Trade Center,* 2255 Kuhio Ave. (phone: 924-2533). Moderate.

Mezzanine – Devotees of dining that teeters on the cutting edge will appreciate the unusual "designer" pizza served here, where toppings include everything from goat cheese to cilantro (a licorice-tasting type of parsley). Less adventurous folks can try the rack of lamb grilled over local kiawe wood, numerous pasta dishes, as well as sautéed and blackened fish dishes. There's indoor and alfresco seating to suit your fancy, as well as nightly entertainment. Open daily; on weekends, open for breakfast and dinner only. Reservations advised. Major credit cards accepted. In the *Waikiki Terrace Hotel,* 2045 Kalakaua Ave. (phone: 955-6000). Moderate.

Monterey Bay Canners – The Waikiki branch of this restaurant, in the *Outrigger Waikiki* hotel, offers a limited number of alfresco tables that take full advantage of the beachfront location. The best bet on the menu is one of the catch-of-the-day specials, which are reasonably priced and delicious. Open daily. Reservations advised for dinner. Major credit cards accepted. 2335 Kalakaua Ave. (phone: 922-5761). Moderate.

Parc Café – Although the menu is limited to four entrées a night, plus a buffet, the food is delicious and the prices are reasonable. Prime ribs, pasta, chicken, and the catch of the day are usual fare. Sunday brunch is recommended. Open daily for lunch and dinner. Reservations advised. Major credit cards accepted. In the *Waikiki Parc Hotel,* 2198 Kalia Rd. (phone: 921-7272). Moderate.

Siam Inn – There has been high praise for this Thai place in the heart of Waikiki, where imported spices and fresh local produce and seafood are combined to advantage. Normally fiery Thai dishes are prepared with Western tastebuds in mind. Open daily for lunch and dinner. Reservations unnecessary. Major credit cards accepted. 407 Seaside (phone: 926-8802). Moderate.

Singha Thai – This spot serves authentic Thai appetizers, soups, curries, seafood, and noodle and rice dishes, prepared by Chef Chai Chaowasaree. Before he came to Honolulu, Chaowasaree owned an award-winning restaurant in Bangkok. Open Mondays through Saturdays for lunch, daily for dinner. Reservations advised. Major credit cards accepted. 1910 Ala Moana Blvd, across from the *Hilton Hawaiian Village* (phone: 941-2898). Moderate.

Spats – Dinner in a well-known disco might not sound very promising, but don't let what goes on after 9 PM deter you from coming here. The decor recalls a rather lavish speakeasy, with beveled glass, highly polished wood, and waiters in cutaways and suspenders. Try the chicken *alla cacciatore* or shrimp *all' aglio e olio* (with garlic and oil). Fettuccine Alfredo is the star attraction among the pasta. Open daily. Reservations advised for dinner. Major credit cards accepted. *Hyatt Regency Hotel,* 2424 Kalakaua Ave. (phone: 923-1234). Moderate.

Trattoria – The chef doesn't overload the menu with tomato paste, and many dishes are cooked al burro — delicately, in butter — instead of doused in olive oil. The lasagna in this charmingly decorated restaurant is well worth tasting. So are *cotoletta di vitello alla parmigiana* and *pollo alla romana.* The *cannelloni milanese* is definitely a "don't miss." Open daily for dinner. Reservations necessary on weekends. Major credit cards accepted. *Outrigger Edgewater Hotel,* 2168 Kalia Rd. (phone: 923-8415). Moderate.

W.C. Peacock – Mr. Peacock developed the *Moana* hotel in 1901 and helped develop Waikiki Beach as a tourist destination; now his name has been immortalized by this Waikiki restaurant. An open-air seaside spot with a big beach view, specialties of the house include Kona crab cakes, lamb chop Java in a special peanut sauce, duck Chinatown with ginger and mango relish, and lilikoi chiffon cake. Open nightly from 5:30 to 10:30 PM. Reservations advised. Major credit cards accepted. *Sheraton Moana Surfrider Hotel,* 2365 Kalakaua Ave. (phone: 922-3111). Moderate.

Dynasty I – An excellent, family-style Chinese eatery in Waikiki, this spot is best known for its sizzling platters, fresh prawns, roast duck, and reasonable prices. Open 24 hours. Reservations unnecessary. Major credit cards accepted. In the *Hawaii Dynasty Hotel,* 1830 Ala Moana Blvd. (phone: 947-3771). Moderate to inexpensive.

Hard Rock Café – The Honolulu branch of this trendy international chain attracts a young crowd out to be part of "the scene." Food is good, crowds are standard day or night, and the noise level is decibels higher than that which allows comfortable conversation. But, then, that's intended to be part of the appeal. Guitars of famous rockers are part of the decor, as are other blasts of rock 'n' roll memorabilia, and patrons come as much to buy T-shirts and other signature souvenirs as to eat or drink. Valet parking. Open daily from 11:30 AM to midnight. No reservations. Major credit cards accepted. 1837 Kapiolani Blvd. (phone: 955-7383). Moderate to inexpensive.

Caffè Guccini – The warm welcome at this low-key café is followed by fine pasta, rich cappuccino, and tempting desserts. Guests may bring their own wine or beer, but there's also a full bar. Open daily from 3 to 11:30 PM. Reservations unnecessary. MasterCard and Visa accepted. 2139 Kuhio Ave. (phone: 922-5287). Inexpensive.

Eggs 'n Things – In the wee hours after Waikiki's nightclubs close, this popular all-night breakfast club starts to hum. Open daily from 11 to 2 PM. No reservations or credit cards accepted. 1911B Kalakaua Ave. (phone: 949-0820). Inexpensive.

Ono Hawaiian Foods – In Hawaiian *ono* means delicious, and for years the search for good Hawaiian food in Honolulu has ended here. Try the chicken long rice soup (slender noodles and chicken in a clear broth) or kalua pig (shredded roast pork). Open 11 AM to 7:30 PM Mondays through Saturdays. No reservations. No credit cards accepted. 726 Kapahulu Ave. (phone: 737-2275). Inexpensive.

Tahitian Lanai – Better hurry before the long-rumored wrecker's ball destroys this last remnant of early Polynesian–style Waikiki. Here you dine by the sea under thatch-roofed shacks, and on a steamy Honolulu night, when ukuleles plink in the bar, there's no greater fun this side of Bora Bora. Seafood is recommended here, and Sunday brunch features eggs Benedict and Portuguese sausage. Open for breakfast, lunch, and dinner daily. Reservations advised. Major credit cards accepted. *Waikikian Hotel,* 1811 Ala Moana Blvd. (phone: 946-6541). Inexpensive.

DIAMOND HEAD

Michel's – At most beachfront restaurants in Honolulu, the cooking takes a back seat to the view. Not here. For a start, the decor does not suggest a mere extension of sand and sea. The dining room is elegant and subdued. Although there are occasionally deft local touches, such as prosciutto served with papaya, most of the dishes tend to be classic. Even the opakapaka is served *Véronique* — with champagne sauce and grapes. Jacket required for dinner. Sunday brunch here is a tradition (see *Quintessential Honolulu,* DIVERSIONS). Open daily for breakfast from 7 to 11 AM, lunch from 11:30 AM to 3 PM, and dinner from 5:30 to 10 PM. Reservations necessary. Major credit cards accepted. In the *Colony Surf Hotel,* 2895 Kalakaua Ave. (phone: 923-6552). Very expensive to expensive.

Hau Tree Lanai – One of the best alfresco locales in Waikiki, with beachside patio seating beneath the ancient tree that gives this restaurant its name. Soft-shell crabs, New York strip steaks, and Cajun sashimi are some of the dinner offerings. Open for breakfast from 6:30 to 11 AM, lunch from 11:30 AM to 2:30 PM, and dinner from 5:30 to 9:00 PM. Reservations advised. Major credit cards accepted. In the *New Otani Kaimana Beach Hotel,* 2863 Kalakaua Ave. (phone: 923-1555). Expensive to moderate.

Miyako – *Shabu shabu*–style cooking (meat, vegetables, and seafood prepared in boiling water at the table) is emphasized here. Seating is either in the main dining room with its rooftop, oceanside views, or in small tatami rooms where guests sit on mats on the floor. Two days' advance notice will procure the special Kaiseiki dinner, a set menu of 7, 8, or 9 courses, all making use of the freshest produce, fish, and seafood available that day. Open daily for dinner from 6 to 10 PM. Reservations advised. Major credit cards accepted. *New Otani Kaimana Beach Hotel,* 2863 Kalakaua Ave. (phone: 923-1555). Expensive to moderate.

Keo's – This is a fine place to sample Thai fare, which can be flavorful and fiery, although the kitchen will prepare milder versions of its hot specialties if requested. Mint-flavored spring rolls make a delicious appetizer, and cold sweet tea is a good accompaniment for the spicier dishes. The setting is elegant and nearly drenched in orchids; the crowd, Honolulu's cognoscenti. Open daily for dinner from 5 to 10:30 PM. Reservations necessary. Major credit cards accepted. 625 Kapahulu Ave. (phone: 737-8240). Moderate.

MIDTOWN

John Dominis – Spectacularly located on a promontory overlooking the Kewalo Basin and the Pacific, this dramatic eatery has floor-to-ceiling windows to showcase the extraordinary views. Inside the dining room, at a central island lavishly laden with fruits of the sea, a chef shucks oysters, steams clams, and makes broth. In saltwater pools spiny lobsters and fresh local fish clamber and swim around. This is the ideal place to sample island seafood: ono (wahoo), onaga (red snapper), and opakapaka (white snapper) are all available in season. The *cioppino* (fish stew) and fresh fish cooked in tomatoes, herbs, and spices are unbeatable. Open daily for dinner. Reservations necessary. Major credit cards accepted. 43 Ahui St. (phone: 523-0955). Very expensive to expensive.

Nicholas Nickolas – Fine dining amid soft lights and elegance atop the 40-floor *Ala Moana* hotel, which affords magnificent views. The extensive menu focuses on both American and continental specialties, ranging from veal to lamb, with pasta, soups, salads, and catch-of-the-day entrées in between. Open daily from 5:30 to 11:30 PM, with live entertainment from 9:30 PM to 2:30 AM weekdays, to 3:30 AM on weekends. Reservations advised. Major credit cards accepted. 410 Atkinson Dr. (phone: 955-4466). Expensive.

Andrew's – When you're yearning for homemade cannelloni, this place prepares some of the best anywhere. Other favorites on the Italian/continental menu include seafood with linguini and first-rate veal dishes. Hawaiian entertainer Mahi Beamer sings and plays the piano nightly Wednesdays through Saturdays. Open weekdays for lunch; Sunday for brunch; daily for dinner. Reservations advised. Major credit cards accepted. *Ward Center,* 1200 Ala Moana Blvd. (phone: 523-8677). Expensive to moderate.

Café Cambio – Northern Italian fare combines with southern highlights like cioppino and an *antipasto misto.* The owner is from Turin, which helps make this place the real thing. Open for lunch weekdays from 11 AM to 2 PM, and dinner daily from 5:30 to 10:15 PM; closed Mondays. Reservations necessary for lunch only. Major credit cards accepted. 1680 Kapiolani Blvd., adjacent to the *Kapiolani Theater* (phone: 942-0740). Moderate.

Café Sistina – One of Honolulu's hipper establishments, its trattoria atmosphere attracts a mixed crowd, who come for the excellent cooking and live jazz music. The menu, similar to *Café Cambio* (same owner), is northern Italian, with delicious pasta, meat, and fish specialties. Open daily. Reservations taken until 8 PM; after that, there's likely to be a wait at the door for first-come, first-served seating. Major credit cards accepted. 1314 S. King St. (phone: 526-0071). Moderate.

Compadres – Delicious Mexican food, a comfortable setting, and good prices make this a popular spot. Open daily for breakfast from 9:30 to 11:30 AM, lunch from 11 AM to 2:30 PM, and dinner from 5 to 10 PM. On Saturdays and Sundays, a weekend brunch is served from 10:30 AM to 2 PM. Reservations advised. Major credit cards accepted. *Ward Center* (phone: 523-1307). Moderate.

Fisherman's Wharf – Tuna and charter boats tie up at the dock beside this seafront place with a nautical atmosphere. Open daily. Reservations advised. Major credit cards accepted. 1009 Ala Moana Blvd., Kewalo Basin (phone: 538-3808). Moderate.

Il Fresco – High-tech design and tables set with crystal and linen fit its chic location. A varied menu features blackened ahi (tuna) and pasta. Open daily for dinner from 6 to 10 PM; Mondays through Fridays for lunch from 11:30 AM to 2 PM. Reservations advised. Major credit cards accepted. *Ward Center* (enter on Auahi St.; phone: 523-5191). Moderate.

Horatio's – The nautical decor is most appropriate in this tavern overlooking the Kewalo Boat Basin. Among the house specialties worth trying are island seafood and Nebraska beef. Freshly baked Russian rye bread accompanies each entrée. Open daily for lunch from 11 AM to 5 PM, and dinner from 5 to 10 PM. Reservations recommended Fridays and Saturdays. Major credit cards accepted. *Ward Warehouse,* 1050 Ala Moana Blvd. (phone: 521-5002). Moderate.

Salerno – This Italian restaurant serves generous amounts of delicious food (order a half portion if you're not very hungry). Just over the McCully Bridge from Waikiki. Open daily for lunch from 11 AM to 2:30 PM, and dinner from 5 to 10 PM. Reservations advised. Major credit cards accepted. 1960 Kapiolani Blvd., second floor (phone: 942-5273). Moderate.

Yanagi Sushi – Two Tokyo-style sushi bars serve a sushi lover's abundance of specials. The atmosphere is upbeat, the decor simple but appealing, and the sushi first-rate. Open daily. Reservations necessary. Major credit cards accepted. 762 Kapiolani Blvd. (phone: 537-1525). Moderate.

China House – The cavernous dining room of this Honolulu favorite is often full. If shark fin or bird nest soup is your thing, try it here. Four varieties of the former and three of the latter are served. The dim sum is famous throughout the island, and is served daily from 11 AM to 2 PM. Open daily. Reservations advised. Major credit cards accepted. At the top of the ramp from Kapiolani Blvd. in the *Ala Moana Center* (phone: 949-6622). Moderate to inexpensive.

Orson's – Downstairs is a coffee shop called the *Chowder House,* which serves fresh salads as well as seafood; upstairs, a dining room decorated with beautifully stained woods offers more fine seafood. Open daily for lunch and dinner; lunch menu available from 11 AM to 10 PM. Reservations advised. Major credit cards accepted. *Ward Warehouse,* 1050 Ala Moana Blvd. (phone: 521-5681). Upstairs moderate; downstairs inexpensive.

Ryan's Parkplace – Popular for its pasta, vegetable, and fish dishes, desserts, and coffee. Open daily for lunch from 11 AM to 5 PM, and dinner from 5 to 10 PM, with partial alfresco seating. Reservations advised. Major credit cards accepted. *Ward Center,* 1050 Ala Moana Blvd. (phone: 523-9132). Moderate to inexpensive.

TGI Friday's – The Honolulu version of the New York original features antique furnishings, a friendly bar, and surprisingly good food at modest prices (especially for the enormous portions served, which can easily be shared). Best known for its potato skins, this eatery also serves an array of quiches, omelettes, salads, desserts, and more. It's always lively and usually noisy. Open daily from 11 AM to midnight, Fridays and Saturdays to 1 AM. No reservations. Major credit card accepted. 950 Ward Ave. (phone: 523-5841). Moderate to inexpensive.

Big Ed's Deli – This is the place to head if you've got a craving for New York–style pastrami or corned beef. Popular with the lunch crowd, it's much easier to go at dinnertime. Open Mondays through Fridays from 10:30 AM to 10 PM; Saturdays and Sundays from 8 AM to 10 PM. Reservations unnecessary. Major credit cards accepted. In *Ward Center* (phone: 536-4591). Inexpensive.

Chiang Mai – Tasty, home-cooked northern Thai food is served in this tiny flower-filled restaurant by a large Thai family from the town of Chiang Mai. Open weekdays for lunch; daily for dinner. Reservations advised. Major credit cards accepted. 2239 S. King St. (phone: 941-1151). Inexpensive.

Columbia Inn – This family-style café and writers/sports fans bar next to the offices of the *Honolulu Star Bulletin & Advertiser* is decidedly downscale; it's where Honolulu journalists slam-dunk chow in between deadlines. But that's its charm. It's a *saimin* (noodles cooked in chicken or shrimp broth) and macaroni lunch kind of place with ice cold beer. Great for late-night, bright-light dining, too. Open 6 AM until midnight daily. No reservations. Major credit cards accepted. 645 Kapiolani Blvd. (phone 531-3747). Inexpensive.

Fisherman's Wharf – Stop by this shipshape nautical roadhouse on Kewalo Basin waterfront for the clam chowder and fresh mahimahi sandwiches. The dark, cool bar, with its gape-jawed trophy fish on the walls, is also a proper oasis in the tropical heat. Open daily for lunch and dinner. No reservations. Major credit cards accepted. Ala Moana Blvd. and Ward Ave. at Kewalo Basin (phone: 538-3808). Inexpensive.

DOWNTOWN

Black Orchid – American dishes are served here — both indoors and alfresco. There's also a dance floor and a large, beautifully designed lounge. Open weekdays for lunch from 11 AM to 2 PM, and dinner from 6 to 10 PM Mondays through Thursdays, 6 PM to midnight on Fridays and Saturdays. Reservations advised. Major credit cards accepted. Restaurant Row (phone: 521-3111). Expensive.

Ruth's Chris Steakhouse – Some of the best filets and New York steaks in town. Open daily for dinner from 5 to 10:30 PM; open Mondays through Fridays for lunch from 11 AM to 3 PM. Reservations advised. Major credit cards accepted. Restaurant Row (phone: 599-3860). Expensive.

Touch the East – A chic Tokyo-style spot for sushi with a karaoke bar, where patrons lip-synch to their favorite songs. Open for lunch weekdays, dinner nightly. Reservations advised. Major credit cards accepted. Restaurant Row (phone: 521-5144). Expensive.

Coasters – Nestled in a harborside setting at the back of the *Hawaii Maritime Museum,* there's an excellent lunch and dinner menu, with appetizers such as clams casino and shellfish sausage Nantua, plus a full range of seafood, veal, and steak entrées. Open for lunch from 11 AM to 2:30 PM, Mondays through Saturdays, and dinner from 5 to 10 PM daily. Reservations advised. Major credit cards accepted. At Pier 7 (phone: 524-2233). Expensive to moderate.

Café Asia – This Restaurant Row version of *Keo's,* another Thai establishment owned by the same family, also offers the deliciously prepared Thai specialties that made *Keo's* a hit. The decor is upbeat and tropical, while the setting is quiet, which makes it a great place for an intense tête-à-tête. Open daily; closed for lunch on Sundays. Reservations advised on weekends. Major credit cards accepted. Restaurant Row (phone: 536-6889). Moderate.

Café Che Pasta – Homemade pasta is only part of a menu that includes fresh grilled fish, calamari, and other nouvelle-style dishes. *Che Pasta's* original eatery in Kaimuki established the good reputation that's maintained at this downtown branch. Open Mondays through Fridays until 8 PM for lunch, snacks, and dinner. Reservations advised. Major credit cards accepted. 1001 Bishop Sq. (phone: 524-0004). Moderate.

Sunset Grill – The style is California-casual; the food is cooked over kiawe wood to provide a distinctive flavor. Specialties include chicken, veal, lamb, and fish with rotisserie, oven, and grill preparations. Open for lunch from 11 AM to 4 PM, and dinner from 4 to 11 PM daily; breakfast on Sundays only. Reservations advised. Major credit cards accepted. Restaurant Row (phone: 521-4409). Moderate.

Kirin – This bustling Hong Kong–style Chinese restaurant serves traditional Cantonese fare including steaming platters of shrimp, crab, and lobster. Don't miss the minced pork with sesame buns and sesame rice balls in *azuki* bean soup, a warm dessert. Open for lunch and dinner daily. Reservations advised. Major credit cards accepted. 2518 S. Beretania St. (phone: 942-1888). Moderate to inexpensive.

Manzo's – Tony Manzo's see-and-be-seen sidewalk café is noisy, fun and nearly always crowded. Lots of pasta and snappy service, but don't expect culinary creativity. Open daily 11 AM to 11 PM. Reservations advised for lunch. Major credit cards accepted. Restaurant Row (phone: 522-1711). Moderate to inexpensive.

Rose City Café – A 1950s-style diner, featuring outdoor dining. Good food for those seeking basic fare. Open daily for breakfast, lunch, and dinner, from 7 AM to midnight on weekdays, 8 AM to 2 AM on Fridays and Saturdays. Reservations necessary for parties of five or more. Major credit cards accepted. Restaurant Row (phone: 524-ROSE). Moderate to inexpensive.

A Little Bit of Saigon – If Vietnamese food is foreign to your palate, the best place in Honolulu to sample its fare is this bright, cheery Chinatown restaurant. House specialties include beef noodle soup, spring rolls, and shrimp on sugarcane. Open daily 11 AM to 11 PM. Reservations advised at lunch. Major credit cards accepted. 1160 Maunakea St. (phone: 528-3663). Inexpensive.

Ba-Le Sandwich Shop – Started in Chinatown as a lively hole-in-the-wall eatery, this Vietnamese-run operation now has 10 branches. The menu includes Honolulu's best croissants and espresso, as well as sandwiches, fresh fruit, and some hot entrées. Open daily 5 AM to 7 PM. No reservations or credit cards accepted. Chinatown branch, 150 N. King St. (phone: 531-0704). Inexpensive.

Chinese Cultural Plaza – Though not quite as successful as planned, this ethnic enclave does offer a wide range of good Oriental restaurants and cuisines — Cantonese, Hakka, Mandarin, or Mongolian barbecue — as well as shops purveying Oriental bric-a-brac that are fun to browse through. Open daily. Reservations unnecessary. Most major credit cards accepted. 100 N. Beretania and River Sts. (phone: 521-4934). Inexpensive.

Elena's – Sample the tasty home-cooked dishes of the Philippines, including chicken and pork *adobo* (stew), *pancit bijon* (noodles) and *halo halo* (a cold fruit dessert), at this unassuming spot. Open daily from 6 AM to 8:45 PM. Reservations unnecessary. Major credit cards accepted. 2153 N. King St. (phone: 845-0340). Inexpensive.

Grace's Drive Inn – A local lunch favorite, stop here for the beef or chicken teriyaki, served with "one-scoop rice and one-scoop macaroni." You've got to try it. Open daily from 6 AM to 10:45 PM and Sundays 7 to 10 PM. No reservations or credit cards accepted. 1296 S. Beretania St. (phone: 537-3302). Inexpensive.

King Tsin – Known for its spicy Chinese fare, this eatery serves up very tasty hot and sour soup. The crackling chicken is chopstick-lickin' good, as is the Hunan pork sautéed with broccoli. Open daily. Reservations advised. Major credit cards accepted. 1110 McCully St. (phone: 946-3273). Inexpensive.

Murphy's – A San Francisco–style bar (run by a Golden Gate native), this place is full of '49er *Super Bowl* memorabilia. It's popular with the downtown lunch bunch (the menu features soup, salads, sandwiches, and burgers), and in season, Monday night football airs "live" (afternoon in Honolulu) via satellite. Open for lunch weekdays 11 AM to 3 PM, weekends 10:30 AM to 2 PM. The bar stays open nightly until about 9 PM. No reservations. Major credit cards accepted. 2 Merchant St. (phone: 531-0422). Inexpensive.

Quintero's – It's a small, crowded, and *muy authentico* Mexican eatery; the cook's from Guadalajara and the regional Mexican food is *perfecto.* Open daily for lunch and dinner. No reservations. No credit cards accepted. 2334 S. King St. (phone: 944-3882). Inexpensive.

La Salsa – The outdoor bar at this spot on Restaurant Row is a great place to hang out and watch the world go by. Order a cool margarita, and feast on homemade tortilla chips and fiery salsa. This contemporary *tacqueria* is also the place for good, hot, straightforward Mexican food. Open daily 11 AM to 11 PM. No reservations. Major credit cards accepted. 500 Ala Moana Blvd. (phone: 536-4828). Inexpensive.

Wo Fat – This granddaddy of Chinese restaurants in Honolulu just celebrated its 100th birthday. Hong Kong chicken, beef in oyster sauce, and *Wo Fat* noodles draw people here from all over the island for lunch and dinner. Open daily. Reservations advised. Major credit cards accepted. 115 N. Hotel St. (phone: 537-6260). Inexpensive.

Woodlands – A little Chinese eatery run by an ex–Hong Kong wigmaker, who also happens to make what nearly everyone in Honolulu agrees are the city's greatest potstickers (dumplings filled with meat or seafood). Open for lunch and dinner daily except Tuesdays. Reservations advised. Major credit cards accepted. 1289 S. King St. (phone: 526-2239). Inexpensive.

GREATER HONOLULU

Maile – Guests descend through a minor jungle of anthuriums, yellow heliconia, and orchids into this dining room beneath the lobby of the *Kahala Hilton,* where kimono-clad waitresses provide expert, unobtrusive service. The award-winning menu includes roast duckling Waialae and baked chicken supreme. Local fish treated somewhat exotically here include mahimahi glazed with banana and served on creamed mushrooms and baked kumu with fennel and a dash of Pernod. A classical guitarist or a pianist plays during dinner, from 6:30 to 9 PM. Live dance music begins at 9 PM. Open daily for dinner only, from 5:30 to 9 PM. Brunch is served Sundays on the *Maile Terrace* from 11 AM to 2 PM. Reservations necessary. Major credit cards accepted. *Kahala Hilton,* 5000 Kahala Ave., Kahala (phone: 734-2211). Expensive.

Roy's – Owner Roy Yamaguchi combines French, Italian, and Asian cooking styles for first-rate results at his original island eatery. Try the spiny lobster in macadamia nut butter, the thin-crusted pizza topped with Chinese-style chicken, pickled ginger, shiitake mushrooms and sprouts, or the mesquite-smoked Peking-style duck with candied pecans and passion fruit–ginger sauce. Open for dinner daily; open for brunch on Sundays only. Reservations necessary. Major credit cards accepted. 6600 Kalanianaole Hwy., Hawaii Kai (phone: 396-ROYS). Expensive.

Willows – One of the most famous restaurants in the state, and *the* place to sample traditional Hawaiian dishes. The celebrated poi supper offers many of these, including poi itself, sweet potato, chicken luau, and *lomilomi* salmon. If all this seems too exotic, the curry dishes, leavened with coconut milk, are equally superb. It's the perfect place to don an aloha shirt or muumuu for the first time, with the rural tropical atmosphere of palm trees, thatch roofs, and strolling musicians as the backdrop. Poi Thursday lunches are legendary with islanders who come here, so be certain to arrive early (11:30 AM) to get a good seat for a taste of some authentic Hawaii. Open daily for lunch from 11:30 AM to 1:30 PM, and dinner from 5 to 9 PM. Reservations necessary. Major credit cards accepted. 901 Hausten St. (phone: 946-4808). Expensive to moderate.

Al Dente – Quiet and comfortable, with better-than-average Italian food. Steamed Manila clams are a treat, as are the well-flavored pasta, veal, and fish. And the excellent and unobtrusive service wins over patrons' hearts time and again. Open daily. Reservations suggested. Major credit cards accepted. In the *Nui Valley Shopping Center,* 5730 Kalanianaole Hwy. (phone: 373-8855). Moderate.

Alpine Village – Owner-chef Alex Schlemmer offers a menu of schnitzel, chicken, as well as the fresh catch of the day. The soups are delicious, as are the steamed Manila clams, the service is friendly, and the prices are right. Dinner daily from 5:30 to 10 PM. Closed Sundays. Reservations advised. Major credit cards accepted. 2700 South King St. (phone: 949-8889). Moderate.

Castagnola's – An Italian spot that has drawn rave reviews from the day it opened in the *Manoa Marketplace.* Delicate flavorings make for some good veal, pasta, and seafood dishes. Open daily except Sundays for lunch and dinner; lunch only on Mondays. Reservations necessary for dinner. Major credit cards accepted. 2752 Woodlawn Ave. (phone: 988-2969). Moderate.

Che Pasta – Good food served at a casual café. Pasta, veal, and chicken dishes are the specialties. Open daily for dinner. Reservations recommended. Major credit cards accepted. 3571 Waialae Ave. (phone: 735-1777). Moderate.

Hajibaba's – Tony residential Kahala is the unlikely setting for this sophisticated Moroccan eatery. The Fassi Feast for two includes lemon chicken, couscous, Moroccan pastries, and fresh mint tea. The Royal Feast ($32) goes beyond overindulgence. The portions are tremendous, so order accordingly. Most evenings there are two shows that feature the talents of belly dancers accompanied by Moroccan musicians. Open daily. Reservations necessary. Major credit cards accepted. 4614 Kilauea Ave. (phone: 735-5522). Moderate.

Hala Terrace – A *Kahala Hilton* restaurant and a lovely lunchtime spot. Sit in the shade and watch the Pacific across one of the loveliest beaches on Oahu. Meals here are on the light side, so it's worth ordering vichyssoise or a spring salad as a starter. Elegant sandwiches are the main item on the menu, in addition to which there are daily specials such as Kahuku prawns, which are delicious. Open daily for breakfast from 6:30 to 10:30 AM, lunch from 11:30 AM to 2:30 PM, and dinner from 6 to 9 PM. Reservations advised. Major credit cards accepted. *Kahala Hilton,* 5000 Kahala Ave., Kahala (phone: 734-2211). Moderate.

Pacific Broiler – Located in the suburb of Hawaii Kai, this restaurant is in a shopping center on a canal. Specialties include Hawaiian seafood, chicken popcorn salad (the croutons are popcorn), Kauai buffalo steaks, and vegetarian plates. Open Mondays through Saturdays 11:30 AM to 2 PM, Sunday brunch 9 AM to 2:30 PM, dinner daily 5:30 to 9:15 PM. Reservations advised. Major credit cards accepted. In the *Koko Marina Shopping Center,* 7192 Kalanianaole Hwy. (phone: 395-4181). Moderate.

Phillip Paolo's – Just a 5-minute drive from Waikiki, and set in an eclectically decorated private home, this establishment receives high praise for its fine Italian fare prepared by owner-chef Phillip Paolo Sarubbi. Daily specials complement such standard features as *fettuccine Vigario* (pasta with mushrooms and spinach in a light basil cream sauce) and shrimp *parmigiano.* Open daily for lunch from 11 AM to 2 PM, and dinner from 5 to 9 PM. Reservations necessary. Major credit cards accepted. 2312 Beretania St. (phone: 946-1163). Moderate.

Swiss Inn – This is the domain of ex–*Kahala Hilton* chef Martin Wyss, and the crowds tell the story. From simple dishes like Wiener schnitzel to the delightful *émincé de veau zurichoise* (thinly sliced veal) or trout caprice (with mushrooms and bananas), your taste buds are in for a treat. Open for lunch and dinner, from 6 to 10 PM. Closed Mondays. Reservations advised. Major credit cards accepted. *Nui Valley Shopping Center,* 5730 Kalanianaole Hwy. (phone: 377-5447). Moderate.

California Pizza – Pizza fans will find plenty to rave about, with specialties, such as goat cheese pizza, cooked in a kiawe wood-burning oven. They also feature an excellent selection of pasta dishes. Open daily for lunch and dinner, Sundays through Thursdays, 10:30 AM to 10:30 PM, Fridays and Saturdays to 11 PM. No reservations. Major credit cards accepted. In the *Kahala Mall* (phone: 737-9446). Moderate to inexpensive.

Emilio's – Be it ever so humble, this little neighborhood-style pizza place, just outside Waikiki, has very tasty pies and other Italian dishes. The pizza is right on the mark, with crisp crusts, dense tomato sauce, and tasty cheese. Open daily. Reservations unnecessary. Major credit cards accepted. 1423 Kalakaua Ave. (phone: 946-4972). Inexpensive.

La Mariana – This little-known South Seas–style waterfront hangout is too salty to be a yacht club, even though many of those who eat here are sailors anchored in Keehi Lagoon. All the seafood is fresh daily; try the fish and chips made with local mahimahi. Open daily for lunch and dinner. No reservations. Major credit cards accepted. 50 Sand Island Access Rd. (phone: 848-2800). Inexpensive.

ELSEWHERE

Jameson's by the Sea – The setting downstairs is quite casual, while upstairs is a bit more elegant, but both provide their popular baked stuffed shrimp, fresh catch-of-the-day, steaks, or chicken specialties. This Haleiwa eatery is popular with Honolulu day-trippers as well as North Shore residents. Open daily for lunch from 11 AM to 5 PM and dinner from 5 to 10 PM. Reservations advised. Major credit cards accepted. 62-540 Kamehameha Hwy., Haleiwa (phone: 637-4336). Expensive to moderate.

L'Auberge Swiss – Considered the Windward Side's best restaurant, this intimate homey spot, run by Chef Alfred Mueller and his wife, Barbara, features Swiss dishes, steaks, pasta (including outstanding gnocchi) and daily specials such as fresh fish and osso bucco. Best of all are the reasonable prices. Open for dinner Tuesdays through Sundays. Reservations advised. Major card cards accepted. 117 Hekili St., Kailua (phone: 263-4663). Moderate.

Los Arcos – When you crave the best Southwestern-style food in Honolulu, drive over to Kailua to this eatery, where Hank and Mary Magana prepare regional specialties such as *calamares borrachos* (squid marinated in brandy) and *pollo con rajas* (chicken with creamy chili-cheese sauce). Open daily 11:30 AM to 2 PM for lunch, 5:30 to 10 PM for dinner; closed Thursdays. Reservations advised. Major credit cards accepted. 19 Hoolai St., Kailua (phone: 262-8196). Moderate to inexpensive.

Paniolo Café – It's a long way from Texas, pardner, but this Tex-Mex bar and grill on the Windward Coast serves great chili along with ice cold beer in a Mason jars. Try the beef ribs, chicken-fried steaks, and shredded beef enchilada *verde.* Live music on weekends. Open for lunch daily, dinner every day but Tuesdays. No reservations. Major credit cards accepted. 53-146 Kamehameha Hwy., Punaluu (phone: 237-8521). Moderate to inexpensive.

Bueno Nalo – The coconut wireless (as the local grapevine is called) gives this eatery high marks for its Mexican cooking — *chiles rellenos, chimichangas,* and such. It's a casual place, where guests bring their own wine or beer and wait for tables. Open Tuesdays through Fridays, 5 to 9 PM; Saturdays and Sundays from 3 to 9 PM. No reservations or credit cards accepted. 41-865 Kalanianaole Hwy., Waimanalo (phone: 259-7186). Inexpensive.

Kua Aina Sandwich Shop – Stop at this roadside eatery in Haleiwa for juicy hamburgers, shoestring French fries, and outstanding sandwiches, including mahimahi with Ortega chilies and cheese. Open daily 11 AM to 8 PM. No reservations. No credit cards accepted. 66-214 Kamehameha Hwy., Haleiwa (phone: 637-6067). Inexpensive.

DIVERSIONS

For the Experience

Quintessential Honolulu

 You've sat on the beach at Waikiki until you're nut-brown and watched a succession of glorious sunsets from your private lanai. You've quaffed many a mai tai; donned a muumuu or aloha shirt; and sampled opakapaka, *pupus,* and three-finger poi. You've even decided that morning coffee will never again taste as good unless there's a tiny orchid floating in it. But while all of the foregoing are a pleasant part of any Honolulu vacation, only after visiting the places and having the experiences described below — which allow a visitor to be a part of the real Hawaii — can a trip here be considered complete.

ARIZONA MEMORIAL: The Arizona Memorial is a perfect example of what a material tribute to those who died in the service of their country should be: simple, graceful, and intensely moving. The white concrete structure, in the blue-green water off the tip of Ford Island in Pearl Harbor, spans the battleship USS *Arizona,* whose sunken hull lies beneath the memorial, entombing the 1,102 servicemen who were aboard on the morning of December 7, 1941, when Japanese planes attacked the base. The memorial is divided into three parts. There is a museum room, containing among other mementos the *Arizona*'s ship's bell; an open assembly area, from which visitors may look down at the battleship's rusted and barnacled hull; and the shrine, where a marble tablet is inscribed with the names of those who died on the *Arizona.* It reads like a cross section of the immigrant groups who traveled to America in search of freedom, prosperity, and peace: Aarons, Abercrombie, Blake, Blanchard, Blankenship, Jastrzemski, Le Gros, Lynch, McGuire, Tambolleo, Van Horn, Vosti, Zimmerman. The American flag that flies above the memorial is attached to a flagpole anchored in the ship's hull. Each morning and evening, the flag is raised and lowered by an honor guard. Alfred Preis, architect of the memorial, said of it: "The overall effect is one of serenity. Overtones of sadness have been omitted to permit the individual to contemplate . . . his own innermost feelings." The US Navy operates the short boat trip to the memorial from the USS *Arizona* Visitor Center — which is run by National Park Rangers — from 8 AM to 3 PM daily; the visitors' center itself is open from 7:30 AM to 5 PM. Commercial sea tours from Kewalo Basin sail along "battleship row," past where other battleships were sunk during the raid. Only passengers on US Navy boats, however, are allowed to disembark at the Arizona Memorial. As it is Hawaii's most popular tourist attraction, a wait of 1 hour or longer for tours to the memorial is not uncommon. No admission charge. Information: *Arizona Memorial Navy Boat Tours,* Pearl Harbor, HI 96701 (phone: 808-422-0561).

BUY A HAWAIIAN SHIRT: Bold, bright, and brassy, Hawaiian shirts fairly shout aloha with their red and green parrots, hula girls, tropical flowers, and palm trees. Fans of these garish designed duds are legion — among them President Harry S. Truman, who wore an "eye-popper" on the cover of *Life* magazine back in 1951, and Tom Selleck, whose trademark pattern, black with white and purple orchids, remains a magnum best seller throughout the island.

It all began in 1931 when Ellery J. Chun came home from Yale University and found his father's Honolulu garment business in deep financial trouble. Ellery took a bolt of bright floral material and whipped out a shirt that, almost instantly, became all the rage among tourists. The first shirts sold for $1, and the rest, as they say, is history.

Today, vintage Hawaiian shirts (not the run-of-the-mill goods sold at most souvenir shops) have become prized — and often pricey — mementos of a trip to the islands. When buying a shirt, look for one with a dark background and contrasting color — yellow night-blooming cereus on midnight black or white pineapples on a purple field — and buttons made of coconut shells or bamboo. Another option is the so-called "reverse print" shirt, made with the fabric turned inside out to create a subdued look and favored by Honolulu bankers and lawyers; sold at *Reyn's,* which invented them, and other department stores, these shirts are worn tucked in for a more formal effect.

Classic shirts can cost as much as $1,000, but there are designers, such as Paradise Found in Honolulu, who are successfully re-creating old patterns in rayon and silk for about $60. The two best places to find true vintage shirts are *Linda's Vintage Isle* (373 Olohana St.), on the outskirts of Waikiki, or *Bailey's Antique and Thrift Shop* (758 Kapahulu St.). Just make sure you pattern yourself after Tom Selleck and not Don Ho — unless tiny bubbles tickle your fancy.

EAT, DANCE, AND BE MERRY: One of Honolulu's most appealing traditions is the luau, an ancient Hawaiian ceremony of cooking a pig in an *imu,* an earthen pit lined with lava rock and heated by burning kiawe wood. The pig is stuffed with red-hot rocks, wrapped in wet ti and banana leaves, and covered with earth. Other ingredients such as yams, taro, fish, breadfruit, and whatever else is available are placed in the *imu* beside the pig. Hours later, the pig is removed, at which time it is referred to as kalua pork. Removing the pig from the *imu* is a ceremony in itself, often accompanied by songs. Honolulu's most authentic luaus are the ones held in somebody's backyard, celebrating first birthdays, graduations, weddings, and other special events. But for those without a local connection, the next best thing is a commercial luau such as the one at Paradise Cove, perfect sunset-watching country at Ewa Beach on Oahu's western shore. There is an *imu* ceremony, torchlighting ritual, beachfront *hukilau* (communal net fishing), Hawaiian arts and crafts displays, and a Polynesian revue. Information: *Paradise Cove Luau* (phone: 808-973-5828).

If you want to shake those calories — roast pig isn't exactly diet food — the waist-watching exercise of choice in Honolulu is the hula. If you're reluctant to try it, then sit back and relax until the spirit moves you — and it will, we guarantee it.

One of the strongest surviving expressions of the Hawaiian culture, the hula is a subtle, graceful dance, primitive in its ancient form (*kahiko*), more sophisticated in the modern (*auwana*) style. The origin of the hula is lost in Hawaiian legend. One story says that two gods named Laka — one male, one female — arrived from beyond the Great Western Sea in a canoe and danced for the people of Hawaii. After a time the male disappeared, but the female remained. The Hawaiians worshiped her, and she taught them the hula. Originally danced only by men and used only in religious rituals, the hula later evolved into a method of teaching, a form of entertainment and the foundation for the art of *lua,* a style of hand-to-hand self-defense known only to Hawaiians. It also expanded into the opera of old Hawaii, with dancers and singers combining to tell its history and folktales. Banned in the 19th century by the Protestant missionaries, the hula was revived by King David Kalakaua, who reigned from 1874 to 1891. He believed that "the hula is the language of the heart and, therefore, the heartbeat of the Hawaiian people." Under his patronage, more than 300 ancient hulas were saved from extinction, and he created a number of hula chants. The hula renaissance he began has not been forgotten and, as a result, hula dancers aren't hard to find in Honolulu. Look for them at Hawaiian music shows, the *Kodak Hula Show* in Waikiki's Kapiolani Park, and many hotels. For more authentic performances, Oahu's hula *halaus* (schools) have frequent fund-raisers and competitions; the biggest is the *King Kamehameha Hula Competition,* held in late June. Sponsored by the State Council of Hawaiian Heritage, it attracts dancers from New Zealand to Texas.

Though it may be corny, it's almost unpatriotic to leave Honolulu without catching a Don Ho show. Hawaii's best-known entertainer and the first island boy to go big time, Ho is renowned for his smooth croon, still island-boyish looks, and "hang-loose" style, and though it confounds most of us, his fans stand in line for hours just to hear him sing "Tiny Bubbles." Ho performs at the Waikiki's *Hula Hut* at 9 PM daily except Sundays (286 Beach Walk; phone: 808-923-8411). To paraphrase Karl Malden's warning in the American Express commercials, "Don't leave here without it."

POLYNESIAN CULTURAL CENTER: Like the Polynesian people themselves, their artifacts, dance, and music exemplify grace, beauty, and a highly refined artistic imagination. A dazzling array of all these qualities can be seen at the Polynesian Cultural Center on Brigham Young University's Hawaiian campus at Laie, on Oahu's Windward Coast. Students from many distinct Polynesian backgrounds, working in replicas of their native villages, explain the life, customs, rituals, ceremonies, habits, arts, crafts, and food of their homelands to visitors. The things to see, and sometimes participate in, include Tongan women making *ngatu,* or tapa cloth; Tahitian girls, lovely as moonlight, making shell leis and grass skirts; elaborate pint-size wooden tikis outside a small Marquesan village temple; Fijians playing music on pipe organs; Maoris from New Zealand throwing spears in their own unique manner; Samoan men walking unscathed through a curtain of flame; and Hawaiians making poi, something no one should leave the islands without seeing. The villages, authentic in every detail, have been built by students of the university, who are very friendly and carry a storehouse of detailed information in their heads. Fortunately, they also talk about up-to-date clothes, modern music, and baseball scores, which infuse a little real life into this museum village community. Don't miss the Tongan House and the Chief's House in the Fiji village. A film on the cultures of Polynesia is shown at the state-of-the-art (IMAX) theater, with its oversize screen. The center also features a series of musical performances throughout the day, including *Mana: Spirit of Our People,* a canoe spectacle that is included in the $25 entry fee, as well as an extravagant song-and-dance revue performed evenings and selected afternoons. The entry fee, dinner, and show package, at $40.50, is a good buy. For an additional $10, you can substitute the nightly luau for the dinner buffet. Front-row "VIP" seating and dinner cost $80.50. Motorcoach transfers are also available from Waikiki. Information: *Polynesian Cultural Center,* 55-370 Kamehameha Hwy., Laie, HI 96762 (phone: 808-293-3333).

SEA LIFE PARK, Waimanalo: "An educational experience" may sound like just the sort of thing you've come to Hawaii to escape, but the didactic side of *Sea Life Park* is riveting, far more appealing than the show-biz side. The outstanding feature of the park is the Hawaiian Reef Tank, a 300,000-gallon re-creation of an undersea Pacific reef. Spiraling around the tank's transparent sides from top to bottom is a ramp with illuminated panels above the windows. These displays help visitors to identify some of the more obscure marine species, such as hermit crabs, which normally exist at depths of 200 to 300 feet; saddleback fish; and vivid butterfly and banded-angel fish. The panels also give the scientific names of some specimens that may be vaguely familiar already, such as the hammerhead shark, reef shark, brown sting rays, eagle rays, and moray eels. In the *Science Theater,* dolphins and penguins perform, while the recently opened Rocky Shores Exhibit shows a cross section of tidal ecology. At Whaler's Cove, porpoises wearing leis and whales towing a rowboat also take part in a sub-Disneyish scenario, which is about as edifying as watching a poodle turn somersaults. A number of small pools hold sea turtles, whiskered harbor seals, and a variety of seabirds normally found in the chain of islets strung out for 1,000 miles northwest of Hawaii. The *Pacific Whaling Museum* displays the largest collection of whaling artifacts and scrimshaw in the Pacific, not to mention the skeleton of a 38-foot sperm whale. Walls full of brightly illustrated explanatory texts inspire a desire to go probing around full fathom five and deeper. *Sea Life Park*'s location at the foot of a sheer Koolau cliff and beside the ocean at Makapuu Beach is exceptionally beautiful. On Fridays, the park is open until 10 PM; every other day until 5 PM. The last series of shows starts at 6:15 PM, and includes Hawaiian music and dance as well as marine shows. Admission is $14.95 for adults, $7.95 for children 6 to 12, and $4.50 for those 4 to 7 years old. Information: *Sea Life Park,* Makapuu Point, Waimanalo, HI 96795 (phone: 808-259-7933).

SUNDAY BRUNCH AT MICHEL'S: A Honolulu tradition since 1965, brunch here is more than just eggs Benedict. It's breakfast with a view — a luxurious wood-paneled dining room that overlooks Mamala Bay — in a setting that's pure Polynesian. Though by night, *Michel's* is a torch-lit formal French restaurant, by day it's transformed into an open-air beachside bistro, where sparrows perch on velvet chairs, crystal chandeliers glisten in the sun, and the air is heavy with the heady scent of plumeria. Ask for an oceanfront table; you'll find yourself literally on the beach with the gentle surf lapping at the sand, coconut trees swaying in the breeze, and a hint of salt spray on the crisp white linen tablecloths. The atmosphere is elegant, but relaxed; tuxedoed waiters pour from silver coffee pots and balance crystal and china with elan. Stretch out your legs and bask in the warmth of the sun, while you watch swimmers and canoeists enjoy the sparkling blue-green water. Brunch begins with Kona coffee or champagne cocktails and a basket of freshly baked banana and blueberry muffins, sweet rolls, and coffee cake. Then choose papaya with lime, omelettes, eggs Benedict or Florentine, or for those with a heartier appetite, entrées such as opakapaka, shrimp in garlic butter, seafood crêpes, lamb chops, or a New York strip steak. The perfect way to start the day, the memory of this most elegant morning meal will linger long after you've left Honolulu. Brunch is served in two seatings, 11 AM and 1 PM, and reservations are advised. Information: *Michel's,* 2895 Kalakaua Ave. (phone: 808-923-6552).

BANZAI!: If you'd ever seen it, we guarantee you'd remember it. Building strength and rolling higher, ever higher, seeming to reach to the sky before it hurls itself toward the shore, the perfect wave — the quest of everyone from experienced surfers to wannabes — is here for the riding in Oahu. The Banzai Pipeline (*banzai* is a Japanese war cry), with its ferocious tube-shape rollers, guarantees the ride of a lifetime to those brave enough — or foolhardy enough — to pit themselves against the angry surf and the treacherous coral reef lurking below the surface. Though challenging, the waves may seem like nirvana to some and insanity to others; surfing as sport is almost as old as time itself. In fact, man has been testing his mettle here since ancient days — Polynesian surfers are depicted in petroglyphs on lava in the area.

The Banzai Pipeline's most colossal waves don't happen in the summer; in fact, they aren't even reliably present in the late fall or winter, which is when giant surf traditionally hits the North Shore. (Be sure to listen to the Honolulu radio stations before coming here; the daily surf advisory will tell you whether the "surf's up.")

But when weather conditions are right, faraway storms in Alaska and Siberia generate ocean swells that surge across the Pacific and attain monstrous size before pounding the beaches here. At the Banzai Pipeline, these huge waves first crash against a shallow reef and then rise up and form a spectacular curl, almost a completely enclosed tube, before breaking with intense force at the shore. For experts, it's the ultimate challenge to shoot from one end of the tube to the other; at times surfers are completely inside the curl with only a glimmer of light at the other end. The trick is to make it through without being caught by the "guillotine" — the name for the wave's breaking edge. If the guillotine falls, the surfer wipes out and is thrown into the churning, foaming backwash and tossed around underwater until the wave retreats. And if the waves don't get you, the coral probably will: The Pipeline's jagged coral reef has inflicted severe cuts, bruises, broken limbs, and worse to those who run afoul of it.

If you want to test your skill (experienced surfers only) or watch from the beach, head for the North Shore and follow the Kamehameha Highway just south of Sunset Beach — look for the Sunset Beach Elemenary School on the *mauka* (mountain) side of the highway; turn toward the ocean at Ke Nui Road. Follow Ke Nui to the end, then walk 100 yards left along the beach. There are no signs, and the beach is rather nondescript, but look for the graceful, yet awesome tube-shape waves. Even if you never get your feet wet, seeing the Banzai Pipeline is an experience that will stay with you long after you return to colder if calmer climes.

TEA DANCING AT THE ROYAL HAWAIIAN: A grown-up version of Miss Darcy's Dance School, this is where Fred and Ginger wannabes come to relive the good old days. The tradition of tea dancing probably predates most of our dance classes, but on Sunday afternoon at the *Royal Hawaiian* it's as though you've never removed your white gloves.

It all began here in 1933 when a Los Angeles trumpet player named Harry Owens came to work at the *Royal Hawaiian.* For 7 years, *Harry Owens and his Royal Hawaiians* (a take-off on *Guy Lombardo and His Royal Canadians*) brought big-band sounds to Honolulu (Owens wrote scores of songs, including his Oscar-winning hits, "Sweet Leilani" and "Hawaii Calls"). Today, the melody lingers on at the hotel's *Monarch Room,* where Del Courtney, a big-band leader circa 1990s, places guests in a wonderful musical time warp, re-creating the soothing sounds and synchopating rhythms of the postwar (that's World War II) years. Even if you're not of that generation, join the touch-dancers who gather here at week's end, where every Sunday, from 4:30 to 7:30 PM, young and old crowd the floor to jitterbug and dance cheek-to-cheek. To get "in the mood," don your best duds (dresses for the women, jackets and ties for the men), and dust off your two-step — or take a table by the dance floor and watch as elderly swains whirl handsome matrons around the floor — and younger couples try their best to imitate them. Decorated in the hotel's signature pink and burgundy, the glass-enclosed room looks out on Waikiki Beach and majestic Diamond Head; if you tire of twirling, you can always watch the sun slide into the Pacific. Information: *Royal Hawaiian, Surf Room,* 2259 Kalakaua Ave. (phone 808-923-7311).

WAIMEA FALLS PARK, Haleiwa: This is among the most beautiful spots on Oahu, with a gem of a cascade that tumbles into a rock-girt pool straight out of *Tarzan* or *The Blue Lagoon.* Even when the pathways through the gardens and around the natural, waterfall-fed pool are fairly crowded, which they often are on weekends and holidays, it's easy to escape the human traffic by walking rather than taking the park's motorized tram, which tends to drop large numbers of people at its more popular (and crowded) sections only. Apart from its considerable scenic charm, Waimea Falls Park inspires both historical and botanical fascination. The land once belonged to the high priest who served Kamehameha the Great, a man said to be buried hereabouts, though no one is quite sure where. Just off the main path are remnants of an ancient Hawaiian village, terraces where fruit and vegetables were cultivated, temple platforms, and fishing shrines. Psychics tell of feeling distinct vibrations in this area, although whoever is trying to relay a message seems to be placated by the sight and sound of old Hawaiian games such as *ulu maika,* a form of lawn bowling, which is taught and played in a meadow close by. The Waimea Arboretum and Botanical Gardens, on the meadows and hillsides between the visitors' entrance and the falls, is a wonderland of tropical flora. Amid this paradise of trees, shrubs, and plants are plots devoted to heliconia and ginger, hibiscus, ferns, bamboo, and exotic vegetation from such distant places as Bermuda, the Canary Islands, Sri Lanka, and Madagascar. A favorite conversation piece among visitors is the world's only known specimen of a tree called *kokia cookei.* Another is the 35 varieties of banana plants. The park is also home to some species of Hawaiian wildlife, including nene geese, Kona nightingales — wild donkeys — from the Big Island, peacocks, and wild boar. The annual *Makahiki Festival,* held during the first weekend in October, is recommended Hawaiiana. Also worthy of note: The park opens on nights when the moon is full, and free guided walks are conducted. Information: *Waimea Falls Park,* 59-864 Kamehameha Hwy., Haleiwa, HI 96712 (phone: 808-638-8511).

WALK IN A RAIN FOREST: In a city known for its beaches, it's hard to believe that high in the mountains and valleys above sunny Waikiki, there are dense, brooding — and very wet — tropical rain forests. A good way to experience this natural wonderland is to hike Manoa Falls trail, an easy 1-mile walk that ends at a freshwater pool under a waterfall. Begin at the well-marked stone footpath; flaming ti plants, mountain apples, guava and hau trees, and colorful thimbleberry and passion fruit vines grow along either side. As you get farther along, the trees form a thick and tangled canopy, and the cool shadows are punctuated only by misted sunbeams. The air is heavy and moist, heady with the fragrance of sweet wild ginger, and the only sounds you'll hear are the calls of exotic birds, the rustling of the wind in the trees, and the constant drip of water through the lush vegetation. Soon you cross over a bubbling stream and pass though a stand of stately eucalyptus. The trail ends at Manoa Stream; cool off here by dangling your feet in the clear water at the bottom of the 100-foot falls, though if the rains have been particularly heavy — 200 inches in 1 year is not unheard of — it is wise to stand clear in case boulders come tumbling over the cataract. To reach the trailhead, go to the end of Manoa Road just past Paradise Park, and follow the signs to the Manoa Falls Trail.

DINNER AT ORCHIDS: On a soft tropical night, Honolulu can be one of the most romantic spots on earth, and one of the best places to appreciate the atmosphere is *Orchids,* the *Halekulani* hotel's elegant dining room, where tables are set up indoors, on the terrace, and even on the beach. Decorated with hundreds of fragrant orchids (what else?) — with such varieties as Sonia, Jacquiline Thomas, and Oncidium Seasprays — the room's French doors open onto lush lawns that slope gently down to the ocean's edge. Request a table close to the water, so you can get the full effect of Waikiki's sunset — the changing hues of orange, yellow, pink and deep red light the sky and reflect off both Diamond Head and the calm evening sea. Offshore, surfers skim the frothy tops of the last waves before dark, and the sails of the sunset-cruise boats are silhouetted against the distant horizon. To add to the almost stage-set atmosphere, soft Hawaiian music, coming from the nearby lounge, can be heard in the background. The tables are set with crisp white napery, glistening silver, and sparkling crystal, and the service is gracious and attentive. The dinner menu entices with entrées that highlight island ingredients. Don't miss kiawe-smoked opakapaka and charbroiled eggplant with soy sauce vinaigrette; poha-berry bread pudding and coconut tapioca *crème brûlée* top the dessert offerings. Lulled by the soothing sound of the surf, it's difficult to part with the Pacific. Romance is still alive in Honolulu, especially at *Orchids.* Information: *Orchids, Halekulani Hotel,* 2199 Kalia Rd. (phone: 808-923-2311).

WHALE WATCHING: If you are in Honolulu between January and May, your chances of spotting a humpback whale are excellent. Although Maui is where these giant creatures (45 feet long, 40 tons in weight) go to mate and bear their young, they can be seen in all Hawaiian waters. The whales detour around Oahu on the way to Maui from Alaska and then pass by later on their way home with their calves. Humpbacks' water spouts can frequently be spotted on Oahu's windward side, and the whales even cruise Waikiki.

There's no great trick to successful spotting from shore, but a few tips should help first-timers get started. To begin with, use elevated ground for your observation point. Then go early in the morning or late in the afternoon. By midday, the wind is stronger and churns up the water, making it more difficult to spot the whales, but a few hours before sunset, which comes between 6 and 7 PM, the whales tend to come closer to shore. Finally, be patient. Scan the horizon till you see what looks like an explosion of smoke about 18 feet high. That's the blow of the humpback. If you have binoculars, by all means, take them along. They're especially good for spotting the light blow of a calf. When a humpback lifts its head out of the water, an activity dubbed "spy hopping" since its eyes are just above the surface, it's just playing around. But when it lifts its tail straight up out of the water (called a fluke-up dive), it's going under for a prolonged dive and won't surface again for another 20 minutes or so.

To bone up on humpbacks before your whale watch, visit the *Pacific Whaling Museum* at *Sea Life Park,* the *Bishop Museum,* and the *Hawaii Maritime Museum* adjacent to Aloha Tower downtown, all of which feature excellent displays on the great whales and artifacts of the hunt. If you come away as fascinated by these creatures as most people do, treat yourself to Richard Ellis's beautiful and comprehensive work, *The Book of Whales* (Knopf; $25); Bob Goodman's interesting book, *Whale Song;* or a Robert Lyn Nelson, Wyland, or Christian Lassen painting (very expensive), lithograph (affordable), or print (very affordable) at local bookstores or art galleries.

Honolulu's Heavenly Hotels

 Contrary to popular conception, Honolulu does not have a long innkeeping tradition. In fact, most of its hotels, resorts, and condominiums have been constructed in the decades since World War II, when the city experienced a tremendous boom in tourism. Many of these facilities were ill planned and hastily constructed, resulting in hodgepodge development in Waikiki and too many faceless concrete high-rises. Happily, Honolulu and the island of Oahu have some very fine hostelries, notable for their history, architecture, ambience, setting, or luxury, and it is in this context that they are discussed below.

COLONY SURF: With a choice location on Sans Souci Beach on the quiet side of Waikiki, it boasts a loyal following: folks who come back year after year. Almost like your own Honolulu hideaway, the elegant 1- and 2-bedroom cream-colored suites have full kitchens and floor-to-ceiling louvered windows that open for panoramic ocean and island views. Other appealing features are the small, almost private beach, and *Michel's,* the hotel's wonderful French beachside restaurant, which also offers room service (see *Quintessential Honolulu*). If you feel a need for a little nightlife, it's only a short walk to Waikiki. Information: *Colony Surf Hotel,* 2895 Kalakaua Ave. Honolulu HI 96815 (phone: 808-923-5751; 800-252-7873).

HALEKULANI: Considered by many (including us) to be Waikiki's finest, most luxurious hostelry. Incorporating several of the buildings of the original bungalow hotel, the *Halekulani* has 456 rooms, 2 restaurants, and beautifully landscaped grounds consisting of 5 acres of prime Waikiki beachfront. Facing the beach is the hotel's *House Without a Key* open-air lounge — a perfect place to sip cocktails at day's end, listen to Hawaiian music, and admire the fine views of Diamond Head. The oceanfront *La Mer* is one of Waikiki's finest dining spots, the *Orchids* restaurant is also very special (see *Quintessential Honolulu*), and service throughout the hotel provides a personal touch. Altogether, this property seems to provide a sense of exclusivity and romance. Information: *Halekulani,* 2199 Kalia Rd., Honolulu, HI 96815 (phone: 808-923-2311; 800-367-2343).

HILTON HAWAIIAN VILLAGE: With close to 2,600 rooms, Hawaii's largest hotel has been totally renovated and rebuilt (at a cost of nearly $100 million), with very appealing results, not the least of which is the comfortable lounging area by the free-form, beachside pool, complete with waterfalls and grottoes. The posh Alii Tower provides guests with a private pool, luxurious furnishings, and full concierge services. But the best rooms in terms of spectacular views of Diamond Head are those facing the ocean in the Rainbow Tower. Fine dining (the *Golden Dragon* and *Bali by the Sea* are both worthy of note), a full complement of shops and boutiques, two showrooms with headliner entertainment, a nightclub, a catamaran pier, full beach services, and a tranquil location at the west end of Waikiki Beach are also among its many assets. Throughout the week, Hawaiian dance, music, song, and crafts are offered on the hotel's expansive grounds, culminating in fireworks on Friday evenings. Information: *Hilton Hawaiian Village,* 2005 Kalia Rd., Honolulu, HI 96815 (phone: 808-949-4321; 800-445-8667).

KAHALA HILTON INTERNATIONAL: There is something about staying here that is reminiscent of spending a few days at a superbly run country house; considering that there are 370 rooms in the complex, this is no mean feat. It may be the hotel's comparative isolation, surrounded as it is by the *Waialae* golf course and the ocean, or it may be the subdued harmony that exists between the polite, friendly, Hawaiian staff and the rather more formal European management. Whatever the individual ingredients, they add up to an operation that manages to be scrupulously (but unobtrusively) attentive to detail. News of the *Kahala*'s singular reputation and the seductive beauty of its setting has been brought to ears influential enough to persuade the Queen of England and her consort, and the King of Spain and his queen, to spend a few days here, as well as a host of celebrated commoners. Besides the main building, with its bright and airy rooms, there are oceanside bungalows and a 2-story wing overlooking the hotel lagoon. The 30-foot-high lobby is filled with orchids and dominated by two huge chandeliers. The lagoon and adjacent ponds hold sea turtles, more than 1,000 reef fish, and dolphins that are constantly on the lookout for mischief and perform for guests during feedings at 11 AM and at 2 and 3 PM. Among the more than 50 varieties of flora are hau and autograph trees; traveler's and bottle palms; heliconia, bird of paradise, hibiscus, and ginger, Tahitian gardenias (called *tiare*), and spider lilies. The *Maile* restaurant, under the hotel lobby, is one of the best-known, most elegant eating places in Honolulu. The *Hala Terrace,* where luscious lunch snacks and delicious Sunday brunches are served, looks out on the ocean and palm trees. Information: *Kahala Hilton International,* 5000 Kahala Ave., Honolulu, HI 96815 (phone: 808-734-2211; 800-367-2525).

KE IKI HALE, Haleiwa: If your idea of heaven is a quiet cottage shaded by palms on a white sand beach, have we got a resort for you! Located right off the tidepool end of Pupukea Beach, in a North Shore neighborhood between Waimea Bay and Sunset Beach, are 12 one- and two-bedroom cottages, all affording panoramic views (for the soul) and full kitchens (for your practical side). The pleasures here are many, but modest: an outdoor shower fastened to a palm tree, a hammock to lounge the days away, picnic tables for alfresco meals, and a white sand beach where puka shells abound. Don't expect a restaurant or room service; everything you need can be found in the little town of Hailewa, only minutes away. Information: *Ke Iki Hale,* 59-579 Ke Iki Rd., Haleiwa, HI 96712 (phone: 808-638-8229).

MANOA VALLEY INN: Set on a hill in misty Manoa Valley, this small historic inn, just 3 miles from the beach, is straight out of Honolulu's plantation era. Listed on the National Register of Historic Places, the 3-story house was built in 1915 and served as the home of sugar planter John Guild. After many years of neglect, the building was restored by Rick Ralston, a local entrepreneur turned preservationist; he filled it with 19th-century antiques and opened it as Honolulu's first bed and breakfast establishment in 1984. Today, although ownership has passed to the Japanese, the Old World charm has been lovingly preserved. Guests stay in one of 7 luxurious rooms, furnished with brass beds, velvet settees, and stained glass lamps; a separate cottage, decorated in white on white, is popular with honeymooners. Amenities include a sumptuous continental breakfast as well as wine, cheese, and fresh fruit in the evenings. The inn's most appealing feature: the cooling breezes of the Manoa Valley, which serve as natural air conditioning. Information: *Manoa Valley Inn,* 2001 Vancouver Dr., Honolulu, HI 96822 (phone: 808-947-6019; 800-634-5115).

PLANTATION SPA, Kaaawa: Seven lovely acres at the foot of the verdant, saw-edged Koolau Mountains provide a setting perfectly in keeping with this spa's commitment to psychological and physical well-being. Guests visit for a day, a weekend, or a full week-long program of activities that includes everything from kayaking to hiking to aerobics to lectures on subjects both holistic and Hawaiian. You can do all or nothing; the choice is yours. Owners Dave and Bodil Anderson, he from Hawaii, she from Sweden, run a superbly efficient, hands-on operation. Accommodations in the main house (ca. 1935) are quite comfortable, and there are several cottages on the grounds that lead to turquoise waters. The guest list is limited to 18 people at any given time, which further enhances a sense of serenity and privacy. Information: *Plantation Spa,* 51-550 Kamehameha Hwy., Kaaawa, HI 96730 (phone: 808-237-8685; 800-422-0307).

ROYAL HAWAIIAN: It is from Waikiki Beach that the Pink Lady, as she is affectionately known, is seen best. Most of the surrounding buildings tower over her rudely, but the hotel's Spanish-Moorish hacienda lines and gaudy pink color still catch the eye immediately. When it was opened in 1927, amid much pomp and circumstance, the Pink Lady was only the second hotel of any note along Waikiki, a kind of flashy Hollywood rival to the *Moana,* the prim, New England–style, seaside hotel just down the street. But the years when steamer trunks were carried to the *Royal Hawaiian* by Chinese coolies riding on the backs of trucks, when *kamaaina* servants stood around the dining rooms waiting on *haole* ladies wearing vast brimmed hats and flowery frocks, have gone. The restaurants have efficient staffs now, and jogging shorts, jeans, and tennis togs are the current fashions for guests. But some nostalgic touches still linger, such as the romantic pink decor, which is so pervasive that one feels an obligation to blush in order not to appear conspicuous. And visitors sitting on the porch at sunset, listening to the palms rustling in the breeze and the faint music wafting up from the bars along the beach, can't help but imagine that they belong — however fleetingly — to an earlier and much different time. Information: *Royal Hawaiian Hotel,* 2259 Kalakaua Ave., Honolulu, HI 96815 (phone: 808-923-7311; 800-325-3535).

SHERATON MOANA SURFRIDER: When the *Moana* was built in 1901 on Waikiki Beach, there were only a few seaside cottages here, along with a number of mansions used by Hawaiian royalty and a handful of wealthy merchants. In spite of predictions that it was too far from downtown to attract customers, it quickly became *the* place to stay, and was preferred by the blue-blood set even when the *Royal Hawaiian* was attracting millionaires and silent-movie stars. In the era of flappers and Bright Young Things, the Prince of Wales (later Duke of Windsor) and his cousin Lord Louis Mountbatten (later Earl Mountbatten of Burma) stayed at the hotel. In keeping with its historic past the *Moana* was completely restored, at a cost of more than $50 million. The original Greek Revival portico was reconstructed and the rooms redesigned with a combination of turn-of-the-century elegance and contemporary chic. The clutter that nearly obscured the great beachfront banyan was removed, re-creating the atmosphere of bygone days that once inspired Robert Louis Stevenson, who used to sit and write here even before the *Moana* was imagined. The *Moana* has been joined with the neighboring *Surfrider* into a single hotel, and although the Surfrider wing offers rooms with spectacular views of Diamond Head, the historic charm and elegance of the original hotel provides its guests with a more unique experience. Information: *Sheraton Moana Surfrider,* 2365 Kalakaua Ave., Honolulu, HI 96815 (phone: 808-922-3111; 800-325-3535).

Delightful Island Dining

 Although Honolulu is better known for its balmy climate and golden beaches, the city today offers a wide variety of first class restaurants and a broad spectrum of ethnic cuisines. Reflecting its history, Honolulu's culinary repertoire embraces traditional Polynesian, American, and continental dishes, as well as those from other nations around the world, including China, Japan, Korea, the Philippines, Thailand, and Vietnam. Thus menus will often feature a variety of dishes, including *lomilomi* salmon, sashimi, Portuguese bean soup, egg rolls, veal Oscar, teriyaki steaks, *coquilles St.-Jacques,* Korean *kal bi* ribs, macadamia nut ice cream, and lots of fresh fruit. The following selection of restaurants represents the very best of Honolulu's eateries. Reservations are essential at all dining spots.

CAFÉ SISTINA: Michelangelo and a magnificent menu are the major attractions at this energetic establishment. An unfinished re-creation of a section of the Sistine Chapel hangs above the bar, presumably to emphasize the fact that good art is at home anywhere. Plentiful portions of hearty northern Italian fare are served, with numerous antipasti and pasta dishes to tempt the fickle tongue, and simply superb entrées. On weekends the place is jammed, and currently considered an "in" spot with hip Honoluluans and their friends. After 10 PM, noise reaches a high-decibel pitch, when the owner's wife, a superb jazz vocalist, provides upbeat entertainment. Information: *Café Sistina,* 1314 S. King St., Honolulu, HI 96822 (phone: 808-526-0071).

CIAO MEIN: This restaurant serves an unlikely mix of Italian and Chinese cuisines. The masterful results prepared by the restaurant's two chefs are superb from either menu. Appetizers include savory sesame asparagus and black mushrooms in oyster sauce, antipasto misto (buffalo mozzarella, copa ham, calamaza olives, roasted onions, and sun-dried tomato croutons), and hearty minestrone soup with braised sausage. Entrées include roast duck served with carrots and cucumber, broiled prawns with Italian tomato butter sauce, and salmon baked in parchment in sea salt crust. There is indoor as well as alfresco seating on the *Hyatt*'s third-floor deck. Dinner is accompanied by live music. Information: *Caio Mein, Hyatt Regency,* 2424 Kalakaua Ave., Honolulu, HI 96815 (phone: 808-923-1234).

DYNASTY I: Crowded, noisy, and short on decor, this bustling spot serves some of the most authentic Chinese food this side of Hong Kong. You come here to eat, not to savor the ambience. Operated by a successful Hong Kong restaurant chain and located in the *Dynasty* hotel, it offers a broad seafood selection — including Oahu's famed Kahuku prawns, Dungeness crab, and Maine lobster. The prawns, which are the house specialty, are served several ways: panfried with peppery salt, steamed in garlic sauce on a bed of rice noodles, or sautéed in butter and garlic. But there's more than seafood on the nine-page menu: try the roast Cantonese duck, shredded pork with dried tofu, and scalded chicken with ginger and green onion sauce. Open around the clock, *Dynasty* even packs them in at 3 AM, when the last Waikiki club closes and night owls stop by for a snack. Information: *Dynasty I, Dynasty Hotel,* 1830 Ala Moana Blvd. Honolulu, HI 98618 (phone: 808-947-3771).

HY'S STEAKHOUSE: In Honolulu, a fish-and-rice city gone nouvelle, a restaurant devoted to red meat is hard to find. But when you're craving perfectly grilled steaks or chops, this is *the* place to go. Just a block from the beach in Waikiki, the plush dining room, with its velvet chairs and etched glass, is staffed with tuxedoed waiters and dominated by a glass, smoke-free gazebo where the chef works over a gleaming brass broiler. Steaks — from simple T-bones to New York strips studded with peppercorns — are the main attraction, but you can't go wrong with rack of lamb, baby back pork ribs, or even scallops in lobster cognac sauce. If you have room, among the calorie-laden desserts are cherries jubilee and bananas Foster. The thick, leather-bound wine list is heavy with hearty cabernets from France and California. Information: *Hy's Steakhouse,* 2440 Kuhio Ave., Honolulu, HI 96815 (phone: 808-922-5555).

KEO'S: Famed for its reputation as the first restaurant to put Thai food on Honolulu's map, this is one of five Thai restaurants owned by the same family. This particular spot offers the prettiest decor, which is a lush background of bamboo, potted palms, parasols, flowers, and paintings. An eclectic menu offers such delicacies as the establishment's signature dish, evil jungle prince (either chicken or prawns bathed in coconut milk, basil, and red chili), *penang* curry (chicken baked in kaffir lime leaves, fresh ground lemon grass, peas, and coconut milk), and Thai noodles made from sticky rice and stir-fried with bean sprouts, chives, and tofu. Unusual desserts include Thai banana chips with coconut ice cream and iced Thai tea, a traditional drink that tastes something like a milkshake. Just outside Waikiki, at the base of Diamond Head. Information: *Keo's,* 625 Kapahulu Ave., Honolulu, HI 96815 (phone: 808-737-8240).

MAILE: To compensate for the lack of a view, the *Maile* (named for a leaf often made into leis and always worn by a Hawaiian bridegroom on his wedding day) has a sumptuous decor of pools, heliconia, anthuriums, orchids, and a variety of tropical plants. Here the maile motif is seen on the gold-rimmed china, a patrician touch that is further underlined by tablecloths of Belgian lace. Among the items on the menu are some native specialties that receive opulent treatment: mahimahi glazed with bananas served on creamed mushrooms; spicy ahi on balsamic mango coulis with curried wild rice; filet of opakapaka (pink snapper) with *beurre blanc* sauce; and luscious dessert soufflés. Petits fours and chocolate are served with coffee, and unobtrusive background music is provided by a classical guitarist or pianist. Meals are deftly served by ladies in kimonos who seem to sum up all that is traditionally feminine and graceful about the East. There is a touch of enchantment about dining here. Information: *Maile, Kahala Hilton,* 5000 Kahala Ave., Kahala, HI 96816 (phone: 808-734-2211).

LA MER: The *Halekulani's* fine dining room is elegantly subdued, with a menu that is innovative and delicious. Appetizers include salad of sautéed foie gras and sautéed Kahuku prawns, with standard fare turned exotic — entrées such as whole onaga baked in a thyme and rosemary rock salt crust and *papillote* of kumu with shiitake mushrooms and basil — both dishes enhanced with *ogo,* also known as Hawaiian seaweed. Those longing for Paris should order the cheese course; in due time, a cart laden down with the finest cheese this side of the Left Bank arrives for your perusal. Service is attentive and professional. This is a match for the best when it comes to intimate dining. Information: *La Mer, Halekulani,* 2199 Kalia Rd., Honolulu, HI 96815 (phone: 808-923-2311).

MICHEL'S: Scattered across the south of France are scores of medium-size restaurants that scornfully eschew the "folksy-rustic" look in favor of an ambience that suggests upper middle class prosperity. The cooking in these places is usually impeccable. So it is with *Michel's.* Diners sit under crystal chandeliers on banquettes or chairs upholstered in Belgian velvet with Regency stripes, at tables elegantly set with fine china, brilliantly polished glass, and crisp, snow-white napery. Quiet and skillful service is civilized, without fuss or pressure. Most of the dishes on the menu are classics, such as lobster bisque with brandy and roast rack of veal. When local produce is used, it is treated in a classic fashion. Fresh opakapaka, for instance, is poached in champagne and served with hollandaise sauce and grapes to become *opakapaka poche au champagne Véronique* — triumphantly. Information: *Michel's,* 2895 Kalakaua Ave., Honolulu, HI 96815 (phone: 808-923-6552).

NICK'S FISHMARKET: Opened 20 years ago by Chicago restaurateur Nicholas Nickolas, this spot has a loyal mainland fan club. With its luxurious black leather booths and tuxedoed waiters, *Nick's* is not just another seafood spot. Head chef Edward

Fernandez rises before dawn to shop Honolulu's fish market for the best local catch of the day — everything from ono to mahimahi, ulua, opah (Japanese moon fish) and auku (broadbill swordfish). The rest of the seafood, including Mississippi catfish, Alaskan salmon, Idaho trout, and even elusive abalone from Baja, California, is flown in daily. House specialties include Nick's Fishmarket chowder, Thai scallops with Malaysian curry rice, and grilled Burmese tiger prawns. Nothing here is inexpensive, but the prix fixe dinner ($28) — which includes chowder, salad with the house's creamy spinach dressing, and your choice of perfectly grilled local fish — is a real bargain. Who could ask for more? Information: *Nick's Fishmarket,* 2070 Kalakaua Ave., Honolulu, HI 96815 (phone: 808-955-6333).

ORCHIDS: Another one of the *Halekulani's* restaurants, this casually elegant open-air eatery, with rattan seating and pots of colorful orchids, gets high marks for its alluring setting: It's steps from the beach and has expansive views of the sea and the jagged arc of Diamond Head. And the food more than lives up to its surroundings. Sample the three-course table d'hôte menu ($36) that includes such dishes as roasted free-range chicken seasoned with garlic, rosemary-marinated ahi with *tapenade,* or blackened scallops with a salad of fiddlehead ferns and watercress. The desserts are delish — frozen lemon soufflé topped with passion fruit sauce, island fruits served with guava sorbet, or 3-tiered coconut layer cake with raspberry coulis. You'll probably find yourself coming back for breakfast. The ocean view is even better first thing in the morning, and who could resist the wholewheat pancakes with macadamia nuts, Belgian waffles, or the lighter-than-air popovers served with poha berry jelly? Information: *Orchids, Halekulani Hotel,* 2199 Kalia Rd., Waikiki (phone: 808-923-2311).

PRINCE COURT: Two indisputable facts about this dining establishment are its charming, airy surroundings and its polite, unobtrusive staff. A third is the superb menu, whose specialties range from kiawe grilled capon to pan sautéed tenderloin of veal with porcini mushrooms to blackened blue ahi to Hawaiian bouillabaisse. Everything is flavorfully prepared, and the fare is so artistically arranged on the plate that you might be tempted to take a photo to preserve the memory. The Sunday brunch is a knockout. Information: *Prince Court, Hawaii Prince,* 100 Holomoana St., Honolulu, HI (phone: 808-956-1111).

ROY'S/ROY'S PARK BISTRO: Master chef Roy Yamaguchi has created an eclectic Eurasian menu that has catapulted this eponymous place to fame as one of Honolulu's most popular eateries. The lively ambience, with the kitchen on display, the casually elegant dining room, the prompt service, and specialties such as Mongolian loin of Niihau lamb with island vinaigrette and cabernet sauce, and smoked Peking-style duck with candied pecans and a lilikoi ginger sauce, are first-rate reasons to come here. *Roy's Park Bistro* (1956 Ala Moana Blvd., *Waikiki Park Plaza Hotel,* Honolulu, HI 96825; phone: 808-944-4624) in Waikiki has an equally eclectic menu. Specialties include salmon with a goat cheese crust and sun-dried tomato sauce, Muscovy duck in a blueberry hazelnut cabernet sauce, and lobster with macadamia nut butter sauce. Maui-bound visitors may also want to check out *Roy's Kahana Bar & Grill,* a creative culinary counterpart to its Oahu cousins. Information: *Roy's,* Hawaii Kai Corporate Plaza, 6600 Kalanianaole Hwy. (phone: 808-396-ROYS).

WILLOWS: Ah, *The Willows!* Outdoors, indoors, in a grass shack–like longhouse, under thatch umbrella roofs, by a carp pond, or surrounded by palms and hibiscus, wherever you sit you experience the graceful flavor of a bygone era — not the one that existed before the missionaries arrived, but something akin to that found by the early passengers on the Pacific liners that used to call at Honolulu en route from San Francisco to the Far East. While dining, listen to old Hawaiian songs accompanied only by the bass and the ukulele and the intense hush of a tropical night.

A specialty of the house is the Poi Supper, which includes most of the ingredients of a real luau on a smaller scale, such as laulau, a mixture of fish and pork wrapped in ti leaves and steamed; chicken luau, simmered with ti leaves and coconut milk; *lomilomi* salmon, chopped salt salmon mixed with onions and tomatoes; sweet potatoes; and poi itself, the bland, smooth paste made from the taro root that is a Hawaiian staple. Desserts are a specialty, so indulge yourself with the coconut cream pie or chocolate gâteau. An indisputable way to appreciate *The Willows* is to come for Poi Thursday's spirit of aloha. Hawaiian entertainment here is full of spontaneity and is well-attended by many old-timers. It's one of the few places where visitors can experience Hawaiian hospitality at its best. Information: *The Willows,* 901 Hausten St., Honolulu, HI 96826 (phone: 808-946-4808).

YANAGI SUSHI: If you want to splurge on sushi, try this *shoji*-screen restaurant, whose name translates as "willow tree." Located on Kapiolani Boulevard on the outskirts of Honolulu's capital district, *Yanagi* attracts many well-known Japanese visitors, including sumo wrestlers and politicans; their photographs and autographs (dramatic black brushstrokes on sheets of white paper) adorn the walls. Although it's known for serving the city's freshest sashimi and sushi, traditional Japanese dishes are also available, and recommended. Information: *Yanagi Sushi,* 762 Kapiolani Blvd. Honolulu, HI 96826 (phone: 808-537-1525).

Shopping Spree

Most people do more shopping in Hawaii than they originally intended, and not simply because shopping is an integral part of any holiday. It probably won't be long after you've stepped from the plane before you begin to feel constricted and lackluster in your mainland clothing, chic as it was at home. Just as you conclude that absolutely everybody is wearing something loose and billowy, its surface rampant with splashy birds, flowers, and leaves, you'll notice that some commercially minded citizen has had the prescience to place, if not a shopping center, at least a shop, exactly where you happen to be. Before you know it, you will have outfitted yourself in a manner you never dreamed possible, in something you will probably never find occasion to wear again. Moreover, you will more than likely never regret your purchase and, once transformed, will look around to find what else is for sale. The only warning offered here is to plan for these purchases before you go — and leave room in your suitcase for the souvenirs you'll inevitably acquire.

Most of what Hawaii's merchants have to offer falls into the souvenir and gift category — T-shirts, shell leis, woven hats, Polynesian bric-a-brac — or alohawear, a designation that includes any clothes with the casual island look, from elegant evening skirts of hand-painted silk to inexpensive muumuus. These items are in alarming abundance virtually everywhere. As expected, hotel boutiques and shops near popular tourist attractions tend to be more expensive than stores catering to a resident clientele. But if you're only buying a $4.95 T-shirt or carved keychain, it's probably not worth wasting precious vacation time looking for the very best prices.

Beyond the mountains of trinkets and flowered shirts, however, are some goods of a distinctly higher caliber, and chances are there will come a time to contemplate a more serious purchase. Thanks to heightened native Hawaiian consciousness, there has been a revival of interest in traditional crafts. Niihau shell leis, intricately worked garlands of the tiny, lustrous shells found on the leeward beaches of the island of Niihau, and elaborate feather leis are highly prized collector's items found in some Honolulu galleries. There has also been a flowering of contemporary art: Painters, sculptors, ceramists, jewelers, woodturners, and glass blowers are producing a prodigious amount of island-inspired work. Much of it is amateurish, to be sure, but some is attracting the attention of the serious art world.

Since Hawaii has always been a trading center between East and West, it is also the place to pick up such treasures as jade from Burma and Taiwan, Japanese porcelain, Cambodian and Tibetan antiques, Thai silks, or hand-embroidered linen from China. Though not easily found, shops selling Oriental antiques do exist on all the main islands. Ivory carvings are also found in abundance, though visitors are advised against buying them because of the damage trafficking in ivory has caused to remaining wild elephant herds.

BEST BUYS

Following is an item-by-item guide to the best shopping in Honolulu.

Alohawear – Any loose-fitting, casual garment made in a bright floral print qualifies as alohawear. *Liberty House,* Hawaii's best-known retailer, and *Reyn's* (*Ala Moana Center*) are well-known for good-quality island attire. For alohawear a cut above average, try *Apparels of Pauline* (*Royal Hawaiian Hotel* and *Hilton Hawaiian Village*), *Linda's Vintage Isle* (373 Olohana St.), or *Bailey's Antique and Thrift Shop* (758 Kapahulu Ave.).

Arts and Crafts – Paintings, watercolors, prints, sculpture, ceramics, hand-blown glasswork, jewelry, and carved wood, much of it by local artists and inspired by island themes, can be found at a number of galleries. Among them: *Artists Guild* (*Ward Warehouse*), *Ala Moana Center, Pacific Island Arts,* and *Wyland Gallery* (Haleiwa). Also visit the shops at the *Honolulu Academy of Arts* and the *Contemporary Museum,* the Sunday art show at the Honolulu Zoo, and check the newspaper for local craft fairs.

Coral – All those necklaces of pinkish orange bunched twigs are white coral from Japan and Taiwan, dyed to give the coral effect; they are not precious coral. The pink precious coral in island shops comes from the Kaiwi Channel between Molokai and Oahu, and so does the gold coral, which is found only in the Hawaiian Islands. (There is something similar in Alaska, but it is not quite the same color.) Black coral is harvested off the coast of Maui, while the dark, oxblood red coral, considerably more expensive, is a Mediterranean import. *Coral Grotto* (*Hyatt Regency* and *Ala Moana Shopping Center*).

Eastern Art and Artifacts – Exquisite jade and ivory carvings, Japanese ceramics, and Chinese cloisonné are some of the Eastern arts that have found their way to Polynesian America. *Max Davis* (Kilohana Sq.); *Lai Fong* and *Waterfall Gallery* (Nuuanu Ave.); *Bushido Antiques* (Eaton Sq.); *Robyn Buntin, Garakuta-do,* and *Sweet By-Gones* (Maunakea St.); *Bernard Hurtig's Oriental Treasures* (*Kahala Hilton*); *Iida's* (*Ala Moana Shopping Center*).

Edibles – Papayas, avocados, and bananas must be treated before they can be taken to the mainland; coconuts and pineapples may go as they are. Even so, it's best to buy all fruit from airport shops on your way home (so you won't have to lug your lovely bunch of coconuts around the islands) or from "take home" stores elsewhere, many of which will deliver to your flight. Coconuts can also be labeled, stamped, and sent "as is" through the mail. Macadamia nuts, Kona coffee, Maui potato chips (be sure to get "Kitch'n Cook'd"), taro chips, and crack seed — preserved fruits, nuts, and seeds — can be found in many shops catering to tourists, as can the Hawaiian Plantations line of products, including tropical fruit jams and mango chutney. *Honolulu Chocolate Co.* (Manoa Ave. and Restaurant Row); *Lappert's Ice Cream* (*Ala Moana Center*); *Matsumoto's* (for shaved ice, Haleiwa); *Crack Seed Center* (*Ala Moana Center*); *Woolworth's* (Waikiki); *Duty Free Shops* (Honolulu International Airport).

Enameled Jewelry – During the 19th century, Hawaii's royal ladies developed a liking for this jewelry, black enamel on gold inscribed with their names. Modern examples of the art can cost between $100 and $400 for a ring and between $300 and $1,200 for a bracelet. *Precious Metals Hawaii* (Suite 616, 1600 Kapiolani Blvd.); *Rain-*

bow Bazaar (Hilton Hawaiian Village); Royal Hawaiian Heritage (1430 Kona St., across from the *Ala Moana Center*).

Fabrics – Silks from Europe and the Far East, hand-painted Hawaiian panels, and endless yards of tropical prints fill boutiques and department stores all over Honolulu.

Feather Leis – This ancient Hawaiian art has been revived and updated, using the feathers of peacocks and pheasants to create beautiful and fanciful hatbands. A feather lei can cost from $50 to $1,000. *Royal Feather Co.* (Aiea).

Flower Leis – The symbol of Hawaiian hospitality and a joy to indulge in as often as possible during your stay, flower leis are sold at airports, by street vendors, and at hotels and shops all over the islands. There's a fine selection at the lineup of lei stands at Honolulu International Airport, a short walk from the main terminal. Chinatown also features small lei shops on Maunakea, Nuuanu, and King Streets, where prices are generally less than at the airport or Waikiki lei stands.

Hawaiian Music – At first hearing, the falsetto singing of traditional Hawaiian music may sound peculiar to Western ears, but before long most people are seduced by its sweet and strange melodiousness. Musicians and groups for which to look include the *Brothers Cazimero,* Eddie Kamae, Palani Vaughn, the *Beamer Brothers,* the *Sons of Hawaii,* and the *Makaha Sons of Niihau. House of Music (Ala Moana Center); Tower Records* (Keaumoku St.).

Hawaiian Quilts – Introduced by New England missionaries, local quilt-making quickly developed a unique Hawaiian style by introducing designs of native flora and motifs from the royal era. It's almost impossible to buy an authentic antique example, but quilt kits and patterns are widely available. Visit *Elizabeth's Fancy* (767 Kailua Rd., Kailua), *Hawaii Quilts* (S. King St.) or write the *Hawaiian Quilt Collection* (PO Box 632, Kailua, Oahu 96734) for their small catalogue of custom-made quilts.

Hawaiiana – Guides, maps, books on Hawaiian flora, fauna, history, culture, legends, language, food, crafts — any printed material to feed the curiosity of the new Hawaiiphile comes under this heading. *Waldenbooks (Waikiki Shopping Plaza and Ward Warehouse); Honolulu Book Shop (Ala Moana Shopping Center* and 1001 Bishop St.); *Shop Pacifica* (1525 Bernice St.) at the *Bishop Museum; The Museum Shop* at the *Honolulu Academy of Arts* (900 S. Beretania St.); *Little Hawaiian Craft Shop (Royal Hawaiian Shopping Center); University of Hawaii Bookstore.*

Jade – Much of the jade jewelry and objets d'art in the islands are from Burma or Taiwan. Burmese jade, which comes in a rainbow of greens, reds, and lavenders, is the connoisseur's choice. *Monarch Jade; Security Diamond (Ala Moana Center); Liberty House; Ming's; Hildgund;* and various Honolulu antiques stores.

Kukui Nut Jewelry – Called the candlenut because its oil was used in lamps, the nut of the ubiquitous kukui tree is polished to a high sheen and made into necklaces, bracelets, and other jewelry. Black is the least expensive ($8 for a plain choker); brown, slightly higher; and jewelry made of the rare white nut, the most expensive. *Kukui Nuts of Hawaii* (66-935 Kaukonahua Rd., Waialua), Hawaii's only manufacturer of kukui nut jewelry, also offers the widest selection. Also available at *Shop Pacifica (Bishop Museum,* 1525 Bernice St.).

Lau Hala – Products woven from the leaves of the pandanus tree range from big-weave placemats, napkin rings, baskets, and boxes to finely textured hats of distinction. *Products of Hawaii (Ala Moana Shopping Center).*

Leather Goods – Like any ranching country, Hawaii has its share of shops that cater to the needs of cowboys and would-be cowboys who simply appreciate fine leatherwork. *Yokohama-Okadaya (Royal Hawaiian Shopping Center), Bebe's (Waikiki Trade Center), Raku Leather (Royal Hawaiian Shopping Center), Louis Vuitton (Royal Hawaiian Shopping Center), Escada, Hermès, Chanel, MCM, Paniolo, Gucci,* and *North Beach Leather (Ala Moana Center).*

Pacific Art and Artifacts – Balinese paintings, antiques from Borneo and the

Marshall Islands, and Malaysian kites are among the many imports from Hawaii's Pacific neighbors. The *Little Hawaiian Craft Shop* (*Royal Hawaiian Shopping Center*).

Plants – Seeds, cuttings, and potted specimens of Hawaii's abundant and exotic plant life — plumeria, ginger, orchids, birds of paradise, protea, anthuriums, hibiscus, ti, bamboo — inspected by the Department of Agriculture and packed to travel, are available at several airport shops; some of the larger stores will mail plants.

Swimwear – As expected, there's a dizzying selection. Try *Down Under Honolulu* (2139 Kuhio Ave.) and any branch of *Liberty House* or *Reyn's*.

Tapa Cloth – Also called kapa, tapa is the bark fabric worn by Hawaiians before Westerners introduced them to cotton. Most of the tapa found in Hawaii today, in the form of wall hangings, table linen, placemats, boxes, and purses, comes from Samoa and Tonga, although it's possible to get an old piece of Hawaiian tapa for $100 and up. *Shop Pacifica* (*Bishop Museum,* 1525 Bernice St.).

T-Shirts – Even the most out-of-the-way places have them, emblazoned with an endless variety of designs and messages. *Crazy Shirts* (Kalakaua Ave.) is the big name, but there are numerous others, including *Novelty World* (*Ward Warehouse*).

Wood Items – Out of the islands' native woods, woodturners make beautiful art of everyday objects, such as bowls, trays, and boxes. The best known wood, koa, is often called Hawaiian mahogany because of its rich, reddish tone and lustrous finish. Mango wood, whitish to tan in color, is shot through with streaks of pink, yellow, and sometimes green, producing what one artisan calls rainbow wood. Monkeypod ranges from light to dark brown, while milo wood is reddish with patches of beige. A very rare and lovely wood is kaimani, which is light to reddish pink in tone and is finely grained. *Martin & MacArthur Koa Wood Furnishings* (Bishop St.); *Nohea Gallery* (*Ward Warehouse*).

■ **Book Mark:** We immodestly suggest that in addition to the book you now hold in your hands, you also pick up a copy of *Birnbaum's Hawaii 1993* (HarperCollins, $17).

Glorious Gardens

Not surprisingly, there are some splendid gardens in one of the garden spots of the world. Those graced with thumbs of green — as well as anyone who just appreciates the beauty of nature — will enjoy Honolulu's botanical gardens and preserves. These spots are easy to find and each is worth spending at least an hour, perhaps a half day, exploring. Most have picnic facilities — and what better place to enjoy an alfresco meal than a setting of stately trees, fragrant flowers, and exotic birds. Below, our favorite green spaces.

FOSTER BOTANICAL GARDEN: An oasis in downtown Honolulu on the outskirts of the business district, this fertile 20-acre plot is dominated by beautiful old trees, many planted in 1855 by renowned botanist William Hillebrand. There are 26 exotic trees in all, among them the double coconut palm, which bears nuts weighing up to 50 pounds. Also of interest are a "prehistoric glen" filled with ancient fern species, the native Hawaiian plants of the Liliuokalani garden, and 800 varieties of orchids. Open daily 9 AM to 4 PM. Information: *Foster Botanical Garden,* 50 N. Vineyard Blvd. (phone: 808-522-7065).

HALAWA XERISCAPE GARDEN: It's difficult to believe that tropical Oahu could ever experience a drought, but the possibility is real: Researchers predict that in 20 years Oahu's population will have increased to such an extent that its natural groundwater reservoirs will begin to be depleted. In an effort to promote water conservation and educate the public, the Honolulu Board of Water Supply created this unique garden on 3 acres in the bone-dry Halawa Valley above Pearl Harbor, about 12 miles from Waikiki. Here is living proof that Hawaii's abundant flora can thrive with 30% to 80% less water. A variety of drought-tolerant ornamentals, succulents, and trees seem to flourish in these surprisingly lush gardens. An hour-long stroll reveals all kinds of plants — from Hawaii's showy hibiscus to the firecracker plant of Mexico — growing in the desert-like environment. Gardeners — especially from Los Angeles and other drought-prone areas — will learn a lot about low-hydration plant care. Open 10 AM to 2 PM Wednesdays through Saturdays. Information: *Halawa Xeriscape Garden,* 630 S. Perrepania St. (phone: 808-527-6126).

KOKO CRATER BOTANICAL GARDEN: Spread out over 200 acres in an old volcano crater beyond Diamond Head are collections of cacti from the mainland desert, Madagascar, and Africa, as well as a stand of hybrid plumeria, red-seeded wiliwili trees, and some brilliantly colored bougainvillea. To reach this garden, take the small unpaved road near *Koko Head Stables* at the southeast end of Oahu; it's small but well worth the trip. Information: *Koko Crater Botanical Garden,* 50 N. Vineyard Blvd. (phone: 808-522-7064).

LYON ARBORETUM: In the misty Manoa Valley, only a few minutes from the modern towers of Waikiki, is Honolulu's rain forest, green and lush and full of rainbows, showers, waterfalls, tropical plants, and exotic birds. An object of civic pride, every day more than 100 volunteers come to care for this 124-acre wilderness, where ancient Hawaiians once tended taro fields. There are more than 8,500 plants here — 5,000 of them native to Hawaii — including palms, figs, taro, gingers, prayer plants, rhododendrons, and birds of paradise. When you go, be prepared to get wet. Dress for a rainy day even if it's sunny in Waikiki (a slicker will suffice) and wear old shoes, since the trails can be muddy. Open Mondays through Fridays from 9 AM to 3 PM, Saturdays until noon. Information: *Lyon Arboretum,* 3860 Manoa Rd. (phone: 808-988-3177).

MOANALUA GARDENS: Known for their magnificent trees, among them a Buddha tree from Ceylon and a giant monkeypod, purported to be the "world's most beautifully shaped tree," by no less an authority than *Ripley's Believe It or Not,* these gardens are just off the H1 Freeway. Only about 5 miles from downtown Honolulu, this lush spot provides a welcome respite from the bustle of the city. Free guided walks, offered on weekends, will acquaint you with the many intriguing native plants found here; call ahead for reservations. Information: *Moanalua Gardens,* 1352 Pineapple Pl. (phone: 808-839-5334).

WAHIAWA BOTANICAL GARDEN: Created by the Hawaii Sugar Planters Association, this 27-acre garden in the town of Wahiawa in central Oahu, is dense with plants that thrive in the wet, cool mountainous regions of Oahu. Expect to see anthuriums, philodendrons and other native species as well as a spectacular Mindanao gum tree (a eucalyptus with a rainbow-colored bark). Open daily 9 AM to 4 PM. Information: *Wahiawa Botanical Garden,* 1396 California Ave. (phone: 808-621-7321).

For the Body

Dream Beaches

The best beaches of Honolulu? Even the ones considered only ordinary by *akamai* (in-the-know) residents are often exquisite by mainland standards, with their bright seascapes of blue skies and even bluer waters, strands of white ringed by sea palms, pandanus, and ironwood pines, and ocean surf ranging from gentle baby swells to monster rollers up to 30 feet high.

The beachcombing possibilities on Oahu are endless. More than 1,500 varieties of shells wash up on the island's beaches, and in some areas the remnants of wrecked ships can also be found. Some coastlines have wave-washed rocky shores and lava ledges, as well as exposed tide pools and shallow reef flats. Exploring these areas for marine invertebrates can be a fascinating alternative to sun worshiping. Protective gloves and reef walkers (rubber ankle boots available in sporting good stores) are recommended for wading in tide pools and walking on the reefs.

To avoid angering residents by trespassing on private property, look for Public Access to Beach signs. If you're searching for secluded beaches, check around; an unmarked road cut through a sugar plantation will often lead to an isolated, heavenly oceanside site.

Be mindful of sea conditions in Honolulu. Riptides, dangerous undertows, sharp coral bottoms, and other such hazards are not always readily discernible to *malihinis* (newcomers). So check with lifeguards, surfers, or residents before entering the water.

WAIKIKI: This 2-mile arc of sand lined with resort hotels is probably the single most famous beach in the world. Waikiki is relatively clean and free of litter but is often carpeted instead with large numbers of sunbathers. Replacement sand that's been trucked in to bolster "the Beach" is constantly washed out to sea and has altered the contour of the offshore ocean floor. Consequently, the shape and size of Waikiki's famous surfing waves are changing. Surfboard rentals, catamaran sails, and outrigger canoe rides are available at concession stands up and down the beach. The best sections of beach lie closer to Diamond Head, a 15-minute walk from central Waikiki. An acquired taste by day, Waikiki is a great place to go for a moonlight stroll, and the hour immediately after dawn makes rising early worth the effort.

ALA MOANA PARK: Honolulu residents and Waikiki exiles flock to this 76-acre park to build sand castles, fly kites, or spread a picnic in a grassy area. Safe, reef-sheltered waters make it a popular place to bring kids. Deep offshore channels makes it a favorite spot with swimmers. Those bored with sun and surf activities can walk across the street to the *Ala Moana Shopping Center,* a huge complex of more than 200 stores.

HANAUMA BAY BEACH PARK: An extinct volcanic crater shaped into a huge outdoor aquarium by sea erosion, Hanauma Bay is one of Oahu's top areas for under-water exploration, a fact that brings almost ruinous crowds to this once quiet spot. Now a designated marine preserve, it has sand pockets within the reef that provide good swimming, especially the Keyhole and a small inlet with a natural rock-carved hole called the Toilet Bowl. Bring food: The fish will eat out of your hand on the reef. In addition, the tide pools contain many fascinating creatures. Snorkelers should be wary of a turbulent area of the bay known as Witches Brew, as well as the Molokai Express, a strong current that sweeps across the outer edge of the bay. Movie buffs (especially Elvis Presley fans) will recognize Hanauma as the backdrop for the 1961 film *Blue Hawaii.*

LANIKAI BEACH: One of Oahu's best-kept secrets, this slender, 1-mile crescent of sand is situated on a palm-fringed lagoon just south of Kailua on the Windward Coast. At the foot of jagged Kaiwa Ridge, its coral sand is soft and powdery, and the water, in hues ranging from nile green to royal blue, looks as if it was squeezed from an artist's paint tubes. The surf is small and gentle, and Mokulua, two pyramid-shaped islands offshore, are natural subjects for Sunday painters and irresistible destinations for kayakers or swimmers strong enough to to make the three-quarter-mile journey. Lanikai is almost hidden from view in an exclusive coastal community, occupied by artists, writers, and a few Hollywood celebrities who take a proprietary view of this public beach, but don't be intimidated — find the sandy paths between the houses that provide public access to the beach. Most days you'll have the place completely to yourself.

GOAT ISLAND (MOKUAUIA BEACH): Simply wade across a narrow strait of water — on a calm day, at low tide — to reach this small island off the North Shore's Kalanai Point. (Wear sneakers to protect your feet from the coral, and don't attempt to cross if the surf is rough.) The island's sandy beach is protected by an offshore reef that makes swimming ideal, especially for children. Goat Island is a state bird refuge, with many bird species in its ironwood trees.

NORTH SHORE: SUNSET, PIPELINE, WAIMEA, AND EHUKAI: Along with other legendary North Shore surf sites such as Waimea Bay, Banzai Beach (home of the deadly "Pipeline"), and Ehukai Beach Park, Sunset is where towering mountains of water crash into shore during the winter. One of Oahu's largest tracts of sand, Sunset Beach stretches for 2 miles. Be aware that swimming in certain stretches can be dangerous, except for a few weeks in the summer. It may be wiser just to pack a picnic lunch and bring a pair of binoculars to watch the world's most daring surfers challenge the largest surfable waves on earth.

WAIMANALO BEACH – This sandy demi-paradise, about 15 miles east of Waikiki, stretches for more than 3 miles around the curve of Waimanalo Bay, making it the longest continuous beach on Oahu. Bellows Beach, as the northern nexus is known, is part of a military complex and therefore open only on weekends and certain holidays. The gentle but always active surf here makes it popular with people just learning to board- and body-surf. The beach's grassy shoreline park is a popular spot for family picnics, and the coast is a favorite of surf casters who fish for papio (baby pompano, which Hawaiians call ulua), weke, and goat fish. Be aware that Portuguese man-of-war jellyfish are also found in the area; keep your distance, since they impart an unpleasant sting. Stop in Waimanalo town to check out the roadside shell shops and, in season, the fruit stands that sell sweet bananas, corn, and watermelon. Just south of Waimanalo is Sandy Beach, a wide coral strand that is a dream come true for expert body-surfers, but a certain danger for all others. Lifeguards hoist up warning flags here when the conditions are dicey; if they're red, stay out of the water. Come here to sunbathe, fly kites, or watch the experts catch the waves, but be cautious when you go near the water.

MOKULEIA: This mile-long stretch of beach at the western end of Oahu is often nearly deserted, except for local fishermen, picnicking families, and military personnel on a day off (much of the beach is military-owned land). The Waianae Mountains provide a lovely green backdrop, and while swimming is complicated by close-to-shore reefs, there are coastal pools where you can cool off, as well as pockets of deeper water.

KAILUA: Powder-white sand and vibrantly turquoise water make this miles-long beach one of the island's most beautiful. Although houses line much of the shoreline, there is a beach park with shower and picnic facilities on the eastern end and numerous public access points elsewhere along the coast. Steady winds make this a favorite spot for windsurfers.

■**WHO SELLS SEA SHELLS:** If your beachcombing fails to yield your idea of a perfect souvenir of the deep, look for orange horned helmets, tritons, nautilus, and other Pacific shells at Waikiki's *International Market Place* (2330 Kalakaua Ave.; phone: 808-923-9871), or for even better prices, at the roadside stands in Waimanalo. In Honolulu, check out *Shellworld Hawaii* (870 Kawaiahao St.; phone: 808-521-6606), a major dealer with showrooms as well as a warehouse where shells and shell-decorated household items are sold at wholesale prices.

Sensational Surfing

"Let's go surfing now, everybody's learning how, come on a safari with me." So sang the *Beach Boys* and *Jan and Dean* of surfing's heyday during the 1960s, when "woodies" (old wood-sided station wagons loaded with surf-boards), "hanging ten" (putting all ten toes over the front edge of the board), and bleached-blond surfers were the rage. Interest in the sport may have peaked on the mainland, but on Oahu surfing remains an endless summer of sandy beaches, open-air snack bars, and near-perfect surfing conditions.

The individual Hawaiian islands are actually the tops of volcanic mountains rising from the ocean floor, and without a continental shelf to slow them down or shrink them, the North Pacific's winter swells attain monstrous proportions by the time they reach the coastline. The raw energy of these great rollers combines with the contour of the ocean bottom to create the biggest (and best-shaped) surfing waves in the world.

But the beginning surfer need not feel left out here. Waikiki Beach has relatively tame conditions where, in a short time, a novice can learn how to balance the board — and ultimately how to catch a wave. (It takes years to refine technique and develop a personal style.)

One-hour group instruction rates cost about $25, including the use of a board. Private lessons are higher. Surfboard rentals start at $5 per hour and go to $25 per day. The Morey Doyle boards — made from a soft fiber foam that is more buoyant and stable than the hard, fiberglass boards — are recommended for "gremlins" (novice surfers). (A hard stringer running from tip to tail makes these boards firm enough to stand on.) "Boogie boards," short body-surfing boards made of soft polyurethane that are ridden in a kneeling or prone position, are also popular. Rental fees range from $7.50 to $15 for a full day.

The appeal of surfing escapes definition. It is a spontaneous, creative activity that is never the same twice because each wave has its own characteristics. Surfboards have come a long way from the long flat wooden planks used by Hawaiian royalty, who surfed to prove the worthiness of their leadership, but the sensation hasn't changed in 200 years. Said Captain Cook of a surfer he observed in 1777: "I could not help concluding that this man felt the most supreme pleasure while he was driven so fast and so smoothly by the sea." So if the surf's up and you're so inclined, go catch a wave.

Just the thought of Oahu is guaranteed to raise goose pimples on any serious surfer's skin. In part because of its fortuitous location, the island has some of the finest surfing breaks in the world. The North Shore, where giant 30-foot waves arrive in the winter, is still the ultimate proving ground for professionals and top amateurs.

Beginners confine themselves to the mellow swells at Waikiki Beach, where professional "beach boys" are available for surfing lessons at a number of concessions along the beach. The instructors at *Waikiki Beach Services,* for example, go through the motions of surfing on land with students before wading into the "soup" (foamy white water) to get the feel of the board underfoot. "We eliminate the fear aspect of the sport," said one teacher. Once gremlins learn to stand with their feet parallel and wide apart, their knees bent, and their weight forward, they are in position to ride a wave. Willing students with good balance can learn to surf in an hour. Catching a wave takes a bit more practice, but the sensation of being carried along on the board is indescribably exhilarating. Information: *Waikiki Beach Services,* c/o *Outrigger Reef Hotel,* 2169 Kalia Rd., Honolulu, HI 96815 (phone: 808-924-4940 or 808-924-4941), or *Sheraton Waikiki,* 2255 Kalakaua Ave., Honolulu, HI 96815 (phone: 808-922-4422).

In addition to Waikiki, Oahu's other top beginner and intermediate beaches include Ala Moana, Diamond Head, and Koko Head. Black Point near Diamond Head, with the great brown and green slopes of the eroded volcanic cone overlooking the surf, is one of the most beautiful settings for wave riding in the islands.

The *Haleiwa Surf Center* at the Alii Beach Park on Oahu's North Shore is a water sports center, run by the island's Department of Parks and Recreation, where surfing (including using the board) is taught *free of charge* on weekends. The beach park is well south of the more famous North Shore sites, where the waves are often higher than most of the homes in the area! The surf at Alii Beach averages 2 to 4 feet, ideal for beginners. Information: *Haleiwa Surf Center,* 66167 Haleiwa Rd., Haleiwa, HI 96712 (phone: 808-637-5051).

When the great North Pacific swells roll in from Alaska and Siberia in late fall and early winter, the cream of the sport gathers on the North Shore for pro tournaments and competitions. The three top sites, strictly for experts, are Sunset Beach, Waimea Bay, and the Banzai Pipeline. Waves break in a curl and envelop surfers in a tube at the famed Pipeline, but this is probably the most dangerous surfing site on earth, as surfers risk being thrown onto the sharp coral reef bottom. Mistakes here are costly — and painful.

Windsurfing

The fastest-growing sport in the world, windsurfing has found a special home on Oahu. This is because the ideal learning conditions for beginners include a bay with a wide sandy beach, smooth warm water, and a light breeze; Oahu has all of these elements in abundance. The island also has prevailing onshore, or sea, breezes that blow at an angle to shore and prevent a careless novice from being swept out to sea.

In addition to its ideal beginner conditions, Oahu has some of the best expert and competition waters in the world. "Surf-sailing" and wave-jumping, advanced techniques using wind *and* waves to produce an exciting (and often airborne) ride, are among the windsurfing variations that have been pioneered here.

Instructors say novices require a minimum of 2 hours of lessons to acquaint themselves with the rudiments of the sport; dancers, sailors, and skiers tend to pick it up most quickly. One instructor thinks that women often make rapid improvement because they "plug into the feel of the wind and its effect on the sail without trying to resort to sheer strength." Windsurfing lessons start at $30 for a 2-hour session. A half hour is usually spent on a ground simulator to learn wind theory. Windsurfer rentals start at $10 per hour with half- and full-day discounts available.

The Kailua Beach Park area, on the windward side of Oahu, lays claim to some of the finest windsurfing grounds in the world. A mere 30 minutes by car from Honolulu, Kailua is a gathering place for hot shots, gurus, and top board and sail designers, all of whom congregate in much the same way that surfers did on the North Shore in the 1950s to test-ride new fiberglass boards. *World Cup* windsurfing competitions are held here each year.

Windsurfing Hawaii's *Kailua Beach School* offers private lessons for $50, including a 1½-hour lesson and a 2½-hour rental, and group lessons for $35 for the same lesson/rental package, and provides equipment rentals for beginner and advanced sailors. Because there are no hotels on its beaches, the Kailua area is relatively uncrowded and, therefore, ideal for windsurfing. From the water, sailors see a white sand beach ringed by palm trees, with the vivid green and often cloud-encircled peaks of the Koolau Range in the distance. For those who want to purchase a sailboard, the *Windsurfing Hawaii* shop, 5 minutes from the beach, probably has the best selection of beginner and high-performance custom boards and accessories in the islands. Information: *Kailua Beach School,* 155A Hamakua Dr., Kailua, HI 96734 (phone: 808-261-3539).

Best Depths: Snorkeling and Scuba Diving

 As beautiful as Oahu's landscape is, some of the island's most ravishing scenery is found beneath the sea. A fascinating kaleidoscope of coral-lined caves, great lava tubes, and cathedral-size archways, Oahu's underwater terrain is also home to a varied and interesting marine life, with a cast of characters ranging from giant spiny puffers to barber pole shrimp. The overall effect of this sensate world on the visiting snorkeler or scuba diver is one of nonstop, wide-eyed wonder, for nowhere are nature's gifts of life, movement, and beauty more concentrated than around the island's coral reefs.

Underwater visibility is usually 100 feet or more. Water temperature is 74 to 80F, ideal for extended explorations. A scuba diver can bring his or her own mask, fins, snorkel, wet suit, regulator with pressure gauge, and buoyancy compensator. Heavier equipment (tanks, weights, backpack, and so on) can be rented, though most dive shops make scuba equipment available only to certified divers. Certification courses, that is, those accredited by the *National Association of Underwater Instructors* (*NAUI*) or the *Professional Association of Diving Instructors* (*PADI*), are offered by most major dive concessions.

Scuba prices range from $45 for an introductory dive to $350 and up for a 5-day scuba certification class. One-, two-, or three-tank dives can be arranged. Most excursions are run from 25- to 42-foot boats with open decks, from which diving is easy. Because a good portion of Oahu's sea life is nocturnal, night dives are popular. Underwater camera rentals are available at most dive shops.

Snorkelers can bring their own masks, fins, and snorkels, or rent all necessary gear from local dive shops. Beach or boat snorkel tours start at $20, with standard half-day tours at $40 to $50.

Because of the fragility of the underwater environment, undersea explorers are strongly requested to "take only pictures, leave only bubbles."

Oahu is the most "dived" island in the Hawaiian chain, and is especially good for novices seeking instruction. (There is an abundance of reputable dive shops in Honolulu.) Hanauma Bay, on the island's southeast shore between Koko Head and Makapuu Point, is probably Oahu's best snorkeling and scuba dive site. Though daily conditions on this side of the island are variable, Hanauma Bay is protected from water-disturbing winds and enjoys near-perfect dive conditions year-round. Most divers make a beach entry to the inner reef lagoon, though visibility and the variety of fish increase dramatically in the outer bay, where a maze of canyon-life surge channels can be explored. The fish here are quite tame and can be fed from your hand. Hanauma Bay is ideal for the beginning skin or scuba diver. *Hanauma Bay Snorkeling Tours* (phone: 808-944-8828) provides four round trips a day (6:30, 8:30, and 11:15 AM, and 1:45 PM) from Waikiki hotels for $14, including gear. Separate rental gear is available.

Another top site on the southeast shore is Fantasy Reef, off Kahala, where intermediate and advanced divers can ride the back of a turtle or watch manta rays glide effortlessly through the water.

Because of the great distance between beach and reef, diving on Oahu's windward shore is best accomplished from a boat. Manana (Rabbit) Island and Makapuu Point attract experienced divers to depths of 60 feet, where the basalt rock bottom is overgrown with coral. Sharks are sighted here occasionally, but seldom threaten divers.

Oahu's North Shore offers good diving opportunities from late spring to late summer, especially for beginners. (In the winter, the waves at Waimea Bay and other top surfing beaches reach gigantic proportions, creating unsafe conditions.) Large fish and brightly colored sponges can be identified at Pupukea (Shark's Cove), known for its many caves and steep drop-offs (but not its sharks; few are ever sighted here). Nearby Three Tables, accessible by beach entry, has several pockmarked caves and is inhabited by schools of small fish.

In addition to Waikiki Beach, Oahu's top snorkeling sites include Black Point near Diamond Head, where ancient lava flows protrude into the ocean and form the basis of a coral reef teeming with life, the nearby Waikiki marine preserve, and Kahe Point on the Waianae (leeward) coast, where the large shallow-water coral reef gives skin divers enough underwater terrain to keep them happy all day. *Aikane Catamarans'* Bare Foot snorkel sail heads from Kewalo Basin to the marine preserve off Diamond Head on half-day excursions.

Information: *Dan's Dive Shop,* 660 Ala Moana Blvd., Honolulu, HI 96813 (phone: 808-536-6181); *Waikiki Diving Center,* 1734 Kalakaua Ave., Honolulu, HI 96815 (phone: 808-955-5151); *Aloha Dive Shop,* Koko Marina, Hawaii Kai, Honolulu, HI 96825 (phone: 808-395-5922); *South Seas Aquatics,* 870 Kapahulu Ave., Honolulu, HI 96816 (phone: 808-735-0437); *Steve's Diving Adventures,* 1860 Ala Moana Blvd., Honolulu, HI 96814 (phone: 808-947-8900); *Leeward Dive Center,* 87-066 Farrington Hwy., Maili, HI 96792 (phone: 808-696-3414); *Aikane Catamarans,* 677 Ala Moana Blvd., Honolulu, HI 96813 (phone: 808-522-1569; 800-522-1538).

Gone Fishing

Because of its serendipitous position at the crossroads of game fish migration paths, Oahu enjoys some of the best deep-sea fishing in the world. And though the smooth, glassy waters off the Big Island's Kona Coast are revered as the finest Pacific blue marlin grounds on the planet, the Waianae coast of Oahu is also very productive.

Visitors who want to try their hands at deep-sea fishing need not be old salts. As one captain noted, "If we had to depend on experienced anglers for all our business, we'd all be broke." The main thing for *malihinis* (newcomers) to remember is to follow the instructions of the captain and the mate when a fish is hooked.

Oahu's top game fishing ports have both private and share charters. Obviously, a private charter is the way to go, especially if there are three or more people in your party. (Most boats accommodate up to six.) Private charters run from $450 to $650 for a full day (8 hours), $350 to $450 for three-quarters of a day (6 hours), and $275 to $400 for a half day (4 hours). Rates vary according to the type of vessel.

On share charters, anglers pay an individual rate of from $75 to $125 and share time with up to five other cohorts. All boats have a democratic rotation system, where anglers draw lots for position and take turns minding the rods. On all charters, fishing tackle and equipment are supplied; anglers usually bring their own lunch and beverages (don't, however, take a banana on board, as they're considered bad luck for fishing). And don't forget your camera, sunscreen, and broad-brimmed hat.

Deep-sea fishing on Oahu is good year-round, but for folks serious about hooking a marlin, chances of success are best from late June to November. No fishing license is required for saltwater fishing on the island.

Though Pacific blue marlin is *the* premier game fish, the supporting cast of heavyweights is also impressive. The waters of Oahu are rich with ahi (yellowfin tuna), an extremely fast, torpedo-like fish ranging up to 300 pounds; mahimahi (dolphin fish), a beautiful phosphorescent fish known for its leaping, spirited battles; ono (wahoo), a fast swimmer averaging 30 pounds, with a mouthful of sharp teeth; and aku (skipjack tuna), a school fish highly prized by sashimi lovers.

Unless previous arrangements are made, it is customary for the catch to be left with the crew, which usually fillets enough fish for the client's party and then sells the rest at the market. This arrangement permits charter captains to keep prices down. (Most of the larger marlin are ground up into fishcakes. Better-tasting dolphin and wahoo are sold to restaurants.)

A word of advice for the prospective deep-sea angler with time to spare: Go to the harbor in the area you plan to fish and talk to the captain and crews of each charter boat. You'll hear some tall stories, but you'll also get a good feel for who's hot — and who's not.

Because charters here are among the least expensive and most accessible to top fishing grounds, deep-sea fishing excursions on Oahu are considered a bargain. If you've only tried freshwater stream or lake fishing for pan fish, the feeling of a large game fish tugging powerfully at the rod while it tail-dances across the surface of the water may render you speechless for the rest of your vacation.

Honolulu's Kewalo Basin (Fisherman's Wharf), only 10 minutes by car from Waikiki hotels, is the base for a fleet of sport fishing boats ranging from 35 to over 60 feet. These cruisers sail off Koko Head to the Penguin Banks southwest of Molokai or off the Waianae Coast. (The world's largest Pacific blue marlin caught on rod and reel, a 1,805-pound monster now on display at the *International Market Place* in Waikiki, was taken off the Waianae Coast by a Kewalo charter vessel in 1971.)

Boats on Oahu can be chartered for 1- or 2-day trips by reserving them in advance. Although the custom is for a group to book the entire boat for a day, single anglers are placed with private parties when space is available. Honolulu boats stalk a mixed bag of game fish — depending on the size and species of fish running, a variety of artificial plugs and live swimming baits are used to capture marlin, tuna, wahoo, and dolphin. For North Shore fishing, charters are available at Pokai Bay and Haleiwa at slightly lower rates than at Kewalo Basin. Information: *Island Charters,* Kewalo Basin, Honolulu, HI 96814 (phone: 808-536-1555); *Coreene C's II Sport Fishing Charters,* Kewalo Basin, Honolulu, HI 96814 (phone: 808-226-8421); *Golden Eagle Marine Charter Services,* Kewalo Basin, Honolulu, HI 96814 (phone: 808-531-4966).

Sailing the South Seas

For visitors raring to get out on the water, Honolulu offers a wealth of opportunities. Charter a classic sailboat complete with crew, take a thrilling outrigger canoe ride on the gentle swells off Waikiki Beach, paddle a kayak to a desert island in a turquoise lagoon, or climb aboard a glass-bottom catamaran and watch the fish wriggle in the water below. Theme cruises aboard diesel-powered craft or catamarans are also popular, especially late-afternoon sunset sails. In the end, boating opportunities here are as diverse as the island itself.

Outrigger Canoe Rides – An ideal way to get the feel of surfing, without mastering board-balancing skills, is to take an outrigger canoe ride on the modest breakers off Waikiki Beach. By paddling hard at the right moment, passengers can assist the two crewmen in putting the 30-foot surfing canoe on the crest of a wave. A pontoon jutting out from the side of these long banana-shaped boats gives them stability. Paddlers get a good workout, along with three thrilling rides during the 30- to 40-minute experience. The price is $6 to $10. (Several of the canoe concessions also have hour-long catamaran rides.) Information: *Waikiki Beach Services, c/o Outrigger Reef Hotel,* 2169 Kalia Rd., Honolulu, HI 96815 (phone: 808-923-3111); *Beach Services, c/o Outrigger Waikiki Hotel,* 2335 Kalakaua Ave., Honolulu, HI 96815 (phone: 808-923-0711); *Waikiki Beach Services, c/o Sheraton Waikiki,* 2255 Kalakaua Ave., Honolulu, HI 96815 (phone: 808-922-4422).

Cruises – Several companies offer cruises off Waikiki beaches; others provide transportation from Waikiki, with departures set from Kewalo Basin. The following outfits include both free hotel pickups and drop-offs:

Hilton Hawaiian Village offers sails aboard the glass-bottom catamaran *Hilton Rainbow I,* departing from the *Hilton* end of Waikiki Beach. The breakfast sail is from 8 to 9:30 AM. Information: *Hilton Catamaran,* 2005 Kalia Rd., Honolulu, HI 96815 (phone: 808-949-4321).

The state-of-the-art Swath vessel *Navatek* offers an upscale cruise from Kewalo Basin past Diamond Head to offshore Kahala. The 150-passenger ship, designed for comfort and stability, offers a variety of day and evening sails, which include buffet luncheons and formal dinners. Information: *Royal Hawaiian Cruises,* PO Box 29816, Honolulu, HI 96820 (phone: 808-848-6360).

The *Hyatt Regency*'s 48-passenger catamaran *Mani Kai* heads out for hour-long sails and 1½-hour-long cocktail sails from a beachfront location. Information: *Hyatt Regency Waikiki,* 2424 Kalakaua Ave., Honolulu, HI 96815 (phone: 808-923-1234).

Windjammer offers a sunset dinner sail ($45) and a moonlight cruise ($45, including buffet; $24, cocktails only) aboard the 1,000-passenger *Rella Mae.* Those seeking quiet, romantic moments should look elsewhere: The sunset sail includes a Polynesian revue, and the moonlight sail comes complete with a Broadway-style musical. A less noisy option for the sunset sail is first class seating on the upper deck. It's worth the $65 charge for full service, two drinks, and tranquillity if you take the dinner cruise. Information: *Windjammer Cruises,* 2222 Kalakaua Ave., Honolulu, HI 96815 (phone: 808-521-0036).

Aikane Catamarans operates three 150-passenger cats on two nightly dinner sails, with 5:15 and 7:45 PM departures from Kewalo Basin. The sails, at $41 and $48 per person, respectively, both include table service dinner, an open bar, and Polynesian entertainment inviting audience participation. Other sails include an SOS dinner show, which is priced at $52.50. Those in a romantic mood may wish to make a getaway to the upper deck and enjoy the breezes, moonlight, and relative quiet. Information: *Aikane Catamarans,* 677 Ala Moana Blvd., Honolulu, HI 96813 (phone: 808-522-1533; 800-522-1538).

Kayaking – One of Oahu's best outdoor adventures is a kayaking trip to one of the Mokulua islands, located in a turquoise lagoon off the Windward Coast. The ideal time to go is shortly before dawn on a calm day when the lagoon is at its smoothest. Kayakers launch their craft at Lanakai Beach, south of Kailua, and head for the bigger of the two islands with its wide sandy beach. During the half-hour trip, you can watch the sun rise, see tropical fish swimming among the white coral heads, and spot fork-tailed iwa (man-of-war birds) riding the thermals overhead. Whitecaps splash against a reef, and the water turns from turquoise to deep blue as the ocean plunges sharply to several hundred feet. It's an easy paddle, and the island, home to many seabirds, including the red-footed booby, is a serene spot — and well worth the short ride. *Twogood Kayak Hawaii* (171-B Hamakua Dr., Kailua; phone: 808-262-5656) offers lessons ($45 an hour), rentals ($20 for a half day; $25 full day; and $40 weekend), as well as two-person tandem kayaks ($35 for a half day; $45 full day). *Twogood* also offers escorted kayak tours ($65) that travel through Kailua Bay to the Mokulua islands. *Go Bananas* near Waikiki (732 Kapahulu Ave.; phone: 808-737-9514) offers hour-long lessons for $20. Rentals are available for experienced kayakers only. *Ocean Kayak* (phone: 808-239-9803), in windward Kahulu, offers half-day rentals for $15; full-day rentals for $25 for kayaking on Kaneohe Bay. Closed Sundays. Kayaking fans can contact *Hui Waa Kaukahi* (*hui* is Hawaiian for fellowship, or club) for information on conditions or planned excursions (phone: 808-263-6249).

Yacht Charters – *Jada Yacht Charters* offers a two-boat fleet for charter service on 4-hour morning and 4½-hour afternoon sails. Charter options include the 62-foot *Jada I,* a teak-and-mahogany classic sailboat, and the 71-foot, 48-passenger *Jada II,* complete with captain, hostess, and crew of two. *Cloud Nine Limousine* offers crewed charters aboard its custom-built 45-foot sloop. A 3-hour minimum, starting at $400, is required. A Wetsail 43 and a Hunter 54 round out the fleet. Information: *Cloud Nine Limousine,* 45-656 Halekou Pl., Kaneohe, HI 96744 (phone: 808-524-7999); *Jada Sailing Adventures,* 1860 Ala Moana Blvd., Suite 413, Honolulu, HI 96815 (phone: 808-955-0772).

Top Tennis

 While Honolulu's warm sun, blue canopy of a sky and prevailing trade winds create almost perfect year-round playing conditions, visiting tennis players — novice and advanced alike — can find themselves too easily distracted by court settings that range from simply beautiful to dramatically spectacular. Windbreaks, for example, are often bedecked with oleander and bougainvillea, and vistas of green cliffs, blue surf, and white sandy beaches are the rule, not the exception.

Tennis courts here are generally very well kept and constructed with all-weather Laykold or Plexipave surfaces. In addition to hotel and resort tennis complexes, where hourly rates range from $5 to $10 per hour or are free to guests, Honolulu has some well-maintained county courts, where playing time is usually free of charge. Information on tournaments can be supplied by the *Hawaii Pacific Tennis Association,* 2615 S. King St., Suite 2A, Honolulu, HI 96826 (phone: 808-955-6696).

Most hotels and resorts with tennis facilities will arrange a match for an unattached visiting player. Individual lessons for players of all abilities range from $20 to $25 per hour, while group lessons and clinics usually average about $6 per hour. Videotaping and playback are also available.

The top three municipal facilities in the Honolulu/Waikiki area are the 10 Laykold courts at Ala Moana Park, all of which are lighted for night play until 9 PM (phone: 808-522-7031); the unlighted, 9-court *Diamond Head Tennis Center* in Kapiolani Park (phone: 808-971-7150), and the 4 lighted *Kapiolani Park Courts,* also in Kapiolani Park, which are open until 2:30 AM (no phone). Free classes are offered at the Ala Moana facility. Courts are available on a first-come, first-served basis, with a 45-minute cap on play if other players are waiting.

Also in the Honolulu area are the noteworthy *Honolulu Tennis Club* and the *Ilikai* hotel courts. The former is a good place to go to avoid the crowds of *malihinis* (newcomers) that mainland snowstorms have driven to the islands in search of sun. Its

4 Laykold courts have a third-floor rooftop location atop a department store, from which players have a view of the Waikiki skyline on the *makai* (ocean) side of the building and a panorama of the Manoa Valley on the *mauka* (mountain) side. The courts, which are at their busiest from the end of November through April, have a pro on hand for lessons. For the four-wall crowd, there are also 3 racquetball courts. A free pick-up service is available to and from Waikiki hotels from 10 AM to 5 PM. Information: *Honolulu Tennis Club,* 2220 S. King St., Honolulu, HI 96826 (phone: 808-944-9696).

The *Ilikai* has 6 Plexipave tennis courts, including the lighted Yacht Harbor court (open until 10 PM) on top of the hotel's main ballroom, overlooking the Ala Wai yacht harbor. The hotel's other showcase court is the Diamond Head court, with the famous extinct volcano providing background distraction. The remaining courts, on the hotel's seventh floor, provide players with fine views of the ocean and marina below.

All reservations for court time and lessons at the *Ilikai,* which is staffed by two tennis pros, are made through the hotel's Sports Desk. A final note: The *Ilikai* has one of the best-stocked tennis shops on the island. Information: *Ilikai Hotel,* 1777 Ala Moana Blvd., Honolulu, HI 96815 (phone: 808-949-3811).

Outside Honolulu, two Oahu resorts are standout tennis destinations. On the North Shore, the *Turtle Bay Hilton* has 10 Plexipave courts (4 lighted at night) set in a grove of coconut palms near the golf course. The courts, cooled by ocean breezes, are within sight of stark volcanic peaks in the Koolau Range. In the interests of privacy, there are no adjoining courts. The resort's player matching service pairs off partners of equal ability based on its rating system. Clinics and social doubles events are also part of the program. The best times to visit are spring and summer — washouts are not uncommon in late fall and winter. Information: *Turtle Bay Hilton and Country Club,* Kahuku, HI 96731 (phone: 808-293-8811).

On Oahu's leeward coast, in the vast natural arena of Makaha Valley, is the *Sheraton Makaha* resort, a secluded hotel in a country club setting. Four Plexipave courts, 2 lighted, are set in this horseshoe-shaped development. Because there is little wind or rain on the leeward coast, *Sheraton Makaha* guests enjoy near-perfect playing conditions year-round, and since the resort is 40 miles from the bustle of Honolulu, its tennis facilities are not pressed to the limit. The *Sheraton Makaha* is a great place to perfect your backhand without fear of discovery by rivals. "It's just you and the tennis here," commented the resident pro. "People come for the quiet." Information: *Sheraton Makaha Resort,* 84-626 Makaha Valley Rd., Makaha, HI 96792 (phone: 808-695-9511).

Great Golf

 The problem with playing golf on Oahu is that the scenery that surrounds golf holes is as dramatic as can be imagined, and keeping your head down requires a very determined act of will. In all candor, we're not sure it's worth the effort: The normal run of duffer may enjoy looking at the peaks of the Koolau Range much more than watching his or her errant shot disappear into the nearest water hazard.

Unfortunately, some of Honolulu's best courses are private. The *Waialae Country Club* (4997 Kahala Ave., Honolulu; phone: 808-734-2151), probably the most familiar Hawaiian course to visitors (it's the site of the televised *Hawaiian Open* each winter), is one of these oases for members only, as is the *Oahu Country Club* (150 Country Club Rd., Honolulu; phone: 808-595-6331). The *Mid-Pacific Country Club* (266 Kaelepulu Dr., Kailua; phone: 808-262-8161) occasionally allows outsiders to play. There are, however, at least two (often successful) gambits for gaining access to these otherwise exclusive enclaves, the most productive of which is to ask the manager of your Honolulu hotel to try to intercede on your behalf. Alternatively, you might present a letter from your own club president and/or resident pro requesting course privileges — a good idea, incidentally, whenever you travel — and you may be pleasantly surprised at the result. In any event, there's no harm in asking.

TURTLE BAY HILTON, Kahuku: *Turtle Bay*'s new course, designed by Arnold Palmer (18 holes, 7,000 yards, par 72), which opened last year, provides a challenge even for longtime golf mavens. Built amidst an oceanside grove of ironwood pines, it includes numerous water hazards, as well as demanding, forest-lined fairways on the back nine. The old George Fazio layout will be replaced by another Palmer-designed course, and will be ready for play next year. Though golf dominates this remote resort complex, there are many other activities to enjoy: tennis, scuba diving, snorkeling, and horseback riding. And the setting, with the ocean in one direction and the peaks of the Koolau Range in the other, is nearly as memorable as the golf itself. Resident pro, Jody Shaw. Information: *Turtle Bay Hilton and Country Club,* Kahuku, HI 96731 (phone: 808-293-8811).

MAKAHA VALLEY, Makaha: The two William Bell–designed courses here — the *West* course and the *Makaha Valley Country Club* — lie in a deep valley well within view of notorious Makaha Beach, where championship surfers regularly pit their tanned bodies against some of the planet's most violent waves. The golf courses are slightly safer, though the tougher *West* course requires a combination of cool temperament and substantial power. The greens on both courses are undulating and difficult to read, and the fairness of the fairways (and their usually superb condition) will provide scant solace for soaring scores. *Makaha Valley Country Club:* 18 holes, par 71, 6,369 yards; managed by Nitto Kogyo; 84-627 Makaha Valley Rd., Waianae, HI 96792 (phone: 808-695-9578). *West Course:* 18 holes, par 72, 6,398 yards; resident pro, Ron Kiaaina; managed by the *Sheraton Makaha Resort,* 84-626 Makaha Valley Rd., Makaha, HI 96792 (phone: 808-695-9511).

KO OLINA, Ewa Beach: Designed by Ted Robinson, the course at this resort complex is set on a beautiful plain, filled with coconut palm trees, banyans, monkeypods, silver buttonwood trees, flowering bougainvillea, and other flora. Built to accommodate a wide range of players, there are water hazards at eight different holes, making a round even more interesting. Opened at the end of 1990 as the first component of the resort, the course offers exciting play in unusually scenic surroundings. Course: 18 holes, par 72, 6,867 yards; resident pro, Craig Williamson. *Ko Olina Golf Club,* 92-1220 Farrington Hwy., Ewa Beach, HI 96707 (phone: 808-676-5300).

PALI, Kaneohe: Located at the base of the lush, vertical *pali* (cliff) is one of the best municipal courses you'll find anywhere. The magnificent setting and the expert maintenance make it a bargain at $18 for greens fees (an additional $11 for a non-mandatory cart). Open from 6 AM to 6 PM daily. It's necessary to get there early for a decent tee time, as this course is a favorite with residents. Course: 18 holes, par 72, 6,950 yards; operated by the City and County of Honolulu, Department of Parks. 45-050 Kamehameha Hwy., Kaneohe, HI 96744 (phone: 808-261-9784).

Hiking the Honolulu Wilderness

 The only way to experience Oahu fully is to walk along its more remote trails. The paradise of picture postcards and mournful legends reveals itself to those willing to explore regions beyond the vision of resort-bound vacationers. However, visitors need not be able to leap tall cliffs in a single bound.

The trails listed below include easy strolls and nature walks less than a mile long, some with swimming holes and picnic tables along the way.

The key to hiking on Oahu is variety: Trekkers can sample humid rain forests and moonlike volcanic craters, as well as deserted beaches scattered with the flotsam and jetsam of shipwrecks. Sights along the way include groves of sweet mountain apples, slim waterfalls cascading into deep pools, and fertile valleys where nature has all but reclaimed the remnants of earlier civilizations.

Hikers should be aware of Oahu's unique hiking conditions. For example, climbing should not be attempted on volcanic surfaces, which tend to crumble when pressure is applied by hand or foot. (Be sure to wear sturdy boots for hiking in volcanic areas.) In the tropics, night drops like a curtain after sunset; plan to be off the trail a few minutes before twilight unless you're going to spend the night. Carry a canteen — not all of Oahu's water is potable. Bring insect repellent for all hikes on terrain below 3,000 feet — the mosquitoes in low-lying regions can be fierce. As a final note, it is wise to stick to marked trails, since taking shortcuts can disturb the delicate ecological balance of the environment.

Malihinis (newcomers) seeking guidance and companionship can contact the various organizations listed below that arrange group hiking trips. These provide an excellent introduction to the island's wilderness regions. To return home without discovering one or two of them is to miss seeing the real Oahu.

Though it offers few extended wilderness treks for an advanced hiker, Oahu has several fine day hikes, many of them just a few miles from Honolulu. To hike with a group, contact the *Hawaiian Trail and Mountain Club* (PO Box 2238, Honolulu, HI 96804; phone: 808-247-3922) or the *Sierra Club* (212 Merchant St., Suite 201, Honolulu, HI 96813; phone: 808-538-6616). The *Hawaii Nature Center* (2131 Makiki Heights Dr., Honolulu, HI 96822; phone: 808-955-0100) offers detailed trail maps and escorted hikes in the Koolau Mountains urban watershed, which overlooks the city. For trail information and maps: *Department of Land and Natural Resources,* Division of State Parks, 1151 Punchbowl St., Honolulu, HI 96813 (phone: 808-587-0166).

DIAMOND HEAD: Though most visitors know it only as the big green and brown landmark at the far end of Waikiki Beach, Diamond Head also is a fine place for a short hike. Inside this extinct volcano is a trail cut into the crater's interior walls (a flashlight is recommended) that climbs 760 feet to the top of the rim (Point Leahi), where hikers are treated to a panoramic view of Honolulu and the surrounding mountains. Military fortifications built inside the crater during World War II are still there. The trail starts at the parking area near the firing range in the middle of the crater, and is open from 6 AM to 6 PM daily, allowing sunrise and sunset climbs from late November through April. Information: *Department of Land and Natural Resources,* Division of State Parks, 1151 Punchbowl St., Honolulu, HI 96813 (phone: 808-587-0166).

KAHANA VALLEY STATE PARK: A 5,220-acre preserve that includes picnic grounds and a variety of valley and mountain trails that head into the Windward Coast's portion of the Koolau Mountains. No camping is allowed here, but the city and county maintain campsites nearby at the Kahana Bay Beach Park. Information: *Department of Land and Natural Resources,* Division of State Parks, 1151 Punchbowl St., Honolulu, HI 96813 (phone: 808-587-0166).

JUDD MEMORIAL: This 1.3-mile loop trail, in the Nuuanu Valley, may well be the most entertaining hike in the state. After passing through a stand of eucalyptus, Norfolk pine, and bamboo trees, the trail comes upon one of the best mud-sliding chutes on the island. In the rainy winter months, bring a sheet of heavy plastic for a slick ride down a muddy hill. A fork in the trail leads to Jackass Ginger Pool, a fine place to swim (or wash off the mud). There is a short waterfall slide at the pool for the clean fun crowd.

MANOA VALLEY: One of the more popular and easiest hikes on Oahu, this trail begins at the end of Manoa Road, just past Paradise Park, and winds through a rain forest amid lush tropical plants, mountain apples, and passion fruit vines. The reward at the end of the 1-mile trail is Manoa Falls, with its crisp, clear pool.

BLOWHOLE TO HANAUMA BAY: This seaside trail (2 miles, one way) follows a rock shelf past a variety of fascinating formations created by the erosive action of the sea, including caves and tidal pools. Wear a bathing suit and sneakers for this hike — waves wash over the shelf in some places. Start the hike at the Blowhole and walk back to Hanauma Bay, where a tide pool known as the Toilet Bowl can be seen filling and flushing with each wave. Caution is urged: Several people have been killed diving into its surging waters.

LANIPO TRAIL: An all-day hike on this 7-mile trail affords enough spectacular views of Windward Oahu to convince anyone of the island's great beauty. On the climb up to 1,600 feet, hikers can cool off in one of the many swimming holes found in Waimano Stream. The *palis* (cliffs) of the Koolau Range rise up majestically along this trail. Hikers should be in good shape for this trek.

For the more robust hiker, the Mauumae Trail offers a 6-hour jaunt through groves of ohia and koa trees to a 2,500-foot elevation. Along the southeastern edge of the Koolau Range, the hike provides a rare look at Kaau Crater. Other popular Oahu hikes include Makua Gulch on the northern Windward slopes of the Koolaus, an easy trek in Makaha Valley, and the 2-mile Koko Head Cliff Walk near Hanauma Bay.

MAUNAWILI: Originating at a point near the Pali Highway's hairpin turn, this trail meanders through the Maunawili Valley highlands and ascends to the Aniani ridgeline atop the Koolau Mountains. It is being built by the *Sierra Club,* and while the ultimate completion of the 15-mile complex is still several years away, the first 2½ miles are now open to hikers. Higher portions of the trail display panoramic views of the Windward Coast, and at one point, the trail passes by the 200-foot-long O'Shaughnessy Tunnel.

Camping

Better known for its extravagant resorts that pamper guests with every luxury, Oahu also boasts a supply of campgrounds for visitors who prefer more primitive accommodations. The range of environments is remarkable: A camper can spend one night surrounded by dense forests of eucalyptus and pine and the next in a beachfront park where tents are pulled taut on a grassy lawn within a stone's throw of pounding surf.

There is more than one way to camp on Oahu: It's possible to hike to a secluded campsite and pitch a tent (or sleep out under the stars). Camping equipment can be brought from home or rented at a number of sporting goods stores around the island. Lightweight tents with a sewn-in floor are best for camping here. Pack warm clothing for mountain camping; the weather can be anything but tropical.

Camping at Oahu's state parks is free and usually allowed for up to 1 week. County park permits cost $1 for adults per night and 50¢ for children under 12. These permits are issued for stays of from 3 to 7 days.

A small caveat for campers: Don't leave valuables unprotected. Theft is not uncommon at campsites. On the bright side, there are no snakes, poisonous insects, or poison ivy in the islands. A review of the top camping sites in the island follows.

KEAIWA HEIAU STATE PARK: In the foothills of the Koolau Range, a few miles from Pearl Harbor, this up-country park has a decidedly non-tropical climate, as well as a fascinating history. Keaiwa Heiau (a *heiau* is an ancient temple) is where Hawaiian medicine men cultivated herbs and other plants used to heal the sick. The campground here is a few hundred yards from temple ruins and herb gardens, all of it surrounded by dense forests of pine and eucalyptus trees. Keaiwa Heiau is best for tent camping; RVs can stay overnight with a permit. Reservations cannot be made more than 30 days in advance. Closed Wednesdays and Thursdays. Information: *Department of Land and Natural Resources,* Division of State Parks, 1151 Punchbowl St., Honolulu, HI 96813 (phone: 808-587-0166).

BELLOWS FIELD BEACH PARK: Though limited to weekend and holiday use, this lovely park, 20 miles east of Waikiki, is actually the small oceanfront corner of a large military base. Its barbecue pits and picnic tables make it popular with day-trippers, and the white sandy beach and calm sea make it a favorite of campers who also like to swim and snorkel. Visitors pitch tents near the forest of ironwood trees that rings the beach. A wonderful pastime here is watching the Pacific mole crabs ("sand turtles") burrow into the sand between waves. Bellows is convenient to Hanauma Bay, a designated marine preserve much enjoyed by snorkelers, and to *Sea Life Park,* where leaping porpoises and trained whales are the main attractions. A permit is required and must be obtained in person. Open weekends only. Information: *Department of Parks and Recreation,* 650 S. King St., Honolulu, HI 96813 (phone: 808-523-4525).

The Division of State Parks operates the *Waimanalo Bay State Recreational Area* adjacent to Bellows Field. Camping is allowed daily, except Wednesdays and Thursdays, and permits are required. Information: *Department of Land and Natural Resources,* Division of State Parks, 1151 Punchbowl St., Honolulu, HI 96813 (phone: 808-587-0166).

KAHANA BAY BEACH PARK: A beautiful grove of ironwood pines on a wide crescent beach, with sawtooth mountains as a backdrop, makes this park on Windward Oahu particularly inviting. The beach is very popular and safe for swimming, with a sandy ocean bottom and a gentle slope. Kahana Bay also offers shoreline fishing, and the park provides shower and barbecue facilities. There is beachfront camping (daily except Wednesdays and Thursdays; permit required) at Malaekahana Beach, several miles up the coast from Kahana. Information: *Department of Land and Natural Resources,* Division of State Parks, 1151 Punchbowl St., Honolulu, HI 96813 (phone: 808-587-0166). Other top campsites in this region include *Nanakuli Beach Park* (tent and trailer camping allowed) and *Lualualei Beach Park* (tent camping only). Permits required for all parks. No camping allowed on Wednesdays and Thursdays. Information: *Department of Parks and Recreation,* 650 S. King St., Honolulu, HI 96813 (phone: 808-523-4525).

Gliding and Hang Gliding

HANG GLIDING: Thanks to recent aerodynamic improvements in flying equipment, hang gliding is no longer considered a "fringe" sport, suited only for potential kamikaze pilots. Oahu, in fact, has some of the world's most beautiful sites for this highly individual pursuit. The *Tradewinds Hang Gliding Center* runs a beginner program for those interested in savoring the immediate and thrilling sense of flight unavailable to those inside an aircraft. According to the *US Hang Gliding Association,* the sport is "great physical and mental therapy for those frustrated by the daily constraints of modern living." (The *USHGA* also believes that hang gliding most closely realizes the flying imagined in dreams.)

Following *USHGA* guidelines, Lani Akiona and state champion Mike Benson of *Tradewinds* organize small classes (no more than six pupils in a group) for introductory lessons, during which novices "tackle some pretty good-size sand dunes." The 2- to 3-hour sessions cost $50. Akiona emphasizes that achieving great height is not necessary to experience the exhilaration of hang gliding. Whether you are 12 inches or 1,200 feet in the air, the excitement of lifting off the ground on a pair of wings is the same. Only the view is different.

Tradewinds' emphasis during the introductory lessons is on fun. The basic course is designed to show beginners how hang gliders fly, to familiarize them with the glider and its equipment, and to enable them to experience the thrill of launching themselves into the air safely. Novices can look forward to 10 mini-flights during the first session. Akiona only teaches when the weather is good, which is about 75% of the time. (In the same way that a surfer needs waves to surf, a hang glider needs wind to fly.) Safety is the overriding concern, but Akiona insists the only injury incurred during her classes was a blister someone received from holding onto the control bar too tightly.

In further support of the sport, Akiona says hang glider equipment at present is vastly improved over "wings" made less than 5 years ago, which are now considered unsafe. The flying characteristics of new certified gliders permit pilots to climb higher, go farther, and land more safely. Turning, handling, and performance are all greatly improved on new models. Accidents caused by design inadequacies are virtually nonexistent these days.

Tradewinds runs excursions for advanced flyers to the main ridge of Makapuu, among the velvety green *palis* (cliffs) of the Koolau Range. Waimanalo is also a favorite ridge-soaring site of accomplished hang glider pilots. Back to the beginners: Akiona says that many visitors who take the introductory lesson pursue the sport back home. No finer setting could be provided for a first taste of do-it-yourself flying, though the timid need not apply. Information: *Tradewinds Hang Gliding Center* (phone: 808-396-8557).

GLIDING: Those who feel more secure flying *inside* even a motorless aircraft can book a *Glider Rides* flight at Dillingham Airfield, near the Mokuleia polo grounds in northwest Oahu. The 15-to-20-minute flights, narrated and piloted by veterans who have logged more than a million miles in gliders, soar to mountain range heights of up to 3,000 feet, depending on lift conditions. Visibility extends more than 30 miles from Kahuku and the patchwork sugarcane plantations at Waialua to Kaena Point, at the western tip of the island. Sights include the famous North Shore surfing playgrounds, brilliant coral reefs, and various Oahu resort complexes, as well as the US Air Force Satellite Tracking Station and leaping schools of dolphin and humpback whales. On a clear day, 80-mile-distant Kauai may be spotted.

The bubble-top gliders seat one or two passengers and leave Dillingham Airfield every 20 minutes from 10:30 AM to 5:30 PM. Rides are $50 for one person, $75 for two. Glider pilot instruction is available by appointment. The service operates year-round; pilots report no more than 30 unflyable days a year. Gliders provide a tranquil, safe, and almost noiseless high-altitude view of Oahu. Information: *Glider Rides,* PO Box 626, Waialua, HI 96791 (phone: 808-677-3404).

Flightseeing

 Perhaps the most interesting aspect of either helicopter or fixed-wing flightseeing tours of Oahu is each visitor's reaction to being borne aloft over sections of paradise inaccessible to all but the air traveler. "Too beautiful to describe," "Absolutely unreal," and "Purely and uniquely of the Lord" are among the entries found in the ledger of one helicopter company.

There is no more glamorous tour on Oahu than a flightseeing excursion. With their champagne picnics at secluded spots and drops on deserted beaches, the helicopter companies are the ultimate trailblazers. "We're not in the transportation business —

we're in the 'experience-providing' business," says one company owner, who calls his trips "adventures set to music." Most helicopters and tour planes are equipped with headsets, through which passengers hear the pilot's narration or music appropriate to the natural wonder below.

Yes, flightseeing prices are high, but many travelers consider them a relative bargain for the quality of the experience delivered. Prices range from under $50 for a short hop along the Waikiki coast to $187 for a flyby over the North Shore and Pearl Harbor. The helicopters, most of them flown by former air force fighter pilots, seat four to six passengers. By all means, bring your camera; you'll have rare opportunities to capture crater rims, deep gorges, sheer cliffs, and other sights to which only birds and other privileged sightseers are usually privy. See *A Shutterbug's View*, in this section, for advice on how best to take photos aloft. In general, March through October is the best season for flightseeing, though it's possible year-round.

Apart from the more publicized helicopter services whose tours are extensively described below, there are several smaller competing flightseeing services over Oahu. Sometimes they offer significant discounts. Check local listings. Fixed-wing commuter aircraft are also used for aerial tours. For those uncomfortable with the thought of helicopter flying, this may be the answer. It also costs less, on the average.

In addition to Oahu's famous surfing beaches on the North Shore and beautiful interior valleys, the island has points of historical interest that take on a new dimension from the air.

Papillon Helicopters runs a series of three tours ranging from a half hour ($79) to an hour. The hour-long Oahu Experience ($99) provides an excellent condensed tour of the island. Passengers fly over Waikiki Beach, the extinct volcano of Diamond Head, and the exclusive residential community of Kahala before hovering near Hanauma Bay, where the love scenes of *From Here to Eternity* were filmed. The helicopter follows the rugged coastline to Makapuu Beach before passing over Sea Life Park near the *palis* (cliffs) of the Koolau Range. Here the aircraft rises suddenly to climb over the twin peaks of 1,643-foot-tall Olomana. The scenic highlight of the trip may well be the visit to Nuuanu Pali, where sheer 1,000-foot drop-offs, sawtooth mountains blanketed in green, and waterfalls whose cascades are blown upward by the wind are sprawled out in the Nuuanu Valley. It is a magnificent vista.

The Oahu Epic ($187) skips Nuuanu Pali but visits the North Shore. Sunset and the Banzai Pipeline, the famous surfing beaches where the waves reach a height of 30 feet in winter, and Waimea Bay, known for its beautiful valley and 45-foot waterfall, also are included. Large fields of pineapple and sugarcane, stretching to the fuzzy blue peaks of the Waianae Mountains, signal the approach to Pearl Harbor, where the elegant, white *Arizona* Memorial can be seen, marking the resting place of the sunken battleship. Information: *Papillon Hawaiian Helicopters,* 421 Aowena Pl., Honolulu, HI 96819 (phone: 808-836-1566; 800-367-7095).

Cherry Helicopters offers two tour itineraries that depart from the helipad at the *Turtle Bay* resort. There's a 15-minute look at the North Shore beaches ($50) and a 30-minute visit to Sacred Falls ($100). Information: *Cherry Helicopters,* 441 Aowena Pl., Honolulu, HI 96819 (phone: 808-293-7588).

Bird Watching

Waikiki's pampered hand-held scarlet macaws and flocks of white beach pigeons are the only feathered friends most visitors notice, but avid birders can spot Honolulu's exotic tropical birds, and if they're lucky, possibly add rare or endangered species to their life lists.

Honolulu's most common birds are exotic, most of which were brought here in cages from Asia, and were then set free or escaped to spread their wings on their own. Like many creatures that took up residence here, the imported birds thrived. But native species (those who came under their own steam and stayed) have faltered as their ecological world changed. According to the *Hawaii Audubon Society*, 200 years ago there were 70 or more species of birds found only in Hawaii. Today, 23 species have vanished, 31 are rare or endangered, and one is threatened.

Hawaii's endangered birds, surprisingly enough, include cousins of species that are common on the mainland, such as coots and gallinules. The alala, the Hawaiian version of a crow, is endangered; only about a dozen are believed to be left in the wild. Among Oahu's native birds are the brown-and-white elepaio and the green-and yellow amakihi, which can be seen in the leafy Koolau rain forests. Stream beds at low tide are where to spot the twiggy legged black-and-white Hawaiian stilt.

The city streets and beach parks are alive with birds, including many Asian and Pacific species: mynah birds, those noisy black rascals with yellow eyes; blue jays; barred and spotted doves; red-whiskered bulbuls, Hawaii's version of red-wing black-birds, who catch and eat live termites on the wing; little green Japanese white eyes, also known as a rice birds. Look for shamas, magnificent singers colored blue-black, orange, and white; fiery red cardinals; and flocks of bad-tempered, fat little gray-and-white, red-billed Java finches.

Marine birds to look or listen for include high-flying black iwas (also called frigate birds or man-of-war); moaning shearwaters, who cry like babies at night; and boobies and albatross, who swoop and wheel over the waves while fishing. Graceful white tropical birds with long slender tails can be seen soaring near the sea cliffs on the Windward Coast and nesting on its offshore islets.

A word about a bird you won't see on Oahu: Hawaii's state bird, the nene goose, lives only on Maui and the Big Island of Hawaii. Named for its two-syllable, high, nasal bark ("nay-nay"), the nene's claw feet allow it to strut about on sharp lava cinders. Also endangered, only about 1,000 wild nenes are left in the wild, officials estimate.

Three places to see Honolulu's birds on your own are at the 1,000-acre Kawainui Marsh, the largest body of water in the state; the slopes of Diamond Head; and the rain forest trails in the mountains behind the city. Contact the *Hawaii Audubon Society* (phone: 808-528-1432) and the *Sierra Club* (phone: 808-538-6616) for information on nature hikes and programs; *The Nature Conservancy* (phone: 808-537-4508) also runs programs to visit their preserves. Check local bookstores for *The Birds of Hawaii and the Tropical Pacific* (Princeton University Press, $24.95 paperback), the best field manual for Pacific birders, and the Hawaii Audubon Society's *Hawaii's Birds*, a small handbook with color illustrations. For more information, contact the *US Fish and Wildlife Service* (phone: 808-541-1201).

For the Mind

Museums, Churches, and Mission Houses

The Hawaiian culture is an ancient one, reaching back more than 1,400 years to its South Seas roots, and several noteworthy Honolulu museums stand as testimony to the city's cultural diversity. Although they are small in size, they are full of delightful surprises. Our museum selection traces Honolulu's multiracial heritage and development, ranging from the early Polynesian settlers to European traders and American whalers, then on to the various Asian groups imported to till the soil. It also includes several churches and mission houses, which so poignantly chronicle Hawaii's conversion to Christianity.

BISHOP MUSEUM: On three separate levels plus a newly opened wing, the museum traces the story of the islands from prehistoric times. Among the exhibits: "Hawaii: The Royal Isles," tracing the islands' monarchy. This section of the museum has portraits of all the islands' kings and queens, together with thrones, crowns, and regalia, plus examples of their uniforms and clothes. Also on display is a fine collection of artifacts common to the islands before the arrival of Captain Cook. A shallow bowl supported by humanoid figurines, an ornate bone fishhook that would be commendable as a brooch, and feather cloaks, capes, and helmets in the royal colors of yellow, red, and black catch the eye here. The second level features a lovely collection of tapa cloth, as well as exhibits on 19th-century whaling. In the Polynesian Hall is a magnificent display of materials from other islands of the Pacific. Look particularly for an elaborate mourning costume from the Society Islands, an ornamental headdress from Samoa, and a highly decorated mask from Melanesia. For a real whale of a time, enjoy all 55 feet, 22 tons, of one right here. A sperm whale is suspended from the ceiling in the Hawaiian Hall, recalling the days when whaling brought Hawaii much of its reputation and prosperity. A stunning array of exquisitely formed mollusks is displayed next to the Hall of Natural History. In the Science Center is an exhibit of rainbow-colored insects arranged like bracelets and necklaces in a jeweler's window. There is more besides: hula and Hawaiian crafts at the Atherton Halau, astronomy shows in the planetarium, special exhibits, classes, lectures, and examples of indigenous trees and shrubs in the charming Garden Courtyard. Admission charge ($6). Information: *Bishop Museum, 1525 Bernice St., Honolulu, HI 96817 (phone: 808-847-3511; 808-848-4129 for a recorded message).*

HONOLULU ACADEMY OF ARTS: A special delight for connoisseurs of small art museums. But even for those who never give paintings or sculpture a second glance, a worthwhile hour or two can be spent here, particularly if you take in one of the excellent special exhibits. The academy's Spanish Court and Chinese Courtyard, both cloistered patios, are the most civilized oases in Honolulu, the perfect escape from the hectic trading in the merchant houses of downtown and from the hedonistic throng on

Waikiki. Handsome as the gallery's design and architecture are — and they are very handsome indeed — it is the collections that give the academy its nationwide reputation. Among the most celebrated of these are its Asian holdings, consisting of ceramics, paintings, furniture, bronzes, lacquerwork, and sculpture; the Kress Collection of Italian Renaissance paintings; and the Michener Collection of Japanese prints. Among items that remain vividly in one's memory are a bronze and silver mirror from the T'ang dynasty of China, between the 7th and 10th centuries; the 14th-century statue *Kuan Yin,* also from China; Segna di Bonaventura's painting *Madonna and Child,* from the early Italian Renaissance; Paul Gauguin's *Two Nudes on a Tahitian Beach;* and one of Monet's superb studies of *Water Lilies.* There's also an intriguing collection of Roman glass and an elegant English drawing room with a table set for tea. Open Tuesdays through Saturdays 10 AM to 4:30 PM; Sundays from 1 to 4 PM. Closed Mondays. Tie in a visit with an alfresco lunch at the *Garden Café* (open Tuesdays through Saturdays from 11:30 AM to 1 PM; phone: 808-531-8865). Information: *Honolulu Academy of Arts,* 900 S. Beretania St., Honolulu, HI 96814 (phone: 808-538-3693).

MISSION HOUSES MUSEUM: "The clapboards are bare and admit quantities of dust which the trade winds bring in such fearful clouds as to suggest the fate of Pompeii. We have three chairs, a table, a bedstead, and a nice little secretary." So wrote Laura Fish Judd, wife of the evangelist Gerrit P. Judd, in August 1828 of the house they shared with the despotic Reverend Hiram Bingham, the first of the Protestant missionaries who were to leave an indelible imprint on Hawaiian life, both socially and architecturally. As if to underscore their uncompromising moral attitudes, the missionaries rejected the practical, relaxed, and airy grass shacks inhabited by the Hawaiians, including the king, in favor of the prim and proper (and stuffy and dusty) dwellings that replicated those they had known in Massachusetts. All over the islands, postage stamp–size versions of New England hamlets sprung up, looking incongruous among the exotic tropical trees and shrubs that surrounded and overshadowed them. The *Mission Houses* are the most elaborate complex remaining that recalls this typical example of Yankee obstinacy. The Frame House, which Mrs. Judd described, was shipped to Hawaii in 1820 from Boston and is the oldest existing house in Hawaii. In the parlors, bedrooms, and kitchen is a collection of the original furniture and utensils. The Printing House next door, built from coral blocks in 1831, contains a replica of the old-fashioned Ramage handpress used by the printer, Elisha Loomis, to produce a Hawaiian translation of the Bible, schoolbooks, and hymnals. On the *makai* (ocean) side of the Chamberlain House, built in 1841 — the latest and largest in the complex — the block and tackle used to haul missionary supplies up to the second-floor storehouse is still visible. Also in the Chamberlain House is a model of the mission station in 1850, which graphically illustrates how Honolulu has changed. Living History events, when visitors mingle with costumed volunteers, are offered twice monthly. Occasionally, candlelit evening walks are also scheduled on the calendar. Open Tuesdays through Saturdays from 9 AM to 4 PM; Sundays from noon to 4 PM; closed Mondays. Tours offered Tuesdays through Saturdays from 9:30 AM to 3 PM. Information: *Mission Houses Museum,* 553 S. King St., Honolulu, HI 96813 (phone: 808-531-0481).

CHURCHES: Along with their zeal and religious convictions, the missionaries who came to the islands in the 19th century brought with them a determination to see their beliefs made solidly manifest in the form of churches. Though architecturally unimpressive, their historical associations and/or decorative details make them noteworthy.

The Episcopal *St. Andrew's Cathedral* (at Beretania and Queen Emma Sts.) was the inspiration of Kamehameha IV and his wife, Queen Emma, Anglophiles both, who adopted the religion of English aristocracy. Although the cathedral's design, and some of its building materials, were imported from Britain, it was the *Kawaiahao Church* (957 Punchbowl St., Honolulu), built by New Englanders and dedicated by Kamehameha III, that became known as the "Westminster Abbey of Hawaii" for the number of royal baptisms, weddings, and funerals held there. In the church gallery is the Hoffstot Collection, 21 portraits of all of Hawaii's rulers and most of their consorts. Especially moving is the portrait of King Kamehameha III, who in the church sanctuary first used the words that were to become Hawaii's motto: *"Ua mau ke ea o ka aina i ka pono"* ("The life of the land is perpetuated in righteousness"). Today, *kahilis* (feather standards) adorn both sides of the sanctuary, and at most Sunday services at least one hymn is sung in Hawaiian. At the *Fort Street Mall* is *Our Lady of Peace Cathedral,* where Joseph de Veuster — Father Damien — was ordained in 1864. The *Queen Liliuokalani Church* (66-090 Kamehameha Hwy., Haleiwa) is special for its old clock with seven dials and seven hands showing the month, day of the week, week of the year, and phases of the moon, and a dial indicating the hours of the day that uses the 12 letters of the queen's name instead of numbers. *St. John the Apostle and Evangelist Church* (95-370 Kuahelani Ave., Mililani Town) is as austere as an early Christian abbey, with its stark granite altar and concrete walls. Highlights are the sculptures depicting the 14 Stations of the Cross, the modernistic stained glass windows, and the bronze statues of the Blessed Virgin Mary and St. John.

Royal Residences

Unlike the Celts and Romans in Europe, the Polynesians built no tombs or burial chambers, no forts or castles, no great walls or monuments. For the most part, nature, not man, still dominates the Hawaiian landscape, and many of the most critical events in Hawaiian history — the death of Captain Cook, the abandonment of the *kapus,* the arrival of the first missionaries and whalers, the overthrow of the monarchy — are marked in memory, not in stone. There are, however, two royal residences in Honolulu, which provide insight into life during the reign of the Hawaiian monarchy.

IOLANI PALACE: This neo-Florentine edifice, with its stone verandahs and Corinthian columns, is the only former royal palace in the United States. It was completed for King David Kalakaua in 1882 and cost more than $350,000. Kalakaua had traveled around the world and had been received by a number of reigning monarchs. He was particularly attracted by the courts of Europe, and he set out to copy their customs, clothes, and houses in his Polynesian homeland. He instituted Royal Household Guards with formal uniforms, complete with epaulets and ribbons; he built a coronation stand, where today the smartly turned out *Royal Hawaiian Band* gives concerts; he had crowns made for himself and his queen, Kapiolani; and on February 12, 1883, he began a coronation ceremony that continued for 2 weeks. Thereafter the palace, with its Victorian armoires and settees, became the scene of balls, receptions, dinners, and musical soirees. These displays of what they perceived as an effete way of life, as well as Kalakaua's high-handed style of government, disturbed and offended the American entrepreneurs in Hawaii. Kalakaua's successor, his sister Liliuokalani, reigned for only 2 years before she was deposed in 1893 by a provisional government headed by the pineapple magnate Samuel B. Dole. For the next 3 years, Iolani was periodically a prison for the ex-queen.

In 1898, sovereignty of the islands was transferred to the government of the United States, and the American flag flew above the former royal residence. The Territory of Hawaii was administered from here, and when the islands became the 50th state, the palace became the executive building. In 1969, the splendid new state capitol was opened, and a group called the Friends of Iolani Palace began looking for funds to restore it to its original opulence. Many of the furnishings and artifacts had been dispersed among Liliuokalani's family, as well as to collectors and museums. But little by little, donations and purchases have enabled a growing number of items to return to their original setting. The mirrored throne room, with its gilt trim and crystal chandeliers, once again evokes a sense of 19th-century court elegance. The main stairwell, made of highly polished koa wood and trimmed with ohia and cedar carvings, glows as it did when Robert Louis Stevenson stopped by to pay his respects and to note that Kalakaua could demolish five bottles of champagne in an afternoon. The walls of the king's bedroom still retain the silver-leaf decoration and eggshell blue paint of his day; and a portrait of Louis-Philippe, King of France, which he presented to Kamehameha III in 1848, still hangs on the first-floor landing. From time to time, people can be seen sipping champagne on the verandahs. Usually these are visiting chieftains from other Polynesian islands being entertained by Edward Kawanankoa, the pretender to the Hawaiian throne. Although Mr. Kawanankoa receives no official recognition from the state, he is extended these minor courtesies in memory of the Kamehamehas, from whom he is descended. Although much remains to be done before the house regains its original palatial status, it nevertheless offers a glimpse of how a semi-Europeanized Polynesian court thought it ought to live. Tours last 45 minutes and are offered from 9 AM to 2:15 PM, Wednesdays through Saturdays; call for reservations. Admission is $4. Information: *Iolani Palace,* Box 2259, Honolulu, HI 96804 (phone: 808-522-0884; for reservations, 808-522-0832).

QUEEN EMMA'S SUMMER PALACE: Unlike the ornate Iolani Palace, Queen Emma's summer retreat up in the Nuuanu Valley above Honolulu looks like the home of a well-to-do plantation owner. Built sometime between 1847 and 1850, it is a simple square building with Doric columns supporting the roof over the front lanai. Queen Emma, wife of Kamehameha IV, inherited the property in 1857, and in 1869 she added a large back room in the expectation of throwing a party for Queen Victoria's second son, Alfred, Duke of Edinburgh. The prince never showed up, but the room is still called the Edinburgh Room. After 1872, Emma no longer lived there. Following her death in 1885, the house fell into disrepair and was about to be torn down when the Daughters of Hawaii rescued it in 1913. Since 1915, they have operated it as a museum, displaying many of the artifacts that belonged to Emma and her family, as well as materials relating to that period in Hawaiian history. Some exotic pieces that visitors find especially appealing among the *kahilis* (feather standards) and Victorian furniture are an elaborate, three-tiered Gothic cabinet bordered with cruciform fretwork and finials, a gift from Queen Victoria's consort, Prince Albert; a stereopticon, presented to the queen by Napoleon III; and a necklace hung with tiger claws decorated with seed pearls embedded in rolled gold. Queen Emma's only son, Albert, died when he was 4 years old. His christening robe, embroidered with the royal coat of arms, hangs in his mother's bedroom, not far from the simple red jacket and brass megaphone given to the infant prince when he was made an honorary member of the Honolulu Volunteer Fire Department. Many of the plants found here in Emma's day still flourish on the grounds, and a delightful view of the house is seen from the driveway, framed by kukui and koa trees and surrounded by roses, geraniums, spider lilies, and serpentine ferns. Admission is $4. Information: *Queen Emma's Summer Palace,* 2913 Pali Hwy., Honolulu, HI 96817 (phone: 808-595-3167).

Honolulu Art Galleries

With little fanfare, Honolulu has evolved into a thriving art center. For years, the *Honolulu Academy of Arts,* founded in 1927, was the only game in town. Today art galleries are popping up all over — most notably in Chinatown with its low rents and interesting storefronts and exhibit spaces — and showcasing the work of the city's talented artists and craftspeople. Beyond the galleries, many island artists display their work on Sundays along the "fence" at the *Honolulu Zoo* on the Diamond Head side of Waikiki, and in Kailua, along the hedge at the main intersection. Restaurants such as *Che Pasta* and *Roy's* have regular art exhibits, and so does the airport. Here then is a gallery guide to Honolulu and its environs.

CONTEMPORARY MUSEUM: Located in a former estate on the slopes of Mount Tantalus, this museum/gallery commands dramatic views of the ocean and the city below. Its focus is modern art, and the exhibits change constantly, spotlighting artists from Hawaii as well as the rest of the country; the gardens and outdoor sculpture are almost as spectacular as the art within.

Begin a visit in the entry courtyard where a Deborah Butterfield horse and *Mirror XV,* a complex James Seawright reflecting sculpture, share the space. To the left, Viola Frey's larger-than-life ceramic *Resting Woman* lounges by the swimming pool, and two more of her seated women can be found on the front lawn. Here too is a George Rickey stainless steel kinetic sculpture, moving gracefully in the breeze. In the garden, look for the wry Robert Arneson ceramic sculpture, *Temple of Fatal Laffs.*

Inside, regular exhibits of contemporary artists change frequently and are supplemented with curated shows of national and international artists. A highlight of the museum is the Cadres Pavilion, a separate building, housing David Hockney's *L'Enfant et les Sortileges,* a fascinating and brilliantly hued environmental installation based on the English pop artist's sets and costumes for Maurice Ravel's opera.

Don't miss the contemporary arts and crafts at the museum shop, including the work of many Hawaiian craftspeople. Look for glass earrings by Patricia Van Asperin-Hume, glass bowls by Bruce Clark, button jewelry by Carol Hasegawa, vests and T-shirts made with kimono material by Patricia Greene, and painted corrugated cardboard pins by Lisa Salazak. The museum's handsome café serves individual pizza, smoked salmon with dill cream, and tempting desserts. Open Tuesdays through Saturdays, 10 AM to 4 PM; Sundays, noon to 4 PM. Information: *Contemporary Museum,* 2411 Makiki Heights Dr. (phone: 808-526-0232).

TENNENT ART FOUNDATION: Artist Madge Cook Tennent, an Englishwoman who lived in Samoa, was influenced at an early age by Gauguin, but her own distinctive style developed when she arrived in Hawaii in 1923. A prolific, internationally recognized artist, Tennent is known for her dramatic oils, especially her studies of Hawaiian people. Elaine Tennent, her daughter-in-law and the co-curator of this museum, describes her work this way: "Swirling masses of paints in bold, explosive colors were applied with a palette knife rather than a brush in her larger paintings. The lyrical portraits of large-bodied Hawaiian women, monumental in size with a sense of elegance, grace and refinement, became her own personal idiom." The pieces here range from her earliest drawings to a series of studies of the masters, her homage to Renoir, Gauguin, and Picasso. Open Tuesdays through Saturdays, 10 AM until noon, and Sundays 2 to 4 PM, or call for an appointment. Information: *Tennent Art Foundation,* 201-203 Prospect St. (phone: 808-532-1987).

GALLERY ON THE PALI: In an old mansion in Nuuanu (now a Unitarian church), this is the oldest private art gallery in Hawaii. Its aim is to promote young and unrecognized Hawaiian artists, though they do present the work of established artists on a regular basis. What the gallery lacks in sophisticated presentation, it more than makes up for with creative enthusiasm. Open weekdays, 9 AM to 3 PM; weekends, 1 to 4 PM. Information: *Gallery on the Pali,* 2500 Pali Hwy. (phone: 808-526-1191).

HART, TAGAMI & POWELL GALLERY AND GARDENS: These beautifully designed Japanese-style galleries are just 45 minutes from Waikiki in the Kahaluu Valley. First opened to the public in 1977, they provide a forum for local artists Hiroshi Tagami and Michael Powell to exhibit their oil paintings and watercolors depicting scenes of nature — birds, trees, the sea, and the Koolau Mountains. Also on display are raku stoneware, ceramics, and wood pieces by other local artists. Part of the pleasure of visiting here is the galleries' garden; carved out of the valley, it's filled with rare orchids, heliconia, anthuriums of unusual color, and exotic palms. By appointment only. Information: *Hart, Tagami & Powell Gallery and Gardens,* 47-754 Lamaula Rd., Kaneohe (phone: 808-239-8146).

In Chinatown, recent restoration efforts have made the area appealing to gallery owners. There are now a dozen or more art enclaves that feature contemporary American, Asian, and European art objects. A notable cluster of them is on Nuuanu Avenue, including the *Pegge Hopper Gallery* (No. 1164; phone: 808-524-1160), which sells Hopper's pastel graphics of lounging Hawaiian women; *William Waterfall Gallery* (No. 1160A; phone: 808-521-6863), specializing in folk art from Bali and Thailand as well as hand-tinted photographs of turn-of-the-century Hawaii; and *Pauahi Nuuanu Gallery* (corner of Pauahi and Nuuanu; phone: 808-531-6088), the place for contemporary Hawaiian art as well as arts and crafts. Nearby, the *Ramsay Galleries & Café* (1128 Smith St.; phone: 808-537-ARTS) features Ramsay's black-and-white architectural etchings and live jazz in the evenings.

At the University of Hawaii, look for the *Commons Gallery* (phone: 808-737-5671), which shows the work of student artists, and don't miss the Pacific Rim artists at the *John A. Burns Hall* (phone: 808-944-7341) in the East-West Center. On the ground floor of the downtown *Pauahi Tower* (phone: 808-537-6838) there is a gallery showing contemporary works of Honolulu artists, and the *Honolulu Advertiser Gallery* (605 Kapiolani Blvd.; phone: 808-526-0232) is the downtown satellite of the *Contemporary Museum.*

A Shutterbug's View

 The dramatic juxtaposition of land and sea, vibrant color, beautiful weather, and a diverse and exotic population are Honolulu's photographic stock in trade. Even a beginner can achieve remarkable results with a surprisingly basic set of lenses and filters or a camcorder. Equipment is, in fact, only as valuable as the imagination that puts it into use.

Don't be afraid to experiment. Use what knowledge you have to explore new possibilities. Don't limit yourself by preconceived ideas of what's hackneyed or corny. Because a hibiscus has been photographed hundreds of times before doesn't make it any less worthy of your attention.

In Honolulu, as elsewhere, spontaneity is one of the keys to good photography. Whether it's a sudden shaft of light bursting through the clouds or a surfer poised on the curl of a huge wave at Sunset Beach, don't hesitate to shoot if the moment is right. If photography is indeed capturing a moment and making it timeless, success lies in judging just when a moment worth capturing occurs and reacting quickly.

A good picture reveals an eye for detail, whether it's a matter of lighting, of positioning your subject, or of taking time to crop a picture carefully. The better your grasp of the importance of details, the better your results will be photographically.

Patience is often necessary. Don't shoot a view of Diamond Head if a cloud suddenly covers it with shadows. A dead tree in a panorama of the Nuunau Valley? Reframe your image to eliminate the obvious distraction. People walking toward a scene that would benefit from their presence? Wait until they're in position before you shoot. After the fact, many of the flaws will be self-evident. The trick is to be aware of the ideal and have the patience to allow it to happen. If you are part of a group, you may well have to trail behind a bit in order to shoot properly. Not only is group activity distracting, but bunches of people hovering nearby tend to stifle spontaneity and overwhelm potential subjects.

A camera or camcorder provides an opportunity, not only to capture Oahu's straightforward beauty, but to interpret it. What it takes is a sensitivity to the surroundings, a knowledge of the capabilities of your equipment, and a willingness to see things in new ways.

LANDSCAPES AND SEASCAPES: The Hawaiian landscape is of such compelling beauty that it is often the photographer's primary focus. Even Honolulu and Waikiki are best captured in the context of their setting, sandwiched between the lush, saw-toothed Koolaus and the variegated blues and greens of the Pacific.

Color and form are the obvious ingredients here, and how you frame your pictures can be as important as getting the proper exposure. Study the shapes, angles, and colors that make up the scene and create a composition that uses them to best advantage.

Lighting is a vital component in landscapes and seascapes. Take advantage of the richer colors of early morning and late afternoon whenever possible. The overhead light of midday is often harsh and without the shadowing that can add to the drama of a scene. This is when a polarizer is used to best effect. Most polarizers come with a mark on the rotating ring. If you can aim at your subject and point that marker at the sun, the sun's rays are likely to be right for the polarizer to work for you. If not, stick to your skylight filter, underexposing slightly if the scene is particularly bright. Most light meters respond to an overall light balance, with the result that bright areas may appear burned out.

Although a standard 50mm to 55mm lens may work well in some landscape situations, most will benefit from a 20mm to 28mm wide-angle. Waikiki, Hanauma Bay, the Punchbowl, and the Pali Lookout are just some of the panoramas that fit beautifully into a wide-angle format, allowing not only the overview, but the opportunity to include people or other points of interest in the foreground. A flower, for instance, may be used to set off a view of Diamond Head; or people can provide a sense of perspective in a shot of the monstrous waves at Waimea.

To isolate specific elements of any scene, use your telephoto lens. Perhaps there's a weird and wonderful plant amid the volcanic debris of Koko Crater, or it might be the interplay of light and shadow on Pali Lookout or a distant waterfall cascading down the windward cliffs of the Koolau Range. The successful use of a telephoto means developing your eye for detail.

PEOPLE: As with taking pictures of people anywhere, there are going to be times in Honolulu when a camera is an intrusion. Your approach is the key: Consider your own reaction under similar circumstances, and you have an idea as to what would make others comfortable enough to be willing subjects. People are often sensitive to having a camera suddenly pointed at them, and a polite request, while getting you a share of refusals, will also provide a chance to shoot some wonderful portraits that capture the spirit of the islands as surely as the scenery does. For candids, an excellent lens is a zoom telephoto in the 70mm to 210mm range; it allows you to remain unobtrusive while the telephoto lens draws the subject closer. And for portraits, a telephoto can be used effectively as close as 2 or 3 feet.

For authenticity and variety, select a place likely to produce interesting subjects. Waikiki is an obvious spot for visitors, but if it's local color you're after, visit China-town, wander into a pineapple field, or go to one of the North Shore beaches that are popular with surfers. Aim for shots that tell what's different about Honolulu. In portraiture, there are several factors to keep in mind. Morning or afternoon light will add richness to skin tones, emphasizing tans. To avoid the harsh facial shadows cast by direct sunlight, shoot in the shade or in an area where the light is diffused. The only filter to use is a skylight.

SUNSETS: Not every Honolulu night is preceded by a brilliant sunset, but there are likely to be some that will seem to typify every magical impression ever dreamed of the tropics. When shooting sunsets, keep in mind that the brightness will distort meter readings. When composing a shot directly into the sun, frame the picture in the viewfinder so that only half of the sun is included. Read the meter, set, and shoot. Whenever there is this kind of unusual lighting, shoot a few frames in half-step increments, both over and under the meter reading. Bracketing, as this is called, can provide a range of images, the best of which may well be other than the one shot at the meter's recommended setting.

Use any lens for sunsets. A wide-angle is good when the sky is filled with color-streaked clouds, when the sun is partially hidden, or when you're close to an object that silhouettes dramatically against the sky.

Telephotos also produce wonderful silhouettes, either with the sun as a backdrop or against the palette of a brilliant sunset sky. Bracket again here. For the best silhouettes, wait 10 to 15 minutes after sunset. Unless using a very fast film, a tripod is recommended.

Orange, magenta, and split-screen filters are often used to accentuate a sunset's picture potential. Orange will help turn even a gray sky into something approaching a photogenic finale to the day and can provide particularly beautiful shots linking the sky with the sun reflected on the ocean. A pale magenta, as in a fluorescent or daylight correction filter, can add subtle color to dull or brilliant sunsets. If the sunset is already bold in hue, the orange will overwhelm the natural colors. A red filter will produce dramatic, highly unrealistic results.

NIGHT: If you think that picture possibilities end at sunset, you're presuming that night photography is the exclusive domain of the professional. If you've got a tripod, all you'll need is a cable release to attach to your camera to assure a steady exposure (which is often timed in minutes rather than fractions of a second).

For situations such as luaus, Polynesian revues, and other nighttime entertainments, a strobe does the trick, but beware: Flash units are often used improperly. You can't take a view of Diamond Head with a flash. It may reach out 30 to 50 feet, but that's it. On the other hand, a flash used too close to your subject may result in overexposure, resulting in a "blown out" effect. With most cameras, strobes will work with a maximum shutter speed of 1/125 or 1/250 of a second. If you set the exposure properly and shoot within range, you should come up with pretty sharp results.

CLOSE-UPS: Whether of people or of objects such as lava, close-ups can add another dimension to your photography. There are a number of shooting options, one of which is to use a 70mm or a 210mm lens at its closest focusable distance. Unless you're working in bright sunlight, a tripod will be worthwhile. If you are very near your subject and there is a good deal of reflective light, it may pay to underexpose a bit in relation to the meter reading.

If you do not have a telephoto lens, you can still shoot close-ups using a set of magnification filters. Filter packs of one-, two-, and three-time magnification are available, converting your lens into a close-up lens. Even better is a special macro lens designed for close-up photography.

AERIAL VIEWS: An inter-island flight or a helicopter tour can inspire some great pictures, but you have to be prepared. Get your equipment ready as soon as you're seated, test the meter against the horizon's light, and set for the proper exposure. Have spare film unpackaged and handy so you can change it quickly, and try to start off with a full roll rather than waste time (and photo opportunities) while airborne.

You can use a wide-angle lens from the air, although it will flatten things out and may well include sections of the plane in the picture. A 50mm can be used, and a telephoto will pick out details. Don't shoot through glass (or plexiglass) that is curved or at too extreme an angle; it will cause distortion. If there's bright sunlight, it's possible to underexpose a bit, yet still have enough light to shoot at speeds of 1/500 or 1/1000: fast enough to get results. Below 1/125 the outcome is questionable.

Below, some of our choice of Honolulu's most photogenic places.

A SHORT PHOTOGRAPHIC TOUR

DIAMOND HEAD: For the definitive shot of Diamond Head, wait until afternoon and head down the beach to the jetty in front of the *Outrigger Reef.* The beach to the right of the *Hilton Hawaiian Village* and the Magic Island section of Ala Moana Beach Park also have clear, uncluttered views. So do the lounge and restaurant atop the *Sheraton Waikiki.*

THE BEACHES: A visit to any of Oahu's beaches will provide endless vistas of white sand and blue water as well as lots of subjects: Try Waikiki for all sorts and shapes of sunbathers; Diamond Head and Kailua Beach for windsurfers; Sunset and the Banzai Pipeline for championship surfers. You might try an 81B (brown) filter to warm up beach shots or underexpose a bit if you're using a skylight to compensate for reflective glare.

CHINATOWN: For people shots and atmosphere, you can't beat Chinatown, particularly the early morning market on King Street.

TANTALUS LOOKOUT AND PUNCHBOWL NATIONAL CEMETERY: A drive to Tantalus Lookout affords spectacular cityscapes that include Diamond Head, Waikiki, and downtown Honolulu. The lookout at Punchbowl National Cemetery also offers panoramas of the city. Early morning is the best time to shoot; those in search of the perfect sunset can sleep — or swim or surf — until late afternoon.

HANAUMA BAY: Photographers come here for shots of snorkelers, marine life, and one of Hawaii's largest reefs. For the latter, you'll need an underwater casing.

WINDWARD COAST: For one of the most encompassing views in Hawaii, follow the Pali Highway to Pali Lookout, which offers picture possibilities anytime during the day before 4 PM, when the Windward Coast becomes covered in shadow. Photographic possibilities on the coast include sunrise at Lanikai Beach, with the sun coming up behind two pyramid-shaped islands in a turquoise lagoon, and the windsurfers skimming over the blue-green water of Kailua Bay.

NORTH SHORE: Take a morning's drive up the coast to the North Shore and beyond for the photographic possibilites in its 2-hour sweep of rugged mountains, ribbon beaches, ever-changing seas, and thick green vegetation. Also noteworthy are the pineapple fields of the Schofield Plains, especially during harvest; the charming town of Haleiwa, which sees some stunning sunsets; and Waimea Falls Park with its waterfalls, tropical flowers, and hula dancers.

DIRECTIONS

Introduction

Honolulu is something of an enigma to most mainland US residents. As the capital of our 50th state, it invites comparisons with other state capitals, but Honolulu is not just a city — it's a county too, streamlining what is generally two levels of government into one. Officially, it is the city and county of Honolulu, and includes the entire island of Oahu within its Pacific perimeters.

Like most capital cities, Honolulu consists of busy city streets lined with office buildings, high-rise hotels, and ultramodern shopping centers — but that's not all: Also within the city, far from the bright lights and bustle, are such rural pleasures as pineapple fields, rain forests, papaya plantations, and glorious beaches. And just to make the concept even more startling, for administrative purposes, the city and county also encompass more than 100 islands, islets, atolls, and other projections above the surface of the ocean, most of which are bird sanctuaries and are not open to the public. Whew!

All of this makes Honolulu a fascinating, but complex, place to visit. To discover the 608 square miles that make up the medium-size island of Oahu, we offer five easy and entertaining excursions. Three are walking tours: The first follows the famous beach at Waikiki; the second meanders through the narrow streets of Chinatown, chockablock with open-air markets, noodle factories, and tiny shops; and the third visits historic Downtown Honolulu, with its reminders of Hawaiian royalty and the island's first missionaries. A fourth excursion combines a short drive with a healthy hike — the trek to the top of Diamond Head. The last route is a driving tour, cutting through the pineapple and sugar fields of central Oahu to the North Shore, with its world-famous surfing beaches.

So stroll or drive with us. You'll discover that Honolulu is much more than just another pretty stretch of sand.

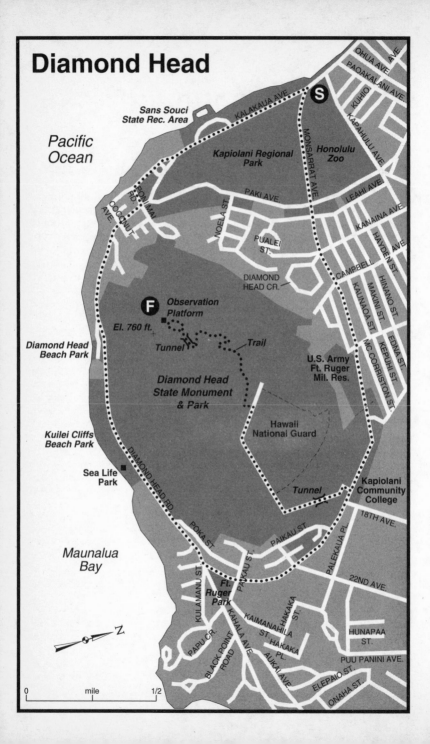

Tour 1: Diamond Head

Diamond Head, the extinct volcanic crater whose dramatic silhouette provides a backdrop to the gentle curve of Waikiki Beach, has become a symbol of Hawaii known around the world. Although it is just one of several craters on Oahu, it's the most famous: In fact, it's a state monument.

Two centuries ago, in the days of sailings ships, fires were lit on Diamond Head's summit to guide the boats safely to land, and lookouts were stationed here to relay the first news of approaching vessels. Prior to World War II, when nearly all visitors still came to Hawaii by ocean liner, passengers vied for prizes given to the first one of them to spot Diamond Head's craggy arc on the horizon.

The ancient Hawaiian name for the landmark is Leahi (pronounced Lay-ah-hee), because the ancient Hawaiians thought the peak's profile resembled the forehead (*le*) of the yellowfin tuna (*ahi*). Dubbed Mount Leahi by the first *haoles* (non-Hawaiians), the name lives on today in a nearby street and a hospital.

One theory purports, however, that the original name came from lei (a wreath), and *ahi* (which also means fire). But although Diamond Head may have been a wreath of fire at one time, it would have been long before even the first Hawaiian occupied the island. The crater exploded into existence 150,000 years ago, give or take a few millennia, and it is not expected to erupt again in the foreseeable future. Its characteristic shape, with the leeward, or southwestern, slope higher than any other point in the rim, indicates that the northeast trade winds were blowing when the eruption occurred.

Diamond Head received its alluring modern name in 1825, when British sailors found calcite crystals, resembling diamonds, on its slopes. These crystals are also known in Hawaii as Pele's tears (Pele — pronounced *Pay*-lay — is the Hawaiian goddess of volcanoes).

Although Diamond Head can be called a volcano, it can hardly be called a mountain. Although it appears to be much higher, its rim is only 760 feet above sea level, tantalizingly low for hikers, but beware: Many who have tried to scramble up its face have been injured and have had to be rescued by helicopter from its slopes.

If approached in a logical way, however, Diamond Head is one of the most accessible peaks in Hawaii. The secret is to make the ascent from *inside* the crater, and to make the trip in the morning, when the weather is still relatively cool — and the light just right for taking pictures along the way. The actual climb takes about 45 minutes and is so easy that most locals say if you can climb stairs, you can can climb Diamond Head.

Wear jeans or shorts and good walking shoes, and bring binoculars, a camera, a container of drinking water, and a flashlight (you'll be navigating some dark tunnels); some hikers carry a picnic in a backpack. When planning your hike, keep in mind the road into the crater is only open from 6 AM to 6 PM.

There are two ways to get to the beginning of the trail, each about 2 or 3 miles from Waikiki. The longer, and more scenic, route is via Kalakaua Avenue alongside Kapiolani Park going "diamondhead." (Directions in Hawaii are more often given by naming geographic features rather than traditional compass readings.) The avenue here is shaded by scores of ironwood trees, a type of fuzzy Australian pine imported to Hawaii a century ago to be used as windbreak.

Go past the Dillingham Fountain and follow the road to the left on Poni Mai Street for a block and then turn right into Diamond Head Road. On the right are flowered gateways that lead to some of Honolulu's most luxurious — and secluded — private estates; two tiny green parks used by local residents; a small white Coast Guard lighthouse; and several parking areas — great spots at which to stop and watch windsurfers skimming across the waves below. Look to the southeast for the islands of Molokai, Lanai, and on a clear day, even Maui, 90 miles away. (Keep strictly to the speed limit in this area; it is well-patrolled by the Honolulu Police Department.)

Just beyond the parking lots at Ft. Ruger Park, a triangle-shape, tree-shaded space with a playground, Diamond Head Road curves to the left (if you continue straight the road becomes Kahala Avenue, leading to a silk stocking residential area and the *Kahala Hilton* hotel). Follow Diamond Head Road past the Department of Defense building (on the right) into the old grounds and blocked-off streets of Ft. Ruger, and then turn left at the yellow-and-brown sign with an arrow indicating Diamond Head Crater.

To go by the shorter (less scenic) route, the opposite way around Diamond Head, follow Monsarrat Avenue through Kapiolani Park until it becomes Diamond Head Road at the entrance to Ft. Ruger. (If you don't have a car, take a taxi or bus No. 58 or 22 — marked *Hawaii Kai* and *Sea Life Park* — on Kapahula Avenue and get off at Kapiolani Community College. To be sure, tell the driver you're going to Diamond Head Crater.)

Follow the old asphalt road with the faded yellow line to the narrow tunnel that has been drilled through the back wall of the crater. Drive slowly; and watch out for pedestrians.

Take the road into the crater; the buildings on the crater floor, most of which are blocked off by a high fence, belong to the FAA air traffic control station, which oversees most of the air traffic in the central Pacific. (Now that Diamond Head has gained state monument status, the existence of the center on this site has been deemed by many to be inappropriate.)

Follow the road through the crater to Diamond Head Park, which has a couple of picnic tables, a comfort station, a drinking fountain, and a public phone. Park in the lot (be sure to lock your car) and look up to the rim of the crater; the old cement military structures at the top are your final goal.

Begin the trek on the only trail (paved at first but dusty soon enough) that leads from the area, through the tall grass on the crater floor. If your nostrils are assaulted with a pungent smell, it's probably an unseen patch of Chinese parsley. Please don't stray from the beaten path; the pathways that occasionally branch off the main trail are no longer safe.

Gradually the trail becomes steeper and then winds upward, switching back and forth through the ubiquitous tropical Pacific brown seed-pod underbrush known in Hawaii as *haole koa*. During the summer, the way is brightened by miniature red tomatoes, as well as orange ilima blossoms. (The official flower of Oahu, ilima is used in specially prized leis.)

A half hour into the climb (usually about two-thirds of the way), catch your breath on the crater rim next to an old winch, probably used by the military posts on Diamond Head some 50 years ago to crank up supplies from the streets far below. Some turn around at this point, but don't: The best is yet to come.

Climb the flight of 36 or so cement steps that lead to 100 yards of the darkest tunnel you ever *didn't* see. Electricity was cut off decades ago, and those who bring flashlights will be glad for their foresight. Those not so equipped will make it through by whistling in the dark and keeping a steady hand along the guide rail. At the end of the tunnel are even more steps leading straight up.

Bunkers, tunnels, and other empty cement-wall rooms can be seen on either side of the stairs. Although it's tempting to explore, it's far safer to continue up the winding stairways though 3 levels of dark, musty fortifications until you emerge into full daylight at the summit. From the windy platform, admire the panoramic 360° view, with Waikiki in the foreground and the rest of Honolulu beyond — including the airplanes landing and taking off at Honolulu International Airport and, on a clear day, the Waianae Mountains farther off to the west. Think about the fact that members of the ancient Hawaiian nobility cut a path down to Waikiki and rode *holua* (sleds), made of large leaves or wood, to the bottom. If you want to show your friends back home proof of your accomplishment, look for the US Coast and Geodesic Survey marker on the platform and make a crayon or soft-pencil rubbing of it as a souvenir.

■**Diamond Head Data:** For more detailed information on climbing Diamond Head, go to the front desk of the *New Otani Kaimana Beach* hotel (2863 Kalakau Ave.) and ask for their Diamond Head climbing kit, which includes a flashlight, a 38-page booklet (written by hotel manager Steve Boyle), a crayon, and rubbing paper. After the climb, go back to the hotel, return the flashlight, and present your rubbing; the desk clerk will then issue you a certificate, suitable for framing, verifying that you made the climb. The cost: a charitable donation (perhaps $5 or $10), which the hotel passes on to those helping the homeless of Honolulu.

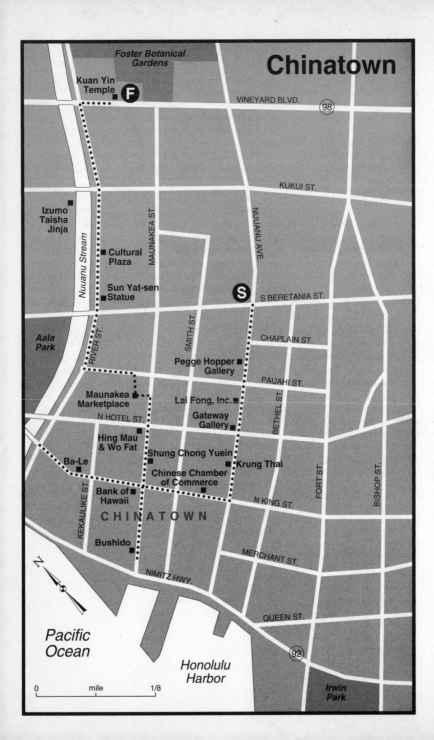

Tour 2: Chinatown

It was July 1865 when the first Chinese workers, under contract to the Hawaiian government, arrived on Oahu to toil in the sugar fields. Over the next few decades, they would be followed by more than 45,000 of their countrymen, some of whom came from California when work petered out in the gold fields or on the railroad. The Chinese were the first, but not the last, 19th-century contract laborers to come to the islands; there were also Japanese, Koreans, Filipinos, and even groups from the Portuguese Azores. But it was the Chinese who were the first to leave the sugar fields and establish themselves as craftsmen, merchants, and restaurateurs.

Many opened shops, with their homes upstairs, in about 14 square blocks just northwest of downtown Honolulu; by 1870, the area became known as Chinatown. But Honolulu's Chinatown never quite became the enclave that exists in many North American cities. Once established, many Chinese — often called *pake* (pronounced pah-*kay*) by locals — moved their homes and businesses into other parts of the city.

Almost all the buildings extant in Chinatown today were built after 1900, when an outbreak of bubonic plague was traced to this neighborhood of rickety wooden row houses; and city fathers decided to burn a small part of the area in order to eliminate the source of the disease. Unfortunately, a strong wind whipped through Honolulu that night, and the fire burned out of control. By the time the smoke cleared, the fire had spread out over 38 acres and several thousand people had lost their homes and businesses. The plague, by the way, was also wiped out.

Today, Chinatown is a neighborhood of brick, stone, and stucco 2-story buildings, not unlike many a 19th-century business district in small-town America. There are two notable differences: Most of the buildings have a corrugated metal overhang to protect shoppers or strollers from the sun and rain, and many signs are written with Chinese characters. In open-air meat, fish, and vegetable markets stocked with exotic produce, elderly people still dress in the costume of their native or ancestral land. And sleazy pool halls and seedy bars still compete for customers with family-style chop suey houses.

Most of the Chinese in Chinatown today were born in Hawaii. (If you hear them speak anything other than English, it is probably Cantonese, not Mandarin, since most originally came from the southern part of China.) But these days, the languages spoken here may also be Filipino, Laotian, Samoan, Korean, and Vietnamese. Today very few Chinese actually live in Chinatown, although many reside just outside its boundaries, and come to the area for cultural activities and shopping. The predominant ethnic group living here today is Filipino.

Urban renewal has brought changes to Chinatown — some bad and some good. In 1973, the entire area, which is bounded by Nuuanu Avenue, Nimitz

Highway, and River and Beretania Streets, was placed on the National Register of Historic Places. Prior to this designation, many buildings were lost to the bulldozer and the wrecking ball; but since then, structures have been preserved and redesigned and are attracting new business to the area; a major lure is the inexpensive rents.

During World War II, servicemen used to come to Chinatown for entertainment. Many elements of this honky-tonk atmosphere still exist, mostly along Hotel Street, a typical urban "combat zone" of rowdy bars and dance halls, tattoo parlors, strip shows, prostitutes (gay and straight), and adult bookstores. Tame in comparison to other such urban areas, no one need avoid this bustling sector by day. Some women, however, may not be comfortable in the neighborhood at night. (There is a police substation at the corner of Nuuanu Avenue and Hotel Street, almost in the center of the action.)

If you drive to Chinatown, park in the city lot on Smith Street between Beretania and Pauahi (the meters take quarters only and charge 25¢ per 15 minutes), or a private lot, which can cost as much as $2 a half hour. Bus Nos. 2, 19, and 20 go to the downtown area and Chinatown from Waikiki.

Begin an exploration of Chinatown on the north side of Nuuanu Avenue at Beretania Street and walk *makai* (seaward — the opposite of *mauka*, toward the mountains). Little on Nuuanu today is recognizably Chinese (*Yung's Kitchen* at No. 1170 is an exception); this street is now home to art galleries and specialty shops. (Note that many of these are closed on Sundays.)

The *Pegge Hopper Gallery* (No. 1164) showcases the work of Ms. Hopper, one of Hawaii's most popular contemporary artists. At the *Waterfall Gallery* (No. 1160), expect posters, photography, and modern Asian art; owner William Waterfall is an accomplished local photographer, and his gallery is surprisingly eclectic in content.

Nearby, just across North Pauahi Street on the corner, is the *Pauahi Nuuanu Gallery,* which specializes in crafts made from native Hawaiian koa wood. The *Moratin Downtown Gallery* (3 N. Pauahi) features paintings by Hawaii artists as well as Oriental antiques; *Art Treasures Gallery* (9 N. Pauahi) also sells art and antiques.

Back on Nuuanu, continue on to the venerable *Lai Fong, Inc.* (No. 1118); this is the spot for antique Chinese furniture and figurines. Ask about Lai Fong's *cheongsams* (Oriental slit-skirt dresses); he will make them to order. Look across the street at the two stone buildings with rounded upper-story windows; one survived the 1900 fire (the Perry Block, ca. 1886) and the other was built just after it (the McLean Block, 1903).

Cross the street to *City Art Works* (No. 1133) for Honolulu's best prices on film and other photo supplies. Nearby is *Kam Sing Shun* herbalist and acupuncturist (the two health-care professions often combine their curative powers in Chinatown). *Magner's on the Park* (No. 1121) is a trendy eatery that serves continental fare and features New Zealand beer on tap; the best tables here are in the back garden. Next door, *Chinatown Pasta Bar* is part of the same operation.

At Hotel Street, on the north side of Nuuanu, visit the *Gateway Gallery* (No. 1050), which specializes in painted furniture, and *Something's Up* (No.

1034), featuring hand-painted baskets and kitchenware. Stop for lunch at *Krung Thai* (No. 1028), a Thai restaurant where the food is inexpensive and tasty, and there's an attractive dining patio out back. Try the chicken Penang, with peanut curry, coconut milk, and basil.

Cross King Street, and turn right. On the left, on street level (despite its name) is the *Penthouse,* featuring closeouts and other marked-down goods from the *Liberty House* department stores. About midway down the block, the Hawaii National Bank makes a nod to its surroundings with the two white lion statues that guard against evil spirits — and presumably ward off would-be bank robbers. Rub the head of the male lion (the one with its paw on the ball) on the right for prosperity and good luck; rub the head of the female to ensure fertility. Check the bank's windows for Chinese cultural displays, featuring such items as prayer beads, Chinese lion's heads, and Mandarin costumes; inside, dip into the big glass jar of free fortune cookies. Across the street and upstairs is the Chinese Chamber of Commerce (42 N. King St.; phone: 808-533-3181). Stop in or call them for information about their inexpensive guided tours of Chinatown.

Continue up King, crossing Smith Street. The *Concord Trading Company* (75 N. King) is the first of many Chinese specialty stores and family markets on this street. Great for browsing (or buying), the markets sell all kinds of exotic Chinese fruits and vegetables.

At the corner of King and Maunakea Streets, the Chinatown branch of the Bank of Hawaii has a roof with traditional upturned corners and red pillars encircled by golden dragons. A block detour *makai* (seaward) on Maunakea leads to *Bushido* (No. 936), a gallery selling Japanese swords, Korean ceramics, and other items from the Far East. *Robyn Buntin of Honolulu* (No. 900) features traditional Oriental art on the right side of the store and contemporary Hawaiian works in the corner studio on the left. In the 19th century, this area was a major fish market; the building now occupied by Buntin was a smokehouse for fish. The smell, fortunately, is long gone, but ask and they'll show you the brick pillars still stained with smoke.

On your return to King Street, look for a building with a sign that reads "C. Q. Yee Hop & Co., Ltd." (in the alleyway at No. 948 Maunakea); it's an example of the lava rock construction that was popular around the turn of the century. Many old Chinatown and downtown buildings were similarly built, but most have been replaced with cement facing.

Walk down King as far as River Street, returning again to Maunakea via the other side of King. This stretch is lined with small cafés, open-air markets, and pastry shops, selling delicious dim sum (Chinese appetizers, including dumplings), candied ginger root, rice cakes, and almond cookies. Need an Asian conical peasant hat? Check out *Viet's Mart* on the corner of North King and River Street. Delicous sandwiches and croissants can be found at *Ba-Le* (150 N. King), and next door, at the tiny *Yat Tung Chow Noodle Factory,* you can watch the pros noodle around with the dough. At the North King markets, expect unusual displays — from such simple offerings as *limu,* a popular seaweed, to a whole pig's head suspended by a wire running through its eye sockets (ugh!).

Back at Maunakea, once considered the main street of Chinatown, walk *mauka* (mountainside). On the south side of the street is the *Chinatown Mall,* home to several Oriental gift and jewelry shops. Look here for fancy chopsticks, tea service items, stoneware, and jade.

Maunakea Street is known for its lei shops, and several are located along the 3-block stretch between King and Beretania Streets. You can buy fresh strands of plumeria, carnations, orchids, ginger, jasmine, ilima, and several rarer types — and at lower prices than those in Waikiki.

Shung Chong Yuein (No. 1027 Maunakea), a Chinese cake shop, has mouth-watering displays of moon cakes, banana rolls, almond cookies, black-and-yellow bean pastry, *char siu bao* (steamed barbecued pork buns), and melon cakes. Peek in at the Chinese herb shop (No. 1033) next door; along the walls are hundreds of little drawers containing long-dead sea horses, shriveled donkey skin, powdered clamshell, ginseng root, and other dried concoctions sure to cure whatever ails you.

Across the street, on the corner of Maunakea and Hotel Streets, is *Wo Fat,* Chinatown's oldest restaurant, established in 1882. The restaurant itself is upstairs; on the street level is *Hing Mau,* a Chinese grocery.

Cross Hotel Street, walk on the north side of Maunakea, and then turn in to the gateway at No. 1120. This is *Maunakea Marketplace,* which has an open-air patio, delightfully insulated from the sound of traffic, and dominated by a clock tower and a statue of "Confucius — 551–479 BC," according to the sign. (Local Chinese admit that no one is sure what Confucius looked like, only that he was supposed to have been born with two horns, which are *not* evident in this representation.) Although most of the shops here are rather precious, the food hall, with its many ethnic food stalls, is worth a stop. Take-out food representing the diverse cuisines of Japan, China, Korea, Malaysia, Thailand, the Philippines, Puerto Rico, and Italy is available.

Leave the marketplace via the Pauahi Street gateway, turn left and walk for a half block to River Street, and turn right, following the Nuuanu Stream (actually a mountain water drainage canal). See if you can spot tilapia, a hardy fish that flourishes almost anywhere. Cross Beretania Street, leaving the traditional boundary of Chinatown behind; look for a statue of Sun Yat-sen (1866–1925). Considered to be the father of modern China — by both Taipei and Beijing — Dr. Sun began plotting his successful 1911 revolution against the Manchu Dynasty while living in Hawaii. Many Hawaii *tongs* (Chinese societies) helped finance the cause. On the opposite side of the stream, there's a statue of José Rizal, the Philippine writer and patriot, executed by the Spanish colonial government in 1896, because of his rebellion against Spanish rule in the Philippines.

Walk along the wide embankment by the stream; on the right is the Cultural Plaza, a collection of ethnic restaurants. The pedestrian mall is marked by a large, distinctive square sculpture, a modern representation of a Chinese emperor's seal, and a trellis that shades tables where senior citizens, most of them Oriental, gather to play such games as checkers, dominoes, and mah-jongg. Across the river is Izumo Taisha Jinja, one of the oldest and largest Japanese Shinto shrines in Hawaii. Complete with traditional *torii* gate, the shrine is built of light and dark wood, and its roof beams come together outside and cross in an "X" at the top. Cross Kukui Street and continue underneath the royal poinciana trees, which blaze with red blossoms in June and July.

Then cross busy Vineyard Boulevard to Kuan Yin Temple, a lovely Buddhist sanctuary honoring Kuan Yin Boddhisattva, the goddess of mercy, represented here by a large statue seated on a lotus blossom. The tour concludes here, but it's worth noting that the adjacent city-operated Foster Botanical Garden (see *Glorious Gardens* in DIVERSIONS) is a peaceful haven and deserves to be a destination in itself. Open daily from 9 AM to 4 PM, it's a green oasis in the midst of the city, displaying several thousand species of plants: the perfect spot to rest your bones after a walking tour of Chinatown.

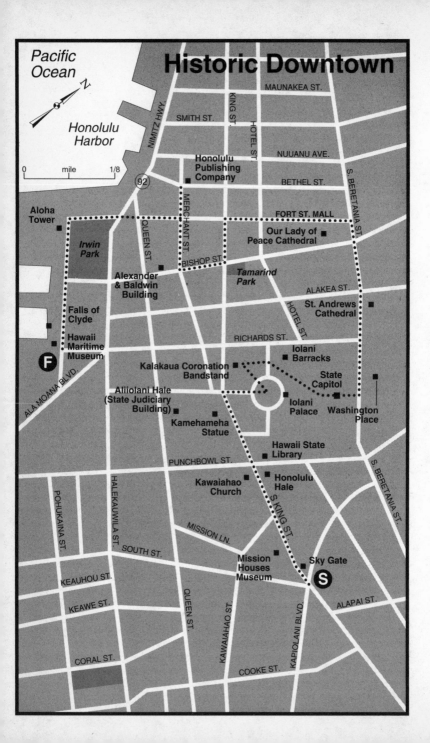

Tour 3: Historic Downtown

Before the *haoles* (foreigners) came to Hawaii, there was an often-muddy thatch-roofed village not far from the point where Nuuanu Stream entered the ocean on Oahu. When the *haoles* did come, they arrived in big merchant ships that needed deep, protected waters — conditions that existed near this unattractive shoreline settlement. As a result, the Hawaiian *alii* (nobility) made this undistinguished spot with the lyrical name Honolulu the center of commercial action for the island of Oahu, and all of the kingdom.

Though the exact meaning of the name Honolulu is still debated, it is usually translated as "safe haven." *Hono* does mean "bay" in most contexts and *loulu* is a type of large palm leaf used for shelter from the rain. Strictly speaking, it should be pronounced with long o's (Hoh-noh-*lu*-lu).

But no matter what it means, over the years, Honolulu has come to embrace a much wider piece of real estate. To many it signifies the sprawling area between the suburb of Hawaii Kai and Pearl Harbor, but the area that was called Honolulu in the 19th century is today referred to simply as Downtown (and usually capitalized). During much of the 19th century, this was the extreme "diamondhead," or southern, end of town.

Begin this tour of Downtown at the point where Kapiolani Boulevard meets South King Street. From Waikiki, take Bus No. 2 to the corner of Beretania and Alapai Streets. Get off in front of *BJ Furniture* and walk 2 blocks *makai* (oceanward) to King Street. If you come by car, be forewarned that parking is difficult in this neighborhood, although it's possible to find a meter on a side street and then proceed on foot.

Look for a waterfall; the triangular island in the midst of the traffic at King Street and Kapiolani Boulevard would seem to be the most unlikely place in town for a waterfall, but there is one — albeit artificial — behind *The Net Mender,* a sculpture by Charles Watson. This is a busy spot, so watch your step if you try to inch your way along the curb to find a good place from which to photograph the statue.

Cross the street toward Kawaiahao Plaza and turn right (north) on King Street. On the opposite side of the street, look for *Sky Gate,* an unusual three-legged black tubular sculpture by Isamu Noguchi, which has graced the spot since 1979. Concerts and other outdoor community gatherings are sometimes held here.

Continue along King Street; underneath a hala (pandanus) tree next to the sidewalk is the beginning of a low coral-stone wall, lined in some places with a hedge of aloe. Behind the wall and across a well-kept lawn is one of the most important heirlooms in the state — a clapboard mission house. The first

Western structure in Hawaii, the first missionaries had it prefabricated in New England, shipped it around Cape Horn, and then assembled it on this spot in August 1821. Grouped with two coral block buildings, the stone Printing House (1823), which produced religious material in Hawaiian, and the Chamberlain House (1831), another New England design used by the mission's purchasing agent, the three structures now make up the *Mission Houses Museum* (see *Museums, Churches, and Mission Houses* in DIVER-SIONS). Operated by the Hawaiian Mission Children's Society, descendants of the first people to preach Christianity in the Sandwich Islands, the museum is open Tuesdays through Saturdays from 9 AM to 4 PM; Sundays from noon to 4 PM.

Cross Kawaiahao Street and walk under the stone arch there, which once served as the entrance to the main footpath into town. You are now in the back yard of Kawaiahao Church; designed by Hiram Bingham, its first minis-ter, it was constructed by the first Hawaiian converts to Christianity. Built with 1,000-pound coral stone blocks painstakingly cut and removed by skin divers from the reef under the waters of Honolulu Harbor, this Congrega-tional church was completed and dedicated in 1842. A sign near the front door tells the church's story in more detail. Look inside; the church normally is open. Or come back on Sunday: Services, partly in Hawaiian, are conducted here at 8 and 10:30 AM, and visitors usually are invited to tour the building afterward.

Don't miss the small cemetery behind the church, with graves of the early missionaries and their families; the stones bear some of the most revered names — *kamaaina* (old-time resident) families including Alexander, Bald-win, Dole, and Bingham — in the islands. On the King Street side of the church is a rough-hewn fountain that commemorates the spring that once flowed on this spot. In fact, Kawaiahao means the water of "Hao," which is the name of the man who lived here. Almost in the church's front yard is the tomb of King Lunalilo, who died in 1872; on his deathbed, he asked to be buried here near his people rather than in the Royal Mausoleum in Nuuanu Valley.

On the other side of King Street is Honolulu Hale (pronouced *Ha*-lay), or City Hall. Built in 1927, the Spanish-style structure houses the offices of the mayor and the city council, and the council chambers.

Cross Punchbowl Street and walk past the rectangular World War I memo-rial, with the names of Hawaii's war dead inscribed on its sides, and the Art Deco–inspired Old Territorial Office building. (On the other side of King Street is the recently refurbished Hawaii State Library, a 1913 gift from steel magnate and philanthropist Andrew Carnegie.) In front is a statue of Kamehameha the Great, the conqueror of all the islands and the first ruler of the unified island kingdom. This gold-and-black likeness of His Highness, decked out in feather cloak and helmet, is actually a molded copy of the original, which went down in a Falkland Islands shipwreck en route to Honolulu from Italy. (The original was eventually salvaged, however, and re-erected on the Big Island of Hawaii, birthpace of the king.) Kamehameha stands in front of Aliiolani Hale (House of the Heavenly Chief), a handsome Spanish-style structure with a clock tower and terra cotta courtyard. Built in

1874, it was originally designed as a palace, but instead became the House of Parliament; the overthrow of the monarchy was proclaimed here in 1893. Today, it serves as the State Judiciary building; on weekdays it's worth a stop at the Judiciary History Center, where exhibits such as "Hawaii Under Martial Law" can be seen.

Traverse busy King Street on the nearby crosswalk and go through the gate with the royal Hawaiian coat of arms to the expansive, tree-shaded grounds of Iolani Palace, usually billed as the only royal palace in the United States (see *Royal Residences* in DIVERSIONS). Built by King Kalakaua in 1882, this Victorian masterpiece was inspired by the style of architecture the king saw on a European tour. Following the monarch's death in 1891, the palace and the throne were occupied by his sister, Queen Liliuokalani — the last monarch of Hawaii. She was placed under house arrest in the palace by revolutionaries for a time in 1893, and legend has it that this was when the queen composed the haunting song "Aloha Oe," probably the best-known piece of Hawaiian music ever written. After the revolution and the annexation of the Republic of Hawaii to the United States in 1898, the palace became the seat of government; until the new capitol was built in 1969, the House of Representatives met in the throne room and the Senate in the dining room.

In recent years, the building has been painstakingly restored by the Friends of Iolani Palace, who are overly solicitous in its care and upkeep. Be forewarned: An alarm sounds if you try to stand on the front steps, no photographs are permitted inside, and special padded slippers must be worn over your shoes to avoid scuffing the floor. No matter: The 45-minute tours, offered every 15 minutes from 9 AM to 2:15 PM Wednesdays through Saturdays, are well worth the slight inconvenience.

On the palace grounds, walk past the kapok tree (with its elephant-skin bark) to the *Kalakaua Coronation Bandstand.* The small gazebo-like pavilion was built in 1883 so that David Kalakaua could stage a lavish, belated coronation ceremony (at that point, he had already been on the throne for 9 years). The bandstand has a copper dome with eight concrete pillars, symbolizing Hawaii's eight major islands, supporting it. Today, the structure is used for concerts by the *Royal Hawaiian Band* (often held at noon on Fridays) and other public events. Don't count on it for shelter from a sudden shower; it's now *kapu* (forbidden) to the general public.

On the north side of the palace is Iolani Barracks. Built in 1871 for the Royal Household Guard, it looks like a miniature fort and was moved stone by stone from the site of the state capitol to its present location. It now houses a gift shop, and is the place to pick up tickets for tours of the palace. Look behind the palace to see one of the largest banyan trees in Hawaii. Well over 100 years old, the tree has spread over a wide area (although much of it has rotted or has been eaten away by termites). According to some, the Iolani Palace banyan began as two trees but joined together over the years.

Outside the back fence of Iolani Palace is a bronze statue of Queen Liliuokalani, installed here in 1982. In her hands she holds several documents, including the manuscript for "Aloha Oe." The queen has her back to the royal palace and her hand extended toward the state capitol (hell hath no fury like a queen overthrown).

Across a green lawn is the State Capitol, considered one of modern Hawaii's premier architectural triumphs; it was opened in 1969, 10 years after Hawaiian statehood was granted. This dramatic building, which has been recently renovated, is a massive structure whose cantilevered concrete ribs, separated by glass mosaic tiles, suggest the form of a volcano and the wave action of the ocean. The 4-story interior courtyard is open to the sky, flooding it with natural light. If you like, take the elevator and walk the open-air corridors on the upper levels. The governor's office is on the top floor; a massive koa wood door is marked in Hawaiian *E Komo Mai* (Please come in).

Exit the building on the Beretania Street side, and look for the still somewhat controversial metal statue of Father Damien (born Joseph de Veuster), the Belgian priest who worked with the leprosy victims on Molokai from 1873 until 1889, when he contracted the disease and died. The modernistic interpretation, which shows Father Damien, deformed and bloated from leprosy, is by Venezuelan sculptress Marisol Escobar. Walk a little north on Beretania; look for a safe place to cross — probably with the light at Richards Street — and then backtrack a few yards. Look for No. 320 South Beretania; through the iron gates you can see Washington Place, a stately white mansion that was the residence of Queen Liliuokalani, and the home to which she returned after her government was overthrown. Built in 1846, Washington Place is the oldest building in Hawaii used continuously as a dwelling. Now, however, it is the governor's official mansion and is not open to the public.

Continue in the same direction on the *mauka* (mountain) side of Beretania Street. Almost next door to Washington Place is Saint Andrew's Cathedral, an Episcopal (Anglican) establishment dedicated in 1867 by Queen Emma, the wife of Kamehameha IV. The royal couple were Anglophiles, and the plans and even most of the materials for the complex building were shipped from England. If the front of the main structure seems out of sync with the surrounding medieval architecture, it's because this portion was redesigned in 1958. The statue of St. Andrew, the fountain, and the olive trees also are from the 1950s. If you look inside, you can see images of the king and queen depicted in the lower panels of the huge stained glass window.

Cross Beretania again to the *makai* (sea) side, then continue walking north (you'll cross Alakea Street) to the *Fort Street Mall,* a pedestrian shopping area, formerly the downtown area's center of commerce; today, it's a tree-lined promenade. Look for Our Lady of Peace Cathedral, a Spanish-style, stucco church with classic buttresses and a red tile roof. Dedicated in 1843, it is the center of Roman Catholic activity in the islands. The mall is filled with office workers on weekdays, but it is sometimes a haven for the homeless on the weekends, when many of the shops are closed. There are also far too many pigeons in residence. But you can stop here for a soda or snack, and rest a while on one of the benches. Look for the *King-Fort Magazine Shop* (No. 1122); it stocks hard-to-find publications. Next door, *T & H Leather* still makes leather sandals to order (prices begin at around $90).

If time is short, continue down Fort Street to the waterfront. But if you still want to wander a bit, follow this 1-block detour: Turn left on King Street to Bishop and visit Tamarind Park. In this green open space, there is a reflecting pool graced by *Upright Motive No. 9,* an 11-foot Henry Moore sculpture; Honolulu residents like to come here to listen to the frequent noontime concerts. On the south side of the square are several popular lunch spots, among them *Heidi's Bread Basket,* known for its sandwiches made with freshly baked bread, and *Harpo's Pizza,* worth a stop for its vegetarian pie.

Catercorner from the park is the Financial Plaza of the Pacific, a banking center taking up the entire block. When it was constructed in 1968 it was the largest commercial condominium in the United States. Note the circular metal sculpture, reminiscent of a bank vault door, in front of the Bank of Hawaii.

Then continue down Bishop to Merchant Street. Check out the Alexander & Baldwin Building (No. 822); built in 1929, it's considered a local gem by traditional architects. The beautifully proportioned building has a balcony on its upper floor and a classic Dickey roof (named after architect C. W. Dickey), with a high peak and low, widespread eaves. Now turn north on Merchant; at the corner of Merchant and Bethel, next to a mini-park, is the Kamehameha V Post Office, a yellow edifice with a distinctive wooden fascia screen on its sloping roof. No longer in service, when it was built in 1870 it was Honolulu's first all-concrete structure. You'll find it mentioned in Earl Derr Biggers's first Charlie Chan novel, *The House Without a Key.*

Across Bethel Street is the ornate 1910 structure that was, until December 7, 1941, the Yokohama Specie Bank. Today it houses the offices of the Honolulu Publishing Company, which has preserved its architectural detail, including the copper accents on the door and windows. Diagonally opposite the old post office is a former police station, now called the Walter Murray Gibson Building, incongruously named after a former gunrunner who was a scandalous character in Hawaiian history.

Retrace your steps for a block to the *Fort Street Mall* and turn *makai.* Cross Queen Street and cut through the small park in front of the twin-tower Amfac Center complex. These buildings are on the site of a fort built by King Kamehameha I — thus the name Fort Street. The only remaining evidence of this bulwark is the park's solitary cannon still pointing toward the harbor.

At the traffic light, cross Nimitz Highway to Irwin Park and take the outdoor escalator to reach the second level of the cruise ship complex. When an ocean liner docks, this is a busy place, bustling with lei sellers, taxis, and those meeting arriving passengers, but most of the time, it's very quiet. Follow the signs to the elevator that goes to the 10-story Aloha Tower. Built in 1921, it was the tallest structure in Hawaii until the 1950s, when high-rise hotels began to dominate the Waikiki skyline. It was from the tower that the harbormaster would control the movement of ships in and out of Honolulu Harbor, originally by manipulating colorful signal flags.

Unfortunately, the sheds that have now sprouted around the tower make it less attractive from the outside, but the 360° view of Honolulu and the surrounding area from its 10th-floor observation platform, which is open daily, remains unsurpassed. Informative panels point out the major sights.

After leaving the tower, walk "diamondhead" (generally south) and then down the long ramp that parallels Nimitz Highway, below. On the right, look for the *Falls of Clyde,* a 266-foot square-rigged sailing vessel that often called at Honolulu during the days of the tall ships. Today, it's a part of the *Hawaii Maritime Museum,* which traces the role of the sea in island life. Open daily from 9 AM to 5 PM. Also often docked at the center is the *Hokulea,* the Polynesian voyaging canoe that made history by re-creating the open-ocean voyages of Hawaii's first inhabitants. This walk concludes at *Coasters* (see *Eating Out* in THE CITY), an attractive open-air restaurant and bar overlooking the water in the same complex — a pleasant stop before heading back to your hotel.

Tour 4: Waikiki Beach

Long before Captain Cook — Hawaii's first tourist — arrived in what he called the Sandwich Islands, Waikiki was a popular playground. This lovely and serene stretch of sand, with its backdrop of coconut groves, luminous rainbows, and the romantic Koolau Mountains, was already a favorite swimming and surfing spot for Oahu's ancient *alii* (nobility). In the early 19th century, Kamehameha I, the warrior king, built a *pili* (grass shack) on Waikiki Beach for his favorite wife, Queen Kaahumanu. Subsequent monarchs built cottages; and eventually two hotels, the white, New England–style *Moana* and the raffish and roseate hacienda-style *Royal Hawaiian,* both still flourishing, were constructed to accommodate the mainlanders who had been attracted by Mark Twain's *Letter from the Sandwich Islands* and Isabella Bird's *Six Months in the Sandwich Islands.*

Military personnel who knew Hawaii only in the days of World War II tell of long and lonely stretches of beach; in the 1940s, Waikiki was a relatively undeveloped area. The great building boom started in the 1950s, and today the *Royal Hawaiian* and the *Moana* are dwarfed and obscured by concrete high-rises that have mushroomed around them, with dozens along the beach and Kalakaua Avenue alone. The coconut groves that once merged with the taro fields and swamp between the beach and the mountains are all but gone. The swamp in turn has been drained, and Waikiki is now defined on its *ewa* (west) and *mauka* (inland) sides by the Ala Wai Canal, a moat shaped like a hockey stick, with the handle pointing toward Diamond Head and the blade into the Yacht Harbor across from Ala Moana Park. The canal and Diamond Head provide Waikiki with neat boundaries encompassing an area about 2 miles long and a half-mile wide.

Begin at the corner of Kapahulu and Kalakaua Avenues at 170-acre Kapiolani Park — a gift to the people of Hawaii in 1877 by King Kalakaua, in honor of his wife, Queen Kapiolani. (Look for the information kiosk on the corner; there is a map of the facilities as well as a short history of the park posted on its walls. Also see *Special Places* in THE CITY). One of Honolulu's most popular green spaces, this is the spot for company picnics, rugby and soccer games, archery demonstrations, tennis matches, band concerts, and kite-flying contests. Humans aren't the only creatures who covet Kapiolani: People share the space with a multitude of birds, including white pigeons, Hawaiian doves, mynah birds, sparrows, red-headed Brazilian cardinals, and, during the winter, golden plovers (avian visitors from Alaska and Siberia).

Follow Kalakaua Avenue for 1 block toward Diamond Head until you reach Monsarrat Avenue, which cuts through the park. Turn left on Monsarrat and look for the *Waikiki Shell,* an open-air amphitheater, the site of evening concerts, featuring Hawaiian entertainers such as slack key guitar virtuoso Peter Moon, and visiting pop, jazz, and rock stars. Although you can

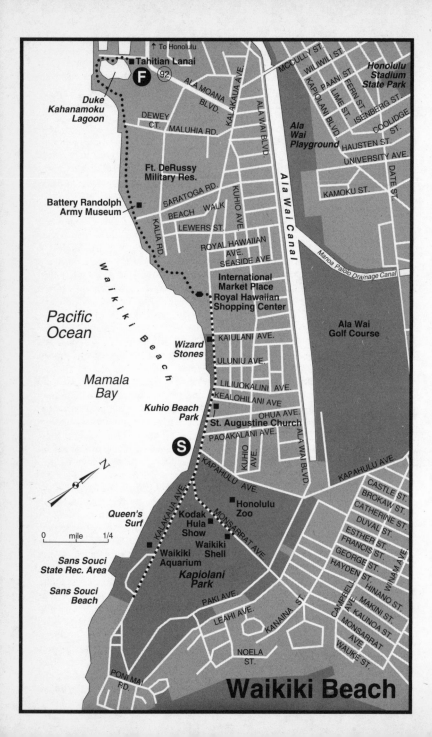

Waikiki Beach

reserve seats in the amphitheater, locals come early and bring their own tatami mats or beach chairs and picnic before the performance on a grassy knoll a short distance from the stage. There is free parking at a large lot nearby; space is usually available on weekdays, but on weekends it may be a different story.

Next to the *Shell* are the bleachers for the *Kodak Hula Show,* a Waikiki tradition since 1937. Some of the performers have been swinging and swaying here for more than 50 years, starting as *wahines* — young women — and now continuing to dance and sing as *tutus* — grandmothers. There is an admission charge for the show, which is held at 10 AM Tuesdays, Wednesdays, Thursdays, and sometimes on Fridays.

Walk back toward Kalakaua Avenue; on the left look for the squared-off roof of the *Waikiki Bandstand.* Events held here — including concerts by the *Royal Hawaiian Band,* the oldest municipal band in the US (2 PM Sundays) — are usually free.

Cross to the other side of Montsarrat to the Honolulu Zoo, which has many of the same animals you would see in a mainland menagerie, concentrated in a relatively small, tropical setting. Don't miss Hawaii's official state bird, the nene, which is related to the Canada goose, and the mongoose, a mammal sometimes called the "Hawaiian squirrel"; these fast and furry fellows are sometimes seen scampering across suburban and country roads. The zoo is open daily from 8:30 AM to 4 PM. On weekends, check out the *Weekend Art Mart,* where local artists set up card tables and prop up paintings against the fence bordering the Monsarrat Avenue side of the zoo.

Back on Kalakaua Avenue, cross the street and walk toward Diamond Head to the *Kaimana Beach* hotel; look for the ruins of the Waikiki Natatorium, a saltwater swimming pool built in 1927. Dedicated to the dead of World War I, it was the scene of aquatic exhibitions by *Olympic* swimmers Buster Crabbe, Johnny Weissmuller, and Hawaii's own Duke Kahanamoku. The debate as to whether or not to tear this place down has been ongoing for the past 20 years.

The beach in this area bears the name Sans Souci (French for carefree), after a rooming house that stood here in the 1890s. Robert Louis Stevenson was once a guest, and wrote admiringly of his surroundings, describing the "heavenly sunsets over the Pacific."

Turn around (heading away from Diamond Head) and walk back along the beach side of Kalakaua Avenue, which is shaded by a series of tall ironwoods; there is a paved walkway along the edge of the sand for those who prefer to wander near the waves. Coconut palms, banyans, and eucalyptus trees also grow along the beach, many of them protecting picnic tables from the sun. Changing rooms, showers, restrooms, and drinking fountains complete the picture.

Follow Kalakaua to the compact but well-designed *Waikiki Aquarium,* run by the University of Hawaii. The third-oldest public aquarium in the country, its tanks are home to more than 300 species of Pacific sea creatures, including sharks, giant clams, sea turtles, and even freshwater crocodiles from the Pacific island of Palau. The aquarium is known for its success in raising the rare chambered nautilus, a deepwater survivor of a pre-dinosaur age. Open daily from 9 AM to 5 PM; shark feedings are at 10:30 AM. There is a small admission fee.

The beach changes its name here to Queen's Surf, since it was once favored by Hawaiian royalty. To enhance its "regal" name, old-style street lamps with delicate glass globes have been installed along the walkway along this part of the strand. At the intersection of Kapahulu and Kalakaua, Waikiki begins in earnest, with its trademark hotels, condominiums, and shops selling suntan lotion.

Across from Kapahulu Avenue, look for Kuhio Beach Park. Protected by a seawall that runs parallel to the beach several yards from shore, it is a popular place for the youngsters, because of it gently sloping sandy bottom and the calm surf created by the seawall. Along the shore is a belvedere lined with benches, picnic and game tables (some with built-in checker and chess boards), drinking fountains, and planters, as well as several arbors, pavilions, and trellises.

Across the street, look for St. Augustine Catholic Church, with its steep A-frame roof and colorful stained glass windows. Recently, the bishop announced plans to tear down the building and sell the valuable land (it was built when property values were much lower than they are today), but the outcry of its parishioners and other preservation-minded citizens saved the day — and the church.

On the beach side, notice the beachboy stands, where surfboards, bogie boards, and wave skis are available for rent; lessons are also available. Nearby, look for the bronze statue of a Hawaiian beachboy complete with massive surfboard; this is the beloved Duke Kahanamoku (1890–1968), Hawaii's most famous surfer and an *Olympic* swimming champion. (He won a gold medal in 1912.) The recently erected image is controversial for at least two reasons: The Duke is facing away from the ocean, and there is no plaque to tell visitors who he is — although virtually every Hawaii resident knows about him.

At the end of Kuhio Beach Park, next to the police substation, look for four massive boulders known as the Wizard Stones. Supposedly placed there 400 years ago by four Tahitians with magical powers, they predate anything else in sight. The Tahitians disappeared, or perhaps left for their native land, leaving behind the stones as repositories of their *mana,* or magical powers.

Cross Kalakaua again to check out a couple of favorite shopping sites. *King's Village,* a shopping complex with a 19th-century monarchy theme, is on Kaiulani Avenue just behind the *Hyatt Regency Waikiki* (see *Shopping* in THE CITY). A drill team in period uniforms perform a "changing of the guard" ceremony daily at 6:15 PM, and the *Rose and Crown,* a British-style pub, is a popular singles meeting place, especially for young members of the British Commonwealth. Nearby is the *International Market Place* (2330 Kalakaua Ave.), an outdoor bazaar in a courtyard surrounding a giant banyan tree (see *Shopping* in THE CITY). Here you'll find legions of trinket vendors, many of them recent Asian and Pacific immigrants; have your caricature drawn, your picture taken with a parrot, or your fortune told by gypsies. The market is a hodgepodge, but it's also a cherished local souk with a tradition dating back nearly 50 years. (At press time, plans to erect a convention center on this site were still under discussion.)

Back on the *makai* side of Kalakaua, almost opposite the *International Market Place,* is the *Sheraton Moana Surfrider* hotel (see *Heavenly Hotels* in DIVERSIONS). This airy, 4-story Victorian building is Waikiki's oldest hotel; it first opened its doors in 1901 and is now on the National Register of Historic Places. With its wide verandahs, rocking chairs, and wicker furniture, the *Moana* is reminiscent of a more leisurely time in now bustling, built-up Waikiki. Stop at the hotel's *Banyan Court* and sip a mai tai underneath the century-old tree. Musical entertainment is often on tap, and there's an additional show — provided free by a score or more of surfers riding the waves.

Continue along Kalakaua Avenue on the earth-toned tile sidewalk. Turn left to enter the massive *Royal Hawaiian Shopping Center.* Follow the signs to the rear of the center to the *Royal Hawaiian* hotel; take the hibiscus-lined walkway across the green lawn to enter.

Known affectionately as the "Pink Lady," this Moorish-style hotel was considered the epitome of luxury when it opened in 1927. Happily, it has maintained its royal reputation over the decades, and its restaurants and night club continue to be popular. The *Surf Room,* right next to the sand, is favorite and certainly scenic for breakfast, lunch, or a sunset supper. Incidentally, the *Royal* has one of the best luaus in Oahu, usually beginning on the oceanside lawn at 6 PM on Mondays.

Exit the hotel near the pool, take off your shoes, and walk along the sand. The beach will narrow and practically disappear as you pass by the *Sheraton Waikiki* with its two swimming pools, and the modern *Halekulani* hotel, which incorporated into its modern design an original 1917 building (see *Heavenly Hotels* in DIVERSIONS). *La Mer,* the hotel's premier restaurant, is on the upper floor of this older building and is one of Honolulu's best — and most expensive — dining rooms. *The House Without A Key,* an outdoor bar, was inspired by the title of the first Charlie Chan novel by Earl Derr Biggers. Stop to admire the hotel's beautiful pool, with the world's largest tile orchid on its bottom.

Go back to the sand for a few yards; you'll pass the *Outrigger Reef* hotel and a small apartment building before emerging at what appears to be another public park. These are the grounds of Ft. DeRussy, a 72-acre military installation now devoted largely to recreational activities of active and retired service personnel.

At the beginning of the grounds of Ft. DeRussy, look for an unusual low-profile building whose walls on the *makai* (sea) side seem to be reinforced with dirt embankments. This is the Battery Randolph, a former coastal artillery installation built on this site in 1911. Its walls — more than 20 feet thick — were too sturdy even for the wrecker's ball; when attempts to raze the installation failed, it was turned into the *Army Museum.* Exhibits here range from weapons used in ancient Hawaiian battles to those utilized in the Vietnam War; the museum's collection, not surprisingly, emphasizes World War II in the Pacific. Notice the tanks, half-tracks, and artillery pieces outside the *mauka* side of the building. The museum is open from 10 AM to 4:30 PM daily except Mondays; no admission charge.

Continue along the beach sidewalk past the US Army's own *Halekoa* hotel (*hale* means house, and *koa* means warrior), which charges unusually inexpensive room rates to the military. At the end of Ft. DeRussy, on private turf again, is the huge *Hilton Hawaiian Village* (see *Heavenly Hotels* in DIVERSIONS), with its six towers spread out over 20 acres.

To many, this is the widest, prettiest section of Waikiki Beach, with palm trees growing right up out of the sand, creating an attractive pattern of sun and shade. One of the best views of Waikiki Beach and Diamond Head — the one most often seen on postcards — can be gained from this vantage point. Stop for a drink at one of the *Hilton*'s two beachside bars — *Tropics* or the *Hao Tree*. Walk through the grounds among the pools and ponds, admiring ducks and other water birds, to get to the *Rainbow Bazaar,* a shopping village with Asian architectural accents (see *Shopping* in THE CITY).

Go back out to to the beach and continue clockwise for about half a circle around the Duke Kahanamoku Lagoon. Look for the *Tahitian Lanai* restaurant, part of the small *Waikikian* hotel. The restaurant's popular, fan-cooled bar, with its poolside setting and Polynesian ambience, harks back to the 1950s; when it was announced not long ago that the hotel would be torn down, there was a hue and cry heard throughout Oahu. Happily, this atmospheric spot was granted a deserved reprieve — for us, it's a good place to end a day in Waikiki.

Tour 5: The North Shore

Although it looks accessible enough on a map, there simply is no way to make a complete drive around the island of Oahu. The stumbling block is Kaena Point, a rugged outcropping at the extreme western end of the island that is virtually impassable by any kind of vehicle (more about that later). In the old days (prior to World War II), the *Oahu Railroad* went around the point, but the railroad is long gone, and the tracks have been washed away or ripped up.

Given these constraints, the best route for an all-day excursion is to head for the North Shore, cutting through the sugarcane and pineapple fields in the approximate center of Oahu, and then return to Honolulu along the long Windward (northeast) Coast of the island. It's a distance of about 150 miles, and will take 3 hours if you don't make any stops — in which case there isn't much point in making the trip. Try to plan the drive for a weekday so that you can avoid the crowds. There's a lot to see, so get an early start, too. Be sure to get a recent map (preferably one you buy, such as the maps produced by Hawaii TMK Service or Bryan's, not one of the free tourist publications), and appoint someone to be navigator. Don't forget a pair of binoculars and a camera. (If you don't have a car, an approximation of this route is run by bus No. 52; pick it up at the *Ala Moana Center.*)

From Waikiki, take either Kapahulu Avenue or McCully Street to the Lunalilo Freeway (H1) and head west. (By the compass, it's northwest, but given the island's angular shape, traditional directions mean little.) Locals would say that you get on the freeway and head *ewa* (pronounced *eh*-vah), which means in the opposite direction from Diamond Head. From 7 to 9 AM weekdays, the freeway is busy with rush-hour traffic for the first few miles as you join commuters coming into town from such suburbs as Kahala and Hawaii Kai. Be patient: In short order you'll whiz right by Downtown and Chinatown. Keep an eye out for the *Bishop Museum* (see *Museums, Churches and Mission Houses* in DIVERSIONS), an old dark-stone mansion on the right, which is definitely worth a stop another day. It's located at just about the point where the Likelike (pronounced *Lekay-Lekay*) Highway joins the freeway; if you follow the circuitous route recommended below, this is the point at which you'll rejoin the freeway for the trip back to your hotel.

Soon after that the highway splits — H1 continues on a right-hand ramp that swings over the freeway and then *makai* (seaward) around the airport. Stay in the left two lanes, which will now become the Moanalua Freeway (Rte. 78). Don't worry if you inadvertently take H1 at the split; even if you stay on H1, it will eventually join up with this route.

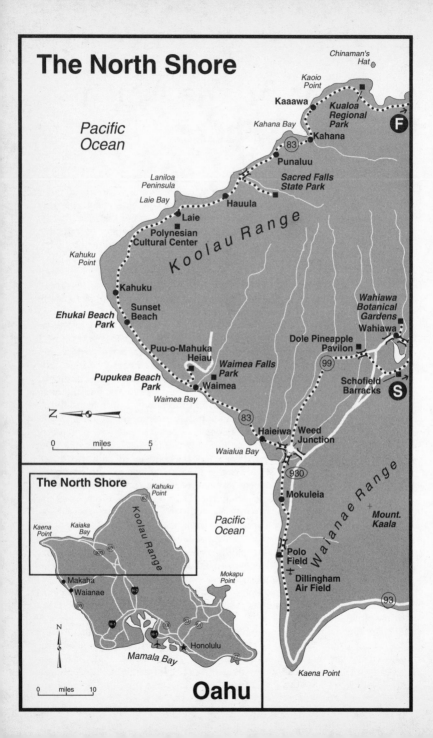

If time permits, take the "Puuloa Road–Tripler Hospital" exit; make an almost immediate right turn to the Moanalua Gardens, a 26-acre park with some dramatic monkeypod trees, a stream, and the old wooden cottage where King Kamehameha V used to play whist and fan-tan with his friends. This is a great spot for a picnic — even if it's early in the morning, have coffee and doughnuts under the trees (see *Glorious Gardens,* DIVERSIONS).

Return to the freeway and continue heading *ewa* (away from Diamond Head); the pink building on the right is the Tripler Army Medical Center. Built in 1948, it serves military personnel and their dependents. As you round the curve over Red Hill, the 50,000-seat *Aloha Stadium* and the waters of Pearl Harbor dominate the scene. Follow the signs to H1 West. (Those who took the wrong road back in town can now rejoin this route near the stadium.) Continue on the freeway, past new condominiums and golf courses. Ahead are the long, jagged green peaks of the Waianae Mountains. The low point in the range is called Kolekole (pronounced *Coaly-coaly*) Pass. Watch your speedometer: The speed limit drops from 65 mph to 55 mph here.

Take Exit 8A off the Lunalilo Freeway; you are now on the H2 Freeway, heading north on Oahu's central plateau between its two mountain ranges. Oahu was once two islands, consisting of two separate volcanoes, which became one when the sea level receded. Thousands of acres of sugarcane used to cover this fertile flatland, but today, much of it has succumbed to creeping urbanization.

Continue north on the H2 Freeway until Wahiawa (Exit 8). A former plantation town, Wahiawa does have several rickety wooden buildings left from that period. But as the closest community to Schofield Barracks, it has now taken on some of the unfortunate characteristics — pawnshops, used furniture stores, cheap bars — of a town catering primarily to a soldier's paycheck.

You are now on Kamehameha Highway; follow this road to California Avenue, a major intersection, and make a right. Ignore all the country-and-western bars and video, pizza, and tattoo parlors. In about a mile or on the left is the shaded entrance to the Wahiawa Botanical Garden. An island of floral tranquillity in this apparently philistine neighborhood, it is open daily 9 AM to 4 PM. This 27-acre glen originated as an experimental forest during the 1920s; a free brochure (available at the entrance) describes the trees, plants, and flowers (see also *Glorious Gardens,* DIVERSIONS).

Drive back down California Avenue and make a left on Kamehameha Highway (called "Kam" Highway by locals); cross the bridge and turn right at Wilikina Drive (Rte. 99). This leads to Kunia Road and, a little farther on, to the road to Foote Gate, the main entrance to Schofield Barracks. There's an MP here, but unlike other military posts on Oahu, Schofield is generally open to the public. You don't have to stop for him — unless you want to ask directions.

Schofield was immortalized by author James Jones in his novel (later made into a film) *From Here to Eternity.* Drive around the area; Jones called Schofield the most beautiful military base in the country, and it still has expansive green lawns, tall shade trees, and neatly kept gardens planted with colorful flowers. Fans may eventually find the quadrangle where Private Pruett (portrayed in the movie by Montgomery Clift) played taps.

If you want to stretch your legs, ask the MP for directions to Kolekole Pass. In fact, there is a road up and over the Waianae Mountains, but while the Army will let you up their side, the Navy — which controls everything on the western side of the pass — won't let you drive through its territory without military ID. (That's where it purportedly stores ammunition including, some say, nuclear missiles.) But do proceed on foot: You can hike through the woods and, once at the top of the pass, admire the panoramic views of inland Oahu. Then return to Schofield and go out the way you came in.

When you leave Schofield Barracks, do *not* turn right (south) on Kunia Road (it's an easy mistake to make). Instead go left on Kunia, and left again on Wilikina Drive (Rte. 99). On the right, look for *Kemoo Farms,* once a fine restaurant overlooking Lake Wilson reservoir. Today it's reduced mostly to a homespun museum and souvenir shop. Cross the red-dirt-encrusted cement bridge, and keep to the right at the Y in the road. Here Route 99 becomes Kamananui Road. This is Oahu's own big sky country, fields of iron-rich soil planted with neat rows of spiky pineapple that seem to pave the way to the horizon. On the right, Del Monte's Pineapple Variety Garden is worth a stop; the vast number of pineapple plants and their accompanying displays provide a living history of how this hybrid terrestrial bromeliad was developed in Hawaii.

Follow Route 99 until it merges with Kam Highway. On the left, notice a few plantation workers' houses almost hidden in the banana palms and other vegetation; if it's harvest time you'll be able to see the pineapple-picking machinery in operation. In about a mile is the eucalyptus-shaded Dole Pineapple Pavilion. Ignore the tourist-trap atmosphere and make your way past the T-shirts and lava-rock figurines to sample some delicious fresh pineapple spears. (Note: Each spear has a sweet end and a slightly sour end. Best to start at the sour end — usually lighter in color — and munch your way toward the sweet.)

Continue on Kam Highway; look to the Waianae Range on the left to pick out the peak known as Mount Kaala. (The name should be pronounced Kah *ah*-lah. In Hawaiian, two vowels are separated by a short stoppage of breath, especially if they are the *same* vowel, forming a type of consonant that doesn't exist in English. For more information, see USEFUL WORDS AND PHRASES.) At a little over 4,000 feet, it is the tallest point on Oahu — much higher than any in the Koolau Range, the mountains east of Honolulu.

As you continue north, the carpet of spiky pineapple suddenly turns into a prairie, vast fields of green shoots that grow as high as cornstalks at some times of the year. You are in the middle of one of Oahu's last remaining sugarcane plantations, still producing the product that was the lifeblood of most of the Hawaiian islands 50 to 100 years ago. As you drive, the road rises; look down to see the ocean and the villages appearing like so many small dots along the shoreline. If you see a fire in one of the sugar fields, don't be alarmed: sugarcane is often harvested using a controlled burn. The cloyingly sweet smell and the white "snowflakes" that float through the air are all part of the process.

Follow Kam Highway to the Weed Junction traffic circle; here you have a choice of three destinations — Mokuleia, Waialua, or Haleiwa. If it's still reasonably early in the day, follow the sign for Mokuleia, taking Route 83 (Kaukonahua Rd.) initially and then at the next junction — Thompson's Corner — taking Route 930 (Farrington Hwy.). You'll pass the *Hawaiian Kukui Nut Company,* which produces kukui nut oil and other related products. Sometimes called the candlenut, the kukui is also the state tree; the ancient Hawaiians used its nuts for leis and candles. Continue on Route 930; the road turns almost due west, past a polo field (matches are held here Sundays at 2 PM, March through August). On the left past the field is the former Dillingham Air Force Base, now primarily used as headquarters for glider rides and sky diving; both activities are available to fearless travelers. Contact the *Hawaii Soaring Club* (phone: 808-677-3404) to ride the wind currents in a glider, or *Skydive Hawaii* (phone: 808-637-9700), if you feel a need to jump out of a plane.

Continue to the end of the paved road; only 2 miles away is the aforementioned Kaena Point, and it's easy to see why it's too difficult to continue. Notice the kiawe trees, permanently bent over by the force of northeast trade winds. Get out of the car, feel the wind, and watch the waves roll in onto the beach below.

Retrace this route to the Weed Junction traffic circle; follow the sign for Haleiwa (pronounced vaguely like two female names, *Holly-Eva*), which leads back to the Kam Highway. During the late 1960s and early 1970s, mainland hippies "discovered" Haleiwa, much to the chagrin of the islanders who coveted its charms. Today, in spite of a growing number of specialty shops, it still manages to retain the feeling of being small-town Hawaii. Suburban villas facing the ocean make it too big to be a slumbering tropical village, and there aren't quite enough decorative clapboard shopfronts to compare it to cattle towns in the Old West, yet it does have character. With an emerging identity as an artists' community, Haleiwa also offers a touch of the avant-garde, with several galleries, restaurants, shops, and even a displaced Greenwich Village coffee shop, the *Coffee Gallery* at the *North Shore Marketplace,* a popular haunt of artists and intellectuals.

Stop here to browse among the shops and art galleries and perhaps have a bite to eat. A traditional treat is a "shave ice" (finely shaved ice covered with fruit syrup), a specialty at *Matsumoto's Grocery.* Other worthwhile spots (in no particular order) include the *Kua Aina Sandwich Shop,* known for its giant, juicy hamburgers; *Café Haleiwa,* for great breakfasts; *Kaala Art,* which sells tapa cloth (fabric made of bark) as well as colorful pareus; and *Steamers,* a reliable restaurant with a deck for alfresco dining. Just over the landmark 1921 bridge, look for *Jameson's by the Sea,* an atmospheric place for sunset drinks or dinner.

Outside of Haleiwa, continue on Kam Highway (Rte. 83), with the shoreline running on the left. After about 4 miles, look for Waimea Bay, a lovely curve of beach with good swimming during the summer. In the winter, enormous waves pound the shore and the beach is transformed into one of the world's premier surfing spots; swimming is off-limits for everyone except the most experienced surfers, but spectators are welcome to watch.

Near the beach park, but across the road, is the entrance to Waimea Falls Park. With its well-labeled flowers and trees, the park is lovely and definitely worth a longer visit (at least 2 hours). If time is short, leave it for another trip.

In ancient times, thousands of Hawaiians lived in this valley; today, there are several ongoing archaeological investigations. Swim in the park's pool under a 55-foot waterfall or, during occasional exhibitions, watch the cliff divers soar from the rocks high above (see *Quintessential Honolulu* in DIVER-SIONS).

Just down the highway, opposite Pupukea Beach Park, turn up the hill on winding Pupukea Road (next to *Foodland*). Follow this road for just over a half mile, take the right-hand turnoff, and drive about the same distance again to the Puu-o-Mahuka Heiau, one of the few *heiaus* (temple-like platforms) at which human sacrifices were made — including, in 1773, three unfortunate British sailors.

A little farther along the Kam Highway is Ehukai Beach Park, the site of the infamous Banzai Pipeline, known for its perfect tube-shape waves and the sharp reef, lurking just under the surface, that can be extremely dangerous for those who wipe out (see *Quintessential Honolulu* in DIVERSIONS). Just past the Pipeline is Sunset Beach, the site of winter surfing meets that attract contestants from all over the world.

Continue past the University of Hawaii's cattle research facility and other dairy farms; on the left is the entrance to the *Turtle Bay Hilton* hotel (see *Checking In* in THE CITY). Situated virtually on the extreme north point of the island, this pinwheel-shape Hilton property has two 18-hole golf courses, lots of tennis courts, plus other outdoor activities such as horseback riding and scuba diving. Two restaurants and a disco complete the picture.

Back on Kamehameha Highway again, notice the commercial aquaculture farms, marked by small ponds where several kinds of underwater life are cultivated. Watch for a little red shack on the left; sometimes shrimp and prawns are for sale here. In the hills, you'll see experimental wind farms, generating electricity with a battery of windmills.

Follow the highway to Kahuku, a sugar town until the mill closed in 1971; some of the small, simple houses are still inhabited. Recently, there was an unsuccessful attempt to turn the mill into a sophisticated theme park, but it has become a shopping center instead. Still, the mill's machinery, including brighly painted gears and conveyer belts, has been retained, and it's worth a stop to get an idea of what a sugar mill looks like close-up. *Ahi's Kahuku* restaurant, just behind the mill, specializes in seafood.

Continue on to the Mormon community of Laie, Hawaii's center for the Church of Jesus Christ of Latter-Day Saints. The Mormon Temple here was built in 1919, but the town's premier sight is the *Polynesian Cultural Center,* also run by the church. Here, seven thatch-roofed "villages," inspired by islands in the South Pacific, showcase the arts and cultures of Polynesia. Many of those who guide, demonstrate, and entertain are students from those islands, who attend the Hawaiian branch of Brigham Young University next door. This is an all-day experience, worth a separate visit (see *Quintessential Honolulu* in DIVERSIONS).

The road winds its way along the shoreline back toward Honolulu, passing several villages and official county beach parks. Between Hauula and

Punaluu, stop at Sacred Falls State Park; here you can take a 4-mile hike along a stream to an 80-foot waterfall, where you can swim if you like. Allow 2 hours for the round trip — and don't go if the weather is bad; rains in the mountains sometimes cause flash floods in the area. A popular restaurant, *Pat's at Punaluu,* is on the ground floor of a huge, green beachside condominium not far from the park.

Farther along, the sparsely populated beach at Kahana Bay is one of the best on the island, with gentle waves perfect for swimming year-round. Rounding the point, look for the *Crouching Lion* restaurant, and the rock formation that inspired its name. Once you look at just the right outcropping of rock in the mountains, it doesn't take much imagination to see the lion — although he looks as if he's resting than crouching. The restaurant, a Tudoresque staple since the 1920s, is often extremely busy at lunch — it's a better bet for dinner, except for the long drive home in the dark.

Follow Kam Highway to the town of Kaaawa; its most interesting feature, outside of all those "a's" jammed together to make four syllables, may just be its fire station. It's just over the bridge on the right: a big yellow truck parked in what looks like the family garage — fire fighting is simpler in rural Oahu. Farther along, the smokestack beside the road is part of an old sugar mill built in 1863. Looking out to sea, try to spot the unmistakable shape of the little island called Chinaman's Hat; stop at the beach at nearby Kualoa Regional Park for a better view. Some folks wade out to the Hat during low tide; but you'd better be a good swimmer if you're going to try to make it back later.

All along this coast are family-operated fruit stands selling everything from passion fruit to mangoes and coconuts. Be sure to try the local bananas. (Ironically, there aren't enough bananas to go around in Hawaii, and supermarkets often import them from South America.) Another "agricultural" activity you may notice is a little "village" or two of rooster houses. Cock-fighting is illegal in Hawaii, yet despite police raids and other measures, matches are occasionally held.

At Kahaluu, near the *Hygienic Food Mart,* follow the road straight, rather than taking the left-hand fork. You are now on Kahekili Highway (Rte. 83). A couple of miles down the road, look for the Valley of the Temples Memorial Park, which is — you guessed it — a cemetery. But this is no ordinary graveyard; hidden in a valley in the back is the Byodo-In Temple, one of the most beautiful buildings on Oahu. This rose-colored reproduction of a Buddhist temple in Kyoto, Japan, has a dramatic setting, with the sculptured green *pali* of the Koolau mountain range behind it. Ring the 3-ton bronze bell (just once) for luck. Wander through the building and the beautifully landscaped grounds; look for colorful peacocks and perhaps some tame rabbits looking for a handout. The park charges a small admission fee, and it is open daily until 4:30 PM.

Back on the highway, continue to Likelike Highway (Rte. 63), and turn right at the light. The four-lane highway slices though banana patches and past other tropical trees and then skirts the dramatic green buttresses created by the erosion of the Koolaus. Passengers (not the driver, please) should look back to get a dramatic view of Kaneohe Bay. Then, when it seems you can go no farther without bumping into the precipices ahead, you dive into the Wilson Tunnel, emerging on the leeward side of the island.

The highway continues through a forest and then gradually begins to skirt alongside housing developments in the upper Kalihi Valley. Finally it connects with the Lunalilo Freeway (H1) again near the *Bishop Museum* to complete the circuit. Take H1 East to return to Waikiki.

INDEX

Index